ERASMUS OF ROTTERDAM

The Man and the Scholar

ERASMUS OF ROTTERDAM

The Man and the Scholar

PROCEEDINGS OF THE SYMPOSIUM
HELD AT THE ERASMUS UNIVERSITY,
ROTTERDAM, 9–11 NOVEMBER 1986

EDITED BY

J. SPERNA WEILAND AND W.TH.M. FRIJHOFF

E.J. BRILL
LEIDEN · NEW YORK · KØBENHAVN · KÖLN
1988

This book is published with financial support from the Prins Bernhard Fonds and the Stichting Universiteitsfonds Rotterdam.

Library of Congress Cataloging-in-Publication Data

Erasmus of Rotterdam, the man and the scholar : proceedings of the
symposium held at the Erasmus University, Rotterdam, 9–11
November 1986 / edited by J. Sperna Weiland and W. Th. M. Frijhoff.
    p.   cm.
    Includes bibliographies and index.
    ISBN 9004089209
    1. Erasmus, Desiderius, d. 1536--Congresses.   2. Humanists-
-Netherlands--Biography--Congresses.   3. Scholars--Netherlands-
-Biography--Congresses.   4. Learning and scholarship--History--16th
century--Congresses.   I. Sperna Weiland, Jan.   II. Frijhoff,
Willem.   III. Erasmus Universiteit Rotterdam.
PA8518.E78 1988
199'.492--dc 19   88-29317
                                                            CIP

ISBN 90 04 08920 9

PRINTED IN THE NETHERLANDS

CONTENTS

PART TWO

EDUCATION AND THE WORLD OF LEARNING

PART THREE

IMAGES

PREFACE

Desiderius Erasmus Roterodamus died at Basel in 1536. In 1986 four hundred and fifty years had passed by since his death. For the university which rather boldly bears his name, the Erasmus University of Rotterdam, this was a good reason for making a special point of calling to mind the great humanist. The commemoration took place in November 1986. The celebrations were opened by the Prime Minister of the Netherlands in the beautiful surroundings of the Boymans-Van Beuningen Museum. There were concerts of Renaissance music, exhibitions devoted to Erasmus and sixteenth century Rotterdam, lectures on Erasmian topics for the general public. A fine book was published as part of the commemoration,—*Erasmus, de actualiteit van zijn denken*, a German translation of which will be appearing at roughly the same time as the present volume. On the final day of the celebrations, the *Præmium Erasmianum Foundation* awarded the Erasmus prize 1986 to the Czech author Vaclav Havel.

From a purely scholarly point of view, the most important part of the celebrations was the three-day symposium *Erasmus, the man and his work*. We were very pleased that so many distinguished scholars, from all over the world, should have accepted our invitation to come to Rotterdam and contribute to the conference. Now that we have the texts of their contributions here before us, published as the proceedings, we are indeed greatly impressed by the richness and the variety of the *Erasmiana* we have been able to garner together between these covers. There seems to be every likelihood that this work will become widely recognised as a storehouse of information on current research into Erasmus and his times.

In order to bring out certain general lines of enquiry, we suggested at the outset that our guests might allow their contributions to fall under the broad headings of *Power relations, Education and the world of scholarship* and *The Erasmian tradition*. We thought that the discussions at the conference would benefit from our allowing them a large degree of freedom, while also directing them toward these central topics. The result of this structuring is to be found in the layout of the book we are now offering to the public. We hope that the material we have brought together will serve as a beacon to future scholars, and that these contributions to the symposium held in Rotterdam in 1986 will prove to be something of a milestone in the co-ordination of Erasmus research. Finally, we thank Mrs Carien de Ruiter for her help in organizing the celebrations, including the symposium, and Mrs Marlotte Schoorlemmer for her help in preparing this book.

J.S.W.
W.F.

ABBREVIATIONS

Allen = *Opus Epistolarum Des. Erasmi Roterodami*, denuo recognitum et auctum, ed. P.S. Allen, Oxonii 1906–1958, 12 vols.—References are to the number of the letter and to the lines in the printed text; *Allen* 305, 214–217 refers to the lines 214–217 in letter 305 in the Allen edition. Sometimes there is a reference to a volume of this edition; *Allen* VI = volume 6 of the edition.

ASD = *Opera omnia Desiderii Erasmi Roterodami*, Amsterdam-Oxford.—References are to the number of the Series, the volume in the Series and the pages in the printed text; e.g. *ASD* IV–1, 142–155 refers to the pages 142–155 in volume 1 of Series IV in the new and ongoing Amsterdam edition.

CWE = *Collected Works of Erasmus* in the ongoing translation, Toronto.—References are to volume and page; e.g. *CWE* 24, 662 refers to page 662 of volume 24 of *CWE*.

LB = Desiderius Erasmus, *Opera omnia*, ed. J. Clericus. Lugduno Batauorum 1703–1706, 10 vols.—References are to volume, column and section; e.g. *LB* IX, 1219F refers to section F of column 1219 in volume IX of *LB*.

PART ONE

POWER RELATIONS

INTRODUCTION

La première partie de ce livre traite des relations d'Érasme avec les pouvoirs de son époque, les États européens et leurs princes d'une part, l'Église catholique de l'autre. Cela veut dire qu'elle traite d'un monde dans lequel le moine érudit n'a pas été à l'aise et qui lui est toujours resté étranger. Ces relations ont le plus souvent été des affrontements, surtout avec les pouvoirs ecclésiastiques, le Saint Office et l'Inquisition par exemple. Cela n'empêche pas qu'Érasme, ambitieux et désireux d'obtenir lui-même de l'autorité, s'est mêlé aux affaires politiques, surtout en tant qu'éducateur et moraliste, et plus encore aux tribulations de l'Église qu'il a aimée et fortement critiquée à la fois, puisque—disait-il—la sottise se trouve partout, même dans l'Église.

Le cadre dans lequel la vie d'Érasme s'est déroulée, est assez bien connu. Il n'est point nécessaire, dans cette introduction, de décrire et d'interpréter encore une fois les grands bouleversements que connut le monde européen à la fin du XVe et au début du XVIe siècle. Pour Érasme, à part la redécouverte des *bonae litterae*, le plus grand événement de son temps fut la Réforme. Dans la Réforme, déclenchée par un autre moine augustin, Érasme a reconnu des éléments de sa propre critique amère de l'Église. C'est pour cela qu'il a hésité, trop longtemps sans doute. Mais après un certain temps il a résolument rejeté un mouvement qui en fin de compte ne pouvait que déchirer l'Église et détruire l'unité de cette Église qui, après tout, etait l'*Ecclesia amabilis*. La réforme qu'Érasme a voulue et qu'il a effectuée, la réforme humaniste—érudition, tolérance, charité, paix—, était autre chose que la foi dévorante dans la grâce inconditionnée de Dieu que proposait la Réforme luthérienne.

D'ailleurs, il n'est pas possible de séparer rigoureusement les pouvoirs politiques et ecclésiastiques. Souvent, les autorités de l'Église jouaient un rôle assez important dans la politique; d'autre part, la politique s'empara bientôt du mouvement d'abord purement spirituel de la Réforme.

C'est dans ce cadre que s'inscrivent les contributions que nous avons reprises dans la première partie de notre receuil.

Sans être obsédé par une folie de grandeur, le jeune Érasme, humble moine dans le monastère de Steyn, était attiré par le monde du pouvoir et de la grandeur. C'est la raison pour laquelle il saisit joyeusement l'occasion qui luit fut donnée d'échapper à la vie monastique en devenant secrétaire de l'évêque de Cambrai, Henri de Berghes, qui appartenait à une famille riche et respectée, liée à la cour de Bourgogne alors établie à

Bruxelles. *R.J. Schoeck* (Erasmus as Latin Secretary to the Bishop of Cambrai) dessine le portrait de l'évêque humaniste et l'entrée assez timide d'Érasme dans le monde du pouvoir. En même temps, il décrit le traité en forme de dialogue *Antibarbari*, défense de l'humanisme et critique de la 'barbarie' (de la théologie médiévale par exemple) à la fois.

Plusieurs années plus tard (1516), Érasme, déjà devenu une célébrité, devait écrire le petit livre intitulé *Institutio principis christiani*, qui traite de l'éducation du prince chrétien et des devoirs de celui qui est destiné à gouverner l'État. *Maxim Marin* (L'Institution du prince' d'Érasme et de Guillaume Budé) compare l'ouvrage d'Érasme avec celui de l'humaniste français. Je mentionne cet essai, classé dans la deuxième partie de ce livre, en tant que témoin de l'intérêt manifesté par Érasme pour une politique chrétienne.

Vers la fin de sa vie, Érasme fut critiqué et attaqué d'une façon parfois malveillante. Les attaques le gênèrent et de temps en temps il se sentit véritablement menacé. Dans un de ces cas, il chercha et obtint l'appui de l'Empereur Ferdinand de Habsbourg, ainsi qu'on le lira dans deux lettres de l'Empereur à l'humaniste, écrites le 11 et le 22 août 1531 et jusqu'ici restées inédites. Dans sa contribution intitulée «Érasme et Ferdinand de Habsbourg d'après deux lettres inédites de l'Empereur à l'humaniste», *J.C. Margolin* donne une transcription des deux lettres, une traduction et un commentaire. L'Empereur rassure l'humaniste en lui disant qu'il peut compter sur lui en toute occasion. Dans les lettres se lit une affection remarquable: «Le Roi sérénissime vous entoure toujours de sa bienveillante sollicitude, ainsi que l'exigent vos mérites».

Dans ces années-là, les Turcs s'emparèrent du sud-est de l'Europe. En 1529, Vienne fut assiégée. La guerre contre les Turcs était un des grands sujets de discussion. Devant cette situation assez menaçante, Érasme esquissa ses idées sur la guerre contre les Turcs, dans la forme d'une *Enarratio in Psalmum XXVIII*. *A.G. Weiler* (The Turkish Argument and Christian Piety in Desiderius Erasmus' «Consultatio de Bello Turcis Inferendo» (1530)), analyse la *Consultatio*, son contexte historique, son contexte littéraire, etc. Il met en évidence que, pour Érasme, les Turcs n'ont eu l'occasion d'avancer, puis de vaincre les peuples chrétiens, que parce que les chrétiens n'ont point lutté sous l'étendard de Jésus-Christ, avec une âme pure; en effet, sans s'en apercevoir, les chrétiens sont devenus des Turcs eux aussi: «Turcae pugnamus cum Turcis». Tout comme dans l'*Institutio principis christiani* et dans un grand nombre d'autres textes, l'humaniste traite les choses politiques d'une façon tout à fait moralisatrice, sans aucune interférence avec les réalités politiques elles-mêmes. Les soi-disant chrétiens ont, selon lui, besoin d'une *universalis et insignis vitae correctio*, d'une lutte contre le Turc qui habite leur propre coeur; ensuite seulement ils pourront battre les Turcs.

Margherita Isnardi-Parente, dans sa contribution intéressante intitulée «Érasme, la République de Platon et la communauté des biens», aborde un problème qui a préoccupé Érasme pendant toute sa vie: celui de l'ordre social et de la justice. A côté de richesses énormes et d'un gaspillage indicible il existe une misère intolérable; d'autre part, dans l'héritage de l'Antiquité on trouve le rêve d'une communauté des biens. Dès lors la question suivante se pose, pour Érasme aussi bien que pour son ami anglais Thomas More: ce 'communisme' est-il possible? *Amicorum communia omnia*, dit le premier des *Adages*. Toutefois, une utopie pareille est-elle réalisable dans le monde actuel? Érasme hésite, mais vers la fin de sa vie, alerté par les efforts farouches des *infelices Anabaptistae*, il se montre tout à fait résolu: il existe un droit inaliénable à la propriété, qui doit être respecté. Et pourtant: si tout le monde était vraiment chrétien ...

Tout cela confirme notre image d'Érasme. Dans les questions politiques et sociales (ou socio-économiques), l'humaniste fut avant tout un moraliste, moins impressionné pas les raisonnements politiques, par la raison d'État par exemple, que par les commandements de son Seigneur Jésus-Christ. Ce ne fut qu'à contrecoeur qu'il s'éloigna de l'idéal 'monastique' de la communauté des biens.

On sait qu'Érasme s'est plongé dans les affaires de l'Église avec beaucoup d'intérêt, avant la Réforme et plus encore après son explosion, et qu'il n'a pas été avare de paroles, parfois d'ailleurs quelque peu mystérieuses. *Nelson H. Minnich* (Erasmus and the Fifth Lateran Council (1512–1517)), décrit soigneusement l'attitude de l'humaniste envers le Concile qui fut convoqué par le pape Jules II, homme frivole et méprisable, et qui après sa mort fut présidé par le pape Léon X. Érasme doute de l'orthodoxie du Concile: les vrais conciles sont *concilia rite in Spiritu Sancto congregata, peracta, aedita et recepta*.

Vers la fin de l'année 1521, la légation de Jérôme Aléandre auprès de Charles-Quint, aboutit, dans les Pays-Bas, à la création d'une Inquisition d'État. Le 6 octobre 1522, l'Inquisition fit arrêter tous les augustins du couvent d'Anvers; le 1cr juillet 1523, deux d'entre eux, Voes et Van Esschen, moururent sur le bûcher. *M. Gielis* (Érasme, Latomus et le martyre de deux augustins luthériens à Bruxelles en 1523) compare les commentaires d'Érasme, dans une lettre adressée à Zwingli, le 31 août 1523, et dans quelques autres textes, avec ceux du théologien louvaniste Jacques Latomus, qui avait collaboré avec l'Inquisition. Pour Latomus, Luther était l'hérésie même, tandis qu'Érasme, en mettant l'accent sur la charité et l'unité, ébranla des dogmes inéluctables de l'Église.

Voilà un thème qui va se répéter. Après 1517, Érasme devient de plus en plus hésitant. Dans son attitude à l'égard de Luther et de la Réforme,

l'on trouve une ambiguïté difficile à accepter et qui n'a pas manqué d'é-
veiller la suspicion. Suivent l'irritation, les intrigues, les insinuations, les
accusations, les attaques plus ou moins directes. Érasme est choqué, il
s'agite, sa réputation est en jeu, il se plaint, parfois d'une façon un peu
larmoyante, il se défend. Dès 1526/7, en Espagne, l'Inquisition rédige
une anthologie de *propositiones* d'Érasme «pour saisir l'hérétique»: les articles de Valladolid. Érasme écrit une *Apologia ad monachos hispanos* et *E.
Rummel* (Erasmus and the Valladolid Articles: Intrigue, Innuendo, and
Strategic Defense) nous donne un résumé passionnant de cette affaire.

C.L. Heesakkers (Argumentatio a persona in Erasmus' second Apology
against Alberto Pio), de son côté, analyse la controverse entre Érasme et
l'humaniste italien Alberto Pio, controverse qui se termina seulement
après la mort de l'italien en 1531. Ce qui a le plus choqué Érasme, c'est
que son 'adversaire' et 'calomniateur' a lié son nom à celui de Luther.
C'est toujours et sans cesse la même insinuation: Luther et Érasme, au
fond c'est une même affaire d'hérésie. Heesakkers met en évidence que
le prince des humanistes fut parfois un homme malveillant et désagréable. Ce qui me surprend dans l'*Apologie* et surtout dans les *Exsequiae Seraphicae*, écrites après la mort de l'italien, c'est le manque total de tolérance
et de générosité. Il y a raison de craindre que ce manque n'existait pas
seulement à ce moment précis.

La mort d'Érasme ne mit pas fin aux mesures de l'Inquisition et du
Saint-Office contre l'humaniste et contre les érasmiens. Dans son article
«Erasmus vor dem Inquisitor», que nous n'avons pas repris dans ce recueil, *S. Seidel-Menchi* montre qu'en Italie, surtout depuis 1555, l'Inquisition demeurait très sévère pour tous ceux qui possédaient ou avaient lu
des livres d'Érasme: si l'humaniste n'avait pas été un hérétique, voire un
luthérien, il était du moins *de haeresi suspectus*.

Cinq mois avant sa mort, le 12 février 1536, Érasme écrivit sont dernier
testament. *P.P.J.L. van Peteghem* a fait une étude approfondie des testaments d'Érasme et des complications relatives à l'exécution de sa dernière volonté. Son article «Erasmus' last will, the Holy Roman Empire
and the Low Countries» est une contribution importante à la recherche
sur les aspects juridiques et même politiques du testament.

J.S.W.

R.J. SCHOECK

ERASMUS AS LATIN SECRETARY TO THE BISHOP OF CAMBRAI: ERASMUS' INTRODUCTION TO THE BURGUNDIAN COURT

In an age that like ours was fascinated by power and high office, Erasmus was not diverted from his scholarship by the lure of power or the *folie de grandeur*. Although we know little about the steps which led to the appointment of Erasmus as secretary to the Bishop of Cambrai, Hendrik van Bergen (1449–1502), much is known about the bishop himself, and from that we can thus infer something more of the nature of that appointment and its importance for Erasmus. To be a bishop's secretary is one thing, but to be this bishop's secretary was something quite special at that time and it introduced Erasmus to politics and power.[1]

Hendrik van Bergen was the second son of Jan van Bergen, who died in 1494 and was known as *Jan metten lippen* and was the lord of Bergen and Glimes; Hendrik was thus a member of a family of wealth, standing and influence. Among his brothers was one, Jan, who was a knight of the Order of the Golden Fleece and chamberlain to Maximilian I in 1485 and to Philip the Handsome in 1493; another, Dismas, was master of requests under Margaret of Austria and in 1517 became a member of the privy council of the future Charles V. Still another brother, Antoon, was a Benedictine abbot, and like Hendrik a patron of Erasmus. In his service with the bishop, Erasmus met them all and learned much about court life; and he made a number of acquaintances that were useful in later life.[2] All of this experience helps to explain his easy access to so many nobles and aristocrats in later years. Yet he was not overwhelmed, for in 1499 he wrote to Adolph of Burgundy (whose mother, Anna van Borssele was a patronness of Erasmus) about his own experience at courts:

> ... for I know by experience that royal courts contain those who neither hesitate to believe, nor blush to say, that Christ's teaching is no matter that need concern noblemen but should be left to priests and monks. (Ep. 93, CWE 1: 185)

Let us look more closely at this bishop. Hendrik van Bergen had studied first at Louvain and Orléans, then at Perugia and Rome, and he had received his doctorate by the age of twenty-six. A protonotary apostolic, Hendrik was sent by Charles the Bold on a mission to Rome in 1476, and the Milanese ambassador could not praise him too highly. ''At the age of only twenty-six, he was 'affinato in tutto, litterato, dottore, docto, gentile, costomato, grave, riverente, prompto, eloquente, humano, praticho,' and so on . . . [and] . . . he spoke Italien as if he had been born in Tuscany itself!'' Thus Richard Walsh in his monographic essay on the Coming of Humanism to the Low Countries.[3] This remarkable young ecclesiastic became abbot of St. Denis-en-Broqueroie near Mons in 1477 and was named Bishop of Cambrai in 1480. Cambrai was then an unusually large diocese comprising about a thousand parishes, covering an area of what is now northern France and southern Belgium; and it is a mark of the importance and the spiritual life of this diocese that the renowned Pierre d'Ailly (1350 – 1420) had been Bishop of Cambrai earlier, and his work in the religious formation of his clergy had been widely acclaimed. In the bull naming Hendrik to the bishopric of Cambrai, Sixtus IV praised his knowledge of letters, the purity of his life, his integrity, and other virtues. In the nature of such documents of nomination, one might suspect that this was largely the conventional rhetoric of praise, but we have seen that Hendrik indeed merited it. He seems to have been an exemplary bishop for his age, and his portrait indeed suggests an aura of piety.

As well as having ecclesiastical responsibilities for the diocese, Hendrik was head of the council of Philip the Good; and in April 1493, almost certainly while Erasmus was his secretary, Hendrik was named chancellor of the Burgundian Order of the Golden Fleece—that most prestigious order in which other members of his family were knights. But in 1477, with the marriage of Marie de Bourgondie to the Archduke Maximilian, the grand mastership of the Order had passed into the house of Habsburg. I do not know where chapters of the order were held in the 1490s while Erasmus was the bishop's secretary, but it is known that in 1473 chapter was held at Valencienne, and in 1500 at Brussels. As chancellor of the Order Hendrik would have travelled for its chapters, and it is not improbable that Erasmus would have journeyed with him. For Hendrik moved continually from Cambrai to Bergen, the court in Brussels, and the country home at Halsteren, near Bergen. Preserved Smith has commented that ''Erasmus must have caught some glimpse of the gorgeous and polished Burgundian court''; but surely it was more than a glimpse in the two or three years of Erasmus' service.[4] Hendrik's place of importance as the highest ecclesiastic at the court and in the council of Philip the Good also commands our attention, for the secretary to such a bishop would have been called upon to handle a varied official—and at times doubtless personal—correspondence, and there were surely other duties and functions to perform. While Erasmus in his letters tells us that he was very busy, the exact nature of his duties is not known—beyond our assumption that his principal responsibility was for Latin correspondence and orations. Yet occasionally there were opportunities that related more closely to Erasmus' own interests, as, for example, to visit monastic libraries, as he did at the Augustinian priory of Groenendael (of which the Bishop of Cambrai was a benefactor), in the forest of Zonia near Brussels, and it was there that he discovered manuscripts of Augustine, which he took to his cubicle. One of the monks later wrote in a letter to Martin Lipsius (1522 or 1523), that "they were all amazed and amused that a cleric should prefer one of those large codices to other things, and they could not understand what he found in the saint to delight him so."[5] As well as such visits, there was at least during the spring of 1494 some leisure at Halsteren (to which place the bishop had been compelled to flee because of the plague), and he worked upon his *Antibarbari*, as he wrote to Cornelis Gerard in Epistle 37. In this letter, which is dated by Allen as Spring 1494, Erasmus asks, "What curse could I, then, most suitably call down upon those who made you an administrator? Why, that they should become administrators themselves!" (CWE 1: 71/4–6). Erasmus' word, *procuratores*, is aptly translated as administrators, in our contemporary sense. And he continues: ". . . I have in hand at present a work on literature which I have been threatening for a very long time to write and have been attending to during my retreat in the country . . ." (ibid., lines 11–13) By this date, Spring 1494, it seems clear from the evidence of the *Antibarbari* and certain of Erasmus' letters, that the bishop's expectations of being made cardinal have been frustrated and therefore the anticipated trip to Rome has been abandoned. Erasmus was clearly disappointed, perhaps even for a time depressed. For the abandonment of the journey to Rome coincided with Erasmus' growing realization that life at court was not conducive to study. Relations between Erasmus and his bishop seem, not surprisingly, to have cooled off at about this time.

But to return to the bishop himself. That Hendrik van Bergen was a prelate of status and influence is now evident; but his connections with the Burgundian Court, and the consequent effect upon Erasmus, need further study. In addition, there are other areas for investigation. There were many connections between Hendrik's archiepiscopal court and the religious houses of the Netherlands, the house of the Windesheim Congregation near Brussels among them. For we know that the Master of the Mary of Burgundy Book of Hours actually "worked at Rooclooster, where Hugo van der Goes spent the last years of his life," and this just preceding Erasmus' years in the entourage of the bishop. We also know, thanks to the foundational study of Jozef IJsewijn on "The Coming of Humanism to the Low Countries" (1975) and the more specialized study by Richard Walsh which concentrates on some Italian influences at the court of Charles the Bold, that there was "a marked increase in Italian influence and personnel at the Burgundian court which took place during the reign of Charles the Bold": given Erasmus' growing interests in Italian humanism, this is a question to be investigated further. The Burgundian Court has long been known for its patronage of music and art, and it now is clear that in the 1470s it became a center of humanistic concerns as well.

What can be urged is that we must no longer rest content with simply characterizing Hendrik van Bergen as an influential prelate, and we must recognize that there were aspects of the life and activities of his court (and of his connections with the Burgundian court) which would have been significant in the development of a young and ambitious cleric who was struggling to find his place in the sun of the Burgundian world. Hendrik, let us recall, had studied six years in Italy himself, and he would have had many friendships and contacts there. Perhaps his years in Italy provide the key for our understanding his offering Erasmus the Latin secretaryship: he would have had a better sense of the importance of the new humanistic style than the majority of his fellow prelates north of the Alps. Not only was Hendrik an important prelate in the Church, then, he had entertained hopes of cardinalate, which the influence of his family and his own contacts in Italy would have encouraged; and Erasmus' hopes of an extended visit to Italy seem the more reasonable, in this light.[6] A few years later, after Erasmus left the bishop to go to Paris but still had relations with him, it is clear that the bishop's embassy to England for the prince in the summer of 1498 was at least in part to enlist English help in his renewed bid for the cardinalate (see Epistles 76 and 77, and the first volume of *Contemporaries of Erasmus*); but Hendrik's new hopes for the red hat were again disappointed. At about this time relations between Erasmus and his bishop cooled markedly; the present evidence leaves unanswered questions, and the final story of that relationship remains to be written. Perhaps it is a sense of this shift in the wind, the kind of change in policies and politics, that underlies Erasmus' remark to Batt in 1498 that "the atmosphere at court rather terrifies me" (Allen 80, CWE 1: 160/73), and in December of that year his writing to Willem Hermans, "I have no news of the bishop of Cambrai" (Allen 81, CWE 1: 165/ 96–97).

Hendrik seems to have been a good bishop, and there were what seem to have been genuine expressions of universal regret upon his death in October 1502. Erasmus composed three Latin epitaphs on his bishop's death: the one published in a book of Jacob Anthoniszoon, the vicar-general of Hendrik, *De praecellentia potestatis imperatoriae* (Antwerp: D. Martens, 1502 (along with another poem). The other two epitaphs are printed in Erasmus' *Epigrammata* of 1507. Gilbert Tournoy has shown clearly that the poem in Anthoniszoon's *De praecellentia potestatis* is not an epitaph and argues for yet another text.[7] There was also a Greek epitaph, now lost. For all of this effort, Erasmus complained in a letter of 27 September 1503 to his friend Willem Hermans, he had been sent only six florins. "So as to keep up in death the character he had in life," Erasmus added with some biting, even carping irony.[8] Thus, the Erasmus who would more than twenty years later express his regrets that his friend Thomas More's going into the royal service of Henry VIII in the year 1517 had taken him from good letters, he knew whereof he spoke. Yet he would also have understood from his own firsthand experience the challenge of such service, even the allure of power and influence—but also the dangers, for he wrote his confidant Ammonio early in 1517, "I observe that More too, who used to be impregnable, is swept like you into stormy water" (Ep. 551, CWE 4: 283/21–22).—And perhaps More himself was self-reflexive enough to have made his friend Erasmus, who was connected with the court but not so much a part of it, at least in part, and to some degree consciously, the model for Hythloday in Book I of his *Utopia*, written the year before More's own entrance into the royal service. Certainly all of the conventional arguments of humanists for and against such service are put forward rather skillfully in the dialogue between Hythloday and the two friends, More and Pieter Gillis.

During this period of service with the Bishop of Cambrai, which lasted at least two and possibly as long as three years until late summer 1495,[9] Erasmus made the acquaintance of several people who became strong and supportive friends. The first, and perhaps the most important, was James Batt, who had been schoolteacher at Bergen, and who in attempting to introduce humanistic studies had been harassed by the other teachers, who were committed to the older ways and texts of scholasticism. Their actions led to Batt's having to resign from teaching, and he then became the secretary of his city. Erasmus' own feelings against the barbarians—by whom he meant those opposed to the new humanism and good letters (it was a term he seems to have borrowed from Alexander Hegius, among others)—were stirred up again, and in his moment of leisure at Halsteren he set about reworking an earlier tract called *Antibarbari*, which he now cast into a dialogue with Batt as the main speaker.[10]

The *Antibarbari*, although largely unread today except by Erasmians, is valuable for throwing light upon an early stage of Erasmus' thought, for it contains much of the values and aims of his more mature work. Reworked thus about 1494–95, Book I (of a projected three or four books) is what we now have, and it is a defence of the study of the classics through the dialogue of Willem Hermans, Jacob Batt, the burgomaster of Bergen (Willem Conrad) and the doctor Jodocus. They all discuss rea-

sons for the resistance to the new study of the classics and the decline of
true learning (the stars, Christianity, the aging of the world, and most
seriously of all, bad teachers). It is clear, as Margaret Mann Phillips observes, that Erasmus "is the link which binds these people together." An
attack upon the opponents of good letters, to be sure; but Erasmus' little
book is also something positive or creative. It insists upon friendship, and
it stresses the beauty and calm of its surroundings (should we not acknowledge a debt to the bishop for this, at least?); these elements and the
role of conversation, and the warm appreciation for the living classical
tradition, all contribute to rendering a memorable picture of a civilized
way of life.[11]

This is not the earliest of Erasmus' published works, of course, and it
first saw print only in 1518; but in its way it can be seen as the passport
which would admit Erasmus into the circles of humanist thought and letters in Paris, for he showed the work at once to Gaguin when he arrived
in Paris in September 1495. The *Antibarbari* is also valuable to us by virtue
of the light that it throws on the essential consistency of Erasmus' values
at the same time that there was a continuing deepening of thought. "Consistent does not mean that one should always use the same language, but
that one should always have the same objectives."[12]

We are compelled at nearly every step to infer the nature of Erasmus'
relations with his powerful bishop, and yet much of the evidence we
would like to have is missing. We do not even know how Erasmus was
offered the Latin secretaryship or precisely when it was offered. It has
been suggested that Erasmus himself applied for the post, but no evidence appears to support this notion. From the prefatory letter by Beatus
Rhenanus to Charles V in the *Opera Omnia* of 1540 we read that

> Hendrik van Bergen, bishop of Cambrai, having heard of the fame of Eras-
> mus already ordained, called the young man to himself .... For he saw
> from his elegantly written letters [*epistolis eleganter scriptis*] that Erasmus was
> a person of good character, who possessed some ability in learning and elo-
> quence. (Allen I, 57)

Yet inasmuch as Erasmus' first published letter to Robert Gaguin was
not printed until 1495—and assuming that Erasmus' early letters to Pieter
Winckel, the unnamed nun, Pieter Gerard, Servatius Rogers, Cornelis
Gerard, and other intimate letters (which are all of the early letters that
have come down to us[13]) would not have been shown to the bishop—one
must conclude either that there were other letters, perhaps more public
and literary, like Epistle 32 to Jacob Canter, which were circulating, or
that someone had called them to the attention of the bishop. It is attractive therefore to think that the bishop of Utrecht had recommended his
promising young cleric to his colleague the bishop of Cambrai at one of

their occasions of meeting or correspondence, and perhaps the timing of Erasmus' ordination in April 1492 is to be directly related to the bishop of Utrecht's recommendation and the bishop of Cambrai's offer. If this line of interpretation holds water, then the early letters of Erasmus must be read with a view to the care with which Erasmus composed those letters and to the probability that from about the early 1490s many of them were written as, or became, quasi-public documents. Our interpretation of the letters as biographical evidence[14] must be weighed with this consideration, much as we have now learned to read the *Familiarium Rerum Libri* of Petrarca.

To conclude: for the ambitious young, options must be kept open. Erasmus would increasingly have become aware at Steyn that his credentials fell short of the reach of his ambition: for degrees were necessary then in the professional and ecclesiastical world—perhaps even more than today. And, *a fortiori*, this observation applies to the more sophisticated milieu of the Bishop of Cambrai's household and of course to the Burgundian court.

Finally, it is to be stressed that the Renaissance secretary—whether to a city, prince or prelate—was an important office, and it is probable that Erasmus would have found little time for his studies (or less than he wanted). Increasingly during the Renaissance the office of secretary was held by a humanist, as Kristeller has observed in describing the diffusion of humanism throughout Europe. The list of Renaissance secretaries is a long and distinguished one, and a number of Erasmus' friends were secretaries or performed secretarial functions, as did Pieter Gilles and (in part) Thomas More, to name only two. Yet a secretary's office produced contacts and potential patronage, and these were for Erasmus even more important in the long run than the experience of writing letters and performing tasks for others. But with the hopes of going to Italy no longer alive in the winter of 1494–95, it became all the more important to Erasmus to go on to the university, and so early in 1495 he began his campaign, with the help of Jacob Batt, to be released by the bishop in order to attend the University of Paris. Even here we may look to the influence of the bishop, for the new master of Collège de Montaigu was another Fleming named Jan Standonck;[15] he had worked with Hendrik of Bergen in founding schools at Cambrai and Malines, and there were other relations between the two. Erasmus needed not only the permission of the bishop to leave his service, but also a measure of support; for this he had had to move carefully, as Epistle 42 to Batt (dated by Allen as summer 1495) clearly indicates. Thus, in mid-1495 Erasmus at long last had his bishop's permission and some assurance of support, and in September 1495 he arrived in Paris to begin a new phase of his career.

NOTES

1 James D. Tracy has addressed the question of *The Politics of Erasmus* in his monographic study (Toronto, 1978), and I shall devote a chapter in my forthcoming biography of Erasmus to Erasmus and his bishop.

2 There is a brief introductory sketch of Hendrik in the *Contemporaries of Erasmus*, ed. P. Bietenholz, vol. I, Toronto 1985, 132–33, which is to be supplemented by scattered information in A.J. van der Aa, *Biographisch Woordenboek der Nederlanden* (Haarlem, 1852–78) esp. VII, 204–05, but *passim*. See also R. Walsh, cited below in n. 3. Jacob Anthoniszoon, vicar-general of the bishop, is but one example of such acquaintances—see below, 9.

3 Richard Walsh, "The Coming of Humanism to the Low Countries; Some Italian Influences at the Court of Charles the Bold," *Humanistica Lovan.*, XXIV (1975), 146–97.

4 Preserved Smith, *Erasmus* (1923; rptd. New York, 1962), p. 19; see also Tracy, *Politics*, p. 14. On the length of service see n. 9 below.

5 Allen I, 590; transl. Bainton, *Erasmus of Christendom*, p. 31.

6 On the Italian connections of Hendrik, see Walsh, op.cit., 188; and *Contemporaries*, I, 132.

7 Gilbert Tournoy, "The 'Lost' Third Epitaph for Henry of Bergen, Written by Erasmus," *Humanistica Lovan.*, XXXIII (1984), p. 109.

8 The accounts bear out the figure of six: see *Contemporaries*, I, 133, and Tournoy, op.cit., 109.

9 See *Allen* I—Appendix V, pp. 587–90—where Allen provides a summary of the evidence concerning Erasmus' service with the bishop and concludes that the dates can only be conjectural; but he adds, "it is possible that the whole period with the Bishop was not more than a year, in which case the departure from Steyn must be placed in 1494 and the visit to Halsteren in the spring of 1495" (p. 589). But this is unsatisfactory, and the consensus seems to be that Erasmus' period of service was at least two years. Given the evidence at hand, I conclude that Erasmus went into the Bishop's household just before or just after his ordination in June 1492—the sequence of events is yet another crux—and that he remained with the Bishop until mid-summer 1495.

Allen notes that in one of the Prefaces to Jerome (vol. II, 1516, f. 189) Erasmus mentions a Peter Santeramus as one of his companions in the Bishop's household, and another alluded to in *Adag.* 3031, and a third a William Bollart, afterwards Abbot of St. Amand at Tournay. Jacob Anthoniszoon, vicar-general of the Bishop, is mentioned above, n. 2. On Jacob Batt, see *Contemporaries*, I, 100–01. See further, Tracy, "Erasmus' Friends at the Court of Holland".

Yet another question (one impossible to discuss here) is that of the bishop's school—a regular part of most, if not all, medieval dioceses—and whether Erasmus had any duties in the school; but this is a subject that has not been discussed.

10 See the Introduction of K. Kumaniecki to *ASD* I–1 (1969), 7–32; and in *CWE*, the general introduction by C.R. Thompson to volumes 23 & 24, Literary & Educational Writings (Toronto, 1978), xix ff., and by M.M. Phillips to the *Antibarbari*, pp. 2–15.

11 Phillips, loc.cit., pp. 14–15.

12 Cf. the opening remark in the colloquy 'The Apotheosis of That Incomparable Worthy, John Reuchlin,' that some people are too conservative to change their shoes or dirty underwear, or to eat fresh eggs—Craig R. Thompson, *The Colloquies of Erasmus* (Chicago: University of Chicago Press, 1965), p. 81. And cf. *LB* I, 860 C.

13 There were more, of course: cf. *CWE* 1: xix ff.

14 See now 'The Early Letters of Erasmus: Problems of Interpretation,' pp. 78 ff. in *Erasmus Grandescens* (Nieuwkoop: B. De Graaf, 1988).

15 On Standonck, see *Contemporaries*, III, 1987, and *CWE* 1: 149 n. 11; and A. Renaudet, "Jean Standonck, un réformateur catholique avant la Réforme," in *Humanisme et Renaissance* (1958; rptd. Genève, 1981). He taught at Gouda (p. 119): could his path and Erasmus' have crossed that early?

JEAN-CLAUDE MARGOLIN

ÉRASME ET FERDINAND DE HABSBOURG D'APRÈS DEUX
LETTRES INÉDITES DE L'EMPEREUR A L'HUMANISTE

Les relations d'Érasme avec les plus grands personnages de son temps
nous sont surtout connues grâce à sa Correspondance, éditée par Allen,
et par les nombreux travaux qu'a suscités cette entreprise majeure, inscrite dans la première moitié de ce siècle.[1] Les éditions, traductions,
commentaires des oeuvres d'Érasme, parallèlement aux recherches des
historiens du XVIe siècle, nous ont permis en particulier d'approfondir
et de nuancer la nature des liens, à la fois politiques et personnels, publics
et privés, que le prince de l'humanisme, par ailleurs *homo Batavus*, c'est-
à-dire sujet de l'Empire des Habsbourg, a pu entretenir avec deux des
quatre grands souverains de l'Europe de son temps: l'Empereur Charles-
Quint, qui fut d'abord l'Archiduc Charles de Bourgogne, puis roi d'Espagne,[2] et le frère cadet de celui-ci, le prince Ferdinand, roi de Bohême
et de Hongrie, puis Empereur d'Autriche.[3] On sait que l'humaniste hollandais exerça pendant un certain temps les fonctions, assez théoriques,
de conseiller politique de Charles, pour lequel il avait écrit en 1516 l'*Institution du Prince chrétien*[4] et auquel il dédiera en 1522 sa *Paraphrase de l'Evangile selon saint Matthieu*[5] dans l'intention de le faire renoncer à sa politique
belliqueuse. Quant à Ferdinand, si les circonstances, l'âge du prince, son
éloignement géographique par rapport à Érasme,[6] ne permirent pas à
celui-ci d'exercer à sa cour des fonctions officielles, les liens qui s'établir-
ent et s'affermirent entre le jeune prince et l'humaniste vieillissant furent
de plus en plus confiants, solides, et apparemment plus fructueux que
ceux qu'Érasme avait pu nouer avec son aîné. C'est à Ferdinand qu'il
dédie en 1522 sa *Paraphrase de l'Evangile selon saint Jean*.[7] Mise en garde,
certes comme auprès de Charles, de François Ier et d'Henri VIII, mais
aussi entretien familier avec un jeune homme—Ferdinand avait alors 19
ans—que son éducation, sa piété, son esprit de tolérance, sa vaste culture, son ouverture politique rendaient beaucoup plus apte à recevoir et
à faire fructifier le message érasmien. Ce que nous savons de la politique
autrichienne de Ferdinand,[8] ce que révèle sa correspondance avec
Érasme (Allen a publié 8 lettres[9] échangées entre les deux hommes), et
ce que confirmeront les deux lettres inédites que nous publions ici, c'est
que Ferdinand était, pour l'auteur de l'*Institutio*, le véritable prince chrétien selon le coeur et l'esprit de l'humaniste. D'autre part, à mesure
qu'Érasme avançait en âge, notamment dans la période fribourgeoise de

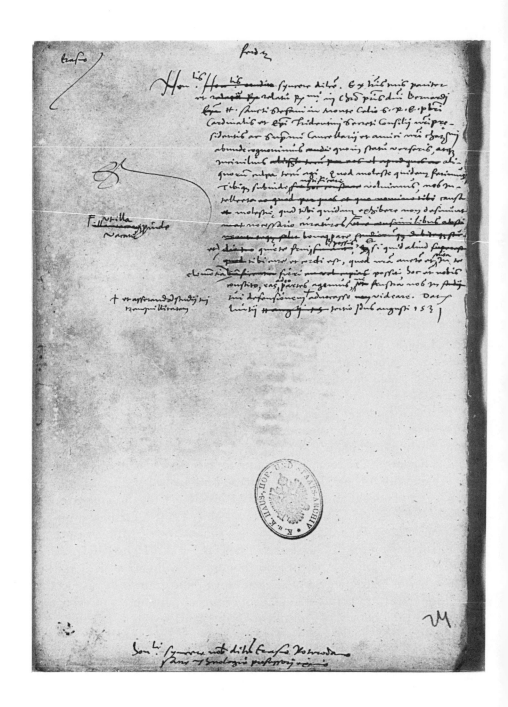

1. Lettre du 11 août 1531

2. Lettre du 22 août 1531

son existence (1529–1535) et que la puissance politique de Ferdinand s'affermissait en dépit des malheurs des temps—développement du luthéranisme, menaces croissantes de la Turquie—les liens de confiance et d'amitié entre le souverain et l'humaniste devenaient de plus en plus forts. Ferdinand avait alors une trentaine d'années, Érasme en avait plus de soixante, ce qui nuançait son attitude déférente envers ce souverain puissant d'une pointe d'affection quasi-paternelle.

Les rapports entre Érasme, l'érasmisme et Ferdinand de Habsbourg nous sont surtout connus grâce à la thèse qu'un chercheur autrichien, Eberdorfer Heinz, a soutenue en 1977 à l'Université de Graz. Dans cette étude, qu'il a intitulée *Ferdinand I und Erasmus von Rotterdam. Ein Beitrag zur Geschichte des Humanismus in Osterreich*, et qui est restée jusqu'à ce jour inédite, il donne en appendice—texte latin original et traduction allemande de son cru—le dossier de la correspondance Érasme-Ferdinand. Mais à côté des huit lettres, bien connues, de l'édition Allen, il a découvert aux Archives d'État de Vienne[11] deux lettres inédites de Ferdinand à Érasme, lettres qui avaient été signalées par ailleurs dans une récente exposition organisée à Vienne sur la Renaissance et l'Humanisme en Autriche.[12] Ces deux lettres étant encore inédites, sauf à figurer dans la dissertation du Dr. Heinz, et après m'être enquis auprès de l'auteur et des autorités autrichiennes responsables de l'autorisation nécessaire, il m'a paru intéressant de les verser au dossier de la correspondance d'Érasme, dont les inédits, comme on sait, sont de la plus grande rareté, même les lettres qui lui ont été adressées. Ainsi qu'on peut le constater, c'est toujours de la période fribourgeoise que datent la plupart des lettres inédites découvertes depuis Allen, période dans laquelle les conditions de vie de l'humaniste, ses déménagements (sans compter son retour à Bâle en mai 1535), un certain détachement de sa part, ont pu favoriser l'oubli de ces textes.

Nous donnerons donc, pour commencer, ces deux lettres, datées respectivement de Linz, le 11 août 1531 et le 22 août 1531. Il ne s'agit pas de brouillons autographes de l'Empereur, dont l'écriture est par ailleurs fort bien connue,[13] mais d'une minute dressée et écrite (en son nom) par son secrétaire de la section latine Johannes Mai.[14] Le papier sur lequel sont écrits ces brouillons de lettres, qui comportent de nombreuses ratures, des renvois, des mentions marginales, etc., et dont la rédaction semble avoir été très rapide et peu soucieuse d'esthétique, n'offre aucune caractéristique digne d'intérêt: c'est un papier typique du XVIe siècle, un peu jauni. Le fol. 24 (lettre du 11 août) a un format de 21,6 cm. sur 31,8 cm. Le fol. 39 (lettre du 22 août) un format de 22 cm. sur 21,5 cm. En fait le premier format paraît bien être celui que l'on utilisait en général, alors que le second résulte d'une coupure qui est intervenue dans la longueur de la feuille (passant ainsi de 31,8 cm. à 21,5 cm.). Nous reproduirons ci-dessous approximativement le filigrane présenté par le fol. 24.[15]

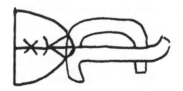

Dans la transcription que nous donnons de ces deux lettres, adressées de Linz[16] à Fribourg (HHStA, Hungarica 18, fol. 24, et HHStA, Hungarica 18, fol. 39), nous indiquons par une barre oblique les fins de ligne du manuscrit, nous résolvons naturellement abréviations ou ligatures et tenons compte, dans un bref apparat, des caractéristiques de la transcription (ratures, etc.)

1. Lettre du 11 août 1531 (Hungarica 18, fol. 24)

HONORABILI SYNCERO NOBIS DILECTO ERASMO ROTERODAMO/
SACRE THEOLOGIE PROFESSORI EXIMIO

Honorabilis syncere dilecte. Ex literis tuis pariter/et relatu reverendissimi in Christo patris domini Bernardi/tituli Sancti Stefani in monte Celio Sanct: Roman: Ecclesie presbyteri/Cardinalis et Episcopi Tridentini secreti Consilii nostri pre-/sidentis ac supremi Cancellarii et amici nostri charissimi/abunde cognovimus quo in statu verseris, atque/incivilius ali-/quorum culpa tecum agi, quod moleste quidem ferimus./Tibique subinde notificare voluimus, nos in-/tellecta causa/molestie, quam tibi quidam exhibere non desinunt/mox necessario curaturos ut illa proinde vacares/bonaque pace/et quiete frui possis, et si quid aliud/tibi cure et cordi est, quod nostra auctoritate et solita in te/clementia fieri possit, hoc etiam nobis/consti[tu]to, eas adeo partes agemus, ne frustra nos in/tui defensionem et asserandam studii tui tranquillitatem advocasse videare. Datum/Lintii tertio Idus augusti 1531.

2. Lettre du 22 août 1531 (Hungarica 18, fol. 39)

Venerabilis et reverendissime syncere dilecte salutem. Accepimus literas/vestras de festo beate Margarete respon-/sivas ad postremas nostras, que nobis gratissime fuerunt/quod ad fratrem Medardum attinet scripsimus/illi et iam denuo scribemus, ut si certo sic habet/quod de illo perhibetur, proinde sit modestior/et nomen vestrum non amplius impetrat./Domum satis commodam vobis obtigisse/gaudemus, qui non solum hanc sed cuncta vobis ex/sententia cedere cupimus. Nec deerunt vobis/pecuniae, cum sint fautores et amici plurimi qui vos iuvare et/augere non dubitant, neque vos arbitramur latere/quanta animi propensione cupierimus aliquid vobis de eo quod/dominus deus nobis concessit et adhuc largitur opitulari vosque/apud nos etiam (si vobis placitum fuisset) fovere et/adiuvare, vehementer autem probamus vos in/ditione serenissimi regis qui vos etiam benigne ut/vestra exigunt merita complectitur, agere/et persistere, sperantes. Hic etiam vobis nihil defore/quod vos scire volebamus. Datum Lintii 22/augusti 1531.

Nous proposons de chacune de ces deux lettres la traduction suivante:

1. A l'honorable Érasme de Rotterdam, éminent professeur de théologie
   sacrée, que nous affectionnons d'un coeur sincère.

Mon honorable ami, bien sincèrement aimé: Par votre lettre, mais aussi
par un rapport du Révérendissime Père en Jésus-Christ, le Seigneur Bernard, prêtre de la Sainte Eglise Romaine, titulaire de Saint-Etienne au
Monte Celio, cardinal et évêque de Trente, président de notre Conseil
secret, chancelier suprême, et de plus notre ami très cher, nous avons été
amplement renseigné sur la situation dans laquelle vous vous trouvez, apprenant que, par la faute de quelques individus, on manquait d'égards
envers vous; ce que nous ne supportons pas sans désagrément. Aussi
avons-nous voulu vous notifier tout de suite, après avoir compris le motif
des tracasseries que certains ne cessent de vous faire subir, que nous allons bientôt prendre les mesures nécessaires pour que vous en soyez
délivré dorénavant et que vous puissiez jouir d'une paix et d'une tranquillité salutaires. Si vous avez en outre quelque autre sujet qui vous
préoccupe et vous tienne à coeur et pour lequel notre autorité et notre
bienveillance coutumière à votre égard puissent intervenir, ici encore
nous prendrons une décision et agirons en sorte que vous n'ayez pas l'impression que nous avons pris en vain la défense de votre cause en voulant
assurer la tranquillité de vos études.
    Fait à Linz, le 11 août 1531.

2. Vénérable et très révérend ami, que nous affectionnons en toute
   sincérité, nous vous saluons.

Nous avons reçu votre lettre, datée de la fête de Sainte Marguerite, par
laquelle vous répondiez à notre plus récente missive, et qui nous a été particulièrement agréable. En ce qui concerne le Frère Médard, nous lui
avons écrit et nous lui récrirons incessamment afin que, mis au courant
des propos qui sont tenus sur sa personne, il fasse preuve lui-même de
plus de modération et cesse de pourfendre votre nom.
    Nous nous réjouissons de l'acquisition que vouz avez faite d'une maison bien confortable, mais nous désirons voir accomplir tous vos souhaits, et pas seulement celui qui concerne cette maison. L'argent ne vous
manquera pas, car vous avez des bienfaiteurs et un très grand nombre
d'amis qui n'hésitent pas à vous venir en aide et à faire prospérer vos intérêts. D'autre part nous ne pensons pas que vous perdiez de vue à quel
point notre désir est vif de vous accorder une partie des largesses que le
Seigneur Dieu nous a concédées et continue de le faire, et de vous appor-

ter, nous aussi (si cela vous agrée) secours et faveur. Mais nous approuvons pleinement que vous demeuriez—et nous espérons que vous continuerez ainsi—sur le territoire du Roi sérénissime qui vous entoure toujours de sa bienveillante sollicitude, ainsi que l'exigent vos mérites. Ici non plus vous ne manquerez de rien: voilà ce que nous voulions vous faire savoir.

Fait à Linz, le 22 août 1531.

Nous examinerons maintenant ces deux brouillons de plus près, puis nous commenterons leur contenu en fonction des préoccupations d'Érasme, telles qu'elles apparaissent à travers sa correspondance des semaines ou des mois qui précèdent les dates de ces deux courts billets, qui se veulent à la fois chaleureux et rassurants.

Comme on peut le voir par l'examen des fac-similés de chacune de ces lettres, le nom d'Érasme (*Erasmo*), écrit de la même main, figure en haut et à gauche. Le fol. 24 comporte, au bas de la feuille, l'adresse: *Honorabili syncero nobis . . . eximio*, écrite, elle aussi, de la main du secrétaire. Le fol. 39 ne comporte aucune indication d'adresse. Dans la lettre du 11 août 1531, deux mots rayés à la première ligne (*Hon.*[lis] *erudite*, le premier ne faisant que redoubler l'épithète liminaire); deux autres mots rayés à la 2e ligne, un à la 6e, la presque totalité de la 7e (. . . *nos et apud quos* . . .), deux à la 9e (. . . *constare*), la presque totalité de la 10e (. . . *quod per quas et quo nomine tibi*), A la 12e ligne, un renvoi marginal (pour inscrire dans la marge ce fragment raturé *ut illa proinde vacares*), et suppression de quelques mots débordant sur la 13e (. . . *a consimilibus abstineant* . . .). Beaucoup d'autres raturés jusqu'à la fin (lignes 13 à 19), d'autres ajoutés entre les lignes (*possis . . . solita . . . adeo . . . ne*), une addition marginale (*et asserandam studii tui tranquillitatem*) qui remplace plusieurs mots rayés plus haut (. . . *debitaque studio tuo* . . .). Aux corrections dues à la syntaxe, comme *adeo . . . ne* remplaçant justement un *adeo . . . ut*, qui n'eût pas correspondu au sens négatif de la proposition, s'ajoute tout à fait à la fin une correction, si l'on peut dire, de style humaniste (il s'agit d'une lettre privée, adressée au prince des humanistes): en effet le scripteur, qui avait commencé par écrire la date en style moderne *11 augusti 15*, s'interrompt—il n'a pas même eu le temps de noter les deux derniers chiffres de l'année 1531—, raye ce qu'il vient d'écrire, et reprend sa feuille pour ajouter: *tertio Idus augusti 1531*. On notera d'ailleurs qu'il n'y a là rien de systématique (comme chez Erasme et les autres épistoliers de l'époque), puisque la lettre du fol. 39 (22 août 1531) se termine sans rature (sinon un *23* transformé en *22*) par la mention: *Datum Lintii 22. augusti 1531*.

Ce brouillon occupe un peu moins de la moitié de la feuille, dans le sens de la hauteur, et ménage une marge, large environ des 2/5 de cette feuille, dans le sens de la largeur.

Il serait intéressant de pouvoir comparer le texte de ce brouillon corrigé avec celui de la lettre qu'Érasme a tenue entre ses mains. Il est tout à fait improbable qu'une telle confrontation puisse se faire un jour. Mais il n'y a aucune raison de supposer l'existence de variantes par rapport au texte que nous présentons ici. Tel qu'il nous est restitué par les Archives d'État d'Autriche, il nous paraît tout à fait conforme au latin correct, clair, généralement concis (sans recherche d'élégances stylistiques) auquel nous a habitués la correspondance latine de Ferdinand Ier.

L'examen de la seconde lettre, celle du 22 août 1531 (Hungarica 18, fol. 39) nous conduit à des remarques analogues. Mêmes abréviations classiques (*Vene^{lis}* pour *Venerabilis,* *re—e* pour *Reverendissime,* *li^{t}s* pour *literas, vrâs* pour *vestras, frám* pour *fratrem, aliqú* pour *aliquid, nt* pour *etiam* etc.), même type de ratures ou de renvois marginaux: *Legimus* (1ère ligne), remplacé par *Accepimus, responsivas* (2e ligne) replacé dans une position syntaxiquement meilleure (2e et 3e lignes), un *penulti[mas]/* (literas) inachevé (dans la marge) remplacé par un *postremas* (sémantiquement plus correct). A la 8e ligne, une périphrase assez redondante (*nobis quoque est volup[tas]*) a été remplacé par le verbe unique *gaudeamus.* L'amorce d'un *deest* (à l'indicatif présent) à la 10e ligne est remplacé par un *deerunt,* au futur, que justifie la suite du texte. Un peu plus loin, *facultas aut* ont été rayés au profit du seul *pecuniae.* A la 12e ligne, *latere* a été disposé à une place stylistiquement meilleure. L'avant-dernière phrase, assez complexe avec son enchevêtrement de propositions a été simplifiée grâce à de nombreuses ratures et une addition marginale.

Le texte occupe un peu moins que la moitié de la feuille dans le sens de la hauteur (en dépit de sa dimension plus réduite) et dispose d'une marge aussi confortable que sur le folio 24. (En bas de la feuille, d'une main moderne: «Hungarica 18, August 1531».

Beaucoup plus intéressant que ces considérations techniques ou graphiques sur ces billets de l'Empereur Ferdinand transcrits par son secrétaire «a latinis», est le sens qu'il convient d'accorder à ces *réponses* par rapport à la vie et aux préoccupations d'Érasme, à la situation à Fribourg-en-Brisgau et au sein des provinces autrichiennes. Une question se pose d'abord: connaissons-nous les lettres d'Érasme qui ont provoqué la rédaction de ces deux billets datés de Linz? On examinera successivement la lettre du 11 août, et celle du 22.

Dans les semaines qui précèdent la lettre du 11 août (et même, si l'on en juge par une lettre d'Érasme à Eobanus Hessus, datée elle-même du 11 août, encore à cette date), l'humaniste vieillissant a deux principales préoccupations: l'une qui tient à son installation dans une nouvelle maison de Fribourg, car la belle demeure «Zum Walfisch» qu'il habitait depuis son arrivée dans la ville impériale ne pouvait plus lui être donnée en location; il devait quitter «Zum Walfisch» pour la Saint-Jean (24 juin)—en fait, il aura un délai jusqu'au mois de septembre 1531—, ce qui le perturbe à tous égards (il s'en entretient dans de nombreuses lettres entre le printemps et l'été).[17] L'autre préoccupation, tout en étant également personnelle, dépasse ce simple problème d'économie domestique et de confort physique: ses ennemis religieux ne cessent de le tracasser, troublant ainsi son confort moral et intellectuel. Ces deux raisons associées font même envisager à un bon ami d'Érasme, l'évêque Bernard de Clès,[18] bras droit du roi Ferdinand, de lui venir directement en aide, en l'invitant à quitter Fribourg et ses ennemis pour s'installer à Vienne, à la cour, et cela d'autant plus vivement que le vieil humaniste avait envisagé de s'installer à Besançon et même écrit à ce sujet (le 26 juillet)[19] au sénat de la ville.

On comprend le ton affectueux et rassurant des lettres de Ferdinand, lui rappelant qu'il peut compter sur lui en toute occasion, et prévenant ses ennemis qu'ils aient à bien se tenir. On comprend en particulier son insistance à évoquer les territoires sur lesquels s'exerce son autorité.

Notons tout d'abord le titre que Ferdinand, nouvellement élu et couronné Roi des Romains, décerne à Érasme dans son adresse: «professeur de théologie sacrée» (ce qui est parfaitement justifié, mais situe immédiatement l'échange épistolaire à un certain niveau). Le prélat Bernard de Clès, dont nous venons de parler, et que Ferdinand gratifie aussi de tous ses titres ecclésiastiques, servait d'intermédiaire entre son maître et l'humaniste. Une lettre de cette époque (Allen la situe en juillet-août),[20] adressée à Érasme de Vienne par Bernard de Clès nous apprend qu'il a fait un rapport à Sa Majesté Royale sur la situation désagréable qui lui est faite à Fribourg. Il n'est pas impossible que ce soit précisément ce rapport de la fin juillet ou du début d'août, qui ait incité Ferdinand à écrire directement à Érasme. On trouve même dans cette lettre de Bernard de Clès une quasi-similitude de certaines expressions: «Je sais que jamais en aucun temps le monarque ne te fera défaut dans tous tes besoins». Et dans la lettre du 11 août, de Linz: «Nous allons bientôt prendre les mesures nécessaires pour que vous soyez délivré des tracasseries que vous subissez ...» Et à la discrète invitation de Bernard de Clès («Tu pourras, si besoin est, te réfugier auprès de nous», c'est-à-dire à Vienne) correspond la non moins discrète allusion de Ferdinand, dans sa lettre du 22 août: «Ici non plus vous ne manquerez de rien».

De quelles tracassaries nouvelles Érasme souffre-t-il précisément à ce moment? La lettre du 11 août est assez discrète à cet égard, puisqu'aucun nom de personne n'est prononcé, il est question de *aliquorum culpa*, de *molestia*, d'insécurité morale dont souffre le vieil humaniste, mais celle du 22 le sera moins, qui cite nommément le Frère Medard (Medardus).[21] Ce qui nous frappe dans la réponse de Ferdinand à la lettre du «plaignant» Érasme et au rapport du Président de son Conseil royal, c'est le ton d'autorité (à l'égard des ennemis de l'humaniste) et de bienveillance à l'égard de celui que nous présentons un peu comme son père spirituel: «nous ne supportons pas sans désagrément» ces tracasseries dont vous êtes victime; «nous allons prendre incessamment les mesures nécessaires» pour que vous en soyez débarrassé. Il se sent l'obligé d'Érasme, en dépit de sa fonction politique, et quand il exprime cette idée qu'il ne veut pas le décevoir («nous agirons en sorte que vous n'ayez pas l'impression que la défense de votre cause aura été vaine»), nous sentons qu'il parle en souverain qui n'admet pas que son autorité soit bafouée, mais aussi et surtout en protecteur particulier de son vieux maître, qui tient par dessus tout à lui montrer qu'il a su rester digne les leçons de morale politique qu'il lui a directement ou indirectement inculquées à travers l'*Institutio Principis Christiani* et ses autres écrits.

En fait le principal ennemi d'Érasme à l'heure actuelle est ce prédicateur franciscain, Metardus ou Medardus (qui deviendra *Merdardus, Frère Merdard*, sous la plume vengeresse d'Érasme dans son fameux colloque *Concio sive Merdardus*)[22], qui était pourtant, par une situation paradoxale, le prédicateur en titre du roi Ferdinand. On comprend que, même s'il éprouvait quelque doute à son sujet, il n'ait pas prononcé son nom le 11 août. Même discrétion relative de la part d'Érasme, dans sa longue lettre du 5 août[23] a son ami Johann Botzheim, dans laquelle il soupçonne le suffragant de l'évêque de Vienne lui-même, de «déblatérer avec grande fougue contre les amants des bonnes-lettres, et contre Érasme en particulier».[24] Ainsi c'est à la cour autrichienne et dans l'entourage de l'évêque de Vienne que prospèreraient en toute liberté les ennemis d'Érasme. On sait notamment que le fameux sobriquet de *Herr Asinus* (Erasmus) est de l'invention du Frère Medardus.

Ces faits laissent entrevoir les limites de l'humanisme érasmien que le roi Ferdinand favorisait à Vienne et dans le reste de l'Autriche, et sur lequel la thèse de Heinz apporte beaucoup de précision, notamment en ce qui concerne le développement de l'imprimerie et les éditions autrichiennes d'Érasme:[25] en dépit de la politique d'ouverture et de tolérance du roi, fondée sur ses propres convictions, son pays était, lui aussi, traversé par un courant d'intégrisme romain, pourchassant luthériens et crypto-luthériens, dénonçant partout des propositions hérétiques, et voyant en Érasme le chef du mouvement réformiste à l'intérieur de l'Eglise catholique. Plus virulent encore, et surtout plus cultivé que Medardus, apparaissait Johann Eck,[26] véritable «bête noire» de l'humaniste, sévissant dans cette même région de l'Empire des Habsbourg, à propos duquel Johann Faber,[27] évêque de Vienne, écrivait à Érasme le 21 juin 1531:[28] «Je l'ai admonesté de mon mieux récemment par lettre ... Ses forfanteries et ses menaces n'ont vraiment pas de quoi t'inquiéter ...»

La seconde lettre de Ferdinand à Érasme, écrite onze jours seulement après la première, fait allusion, elle aussi, à une lettre d'Érasme, «datée de la fête de Sainte Marguerite», c'est-à-dire du 12 ou du 15 juillet, laquelle était une réponse à la dernière lettre du souverain à l'humaniste. Aucune de ces deux lettres, semble-t-il (car un manuscrit inconnu ou inexploité peut toujours surgir de quelque dépôt d'archives), n'a survécu. Mais la lettre du 22 août est suffisamment claire pour que nous puissions imaginer le contenu de celle d'Érasme: plaintes et protestations contre le Frère Medard, cette fois-ci nommément désigné. Ferdinand lui a écrit aussitôt pour lui enjoindre de cesser ses activités calomniatrices et insultantes; il lui a écrit, et il récidivera. Dans l'expression *nomen vestrum impetrat*, on peut prendre *nomen* dans son sens premier de nom, nom de personne (puisque le nom *Erasmus* avait été sciemment déformé pour faire rire les ennemis de l'humaniste) et dans son sens classique de réputation, renom. D'ailleurs en se moquant du nom d'Érasme, Medard nuisait inmanquablement à sa réputation de philosophe et de théologien.

L'allusion à la nouvelle maison d'Érasme (*domum satis commodam*) concerne l'une des deux préoccupations de l'heure que nous évoquions plus haut. Dans une lettre d'Érasme à Eobanus Hessus du 11 août, lettre restée inconnue pendant quatre siècles et demi, et récemment découverte dans un manuscrit de Marbourg,[29] l'humaniste s'exprimait ainsi à propos de cette maison, dans ce mélange d'amertume et d'humour dont il est coutumier: «D'adorateur des Muses, je suis devenu enchérisseur, acheteur, stipulateur, déménageur, migrateur; j'ai affaire aux maçons, aux charpentiers, aux ferronniers, aux vitriers ... Jamais ne m'a paru aussi sage le comportement de Diogène, quand il se réfugiait dans un tonneau. Pour l'achat et les réparations de la maison, j'ai dépensé en argent comptant une somme de 750 florins, et ce n'est pas fini!»[30] Il n'est pas interdit de penser que, sans entrer dans de tels détails dans sa lettre (perdue) au Roi Ferdinand, Érasme ait pu faire allusion à ses difficultés financières. On comprendrait alors mieux les offres pécuniaires du souverain, quand il assure son vieux maître que «l'argent ne lui manquera pas»: parmi les bienfaiteurs et les amis d'Érasme, nul doute qu'il ne se range lui-même en tête! Un tel sujet ou une telle offre d'assistance matérielle sont, il faut le reconnaître, beaucoup moins gênants que l'enregistrement d'une plainte contre le prédicateur en titre du roi Ferdinand, et la promesse de rappeler à l'ordre le frèreur mineur. Le ton, l'invocation de Dieu, dispensateur des largesses dont peuvent jouir certains hommes, mais qui ne leur appartiennent pas en propre, et par conséquent, dont ils doivent disposer avec générosité et intelligence, sont dans le droit fil de la pensée théorique et du comportement pratique d'Érasme: l'argent doit servir à atténuer les inégalités matérielles entre les humains. D'où cette promesse renouvelée d'apporter à Érasme «secours et faveur» (*fovere et adjuvare*). Ici, le verbe *fovere* a pratiquement le même sens que *favere*: il s'agit d'une faveur qui est un réconfort.

L'espoir de voir Érasme continuer à vivre *in ditione serenissimi regis*, c'est-à-dire dans les limites d'un territoire dépendant de l'autorité du Roi (de lui-même) fait allusion à ses velléités de départ pour Besançon[31] ou ailleurs.

La fin de la lettre ne fait que confirmer solennellement les promesses de protection et de sécurité morale pour un hôte de marque qui honore par sa présence et ses travaux les territoires sur lesquels règne l'autorité de l'Empereur ou celle du Roi des Romains.

Un dernier point, qui touche à la stylistique latine de l'*ars conscribendi epistolas*, auquel Érasme a consacré tant de pages, devenues rapidement classiques,[32] mais aussi à la nature des rapports entre le souverain et l'écrivain, tel qu'ils se révèlent à travers ces billets, à la fois très personnels et pourtant officiels: la lettre du 11 août utilise le *tu* latin (*ex literis tuis, tecum agi, tibique notificare voluimus, tibi cure et cordi est, tui defensionem, tui tranquillitatem*), celle du 22 le *vos* plus solennel que les textes du Moyen Age et de la Renaissance réservent aux personnages importants (d'une manière qui n'a d'ailleurs rien de systématique), ce qui est ici le cas (*literas vestras, nomen vestrum, nec deerunt vobis, neque vos arbitramur, si vobis placitum, quod vos scire volebamus*, etc.). Il serait sans doute vain d'insister longuement sur la différence entre l'emploi ou le non-emploi du pluriel dit de majesté, car les rapports de Ferdinand et d'Érasme n'ont pas changé entre le 11 et 22 août. On ne peut pourtant pas nier qu'il y ait une intention dans l'emploi de l'une ou de l'autre formule stylistique: les tracas persistant, les plaintes d'Érasme se faisant de plus en plus pressantes, le souverain a voulu, dans son second billet, souligner davantage que les mesures qu'il a déjà prises ou qu'il s'apprête à prendre vont au-delà de la personne individuelle de l'humaniste; la solennité du ton implique que ses décisions d'ordre politique visent à réparer les offenses qui sont faites à un personnage vénérable, véritable symbole de la culture, de la tolérance et de la paix. Enfin, Ferdinand employant, aussi bien dans la lettre du 11 août que dans celle du 22, la première personne du pluriel pour ce qui le concerne (*cognovimus, ferimus, voluimus, nostra auctoritate, hoc etiam nobis constituto, nos*, etc., d'une part, *accepimus, scribemus, arbitramur apud nos, volebamus*, etc., d'autre part), l'emploi de *nos* et de *vos* dans le second billet souligne davantage ce fait que l'humaniste est traité par le jeune souverain à égalité; le billet a un caractère plus solennel que le premier.

La découverte par le chercheur autrichien, et la publication, par nos soins, de ces deux lettres de Ferdinand Ier à Érasme n'apportent pas d'information exceptionnelles ni en ce qui concerne la vie ou la pensée d'Érasme, ni en ce qui concerne la politique intérieure du souverain d'Autriche. Mais elles précisent un certain nombre de points, que nous connaissions plus ou moins bien par la correspondance du printemps et de l'été 1531. Compte tenu de la rareté des lettres d'Érasme, ou de celles qui lui furent adressées, découvertes après le passage d'Allen dans les bibliothèques et les dépôts d'archives européens, celles-ci méritent de figurer désormais dans l'*Opus Epistolarum*, en appendice au volume IX.[33] Nous proposons de les affecter des numéros *2518B* (pour la première) qui se situe entre la L.2518 envoyée par Érasme à Jean Herwagen le 9 août 1531, et la L.2519 de Boniface Amerbach à Érasme, du 14 août,[34] et *2525A* (pour la seconde), qui se situe entre la L.2525, partie le même jour (22 août) de Fribourg pour Augsbourg et adressée par Érasme à Anton Fugger, et L.2526, adressée par le même Érasme à Reginald Pole le 25 août.

NOTES

1 P.–S. Allen ed. *Opus Epistolarum Desid. Erasmi*, Oxford, 1904–1956, 12 volumes.

2 Nous nous contenterons de ces deux références: Pierre Mesnard, «L'expérience politique de Charles Quint et les enseignements d'Érasme», dans *Fêtes et Cérémonies au temps de Charles Quint II* (Les Fêtes de la Renaissance), CNRS 1960, p. 45–56;—Jean-Claude Margolin, «Charles Quint et l'Humanisme», dans *Charles-Quint, le Rhin et la France*, Strasbourg, 1973, p. 157–182.

3 Parmi les travaux récents portant sur la politique de Ferdinand Ier, nous citerons: Paula Sutter Fichtner, *Ferdinand I of Austria: the politics of dynasticism in the Age of the Reformation*, New York, 1982; Alfred Kohler, *Antihabsburgische Politik in der Epoche Karls V*, Göttingen, 1982. Voir aussi: Wolfgang Hilger, *Ikonographie Kaiser Ferdinands I (1503–1564)*, Vienne, 1969 (Österreichische Akademie der Wissenschaften).

4 Voir *Bibliotheca Belgica*, t. II, p. 844–867, et *Opera omnia, ASD*, IV–1, p. 95–219.

5 Dédicace dans *Allen*, 1255. Texte *LB*, VII, xx1(v°) – xx2(r°).

6 Le prince Ferdinand était resté en Espagne, pendant toute sa jeunesse, et Érasme qui n'y était jamais allé, n'avait pu avoir de contacts directs avec lui que plus tard. Un parti s'était formé en sa faveur, avant même que le nouveau souverain d'Espagne, Charles, son frère aîné, ne vînt en septembre 1517 prendre possession de ses États. Les intérêts de ce dernier étaient d'éloigner au plus vite Ferdinand d'Espagne.

7 Dédicace dans *Allen*, 1323. Texte dans *LB* VII, col. 490–491.

8 Voir notamment l'ouvrage (cité) de P.S. Fichtner.

9 Ce sont respectivement les lettres 1323, 1333, 1343, 1515, 2005, 2090 et 3087, en ce qui concerne celles qu'Érasme a envoyées à Ferdinand, et la lettre 1505, celle que Ferdinand a envoyée à Érasme.

10 Je tiens à remercier l'Administration de la Bibliothèque Herzog-August de Wolfen-büttel, ainsi que celle de la Bibliothèque Universitaire de Vienne, pour les facilités qui m'ont été accordées pour la consultation de ce travail, absent de la plupart des grandes bibliothèques européennes ou américaines. Il s'agit d'un dactylogramme de VI – 353 p.

11 Haus- ,Hof- und Staatsarchiv, Vienne, Minoritenplatz.

12 *Renaissance in Österreich* (Schloss Schallenburg). *Katalog des Niederösterreichische Landes-museum*, Landesregierung, 1974. Les deux lettres inédites sont signalées à la page 112.

13 Voir par exemple un certain nombre de lettres autographes aux Archives Nationales d'Autriche. Voir aussi les facsimilés, dans les volumes de la correspondance de Fer-dinand (en cours de publication).

14 Je dois ces renseignements et ceux qui suivent (concernant la description des deux documents originaux) au Dr. Christiane Thomas, des Archives d'État de Vienne. Qu'elle en soit vivement remerciée, ainsi que pour l'envoi d'un microfilm et de précieuses photocopies.

15 Egalement fourni aimablement par Madame l'Archiviste Thomas. La consultation du répertoire des filigranes de Briquet (voir la nouvelle édition du Briquet en 4 volumes, Amsterdam, 1968) ne présente qu'un intérêt négatif. On pourrait à la rigueur faire quelques investigations dans le tome III (Armoiries, Nos 841 à 2361, en tenant comp-te d'une partie du monogramme) et dans le tome IV (Nos 8441 à 8911 pour cette sorte de lettre qui ressemble à un P), mais le champ est si vaste qu'il n'est pas possible de s'y repérer utilement.

16 Le nom de *Lintium* (ou *Lincium*) employé ici (à la forme du locatif) est l'un des noms latins de la ville de Linz (ou Lintz). On trouve aussi *Aredata, Aredanum, Gesodunum, Len-tia, Lentium, Lincia*, et parfois *Lintiis ad Danubium* (d'après le *Dictionnaire de géographie an-cien et moderne* de P. Deschamps).

17 Voir par exemple *Allen*, 2470 (á Johann Choler), 2478 (à Boniface Amerbach), 2506 (au même), 2507 (de Boniface Amerbach à Érasme), 2514 (Au Sénat de Besançon), 2515 (de Bernard de Clès), 2525 (à Antoine Fugger) . . .

18 Sur Bernard de Clès (1483 – 1539), voir la notice de Ilse Guenther dans le volume I de *Contemporaries of Erasmus*, Toronto / Buffalo / London, 1985, p. 313 – 315. Voir aussi Giulio Briani, «Carteggio tra Bernardo di Cles ed Erasmo di Rotterdam», in *Studi tren-tini di scienze storiche* 25 (1946), p. 24 – 39, et 26 (1947), p. 151 – 164.

19 Voir note 17. La valeur des vins de Bourgogne et le souvenir qu'il en avait ne sont sans doute pas étrangers à ce projet d'Érasme. Il venait pourtant d'acheter à Fribourg une maison fort coûteuse.

20 *Allen*, 2515.

21 Sur ce Franciscain, dont le nom véritable (d'après l'édition d'Allen et Preserved Smith, dans *A Key to the Colloquies of Erasmus*, Cambridge, Mass., 1927) serait Medardus von (der) Kirchen, mais dont on ne sait en vérité pas grand'chose (en de-hors de ses attaques contre Érasme entre 1530 – 1532), voir la notice de P.G. Bieten-holz, in *Contemporaries of Erasmus*, vol. II, 1986, p. 415.

22 *ASD* I – 3, 653 – 666. Deux *famuli* d'Érasme, Hilaire Bertulphe (Hilarius) et Liévin (Levinus) s'en prennent au franciscain. Medardus avait osé attaquer la version éras-mienne du *Magnificat* dans un de ses sermons pendant la diète d'Augsbourg, en 1530. Voir Allen, 2408, 2503 et 2504. On conçoit le parti que l'humaniste pouvait tirer de l'orthographe fantaisiste qu'il avait appliquée au nom de son ennemi.

23 *Allen*, 2516.

24 *Ibid.*, p. 310, l. 45 – 46. Il appelle ce suffragant, avec la liberté qui lui est coutumière, «un Mômos à deux cornes» (allusion à la mitre épiscopale). Cet évêque suffragant venait de remplacer Botzheim comme doyen du Chapitre à Ueberlingen; il était en outre évêque de Constance.

25 *Op.cit.*, p. 193 et suiv.

26 Sur Eck, voir la notice de Denis R. Janz, dans *Contemporaries of Erasmus*, vol. I, p. 416 – 419. Voir aussi: Arno Seifert, *Logik zwischen Scholastik und Humanismus: Das Kom-mentarwerk Johann Ecks*, Munich, 1978.

27 Sur Faber (ou Fabri), voir la notice de Denis R. Janz, *Contemporaries of Erasmus*, vol.
   II, p. 5–8. Johannes Faber (1478–1541), qui avait eu dans les débuts une attitude
   «érasmienne» à l'égard de Luther, était au service de Ferdinand dès 1523. Il maintient
   d'excellentes relations avec Érasme, et servit utilement sa cause en tant qu'évêque de
   Vienne, en dépit de son entourage antiérasmien. Voir aussi: L. Helbling, *Dr. Johann
   Fabri: Generalvikar von Konstanz und Bischof von Wien*, Münster, 1941.
28 *Allen*, 2503.
29 Voir la notice de la lettre *2518A*, dans le vol. XII de *La Correspondance d'Érasme*, Bruxelles, Univ. Press, 1984), p. 8.
30 Trad. J.–C. Margolin, *ibid.*, p. 9.
31 Voir notes 17 et 19.
32 Voir son *De conscribendis epistolis* (Bâle, 1522): *ASD* I–2, 153–579.
33 Mais aucune réédition de l'*Opus Epistolarum* n'est envisagé à l'heure actuelle!
34 Et pour tenir compte de la lettre *2518A*, que nous avons découverte (ou plutôt redécouverte à la Bibliothèque universitaire de Marbourg, après Clemens Bruehl), et qui a été
   publiée *en français* sous ce numéro par nos soins (voir note 29). La disparition de Clemens Bruehl n'a pas permis, jusqu'ici, la publication du texte latin de cette lettre (erreur dans la notice de la page 8 de *La Correspondance d'Érasme*, vol. XII).

A.G. WEILER

THE TURKISH ARGUMENT AND CHRISTIAN PIETY IN DESIDERIUS ERASMUS "CONSULTATIO DE BELLO TURCIS INFERENDO" (1530)[1]

1. *The Consultatio de bello Turcis inferendo and its religious context*

Erasmus presents his consultation concerning the war against the Turks, edited in 1530, in the pious context of an *Enarratio in Psalmum XXVIII*, though he himself indicates that this psalm is only "obiter enarratus". Ps. XXVIII is a very brief song on the wind, called *Vox Domini*, who's force is celebrated and who brings man to the adoration of the power of the Lord. We will see how Erasmus uses the metaphore of *Vox Domini* in application to the Turks. But it is rather important to notice right from the beginning, that this *Consultatio* is embedded in a religious context, and that the religious point of view on the problem of the war against the Turks is dominant. Erasmus—as we could expect from this religious, Christian, biblical humanist—does not offer a thorough analysis of the political situation which might bring the Western princes to decide for a war, nor any analysis of the mutual strength of the two belligerent parties, of the consequences of a lost war or of a victory. Surely, these elements are there, but just to support his religious argument, that concentrates on the need of a *correctio vitae*, a moral and religious renewal of life in Western christianity.

2. *Historical context of the Consultatio*

Since the Turks had crossed the Bosporus and had set foot on European soil, since they had taken Thessalonika (1430), since the battle of Varna (1444) and of Kosovo Polje (1448), Europe lived in anxiety about the course the events would finally take. But since the fall of Constantinople in 1453 it was clear that the Turkish threat would be constantly impending over Europe. The Turks had their capital now in Europe! It is not surprising that Italy was stricken with panic when Mehmed II crossed the sea and took the city of Otranto (in 1480). Pope Sixtus IV intended to escape to Avignon. In the same year, 1480, Rhodes was besieged, in vain as yet, but in 1522 the isle of the Johannite Milites was captured. Again, Europe was in great danger. The catastrophe of Mohács in 1526, where king Lewis II of Hungary died, struck the European nations with terror and sorrow. (Erasmus wrote his 'De vidua Christiana' for Lewis' widow, Mary of Hungary.) Mary's brother, Ferdinand of Habsburg, had to fight for his rights to the throne against the nationalist leader Jan Zápolyai, whose case was supported by the Turks: the outcome would be a division of Hungary between the two rivals, but in 1530, the year that Erasmus published his *Consultatio*, the struggle was not yet decided. And some new hope for victory there was, since Vienna had withstood the siege by Soliman in October, 1529.

3. *Literary context*

Europe was kept informed about what happened in the Ottoman Empire and the attacks it launched at Western Christianity by pamphlets, small books, or "Neue Zeitungen" (New Journals), printed since the end of the fifteenth century. These *Turcica* (German: *Türkendrucke*): printed works concerning the Turks, were spread all over Europe, both in Latin and in the national languages. The woodcarvings on the frontpage gave illustration of the events of the war: battles, sieges, cruelties. The dramatic culminating-points like the fall of Rhodes, the Christian defeat at Mohács, the siege of Vienna, increased this stream of information to a considerable extent. Carl Göllner[2] has made an analysis of the content of some *Turcica*, which appeared on the occasion of the defeat of Mohács. There are eye-witness reports, comments on the social conditions in Hungary as a possible cause for the defeat since Hungarian farmers had fled to the Turks and did not return. The position of Jan Zápolyai is discussed, but also the position of Ferdinand, the Habsburg monarch, and of course the polemics between Catholics and Protestants, which did bear also on the Turkish issue, have all been given full attention. So it is clear, that Erasmus' *Consultatio* is not a strange phenomenon at that time; it has its own distinguished place in the genre of the *Turcica*.

4. *The source of Erasmus' knowledge of Turkish History*

In his treatise Erasmus gives a considerable amount of space to a short history of the Turks, without indicating however where he has got his information on the subject. In our inquiries concerning this point, we came across the unpublished Freiburg inaugural dissertation of Ehrenfried Hermann of 1961, entitled *Türke und Osmanenreich in der Vorstellung der Zeitgenossen Luthers. Ein Beitrag zur Untersuchung des deutschen Türkenschrifttums*. According to Hermann, Erasmus' knowledge of the history of the Turks stems from the work *De origine Turcarum*, published by the Venetian humanist Giovanni Battista Egnazio (Cipelli). Also Michael Heath[3] has identified Egnazio's work as the source of Erasmus' knowledge of Turkish history. *De origine Turcarum* is only a part of a much larger work by Egnazio, viz. his *De Caesaribus libri III*, which appeared at the publishing house of Aldus in Venice, 1516. In a letter of June 21th, 1517, Egnazio writes to Erasmus, that he has sent to him "My Emperors—Caesares meos". In the interpretation of Allen (Ep. 588, 55 note) "Caesares meos" refers to the *Historiae Augustae Scriptores* of Suetonius, which was published by Aldus in 1516 according to an edition by Egnazio. However, this is not correct. In a preface to the reader to Erasmus' edition of Suetonius' *Historiae Augustae Scriptores*, dated June 23, 1518, and perhaps written by Erasmus, the publisher Froben indicates that he used Egnazio's *Caesares*. This statement makes it clear, that also in the letter of Egnazio to Erasmus of June 21th, 1517, "Caesares meos" refers to Egnazio's own book on the Emperors. So we have straight evidence for the source of Erasmus' knowledge of the history of the Turks.

Now comparing both texts, Egnazio's and Erasmus', closely, there is full evidence that Erasmus extensively used the text of Egnazio. He follows Egnazio in his argument, drops some sections, sums up others, and most of all reworks the text in his own Latin. By the use of synonyms he makes slight alterations to Egnazio's text, just as the orthography of Turkish names is sometimes different by Erasmus. We can even find small additions in the text. For example, where Egnazio quotes Pliny and Pomponius Mella as the only two classical authors who mention the Turks in their works, Erasmus gives the texts of Pliny at full length and adds Ptolemy out of his own knowledge of classical Antiquity. His account of contemporary Turkish history, viz. the capture of Otranto in 1480 and the supposed flight of Pope Sixtus IV to Avignon is a little more elaborate than Egnazio's. Is there still another source Erasmus relied on, or is this just "oral history"? More than once Erasmus puts 'dicitur' or 'feruntur' where Egnazio simply has the facts. Is this just a matter of literary style, or did Erasmus admit some historical doubt concerning all that was said and told about the Turks? A fact is, that Erasmus, according to the custom of his time, did not mention the name of Egnazio or of his work. This remains surprising, even considering the customs of that time. But as a matter of fact, no one did at the time, and so scholars find themselves confronted with the problem of the source-relationships, also within the genre of the humanistic historiography on the origins and the history of the Turks. According to Agostino Pertusi,[4] Egnazio also had his own sources, for example, Johannes Zonaras for early Turkish history, further on the *Historia turchesca* of the Venetian Gian Maria Angiolello or some local Venetian chronicles, whereas Johan Spiesheymer (Cuspinianus) (1473–1529) in his work *De caesaribus atque imperatoribus romanis* and

more especially in his excursus *De Turcorum origine*, written c. 1521, copies
the work of Egnazio, though he composes as if drawing on personal knowledge. Erasmus was not the only writer who operated in this way.

5. *The image of the Turks in the West*

In vol. III of his *Turcica*, Carl Göllner has published a study on the image
of the Turks in western literature. He has showed specifically which was
the mental perception of the phenomenon 'Turk' in the western mind,
i.e. the appreciation, the prejudices, the persistent themes and the specific nuances every single author brings in into his description. The reader
is referred to the more detailed studies of Michael Heath, J.W. Bohn-
stedt, C.A. Patrides, Robert Schwoebel and M.E.H.N. Mout.[5]

I for one will confine myself here to the image Erasmus brings forward
on the Turks in his *Consultatio*, indicating already now that he has practically no nuances in this point with regard to his main source, Giovanni Battista Egnazio. Both do use the same denigrating epitheta and commonplaces.

6. *Erasmus' vision of the Turks*

In this paragraph I will first analyze Erasmus' religious metaphorical
way of speaking about the Turks; in the second part I will concentrate on
his historical, more realistic way of talking about them.

a) *Erasmus' religious metaphorical language concerning the Turks*

In the context of his *Enarratio in Psalmum XXVIII* the Turks are seen as the
voice of God, Who calls upon us for inner conversion, for reconciliation
with Him and for a life regulated by His divine law. From the first lines
of the *Consultatio* Erasmus makes it clear that the heart of the European
Christian cause is the correction of life: "de mutanda in melius vita, quod
est totius negotii caput" (Ep. 31, r. 11). God's punishments are meant to
bring about the amelioration of the Christian way of living, but the Christians have become even more recalcitrant. They suffer from wars, robber-
ies, internal conflicts, factions and party-strife, epidemics, and famine,
new diseases like the *scabies Gallica* (syphilis) and the English sweat, and
finally the irreconcilable division in Christianity. All these miseries are
the voice of God, calling us back to Him: *Vox Domini* (Ps. 28), the voice
of God over the waters, viz. over the people that fluctuates to and fro, because of various affections and various doctrines. It is the voice of God
that beats the desert, viz. the Christian heart which is likewise full of wild

and ferocious animals like avarice, lust, cruelty, envy. The voice of God
breaks the cedars of Lebanon, viz. the high-ranked personalities in the
church and the world, and extinguishes the flames of fire, viz. the injustice in the Christian world. Now again God is calling them by means
of the Turks. In Erasmus' view they play the same role in God's plans
of salvation, as all the other internal European stimuli such as the dis-
astrous economical, social, and political situation of his days. Erasmus
pencils a sharply drawn picture of the 'infelicitas nostri seculi', as he
puts it.

b) *Erasmus' view of Turks and Christians in their historical conflict*

Now these religious metaphors concerning the Turks only serve as a vehicle for the religious message Erasmus has to announce to his Christian
audience. And this message has a double tenor: the Turks, being the instruments in God's hand punishing the Christians for their sins, cannot
win a final victory over the Christian armies if only sin be banished from
Christian hearts. So Erasmus will stress the ferocity, the rapacity, the barbarism of the Turks, but finally he puts his trust in God Who will give the
Christians victory if only they fight without sin in their hearts. In Erasmus' way of arguing, the real danger for Europe is not so much the
Turkish power, as the sins of Christians. All his attention is concentrated
on this point, in a typically Erasmian way. And what comes out is more
a portrait of his disappointment concerning the Christians of his days
than a terrifying image of the Turks.

Let us follow his analysis of the conflict-situation more closely. In
Erasmus' vision the Turks could only achieve what they have brought upon Europe because of the indolence of the Christians, not by their own
piety or virtue: "Turcas non sua pietate, non sua virtute, sed nostra
socordia potissimum hucusque crevisse" (p. 38, r. 215–216). It is the
own fault of the Christians, not only to be found in the sinfulness of their
daily life, but also in their social and political disabilities. The Turks do
not have any virtue of their own. Their name is already so unnoble that
one will hardly find it in any of the classical authors.

As I indicated before, Erasmus inserts a rather long history of the
Turks, in order to illustrate how ferocious and barbarous this people is.
Relying entirely on Egnazio Battista, he gives an outline of the Turkish
history, from the moment of their appearance when they invaded Persia
and Asia Minor, to the reign of Selim (1512–1520) and Soliman (1520–
1566). At this moment in history Erasmus brings his story to a stop since
his source, Battista, does not go any further. He sums up what the Turkish "happy impiety" (*felix impietas*: p. 48, r. 312) has achieved, while the

Western nations refuse to dedicate themselves to the pursuit of piety (*pietatis studium*). While they struggle in more than civil wars over every small territory, the Turkish *imperium*, or rather *latrocinium*, has widened tremendously. Erasmus gives a survey of the territories under Turkish control, and recalls the fall of Rhodes (1522), the battle of Mohácz (1526) and the death of king Lewis II of Hungary, the occupation of Hungary, the expulsion of king Ferdinand, the siege of Vienna (1529), and the devastation of Austria, and then comes back to his starting question: "unde igitur illis tantus rerum successus?"

A close analysis of the text of the *Consultatio* shows that Erasmus' way of arguing against the Turks is always connected with the argument against European discord and impiety. At the heart of the text with which Erasmus ends his historiographical survey we find the clue to his argument in the *Consultatio* as a whole: 'Turcae pugnamus cum Turcis' (p. 52, r. 373 – 374). We fight with the Turks in a Turkish way.

We may sum up Erasmus' argument in the following way: the tremendous growth of Turkish power cannot be attributed to their piety or virtue. They owe their victories to the vices of Christians who fought against the Turks while their God was angry with them. The Christians are pushed by the same passions as the Turks, as recent history shows. If the Christians had fought a righteous war with the Turks, in concord and union under the banner of Christ, with pure souls, their Christian territory would not have been so diminished.

7. Erasmus' advice concerning the war against the Turks

Now, what remedy has to be sought for this difficult situation which poses a very complex moral, political and military problem? Erasmus' answer is in line with the analysis of the historical situation he has given before. He rejects the position of those who are clamouring for a war against the Turks, but also the position of those people who dissuade to use the weapons against the Turks. The first formulation we find of Erasmus' position sounds rather ambiguous too: "Just as not every war with the Turks is just and pious, so it can happen that not to resist the Turks is nothing else than to betray the Christian cause to very ferocious enemies, and to desert our brothers who are oppressed by their unworthy servitude" (p. 52, r. 390 – 393). Unexperienced people shout "war against the Turks!", but they forget that the Turks are human beings and semi-Christian. They do not consider whether there is a just cause for the war, whether it is useful to take up arms and to exasperate an enemy who will attack the Christians even more violently. And above all: they do not consider that the most perilous enemies of the church are the impious princes, above all the princes of the church. The Turks are painted as very cruel, but the Christians are, according to Erasmus, no less cruel in their internal struggles: think of what they did to the small town of Aspern in Guelders! The common people think that we may kill every Turk as a mad dog, just because he is a Turk. But that is not allowed by our civil law even with regard to the Jews: when a Jew is punished by a Christian magistrate, it is for his crimes, not for his faith as such. If we were under Turkish domination, the Turks would have the same rights with us. So it is an error to hold that a man who falls in the battle against the Turks goes straight to heaven: only with a pure conscience man will enter heaven. And again Erasmus underlines the necessity of a moral renewal in the European Christian world: "we must repel this most awful kind of Turk from our hearts, viz. the avarice, the ambition, the desire for domination, the presumption, the impiety, luxury, lascivious loves, fraudulence, anger, hatred, and envy". He asks for a just cause, and a religious mind in undertaking a war: we may repel the Turks if at last we take away the reason for God's anger against us.

Erasmus is aware of the fact that his argument might sound as if he was arguing against war with the Turks. More than once in his treatise he makes clear that this is not his intention. He states that all his arguments are directed to this aim "that we might have a succeful war against them, and might win a beautiful victory for Christ" (p. 64, r. 686 – 687). Or again: "A war can only be succeful, if first of all we try to mitigate the anger of God, if our intention is pure and just, if all our trust is in Christ, if we fight under His banner, if He triumphs in us, if we are obedient to God's commandments, if we attack the enemies as if under His eyes" (p. 68, r. 759 – 762). Erasmus is not so much advocating a war against the Turks as against the enemy in Christian hearts. And this pertains not only to soldiers, warlords, or kings, but above all to priests, bishops, cardinals and the pope. Erasmus is very direct in his criticism of all kind of abuses in ecclesiastical circles.

At the end of his treatise Erasmus deals with various more specific arguments. One feels, that Erasmus is hesitating in answering these rather realistic positions. He affirms that he too is not pleased by the prospect of a war against the Turks, unless it is required by unavoidable necessity. With God's help everything is possible, but then we should have God on our side. And again he finds his decisive argument: in the whole Christian world there must first of all be a universal and significant correction of life: "universalis et insignis vitae correctio" (p. 78, r. 31 – 32). He attacks again the princes and their highly increased power, and attacks in strong words the lessening of freedom in Europe, of the authority of the cities and of the *majestas* of the representative organisms in the state. Most of all he attacks the princes of the church, the cardinals, for striving to achieve a prince-like status. The necessary correction of life must start with them!

There was a real fear in Europe that the princes would use the war against the Turks to increase their internal power, that the Pope and the Emperor would betray the Christian territory to the Turks. Still, Erasmus professes his trust in the Pope, in the Emperor, in king Ferdinand, in king Francis and in the German princes. The Turks must finally see that Christianity is not just a stream of words. Christian preachers should be sent to them who only think of Jesus Christ and not of their own interests. Let the Turks live for a while under their own laws, so that they can slowly be assimilated to the Christian way of life. In these words we find the heart of Erasmus' idea about a war against the Turks: it should be more of a missionary operation!

8. *Conclusion*

In the literature that until now has been dedicated to the *Consultatio*, we can find a remarkable consensus among the authors that Erasmus' point of view vis-à-vis the Turks is humane and mild. He disapproves of the idea that merely fighting the Turks is a good and meritorious work and, though he would not reject a war against the Turks, he puts many moral restrictions upon Christian leaders and soldiers. It is not correct to say that Erasmus at the end of his life, when all hope had gone, had himself to sound the trumpet of war, as Geldner[6] puts it. The only trumpet that Erasmus sounded was that of indefatigable criticism of the unchristian attitude of Christians. He appealed to them to slay the Turk in their hearts and to improve their moral life. He appealed to the Christians to win their victory over the Turks by the force of their new morality, to convert them by preaching and by their Christian example. It is interesting to note here that this was also the opinion of Pico della Mirandola, who, just as Erasmus did, severely criticized the papal plans for a crusade and the financial swindling that went hand in hand with it.

More than one author declares that the *Consultatio* belongs to the pacifistic writings of Erasmus and that it also is the most moderate treatise that Erasmus dedicated to the problem of war and peace. Compared to the *Institutio principis christiani*, the *Querela pacis*, the Adagium *Dulce bellum inexpertis* and the *Enchiridion militis christiani*, in which we can find the fundamental elements of Erasmus' opinion on war and peace, the *Consultatio* does not have the radical pacifistic position of his former works. But he shades expressly his own statements, insisting on the all determining moral factor in the Christian position.

As a matter of fact, Erasmus did not dissuade a war against the Turks. In his *Apologia aduersus rhapsodias Alberti Pii* (1531) he states so quite clearly: "Non potest . . . obscurum esse quid de bello sentiam, cum et in principe christiano et in libello de bello suscipiendi adversus Turcas doceam bellandi rationem, haudquaquam facturus, si damnarem omne bellum".[7] But he felt that one should not go reckless to war. In his *Apologia* against Zuñiga he used the same terminology: "Nec vsquam damno bellum in Turcas, sed ostendo qua ratione deceat geri".[8] The *bellandi ratio* refers to the moral conditions of war. Erasmus did not give a systematic elaboration of these moral conditions, but he was constantly solicitous for the morality of those who were to be engaged in warfare: the princes in the first place. He wanted them "to lead an innocent life, to deserve well of their subjects and even their enemies, to tolerate invincibly all injury, to contempt money, to neglect glory, to lead a simple life, in one word: to be good Christians". So he said in the Adagium *Dulce bellum inexpertis* (1516) , so in his letter to Paulus Volz, covering the second edition of the *Enchiridion militis christiani* (1518): "efficacissima Turcas expugnandi ratio fuerit si conspexerint in nobis elucere quod docuit et expressit Christus",[9] and the *Enarratio in Primum Psalmum* of 1515.[10]

Erasmus was well informed of the medieval doctrine on the just war, as this was elaborated by canonists and theologians. He mentions the classical elements: legitimate authority, just cause, inevitability in the last resort (p. 54, r. 422 – 423) but his argument is concentrated on the mind of those involved in war. His favorite advocate of the *recta intentio* (p. 68, r. 759 – 760) is St. Ambrose, who, as Erasmus says, "never approves of a war, however necessary, if there is no religious mind" (p. 56, r. 466); "he does not approve when arms are taken up, unless it is with faith and love of religion, and even then warfare is not in accordance with the evangelical perfection" (p. 60, r. 545 – 548).

Erasmus shows himself not so much to be the advocate of war, as the solicitor of a universal and significant moral improvement of Christian life: "vniversalis et insignis vitae correctio" (p. 78, r. 31 – 32). As such, his *Consultatio* gives the basic principles of any peace movement, even of today.

NOTES

1 The *Consultatio de Bello Turcis inferendo* has been edited by the present writer in *ASD* V – 3, pp. 1–82. The references given in the notes are to this edition. The present article summarizes the *Einleitung*, where the relevant sources and literature are mentioned.
2 C. Göllner, *Turcica. Die europäischen Türkendrucke des XVI. Jahrhunderts*, 3 Bde, Bucuresti 1961, 1968, 1978.

3 M.J. Heath, "Renaissance scholars and the origins of the Turks", *Bibl. d'Humanisme et Renaissance* 41 (1979), 453–471.

4 A. Pertusi, "Giovanni Battista Egnazio ...", in: Vittore Banca, ed., *Venezia e Ungheria nel rinascimento*, Firenze 1973, 479–487.

5 Cfr. *ASD*, V–3, p. 13, n. 60; p. 15, n. 69, 70; p. 27, n. 121; p. 39, n. 192.

6 F. Geldner, *Die Staatsauffassung und Fürstenlehre des Erasmus von Rotterdam*, Berlin 1930 (Nachdruck Vaduz 1965), p. 127.

7 *LB* IX, 1193; *ASD* V–3, p. 25.

8 *LB* IX, 370 D; *ASD* V–3, p. 25.

9 *Allen*, 858, r. 103–104.

10 *ASD* V–2, p. 77; cfr. p. 27.

11 Cfr. A.G. Weiler, "La 'Consultatio de Bello Turcis inferendo': une oeuvre de piété politique", in: *Actes du Colloque International "Erasme de Rotterdam"*, Tours 1986 (à apparaître).

MARGHERITA ISNARDI-PARENTE

ÉRASME, LA *RÉPUBLIQUE* DE PLATON
ET LA COMMUNAUTÉ DES BIENS

On lit dans le premier des *Adages* d'Érasme, *Amicorum communia omnia*: «Et a Platone de legibus quinto. Quo loco conatur demonstrare, felicissimum rei publicae statum rerum omnium communitate constare . . . idem ait, felicem ac beatam fore civitatem, in qua non audientur haec verba: meum et non meum. Sed dictu mirum quam non placeat, imo quam lapidetur a Christianis Platonis illa communitas, cum nihil unquam ab ethnico Philosopho dictum sit magis ex Christi sententia».[1] Il n'y est pas fait référence aux *Lois* de Platon, ainsi que l'expression érasmienne donnerait à croire, mais au cinquième livre de la *République*.[2] La *République* de Platon était plutôt appelée, d'après Marsile Ficin et d'après la tradition, *Respublica sive de iusto*; mais Érasme a l'air de se référer à la *République* comme à l'ouvrage capital de Platon sur les lois et sur l'État.

Dans cet ouvrage, Érasme croit lire l'expression d'une théorie communiste généralisée: la prescription de la communauté des biens est considérée valable pour la société entière. C'est également l'avis de Thomas More, qui, dans le premier livre de l'*Utopia* (là où il affirme par la bouche d'Ithlodée les mérites de la solution communautaire et stigmatise les maux infinis qui descendent de la propriété privée) fait référence lui aussi à la *République* de Platon, interprétant celle-ci dans un sens universel, comme un traité sur la propriété commune des biens.[3] Érasme et More se font tous les deux défenseurs de l'idéal politique de Platon, contre les accusations qu'une tradition chrétienne plus respectueuse de l'orthodoxie et de la coutume n'a pas manqué de soulever contre la *République*, contre cet idéal honteux de la propriété commune des femmes surtout, *lupanar magnum*.[4] Sans doute, la *République* de Platon n'a pas manqué de défenseurs à la Renaissance; mais d'habitude cette apologie est différemment motivée. Bien loin de vouloir considérer les propositions politiques de Platon comme valables pour toute la société, on essaie plutôt de réduire la portée de celles qu'on appelle les *paradoxa Platonis* et de souligner la limitation des normes exceptionnelles aux deux classes supérieures de la cité, celles des philosophes et des guerriers, quelquefois même aux seuls derniers: c'est la voie plus prudente que suivent Francesco Patrizi ou Ubaldo Folieta.[5] Il s'efforcent de démontrer que Platon a limité ces dispositions exceptionnelles à un petit nombre de personnes, exceptionnelles elles aussi; ils n'oseraient pas faire l'apologie de la communauté générale des biens par crainte de glisser sur un terrain dangereux et d'être entraînés à des conséquences plus lourdes. Il faut malgré tout rappeler que la thèse de l'extension généralisée de la communauté des biens dans la *République* est l'interprétation la plus répandue parmi les auteurs de la Renaissance, et qu'elle va survivre jusqu'à l'interprétation proposée par Hegel dans les *Vorlesungen über die Geschichte der Philosophie* et dans la *Philosophie des Rechts*.[6]

Difficilia quae pulchra: un autre des *Adages* érasmiens, le numéro 1012 prend à dessein exactement ce titre, qui dérive d'un dicton platonicien: «Extat apud Platonem in Hippia minore in calce dialogi ... et in Cratylo circa initium», sans compter l'expression χαλεπὰ τὰ καλά de *Resp.* IV. L'idéal de la communauté des biens est si beau qu'il paraît presque chimérique, à cause de la difficulté de sa réalisation; surtout si l'on pense à ce que sont devenues aujourd'hui les 'républiques' et les moeurs de leurs citoyens. Dans un *Adage* ultérieur, le numero 2036 A, premier de la *Chiliade* III,[7] Érasme est encore plus pessimiste: «Extra organum dicetur, quod immodicum est, et extra vulgarem mensuram. Veluti si quis leges Platonis huius aetatis civibus proponeret». En effet, cet idéal est trop sublime pour la société actuelle, et—comme on va bientôt le voir—la république idéale qu'Érasme lui-même va proposer aux princes ne prévoit aucunement l'abolition de la propriété; au contraire, c'est sur le respect de la propriété des sujets que les lois du prince doivent se fonder; prêcher contre la propriéte pourrait, en l'état actuel des choses, être fort dangéreux pour le bien commun. En principe, toutefois, cet idéal demeure supérieur. Dans le *Dulce bellum inexpertis*, le fameux *Adage* 3001,[8] nous trouvons Érasme engagé dans une polémique violente contre Aristote, qui a plaidé contre la communauté des biens. Érasme se plaint que la théologie officielle donne à Aristote une place d'honneur tout à fait particulière: «tandem huc processum est, ut in mediam Theologiam totus sit receptus Aristoteles, et ita receptus, ut huius auctoritas paene sanctior sit, quam Christi. Nam si quid ille dixit, parum incommodum ad vitam nostram, licet interpretamento detorquere: caeterum exploditur illico, qui vel leviter ausit Aristotelicis oraculis refragari. Ab hoc didicimus non esse perfectam hominis felicitatem, nisi corporis et fortunae bona accesserint. Ab hoc didicimus, non posse florere rempublicam in qua sint omnia communia. Huius omnia decreta, cum Christi doctrina conamur adglutinare, h.e. aquam flammis miscere».

La première des deux théories auxquelles Érasme fait allusion ici est celle des «biens extérieurs», ou «biens de la troisième classe», énoncée dans l'*Ethique á Nicomaque*; théorie très chère aux peripatéticiens, combattue au contraire par les stoïciens. Cicéron, dans les *Tusculanae disputationes*, a opté définitivement pour la théorie stoïcienne de la vertu comme bien unique, et c'est de Cicéron qu'Érasme dépend, malgré sa méfiance à l'égard de cet auteur.[9] Mais quand il fait allusion à la réfutation aristotélicienne de la communauté des biens, il se fonde directement sur le deuxième livre de la *Politique*. C'est là qu'Aristote a pris position contre la *République* de Platon. Il a été le premier d'une longue série de critiques à poser le problème essentiel: quelle extension Platon a-t-il voulu donner à la communauté des biens? Voulut-il la limiter aux deux premières classes des citoyens? Mais dans ce cas nous obtiendrons deux républiques différentes, liées ensemble par force, ce qui serait tout à fait contraire aux intentions d'unité que Socrate a proclamées pour la cité dans ses dialogues. Voulut-il, au contraire, la généraliser à tous les citoyens, même à ceux de la troisième classe, les simples sujets? Mais alors n'irait-on pas détruire la cité elle-même, qui, par essence, exige pluralité et articulation puisqu'on ne pourrait plus faire distinction entre cité et famille?[10] Après ces remarques, Aristote poursuit par l'exposition de tous les dangers et défauts d'un régime politique dans lequel les citoyens n'ont rien qui leur soit propre: on se désintéresserait de la chose publique et laisserait tout tomber en ruine; l'absence de limites entre ce qui est 'mien' et ce qui est 'tien' n'emmènerait pas non plus cette amitié et cette paix sociale que Platon nous dit en être la conséquence; bien au contraire, un ordre pareil entraîne l'incertitude et, comme il ôte tout moyen légitime de régler les querelles, il ne peut que les faire augmenter. Les argumentations ont conservé leur valeur paradigmatique chez tous les auteurs qui, après Aristote, ont prétendu se mesurer avec ce problème: il suffit de rappeler Jean Bodin, qui, tout en faisant souvent profession d'antiaristotélisme, se range sur cette question dans le premier livre de sa *République*, chapitre deuxième, tout à fait aux côtés d'Aristote contre la république «en idées, sans effect» de Platon et de Thomas More.[11]

Ce qui nous intéresse ici, c'est que nous voyons encore, dans l'Adage *Dulce bellum*, l'idéal de Platon s'identifier, aux yeux d'Érasme, avec l'idéal chrétien le plus authentique, celui de la communauté apostolique; tandis que la critique qu'Aristote en fait ne peut être acceptée par le chrétien sous peine de dénaturer la véritable théologie du Christ. Érasme se situe dans le sillage de ces humanistes du XVe siècle—un Bessarion, un Pléthon—qui plaidaient pour Platon contre Aristote, reconnaissant dans le premier l'anticipateur du Christ lui-même, le représentant de la *pia philosophia*, un véritable christianisme avant la lettre dans le monde païen. Quand il écrit le *Dulce bellum*, entre 1508 et 1515 (il sera réédité plusieurs fois au cours de la vie d'Érasme),[12] il ne montre ni perplexités ni réserves dans son blâme d'Aristote pour avoir condamné la communauté des biens: il considère cet idéal encore comme l'expression païenne de l'idéal évangelique tel qu'il est décrit dans les Actes des Apôtres, et qui représente le sommet de la perfection chrétienne. Bien sûr, il n'est pas possible de suggérer aux princes la réalisation d'un idéal pareil. L'*Institutio principis christiani*, rédigée en 1516 pour le jeune Charles Quint, peut nous donner une idée claire de ce que fut l'enseignement au sujet de la propriété qu'Érasme dispensa aux princes qu'il souhaita introduire aux arts concrets de la politique: un bon prince est tenu de respecter les droits de ses sujets en ce qui concerne la propriété particulière, sous peine de tomber dans la tyrannie. Érasme jugea en effect *iniquum* tous les procédés contraires aux droits de la propriété et de l'hérédité, tels qu'il put les contempler dans les exploits des princes de son temps.[13] Il n'avait pas pour autant renoncé à l'idéal apostolique anticipé par Platon dans la *République*—idéal qui n'appartenait pas à la réalité concrète, mais était réel d'une façon plus élevée: Platon avait bien enseigné que la réalité de la norme se plaçait sur un niveau ontologique supérieur à celui des simples événements.

Si nous jetons maintenant un regard sur un texte plus tardif d'Érasme, le *De amabili Ecclesiae concordia* (1533), nous n'avons pas de difficulté à reconnaître que bien des choses ont changé. Il n'y a rien d'étonnant à ce qu'Érasme ne mentionne plus expressément ni Platon ni Aristote, car il serait bien étrange de rencontrer des philosophes païens dans un ouvrage pareil. Mais ce qui nous intéresse, c'est qu'il a limité fortement sa confiance dans l'idéal et la pratique de la communauté des biens définis aux temps apostoliques. Il en fait un cas tout à fait particulier, en la réduisant un simple aspect de la société fondée par l'Eglise primitive, qui ne saurait se continuer ni même concerner la totalité des chrétiens, mais seulement une élite très limitée. Il faut citer presque tout le passage en question, pour mieux se rendre compte du contexte dans lequel le discours se place. En plaidant pour la réconciliation des chrétiens et pour la réunion de l'Eglise déchirée, Érasme réfléchit sur les exploits des Anabaptistes, ces extrémistes de la Réforme (et nous ne pouvons ignorer que la tragédie de Munster, à peine commencée, va se dérouler dans les années suivantes jusqu'à son achèvement affreux): «Quis autem malus genius effascinavit infelices Anabaptistas? Nam audio hos errore falli, magis quam incitari malitia, ut ad istum modum in proprium ruant exitium. Non sufficit illis baptismus, qui mille quadringentis annis suffecit Ecclesiae Catholicae? ... Christus ait: date Caesari quae sunt Caesaris. Et Apostolorum principes, Petrus et Paulus, diligenter admonent, ut Christiani cives obtemperent Regibus ac Praefectis, licet idololatris ... Dicuntur exigere a suis rerum communitatem. At ista quidem fuit aliquamdiu temporibus Apostolorum in primordiis Ecclesiae nascentis, ne tum quidem inter omnes Christianos. Nam latius propagato Evangelio non potuit servari communitas, exitura videlicet in seditionem. Hoc ad concordiam erat accommodatius, ut rerum proprietas ac dispensandi ius sit penes legitimos Dominos, caritas vero faciat usum communem».[14]

C'est un passage fort intéressant, qui fournit matière à plusieurs réflexions. Érasme a modifié sensiblement son opinion sur l'idéal de la communauté des biens, ne considérant plus celle-ci, comme le fait Platon, comme une source d'amitié et de concorde, mais plutôt comme une source de querelles et d'inimitiés, si elle déborde ses limites très étroites. Mais il est aussi revenu, en proposant une interprétation nouvelle, sur un passage de l'Evangile de Mathieu, le *quae sunt Caesaris Caesari*, à propos duquel il s'était bien différemment exprimé dans l'*Institutio principis christiani*.[15] Dans cet ouvrage, il avait vu dans le passage en question, tout comme dans le fameux passage de l'Épître aux Romains sur l'obéissance qu'on doit aux autorités politiques, une invitation à se désintéresser des choses de l'État et à ne plus penser qu'aux choses de Dieu; quant à l'invitation à l'obéissance, il avait alors considéré[16] qu'elle s'adressait aux païens plutôt qu'aux chrétiens, ou, tout au plus, qu'elle s'adressait à ces derniers d'une façon absolument provisoire: les païens ne sauraient obtenir l'ordre dans leur société qu'en obéissant aux autorités constituées, tandis que l'obéissance des Chrétiens ne doit s'adresser qu'à Dieu. On voit bien comment dans ce texte tardif, Érasme, sous l'influence d'une situation profondément changée, a été amené à soutenir une interprétation plus conforme à la tradition. Face à la subversion profonde de l'ordre social et politique qu'il voit provoquée par les groupes extrémistes de la Réforme, il est désormais amené à apprécier plus fortement les valeurs de l'obéissance civile et à reconnaître leur source dans le Nouveau Testament lui-même: ce n'est plus la subversion des valeurs ordinaires qu'il y cherche à présent, mais, au contraire, la réaffirmation d'un ordre social établi. Bien sûr, Érasme n'ira pas jusqu'à soutenir que la propriété privée aurait son fondement dans les lois de la nature; d'autres feront ce pas, Jean Bodin parmi les premiers.[17] Pourtant, il fonde le droit de propriété sur une loi d'utilité sociale, même si ce droit contredit quelque peu les règles de la communauté apostolique. Il considère l'idéal chrétien de la communauté des biens comme une règle tout à fait exceptionnelle et provisoire, reservée à un petit groupe d'élus. Et il fait aussi, dans ce contexte, un emploi assez singulier de certaines catégories de nature juridique, telles que *proprietas* et *usus*. Procédé exceptionnel, car on connaît bien la méfiance qu'il a toujours gardée à l'égard du droit codifié.

On pourrait chercher, et aussi trouver, chez les chefs modérés de la Réforme (chez Luther comme chez Melanchton, ou Calvin un peu plus tard) autant de pareilles prises de distance à l'égard des anabaptistes et de leur idéal communautaire. Mais en particulier chez Érasme l'abandon de cet idéal s'identifie avec l'abandon d'une certain forme de platonisme.

Ce n'est pas l'abandon du platonisme politique tout court, car ce dernier va plus loin que l'idéal communautaire de la *République*, et l'on pourrait soutenir la thèse selon laquelle Érasme, tout en s'éloignant de la *République*, demeura fidèle au Platon de la VII Épître, qui lui donna le modèle du philosophe maître et éducateur des jeunes princes. La tâche d'enseigner au jeune prince la science du bon gouvernement et de la véritable philosophie, voilà le seul commandement du platonisme politique capable de survivre à l'expérience traumatisante de la Réforme, sans pour autant entraîner des conséquences dangereuses. Ainsi le terrain glissant de la *République* est abandonné, avec tout ce qui pouvait être soutenu au commencement du XVIe siècle avec une conscience naïve, qui a révélé plus tard seulement son poison caché. Une saison heureuse de l'esprit vient de s'achever en Europe.

NOTES

1 *LB* II, col. 14.
2 *Resp.* V, 462 c et suiv.
3 Éd. J.H. Hexter—E. Surtz, *St. Thomas More Complete Works*, IV, New-Haven—London 1965, p. 100
4 Il suffit de rappeler ici Lactance, *Div. Inst. iii, 21*: les femmes de l'État idéal de Platon, ces femmes auxquelles il concède même les fonctions du gouvernement, ne peuvent être, en effet, que des *prostitutae ac meretrices*.
5 On peut trouver encore un tableau général de ces apologies de Platon à la Renaissance (à commencer par les *Discussionum Peripateticarum libri III*, de Francesco Patrizi) dans la dissertation de G. Pinzger, *De iis quae Aristoteles in Platonis Politia reprehendit commentaria*, Lipsiae 1822, p. VII, n. 2. Mais les arguments sont puisés dans l'ouvrage du Cardinal Bessarion, *In calumniatorem Platonis libri IV*, éd. L. Mohler, Paderborn 1927, p. 493 et suiv.).
6 Cf. M. Isnardi Parente, «La 'Repubblica' di Platone in Germania nel secolo di Marx,» *Belfagor* XXXVII, 1982, pp. 617–632.
7 *LB* II, col. 410 B; col. 725.
8 *LB* II, col. 961 A - B. Voir J.C. Margolin, *Guerre et paix dans la pensée d'Érasme*, Paris 1973, pp. 130–131.
9 *Tusc. Disp.* V, 8, 21 sq passim.
10 *Polit.* II, 1264 a sq.
11 J. Bodin, *Les six livres de la République*, 1576; 1583³, pp. 4, 15–16.
12 J.C. Margolin, *Guerre et paix*, pp. 111–112, donne un tableau de ces différentes éditions.
13 *LB* IV, col. 599 et suiv. *ASD* IV–1, p. 200; je renvoie aussi a Erasmo da Rotterdam, *L'educazione del principe cristiano*, trad.it. a cura di M. Isnardi Parente, Napoli 1977, pp. 138–139, et Intr., p. 24.
14 *De amabili Ecclesiae concordia*, *LB* V, 505 B–D.
15 *LB* IV, 578 D–579 A (éd. Herding, p. 166).
16 *Ibid.* cf. le commentaire du même Érasme sur l'*Epist. ad Romanos*, 13, 1–7, *LB* VI, 636 C–D.
17 Pour cet auteur le droit de propriété appartient aux 'lois de Dieu et de la nature'; cf. J. Bodin, *I sei libri dello Stato*, I, trad.it. a cura di M. Isnardi Parente, Torino 1964, Intr., p. 55.

NELSON H. MINNICH

ERASMUS AND THE FIFTH LATERAN COUNCIL (1512–17)

On 30 March 1522, Erasmus let slip in a letter to Willibald Pirckheimer, the patrician humanist of Nürnberg, the following comment: "As for councils, the only statement I would dare to make is that perhaps the recent Lateran Council was not really a council."[1] Four years later in his colloquy "The Fishmonger," Erasmus, speaking through the butcher, would no longer dare to pass open judgment on this council, but he did observe that the Lateran Council was not presently considered to be among the "orthodox" councils. The criteria for true councils he had the fish salesman enunciate: they must be in the Holy Spirit properly (*rite*) gathered (*congregatis*), carried out (*peractis*), promulgated (*aeditis*), and accepted (*receptis*).[2] In his other writings Erasmus provided evidence for why the Fifth Lateran Council did not meet all of these criteria for validity.

For a variety of reasons Erasmus held that the Lateran Council had not been properly gathered in the Holy Spirit. Most of these arguments focused on the authority of the papal office and its occupant Julius II (1503–13).

Erasmus questioned the power of popes over councils. Given his decade of intermittent theological study at the Sorbonne, that center of Gallican conciliarist thinking, it is not surprising that Erasmus initially sympathized with those who espoused the superiority of councils.[3] In the *Julius Exclusus* he defended the validity of the Council of Pisa-Milan-Asti-Lyon (1511–12) which was based on conciliarist ideas.[4] When the Dominican master general, Tommaso de Vio (known as Cajetan), published two treatises and an oration attacking the Pisan Council as schismatic and arguing that only its rival Lateran Council was valid for it had been called by the pope, Erasmus criticized the friar for writing immoderately about papal power.[5] Erasmus insisted that papal powers were joined to obligations and he feared that a pope's unlimited power could lead to tyranny and become a plague on Christendom. He looked to Christian princes to correct abuses of papal power and praised emperor Maximilian I and king Louis XII of France for carrying out their responsibilities by calling the Pisan Council, when the behavior of Julius II showed that Erasmus' concerns were not groundless.[6]

Another factor calling into question the validity of the Lateran Council was the dubious authority of its convoker. The way Julius II attained the papal office and his conduct in it led to open discussions as to whether he was to be considered a true pope.[7] That he attained the tiara by a simoniacal election was widely suspected. To show that he occupied the chair of Peter unworthily, Erasmus produced a litany of charges against Julius II: sexual misconduct (fathering an illegitimate daughter, sodomy, pederasty, being covered with syphilitic sores), habitual inebriation, simoniac selling of bishoprics, indulgences, and dispensations, ignorance of things spiritual, consulting a fortune-teller, resorting to excommunication for frivolous reasons, violating an oath, inciting others to warfare, and engaging himself in such fighting.[8]

Julius II's war-making activities were for Erasmus perhaps the most serious of the pope's moral failings. While visiting the papal court when the question of fighting Venice was being debated by the pope and cardinals, Erasmus composed an oration in which he argued that to wage war was all the more so forbidden to the pope since it was already prohibited for secular princes, Christians, priests, and bishops. In the *Julius Exclusus* he accused the pope of having caused the death of countless men, but of having gained not one soul for Christ.[9] Did such a man still enjoy the authority of the papal office?

Erasmus felt that the Lateran Council was not properly assembled because another council, that of Pisa, was already in session and producing worthy reform decrees. The Pisan Council had been called to prevent the utter ruin of Christendom. As a condition of his election as pope, Julius had sworn to call such a reform council and had agreed that others could convoke it if he failed to do so within two years. When he neglected his promise, reform-minded cardinals, the emperor Maximilian, and king Louis XII of France joined in calling for such a council and invited Julius II to preside. Despite the pope's refusal to attend and repeated threats against its adherents, the council assembled at Pisa under the presidency of the upright and learned Spanish cardinal, Bernardino López de Carvajal. It enacted reform measures limiting the wealth and pompous display of prelates, ending the pluralism of cardinals, prohibiting simony in the election of pope and bishops, and allowing for the deposition of manifestly criminal clerics. If the Council of Pisa came to be considered schismatic, it was not because of something it did, but because its supporters suffered military and diplomatic reversals.[10]

The motive Erasmus attributed to Julius II in calling the Lateran Council could only diminish its claim to being a true council. In *Julius Exclusus* the pope proclaimed his intention to use the Council to reform himself, Christian princes, and the people as a whole. But in stating this, he was totally cynical, for his only purpose in calling the Lateran Council was to destroy the Pisan, to drive out a nail with a nail. He could have approved the Pisan Council and no schism would have occurred. But Julius claimed that he was exempt from all criticism, even by a general council, and he feared that the Pisan Council, which he could not control, might remove him from the papal office he had purchased simoniacally.[11]

The way in which Julius II gathered and manipulated the Lateran Council's members weakened its claim to be a true council representing the Church. By means he was unwilling to divulge, the Julius of the Erasmian dialogue supposedly seduced former supporters of the Pisan Council, such as emperor Maximilian and some of the cardinals, to switch their adherence to his Council. To pack his Council with men friendly to himself, Julius had it meet in Rome and created a number of new cardinals who would cooperate with his plans. To restrict its membership as much as possible, he advised the local church in each region to spare expenses by spending only one or other representative. Lest too many delegates arrive, among whom would inevitably be some upright men, Julius wrote to them saying he had postponed the opening of the Council. Having thus headed off their arrival, he anticipated the date set for the initial session and convened the Lateran Council with only his friends in attendance. While it is true that Julius was careful to control the Lateran Council, Erasmus' account of his ploys to limit its membership was not based on contemporary events and documents, but on a conspiratorial interpretation of what led to the recall and recomposition of the English delegation which initially had included bishop John Fisher of Rochester who had invited Erasmus to accompany him.[12]

Erasmus' description of the proceedings of the Lateran Council under Julius II suggests that he felt the Council had not been properly carried out and hence was invalid. He summarized the achievements of the first session as the mere faithful following of traditional ceremonies and the delivery of an oration praising the pope. The second session condemned the Pisan cardinals and their proceedings; the third placed most of France under an interdict and transferred the market-fair from Lyon to Geneva. He characterized these measures as nothing more than curses, threats, and cruelty mixed with cunning and declared that the Lateran assembly under Julius was not "a true council."[13]

The death of Julius II on 21 February 1513, five days after the fifth session of the Fifth Lateran Council, not only occasioned the *Julius Exclusus* with its satirical vilification of the deceased pope, but led to the selection on 11 March 1513 of a new pope, Leo X, whom Erasmus initially idealized, claiming he possesses the virtues opposed to his predecessor's vices. Thus noble lineage, an excellent education, and a love of letters replace a menial origin, a youth wasted on oars, and an ignorance of things academic, especially theology. Whereas Leo pursues spiritual and cultural goals and has ushered in an age of gold, Julius was preoccupied with material wealth and questions of jurisdiction and had plunged the world into an age inferior even to that of iron. He sowed discord, and with severity and violence incited men to war, the great disrupter of learning. With military might he harassed his former ally, Louis XII, and thereby rent Christendom by a schism. But by his mildness, Leo has restrained the threats of princes and restored concord and peace, the nurse of letters. His piety and prayers have won over the French king. So thoroughly has he healed the Pisan schism that not even its scars remain. He was elevated to his high office not by the simoniac methods of his predecessor, but by a divine decree, for he had not even desired or expected this honor. His untainted election and Christ-like conduct in office attest that he is unquestionably the supreme pontiff and Christ's vice-regent.[14]

With Leo as pope, Erasmus could no longer denounce the Lateran Council as improperly assembled and carried out. Leo, who inherited the presidency of this Council, was indisputably the supreme pontiff and enjoyed high moral authority. After the demise of the Pisan Council and formal adherence of all major Latin lands to the papal Council, the issues of conciliarist theology and of a rival council embodying its claims all but disappeared. Leo openly encouraged all prelates to attend and Erasmus himself repeatedly stated his own intention to go to Rome.[15]

Such eagerness is not difficult to understand. Among the Council's goals were three dear to the heart of Erasmus: a reform of morals, a restoration of Church unity, and the establishment of peace among Christians. The Council had already or soon would list among its members many prelates whom Erasmus considered his patrons and friends: pope Leo X, cardinals Grimani, Giubé, Pucci, and Riario, and bishops Luigi de Canossa, Giampietro Carafa, Silvestro Gigli, Pietro Griffi, and Thomas Halsey. The ordinary of his native diocese, Friedrich III von Baden, bishop of Utrecht, and the local Bursfelder abbot of St. Adalbert's in Egmond, Meynard Man, both would be represented by procurators. As a place to promote his highest goals for Christendom and to obtain the personal dispensations he so eargerly sought, Rome at the time of the Lateran Council had no equal. Nonetheless, Erasmus never came and his knowledge of the Council's proceedings and decrees remained fragmentary.[16]

What influence if any he had from afar on the Council is difficult to determine. Three of the orators denounced, but not by name, those who attacked the pious customs of the Church. But given their humanistic backgrounds and open esteem for Erasmus, Egidio Antonini and Antonio Pucci probably aimed their comments at others. Giambattista de Gargha, the knight of Rhodes, excoriated those who boldly spurn ecclesiastical custom, but he gave no indication that he had the author of the *Moriae Encomium* in mind.[17]

Among the reforms proposed to the Council were many similar to those favored by Erasmus. Thus, Simun Kožičić de Begna, bishop of Modrus, urged at the sixth session in 1513 that Christ be taken as the exemplar and archetype of a reform which was to begin with bishops—a proposal close to that detailed in Erasmus' *Paraclesis*. Two memorials submitted for the consideration of the Council focused on Sacred Scripture. The Camaldolese hermits Paolo Giustiniani and Pietro Quirini wanted the Epistles and Gospels read at Mass to be translated into the vernacular and the Bible in Latin to become the core, together with the church fathers and canonical decrees, of a cleric's education. Gianfrancesco Pico, count of Mirandola, in 1517 urged that the scriptural text of both Testaments (*utriusque instrumenti*) be purged of their errors by comparing them to copies of the earliest texts—something Erasmus had just attempted for the New Testament. Pico also made the typically Erasmian suggestion that good example may prove more effective than weapons in the struggle with Islam. The call for peace among Christian princes was common to almost all the sermons and memorials.[18]

Erasmus' judgment on what the Lateran Council achieved under Leo X can be found both in his general statements and in his comments on particular decrees. In 1515 he praised the pope for his synodal constitutions which are repairing and restoring the Christian religion and which manifest an apostolic spirit and fatherly concern, rather than a quest for despotic power and financial gain. Which of the Lateran decrees he was thus praising is not clear.[19] The only decrees on which he commented in some detail were those on the soul's immortality and on book censorship.

Whether Erasmus knew all the provisions in the decree *Apostolici regiminis solicitudo* of the eighth session (19 December 1513) is not clear. While he seems not to have cited explicitly its statements on the soul's immortality, he agreed on the importance of this tenet of belief, ridiculed those who tried to find in Aristotle a proof for it, yet freely provided his own arguments based on Platonic philosophy, even though the decree bound only teachers of philosophy to advance such reasons. Erasmus cited approvingly and in detail the final provision of this decree which held that those in sacred orders could not continue the formal study of poetry and philosophy for more than five years after completing their training in grammar and dialectics, unless they pursued at the same time some study of theology or canon law. He used this decree in his battles with theologians who berated as unreligious someone who studied the classics. Given his fear that too avid a study of ancient literature might resurrect paganism, he also approved of this decree's curtailments of such study.[20]

Erasmus initially observed the conciliar decree *Inter solicitudines* of the tenth session (4 May 1515). He admitted to knowing its provision requiring the censorship of books prior to their publication and cautioned his critics to note that the Council had entrusted such censorship to the local ordinary and to those whom he designated as examiners. Erasmus insisted that in the publication of his *Novum Instrumentum* in February of 1516 he was in strict compliance with this ruling, for he had secured the prior approval of the local bishop of Basel, Christopher von Utenheim. He also prided himself in having obtained a letter afterwards from pope Leo who approved this first edition after it was examined by the learned cardinals Grimani and Riario. And the pope went on to give implicit approval even for a revised edition two years later. The demand of Erasmus' English critic, Edward Lee, that he should have secured this papal permit prior to publication, and the suggestion of others that a council should have examined and licenced the *Novum Instrumentum* were both answerable by pointing to the more reasonable provisions of the Lateran Council which allowed for merely episcopal approval, which Erasmus had obtained, and by citing the later Leonine letter.[21]

Erasmus had mixed feelings about censorship. He favored it to silence the combatants in the Reuchlin affair, his own critic Diego Lopéz de Zuñiga, and anyone who published anonymous or calumnious works or urged in print resistance to lawful governmental authority. The effective censorship of all books he saw as unenforceable, given the great numbers produced each year and the numerous opportunities to evade such controls. The law of nations which already banned the printing of seditious and defamatory works, and not some "new constitution," was sufficient to police book publication.[22]

Most of the Lateran Council's decrees elicited no explicit response from Erasmus. He may have had early on only the vaguest knowledge of their contents or have been completely ignorant of their existence. The decrees approving the *montes pietatis* and prohibiting the plunder of cardinals' homes during a conclave seem to have drawn no comment. His statement in May of 1515 that Leo was issuing synodal constitutions which reflect the spirit of Christ and His apostles probably referred to the conciliar decrees reforming curial officials and their fees and to the "great reform bull" of 1514 which regulated cardinals and their households, limited the number of benefices one person could hold, condemned simony, blasphemy, superstition, heresy, and the fictive conversion of Jews, required priests to pray the divine office and lead a chaste life, and prescribed measures to assure the religious education of youths in schools. Given his own situation as the illegitimate son of a priest and as someone in search of more benefices, Erasmus probably had mixed feelings about the Council's condemnation of clerical concubinage and its restraints on pluralism. None of the provisions of the decree restraining the privileges of some of those enjoying papal exemptions touched him personally. Given his often troubled relations with "monks," he may have privately welcomed the decree reining in the friars' privileges.[23]

Although he seems never to have cited the conciliar decree on preaching, many of its provisions were in line with his own thinking: exhortations to preach the Gospel, restrictions on predicting future events, prohibitions on foretelling the end times, abstention from personal attacks on the character of ecclesiastical officials, and the screening by bishops of those permitted to preach to the people. While Erasmus agreed with the general principle that Scripture be interpreted according to the traditional teachings of the doctors of the Church and of professors of sacred theology, he did not want to rule out, as the Council did, any interpretations which were at variance.[24]

In line with Erasmus' efforts to promote Church unity, but apparently never explicitly mentioned by him, were three conciliar items. The healing of the Pisan schism was registered in the acceptance of the French mandate of adherence and any legal basis for its renewal was removed by the abrogation of the Pragmatic Sanction of Bourges and approval of the Concordat of Bologna. Erasmus praised Leo X for ending the Pisan schism. The Council's effort to heal the Hussite schism by sending cardinal Tamas Bakócz to negotiate with the Bohemians a resolution of the conflict, which would allow them to receive the Eucharist under both species, was seemingly unknown to Erasmus. His own proposals were similar to the Council's. The conciliar reaffirmation of the Maronites' adherence to the Roman Church seems also to have elicited no response from Erasmus.[25]

The role of the Lateran Council in promoting peace among Christian princes was not recognized in Erasmus' writings. Instead, he repeatedly gave credit for these efforts to Leo X. On the other hand, Leo was also blamed for urging an armed crusade against the Turks and no responsibility for this undertaking was laid against the Lateran Council, even though Julius II had made this one of its principal aims and Leo's labors can be seen as an attempt to carry out the Council's purpose.[26]

The one decree to which Erasmus may have refused full assent was *Pastor aeternus* of the eleventh session. In the process of abrogating the Pragmatic Sanction of Bourges, this decree made two doctrinal statements. It reaffirmed an earlier teaching based on Sacred Scripture, the church Fathers, and the constitution *Unam Sanctam* of Boniface VIII that it is necessary for salvation that all Christians submit to the Roman pontiff. It also declared that the Roman pontiff, just as he has authority over all councils, so too does he alone have the power and full right of convoking, transferring, and dissolving them. While Erasmus eventually came to ac-

cept the first statement, he probably never would have agreed to the validity of the second if it were interpreted as an outright rejection of the
Haec sancta charter of conciliarism, for he consistently refused to take a
stand on whether a pope or a general council is superior.[27]

This brief review of the Lateran Council's proceedings under Leo X
and of Erasmus' expressed or probable responses to its decrees does not
support a conclusion that he rejected the validity of the Council because
of something carried out (*peractis*) under Leo's presidency—the one possible exception being the Lateran's statement on papal superiority to all
councils.

Could the Council have been nullified by the way in which its decrees
were promulgated or published (*aeditis*)? Most unlikely, for the procedures followed were in strict conformity with existing legal and liturgical
practices. Drafts or *cedulae* of the decrees were read aloud and voted upon
in the formal sessions of the Council. No decree was voted down and,
where opposition was registered by some prelates to particular provisions, Leo X often intervened to assure the opponents that their views
would be taken into consideration when putting the decree into final form
(*Scribatur in forma*). Once its text was finalized, the decree was recorded in
the *acta* of the Council and written up in the form of a papal bull—e.g.
*Leo episcopus servus servorum Dei, ad futuram rei memoriam, sacro approbante con-
cilio*. As a bull it was copied into the papal registers. Usually within several days of the session, papal cursors would publish the bull in Rome by
reading aloud and posting a copy of it on the doors of the basilicas of St.
John Lateran and of St. Peter, on those of the apostolic Chancery, and
in acie of the Campo dei Fiori. Also within days of the session one of the
local Roman printers would usually publish an edition of the bull which
the ambassadors would quickly send to the government they represented.
At the last session on 13 March 1517, Leo and the Council reaffirmed all
that had been carried out in the earlier sessions. Toward the end of July,
1517, Etienne Guillery was apparently commissioned by the Curia to
print a collection of the Council's decrees. A year later on 15 September
1518 another collection was published in Milan by Alessandro Minuzi-
ano. And on 31 July 1521 the press of Jacopo Mazzocchi in Rome issued
the official *acta* of the Council edited by cardinal Antonio del Monte on
order of Leo X.[28]

It is doubtful that Erasmus was either aware of this complicated
process of promulgation and publication or found any fault with it. In the
Julius Exclusus he noted that the pope had taken the decrees of the Council
and published them as bulls to give them more authority. Julius II then
sent these to all princes. While the Lateran decrees were not issued in the
name only of the Council as was done at Basel and Pisa, neither were they

published merely in the pope's name as happened at Florence. The Lateran formula, combining both papal and conciliar authorities, was that laid down in the ceremonial book of Agostino Patrizi a quarter century earlier.[29]

That the decrees of the Lateran Council were not properly received and enforced (*receptis*) was probably the strongest reason Erasmus had for considering that Council invalid. In the final decree of the Council, *Constituti juxta verbum*, the execution and enforcement of the decrees were entrusted to the local ordinaries, but in the jurisdiction of the Roman Curia to the governor of the city of Rome and to the general auditor of the apostolic Camera. Both officials, Amadeo Berruti the governor and Girolamo de Ghinucci the auditor, issued edicts mandating observance, especially of the "great reform bull." The vicar general for spiritual affairs, Domenico Giacobazzi, issued a similar edict. For a while the clergy reluctantly conformed to the dress code. If Leo showed little enthusiasm for the conciliar decrees reforming curial practices and readily granted dispensations, his successors Adrian VI concentrated his efforts on curial reform while Clement VII actively worked to enforce at Rome many of the provisions of the "great reform bull."[30]

Outside of Rome little effort seems to have been made to implement the Lateran decrees. In Italy the ecclesiastical province of Florence promulgated many of the decrees as statutes of the provincial council held in 1517 on order of cardinal Giulio dei Medici. Cardinal Alessandro Farnese implemented the decrees in Parma, Federigo de Sanseverino in Novara, and Antonio del Monte in Pavia. The Venetian government chose to apply the decree on book censorship in its peculiar way. In Spain cardinal Francisco Ximenes de Cisneros worked to put the Lateran decrees into effect. Leo entrusted to cardinal Philippe de Chaumont (or de Luxembourg) the task of seeing that the decrees were given effect in France. But the only decree to be registered as the law of the land, despite much opposition, was the conciliarly approved Concordat of Bologna. The French ambassador to Rome, Guillaume Briçonnet, bishop of Meaux, was specially empowered to apply the Lateran decrees in his own diocese. His brother Denys, fellow ambassador and bishop of San-Malo, was charged to enforce the Lateran decree on clerical garb at the church of St. Martha in the diocese of Avignon. The attempts in 1515 to defend in England the Lateran provision on ecclesiastical immunity were blocked when Henry VIII intervened to protect its critic Henry Standish, O.F.M., and Thomas Wolsey was forced to make a submission for the clergy. In Germany the decrees remained for the most part unknown. By 1520 Luther was criticizing those on the immortality of souls, on the Bohemians, and on the authority of the pope over councils. In his 1523 memorial to Adrian VI, Johann Eck suggested that, if ever implemented, the Lateran decrees on clerical reform, book censorship, and the holding of provincial councils would do much to stem the Reformation in Germany. Even Cajetan, the great defender of the Lateran Council, eventually admitted that many of its censures were probably not binding because their non-observance, by itself, had the legal force of abrogation.[31]

Erasmus followed current practice in regard to observing the Lateran decrees. When he learned of a decree, he tried initially to observe it, as happened when he published the *Novum Instrumentum* with episcopal approval. But most of his contemporaries were either ignorant of or ignored the Lateran's decrees. Since these measures were not put into common practice, he felt no longer bound by them. In the *Ecclesiastes* he stated what can be seen as his justification: "Those things, which the public authority of the Church prescribes, especially in ecumenical councils, and which are approved by public practice over a long period of time, should be reverently observed, nor should those things be spurned which pontiffs have ordered on just grounds for the public weal." Given the great difficulties he could have encountered had the decree on book censorship been put into strict practice, Erasmus must have been relieved that this Council's legislation was not approved by public usage and hence did not bind.[32]

It seems reasonable to conclude that Erasmus' rejection of the Lateran Council as a true council was not based primarily on the way in which it had been assembled, carried out, or promulgated, but rather on the way it had been given only a limited reception at first and then came to be ignored.

Erasmus' keen awareness that both the Pisan and Lateran councils had failed to reform the Church may help to explain his initial reluctance to urge a conciliar solution to the Reformation. Instead, he recommended a court of arbitration whose members would be appointed by emperor Charles V and by kings Henry VIII of England and Louis II of Hungary. But later Erasmus returned to the idea of a church council to reform morals and define central doctrines. Unfortunately, he did not live to see such a council assemble at Trent, and he may have been surprised to learn that this papal council did effect a reform of the Church, in part by reaffirming a number of the Lateran decrees—but this time they were enforced.[33]

NOTES

1 *Allen* 1268, 35–36: "De conciliis non ausim aliquid dicere, nisi forte proximum Concilium Lateranense concilium non fuit."

2 *Ichthyophagia* (February, 1526), in *Colloquia*, I – 3, 508, lines 466 – 67: "Bona verba, ne de conciliis quidem rite in Spiritu Sancto congregatis, peractis, aeditis et receptis." And lines 470 – 71: "... loquor de his qui nunc habentur orthodoxi, ne quid dicam de proximo Concilio Lateranensi."

3 Erasmus did not at first think that papal primacy was instituted by Christ, even though it was necessary for the unity of the Church. He opposed exaggerations of papal power and held that the authority of councils should confirm important papal teachings. Like his friend Thomas More, Erasmus too probably initially looked for such a decree to define whether a pope or a council was superior. He praised the ability of councils to correct errant pontiffs. Those who defended papal superiority were scoundrels like the Julius II depicted in *Julius Exclusus* or like mendicant friars whose exemptions and powers depended on the good will and authority of the popes. See *LB*, V, 90F – 91A, IX, 1087DE, X 1305B; *ASD* I – 3, 508, lines 455 – 64; *Erasmi Opuscula: A Supplement to the Opera Omnia*, ed. Wallace K. Ferguson (The Hague 1933), page 92: lines 465 – 70, 94: 517 – 36, 98: 601 – 14; Harry J. McSorley, "Erasmus and the Primacy of the Roman Pontiff: Between Conciliarism and Papalism," *Archiv für Reformationsgeschichte* 65 (1974), 37 – 54—McSorley, while admitting conciliarist influences (38 n. 10), attempts to play them down (49 – 52), fails to distinguish between Erasmus' early and later thinking on conciliarism (49 – 54), and tries to focus the discussion on whether a council can depose a pope which he calls "the conciliarist question" (49) and "the most notable characteristic of conciliar theory" (51), when Erasmus himself framed the question in terms of whether the pope or council is superior (e.g. *LB*, X, 1305B); and Willi Hentze, *Kirche und kirchliche Einheit bei Desiderius Erasmus von Rotterdam* (= *Konfessionskundliche und kontroverstheologische Studien* XXXIV), (Paderborn, 1974), 121 – 26.

In agreement with the current state of scholarship, this paper accepts the Erasmian authorship of the *Julius Exclusus*. See the excellent historiographical surveys by J. Kelley Sowards in his edition of *The "Julius exclusus" of Erasmus*, trans. Paul Pascal (Bloomington, Indiana, 1968), 97 – 98 n. 32 and that of James K. McConica, "Erasmus and the 'Julius': A Humanist Reflects on the Church," in *The Pursuit of Holiness in Late Medieval and Renaissance Religion*, eds. Charles Trinkaus with Heiko A. Oberman (Leiden, 1974), 444 – 71, esp. 467 – 71.

4 On the conciliarist thinking behind the Pisan Council, see especially Olivier de la Brosse, *Le pape et le concile: La comparaison de leurs pouvoirs à la veille de la Réforme* (= *Unam Sanctam*, 58), (Paris, 1965), and Remigius Bäumer, *Nachwirkungen des konziliaren Gedankens in der Theologie und Kanonistik des frühen 16. Jahrhunderts* (= *Reformationsgeschichtliche Studien und Texte*, 100), (Münster, 1971). On Erasmus' defense of the Pisan Council, see his *Julius Exclusus* in *Erasmus Opuscula*, 38 – 124, esp. 89 – 102.

5 *Allen* 1033, 144 – 46; 1275, 77 – 78; 1412, 49 – 52. In *Allen* 1225, 198 – 203 he praised Cajetan's 1521 defense of papal primacy for its objectivity, temperance, unadorned arguments, and sources cited. On Erasmus and Cajetan, see Christian Dolfin, *Die Stellung des Erasmus von Rotterdam zur scholastischen Methode: Inaugural-Dissertation* (Osnabrück, 1936), 92 – 93 and the entry of Danilo Aguzzi-Barbagli in *Contemporaries of Erasmus* I (Toronto, 1985), 239 – 42.

6 *LB* V, 90F – 91A, 128C, E; *Allen* 872, 16 – 21; *Erasmi Opuscula*, 90: 426 – 32, 98: 612 – 14.

7 *Erasmi Opuscula*, 90: 415, 106: 813 – 17.

8 *Erasmi Opuscula*, 66: 37 – 39, 73: 175 – 79, 88: 392, 90: 413, 114: 953 – 61 (bought papal office); 89: 402 – 03 (illegitimate daughter); 77: 249 – 50, 88: 392, 108: 858 (sodomy, pederasty); 68: 80 – 81, 72: 160 – 61 (syphilitic); 36: 20, 65: 12 – 13, 67: 57, 68: 83, 85, 90: 413 (drunkenness); 73 – 74: 185 – 93, 105: 770 – 71 (simony); 65: 6, 70: 131 – 32 (ignorance); 72 – 73: 165 – 70 (fortune-teller); 69 – 70: 106 – 09, 79: 274 (frivolous excommunications); 90: 417 – 23 (violating oath); 36: 8 – 9, 75: 211 – 14, 108 – 14: 860 – 939, 115: 977 – 80 (inciting others to warfare); 80: 286 – 87 (engaging as a priest in fighting).

9 *Allen* I, 37, lines 7 – 16 and *LB* II, 968C – E; the outlines of this oration seem to have been preserved in *LB* V, 898B – 99A; for other comments on the Venetian war, see *LB* IV, 608AB, IX, 360EF, and *Erasmi Opuscula*, 86: 370 – 79, 118: 1060 – 64.

10 *Erasmi Opuscula*, 90 – 91: 415 – 32, 97 – 99: 595 – 626, 99 – 100: 639 – 57, 102: 708 – 12.

Of the reform measures Erasmus attributes to the Pisan Council, only that limiting the prelates' pompous displays, and that only for the time of the Council, is to be found in its published acts—see the decree of the sixth session at Milan on 24 March 1512, in *Acta primi concilii Pisani . . . item constitutiones sanctae in diversis sessionibus sacri generalis concilii Pisani ex bibliotheca regia* (Paris, 1612), 152–56. Erasmus' knowledge of the Pisan Council came in part from the reports of friends—see, for example, the letters of Andrea Ammonio in *Allen* 236, 42–43; 239, 48–50; 247, 16–18, and the letter of Girolamo Aleandro, *Allen* 256, 44–60. Augustin Renaudet in his *Préréforme et humanisme à Paris pendant les premières guerres d'Italie (1494–1517)* 2nd ed., rev. (Paris, 1953), speculates that Erasmus' knowledge of the Pisan Council came from his contacts with Ammonio, Budé, and Lefèvre and from conversations he may have had in Paris during his June, 1511 visit when he had his *Moriae Encomium* published there. Whether Erasmus ever read the *acta* of the Pisan Council, published in Paris by Jean Petit on 23 August 1512, is not clear. Apparently he may well have read Jacques Almain's *Libellus de auctoritate ecclesiae . . .* (Paris, 1512) in response to Cajetan—see McSorley, "Erasmus and Primacy," 52–53. For the arguments of a modern scholar on the initial legitimacy of the Pisan Council, see Walter Ullmann, "Julius II and the Schismatic Cardinals," in *Schism, Heresy, and Religious Protest*, ed. Derek Baker (= *Studies in Church History*, 9) (Cambridge, 1972), 177–93, esp. 189. For a study of Julius' dealings with the Pisan Council, see my "The Healing of the Pisan Schism (1511–13)," *Annuarium Historiae Conciliorum* 16 (1984), 59–192, esp. 62–96.

11 *Erasmi Opuscula*, 74: 199–201, 91: 440–49, 95–96: 558–68, 99: 628–30, 101: 660–61, 114: 950–55. For a study of the goals set for the Lateran Council, see my "Paride de Grassi's Diary of the Fifth Lateran Council," *Annuarium Historiae Conciliorum* 14 (1982), 370–460, esp. 431–32.

12 *Erasmi Opuscula*, 95–97: 547–83. For Julius' efforts to control the Council and for a detailed study of those who attended, see my "De Grassi's Diary," 436–50 and "The Participants at the Fifth Lateran Council," *Archivum Historiae Pontificiae* 12 (1974), 157–206, esp. 159–60. For Erasmus' failed efforts to attend the Lateran Council in 1512, see *Allen* 252, 2–8; 255, 2–4; 334: 90–94. For the document proroguing the opening of the Council, see *Sacrorum conciliorum nova et amplissima collectio*, ed. J.D. Mansi *et al.*, vol. 32 (Florence, 1759), cols. 692DE, 694C—hereafter this volume is cited as "M".

13 *Erasmi Opuscula*, 101: 661–86, 102: 699. Erasmus' account of what occurred at the Council was deficient. He confused the opening ceremonies with the first session, passed over completely the first session at which the conciliar officials were appointed, and made no mention of the fourth and fifth sessions at which actions were taken against the defenders of the Pragmatic Sanction of Bourges, a reform of curial officials and their fees was confirmed, and an earlier constitution against simony in papal elections was approved. Whether these omissions were from ignorance or deliberately made to strengthen his case against the Council is not clear.

14 *Allen* 288, 83–85; 333, 10–14, 94–95; 335: 37–38, 43 46, 65–66, 77, 80–83, 93–97, 109–113, 122–25, 132–35, 192–99, 202–03, 331–35; 446, 11–13, 38–41, 84–86; and *LB*, IV, 636 D.

15 On the complicated process by which the schism was ended, especially Leo's dealings with the French, see my "Healing of the Pisan Schism," 11–54; on the temporal rulers adhering to the Lateran Council, see my "The Participants," 205–06; on Leo's exhortations to attend and grants of safe conduct, see, e.g., M 783B–D, 793B–D, 815D–816C; for Erasmus' announced intention to go to Rome in the winter of 1514, see *Allen* 296, 225–26, in March of 1515, see *Allen* 324, 26–27, and in the winter of 1515 and 1516, see *Allen* 334, 94–95, 207–09, and 360, 12–14.

16 For some of Leo's early restatements of the goals set for the Lateran Council, see M 783B, 788E, 792E–93A, 816D–17D, 818DE, etc. For Erasmus' patrons and friends as conciliar participants, see my "The Participants," 181–92 nrs. 5, 56, 71, 80, 173, 182, 184, 218, 310, 320, and M 975E and 976AB. The sources of Erasmus' knowledge of what happened at Lateran V are difficult to determine. He may have received in-

formation from his German correspondents such as Konrad Peutinger, Willibald Pirckheimer, and Beatus Bild, but this is not evidenced in their surviving letters. On Peutinger's knowledge of Lateran V, see John Headley, "Luther and the Fifth Lateran Council," *Archiv für Reformationsgeschichte* 64 (1974), 55–78, here 58. How Erasmus obtained copies of the decrees on clerical education and book censorship is unknown. The papal nuncio to England, Giampietro Carafa, may have furnished him with a first-hand report on the Council; see *Allen* 335, 186, 250–65.

17 For Antonini, see M 675BC and the entry of David S. Chambers in *COE*, I (1985), 64–65; for Pucci, see M 893E–94A, *Allen* 855, 6–14, and the entry of Rosemary D. Jones in *COE*, III (1987), 122–23; for de Gargha, see M 853E.

18 For Begna's statements, see M 799D, 805B; for Giustiniani and Quirini, see their *Libellus ad Leonem X. Pontificem Maximum* in *Annales Camaldulenses Ordinis Sancti Benedicti*, ed. J.B. Mittarelli and A. Costadoni, IX (Venice, 1773), cols. 676–79, 681–82. For Pico's statement on the Bible, see William Roscoe, *The Life and Pontificate of Leo the Tenth*, 2nd ed., rev. (London, 1806), VI, Appendix 146, p. 76: "Non in vestibus modo et sumptibus, sed in studiis sacrae literae utriusque instrumenti recognoscendae, et cum antiquis et castigatis primae originis exemplaribus conferendae . . . ."; for the crusade strategy, p. 75.

19 *Allen* 335, 184–91. That Erasmus used the term "synodal" synonymously for "conciliar" is evident from *Allen* 456, 61–63.

20 The decree is printed in M 842A–43C. For some of Erasmus' statements on the soul's immortality, see *Allen* 916, 275–84; 1039, 46–50, 55–56, and *LB*, IV, 621C–E. For his statements on the clerical education provision, see his scholion on Jerome's letter to Eustochius in *Omnium operum Divi Eusebii Hieronymi Stridonensis Tomus Primus . . . una cum argumentis et scholiis Des. Erasmi Roterodami . . . .* (Basel, 1516), fol. 61v, and *Allen* 1164, 15–22. For Erasmus' fear of a revival of paganism, see *Allen* 541, 133–37. For some classical poets who were considered dangerous, see the statutes of the Council of Florence (1517), in Mansi, XXXV, cols. 269C–70A.

21 The conciliar decree on book censorship is printed in M 912B–13D. For Erasmus' statements that he observed this decree, see *Allen* 446, 57–59; 456, 144–57, 215–16. For Leo's approval through Grimani and Riario, see *Allen* 456, 195–213; 843, 331–35; 864, 1–17. For Lee's demand of prior papal approval, see *Allen* 843, 441–46; for his later charges that Erasmus had no letter from Leo or only a counterfeited one and that even an authentic letter was of no weight unless the pope had first examined the work exactly, word for word, see *Erasmi Opuscula*, p. 271, lines 819–33. For Dorp's concern for conciliarly approved texts, see *Allen* 304, 98–108; 337, 768–89; 843, 317–19; for other critics suggesting prior conciliar approval, see *Allen* 456, 27–32.

22 For censorship of the Reuchlin-case pamphlets, see *Allen* 701, 30–31; for censorship of Zuñiga, see *Allen* 1418, 25–28; 2443, 350–55; *LB*, IX, 384E–85B; for reining in the German press, see *Allen* 785, 41–42; for his advice on book censorship to the Basel town council, see *Allen* 1539, 51–74; for his response to Zuñiga and observation that censorship was odious, see *LB*, IX, 383E; on the condemnation of Luther's writings, see *LB*, IX, 353A; on friars as censors, see *LB*, II, 967C; for the disparity between judgments based on expertise and authority, see *Allen* 843, 319–21; for his own licence to teach, see *Ibid*, 491–92. On the impracticality of the Lateran decree, see *Allen* 1539, 64–68.

23 The texts of the following decrees are reprinted in Mansi: *Montes pietatis* M 905C–07B, plundering cardinals' households M 987A–88B, curial reform M 845D–46E, "great reform bull" M 874C–85D, papal exemptions M 907D–12A, mendicants' privileges M 970D–74E. For Erasmus' general statement approving Leo's synodal constitutions, see *Allen* 335, 182–91.

24 For the decree on preaching, see M 944A–47D, esp. 944CD and 946B (criteria for interpreting Scripture). For Erasmus' views on preaching and interpreting Scripture, see *Allen* 446, 61–65; 916, 359–62, and *LB*, V, 798EF, 825D–26C, 1026C–28D, 1068C–69C.

25 For the conciliar texts related to the healing of the Pisan schism, see M 832A–36B, 947E–70D; to the Hussite schism, see M 845AB and the bull granting Bakócz the power to reconcile the Bohemians according to the terms approved at Basel, reprinted in Augustinus Theiner, ed., *Vetera monumenta historica Hungariam sacram illustrantia*, vol. II: *1352–1526* (Rome, 1860), Nr. 807 (20 September 1513), pp. 610–12; and to the Maronite adhesion, see M 942B–43E. For Erasmus' praise of the healing of the Pisan schism, see *Allen* 335, 81–83; for his suggestions on how to resolve the Hussite schism, see *Allen* 950, 45–56; 1039: 81–267, and Konrad Bittner, "Erasmus, Luther, und die Böhmischen Brüder," in *Rastloses Schaffen: Festschrift für Dr. Friedrich Lammert*, ed. Heinz Seehase (Stuttgart, 1954), 107–29, esp. 111, 113–14.

26 For conciliar efforts to promote peace, see M 817A–D, 843D–44E, and 870B–72B. For some of Erasmus' statements extoling peace, urging prelates to work for it, and praising Leo for his efforts, see *Allen* 288: 76–82; 335, 196–204; 541, 6–12, 29–35; 542: 12–15; 694, 41–43; 1202, 9–10, and *LB*, II, 966CD, IV, 636CD. See also Robert P. Adams, *The Better Part of Valor: More, Erasmus, Colet, and Vives on Humanism, War, and Peace, 1496–1535* (Seattle, 1962), esp. 43–121, 158–85. For the conciliar decree calling for a crusade, see M 988CD, 990D–92B. For Leo's efforts, see Kenneth M. Setton, *Papacy and the Levant (1204–1571)*, vol. III: *The Sixteenth Century to the Reign of Julius III* (Philadelphia, 1984), 142–97. For some of Erasmus' statements favoring conversion efforts rather than warfare, see *Allen* 335, 166–84; 775, 5–6; 781, 25–31; 785, 21–23; 786, 24–29; 858, 103–54, 378–87; 891, 24–33.

27 For the doctrinal statements in *Pastor aeternus*, see M 967D, 968E; for Erasmus' acceptance of the necessity to submit to papal authority, see *ASD* I–3 (*Ichthyophagia*, 1526), p. 505, lines 357–61; for Erasmus' refusal to take a stand, see *Allen* 1596, 35–42, and *LB*, IX, 1087D, X, 1305B. For an interesting study which argues that *Pastor aeternus* should not be interpreted as a repudiation of *Haec sancta*, see Francis A. Oakley, "Conciliarism at the Fifth Lateran Council?" *Church History* 41 (1972), 452–63, here 459–63.

28 For the procedures followed in making conciliar law, see Stephan Kuttner, "Conciliar Law in the Making: The Lyonese Constitutions (1274) of Gregory X in the Manuscript of Washington," in *Miscellanea Pio Paschini* (= *Lateranum*, N.S. 15), II (Rome, 1949), 39–81, here 39–44 and 49–50; and Minnich, "De Grassi's Diary," 441–45, 453–57. For copies of decrees which included rubrics testifying to the legal procedures followed, see the *Bulla intimationis Generalis Concilii apud Lateranum per summum dominum nostrum Julium Papam ii edita* (Nürnberg: Johannes Weyssenburger, 1512), Ai^v (Girolamo Ghinucci's verification of lead seal, of the red and saffron colored threads, and of the bull's publication and posting by three papal cursors in the customary places), Biv^r (verification that the text here printed is correct and authorization to print), see M 689DE, 691A–E for how this bull was read and posted (for from one to two hours) in various places around Rome. For the publication of the bull *Cum inchoatam*, see *Bulla Secunda sessionis sacrosancti Concilii Lateranensis approbans et renovans damnationem et reprobationem Pisani conciliabuli et annullans omnes et singula in illo gesta et gerenda, celebrate die xvii Mai M.d. xii* (s.l., s.d.), 4^v. For the formula "*Scribatur in forma*" following a positive vote, see *Bulla Concilii in Decima Sessione super materia Montis pietatis: Lecta per Reverendum patrem dominum Bertrandum Episcopum Adriensem Oratorem Ducis [Ferrariae]* (s.l., s.d.), iv^r. For revision of a *cedula*, see M 886D, 987A; for registration in the *acta* of the Council, see M 930CD; for extant copies in bull form of *Constituti juxta verbum*, see Archivio Segreto Vaticano (= ASV), AA. Arm. I–XVIII, nos. 1905 and 1906. For the printing of the decrees within days and ambassadors' concern to obtain copies, see Baltassaro Turini to Lorenzo dei Medici, Rome, 6 May 1514, Archivio di Stato—Florence (= ASF), Mediceo avanti il Principato, Filza 107, no. 18, fol. 18^v, and Francesco Vettori to the Dieci di Balia, Rome, 25 May 1514, ASF, Dieci di Balia, Carteggio-Responsive, no. 118, fol. 706^v. For a listing of bulls which were printed separately, see Fernanda Ascarelli, *Le Cinquecentine romane: "Censimento delle edizioni romane del XVI secolo possedute dalle biblioteche di Roma"* (Milan, 1972), 145–47, 153–56. For the reaffirmation of the twelfth session, see M 991BC; for the July 1517 printing of the con-

ciliar decrees, see Hubert Elie, "Un Lunevillois imprimeur à Rome au début du XVIème siècle: Etienne Guillery," *Guttenberg-Jahrbuch* (1939), 185–96, (1944–49), 128–37, here 129–30, 137. The Milan collection, which does not contain such important bulls as those abrogating the Pragmatic Sanction and approving the Concordat, is entitled *Bullae sacri concilii Lateranensis*; the *acta* were published at Rome as *Sacrosanctum Lateranense Concilium Novissimum sub Julio II at Leone X Celebratum*.

29 *Erasmi Opuscula* p. 101, lines 674–76; Agostino Patrizi, *Rituum ecclesiasticorum sive sacrarum cerimoniarum SS. Romanae Ecclesiae libri tres non ante impressi*, ed. Cristoforo Marcello (Venice, 1516), fol. 62ʳ.

30 For the delegation of execution, see M 991BC; for the enforcement at Rome, see my "'*Incipiat iudicium a domo Domini*': The Fifth Lateran Council and the Reform of Rome," in *Reform and Authority in the Medieval and Reformation Church*, ed. Guy Fitch Lytle (Washington, 1981), 127–142, esp. 135–42 and ASV, Arm. XLIV, vol. 5, fol. 251ᵛ and Reg. Vat. 1200, fols. 391ʳ–95ᵛ, esp. 391ᵛ.

31 For the Florentine statutes, see Mansi, XXXV, 215A–318C, esp. 229D, 230AB, 232D–34B, 269D, 270D–73A, 274C–75C, 283C, 290C, 304B, etc. For Farnese's efforts to implement the conciliar decrees at Parma, see Ludwig Pastor, *History of the Popes*, 2nd ed., vol. XI, trans. Ralph Francis Kerr (St. Louis, 1923), 20–21; for Sanseverino's efforts at Novara and del Monte's at Pavia, see Angelo L. Stoppa, "Quattro decreti generali novaresi simultanei al Concilio Lateranense V finora sconosciuti e inediti," *Novara* 2 (1968), 48–104, esp. 48, 64–65, 84, 89, and 92; for the Venetian measure, see Marino Sanudo, *I Diarii*, XXI, col. 485; for Ximenes' efforts in Spain, see Joseph Hergenroether, *Histoire des conciles*, VIII–I, trans. Henri Leclercq (Paris, 1917), 564–65. For the registration of the Concordat, see *Recueil général des anciennes lois Françaises depuis l'an 420, jusqu'a la Révolution de 1789*, ed. F. Isambert et al., XII (Paris, 1828), 75–97, 114–18; for the charge to Philippe de Luxembourg and Guillaume Briçonnet, see ASV, Reg. Vat. 1204, fols. 198ᵛ–99ᵛ, for that to Denys Briçonnet, Reg. Vat. 1200, fols. 277ʳ–78ʳ.

For this English effort, see J. Duncan M. Derrett, "The Affair of Richard Hunne and Friar Standish," in *The Complete Works of St. Thomas More*, vol. 9: *The Apology*, ed. J.B. Trapp (New Haven, 1979), 215–46, esp. 226, 229, 231–32.

For Germany, see Headley, "Luther and Lateran," 65–73, and *Acta Reformationis Catholicae ecclesiam Germaniae concernentia saeculi XVI: Die Reformverhandlungen des deutschen Episcopats von 1520 bis 1570*, Band I, ed. Georg Pfeilschifter (Regensburg, 1959), 121–24, for a memorial urging the implementation of the Lateran decrees in the province of Salzburg, see pp. 21, 32.

On the principle of abrogation through non-observance, see Geoffrey King, "The Acceptance of Law by the Community: A Study in the Writings of Canonists and Theologians, 1500–1750," *The Jurist* 37 (1977), 233–65, here 237–38 (for the opinion of Felinus Sandaeus, d. 1503, an auditor of the sacred Rota). For Cajetan's application of this principle to Lateran V in 1523 and his doubts about the binding force of certain decrees, see his *Peccatorum Summula novissime recognita . . . per Gaugericum Hispanum* (Douai, 1613), "Excommunicatio," cap. LXXXII, pp. 295–97. Carranza, in his conciliar collection which first appeared in Venice, 1546, reiterated approvingly Cajetan's doubts, see Bartolomé Carranza de Miranda, *Summa conciliorum et pontificum a Petro usque ad Pium iiii collecta* . . . . (Lyon, 1570), fol. 403ᵛ

32 *LB*, V, 1076E.

33 *Erasmi Opuscula*, pp. 352–61, esp. lines 134–54; *ASD*, IX–2, 481, lines 51–54; *Allen* 2988, 70–72; and for some examples of Lateran decrees reiterated at Trent, see *Conciliorum Oecumenicorum Decreta*, ed. G. Alberigo et al., 664–65 (book censorship), 670 and 763 (preaching), 730 (union of benefices), 761 (provincial councils), etc.

ÉRASME, LATOMUS ET LE MARTYRE DE DEUX
AUGUSTINS LUTHÉRIENS À BRUXELLES EN 1523

Vers la fin de l'année 1521 la légation de Jerôme Aléandre auprès de Charles-Quint aux Pays-Bas aboutit à la création d'une inquisition d'état.[1] Le 23 avril 1522 un laïc, François van der Hulst, membre du Conseil de Brabant, fut nommé inquisiteur dans les «pays de par deça». En réalité, au moment de sa nomination il exerçait déjà cette fonction depuis quelques mois. Maître van der Hulst pouvait se faire assister par deux théologiens afin de convertir éventuellement les suspects. C'est en tant qu'experts en matières religieuses que les théologiens louvanistes, surtout Nicolas Baechem Egmondanus et Jacques Masson ou Latomus, furent mêlés à la plupart des procès que l'inquisition d'état instruisit entre la fin de 1521 et la fin de 1523, quand van der Hulst fut destitué de ses fonctions, par suite de fautes commises dans le procès contre l'avocat hollandais Corneille Hoen.

C'est surtout à Anvers que l'inquisition d'état fut active. Elle y intenta des procès à Jacques Praepositus, le prieur des augustins, et aux humanistes Corneille Grapheus et Nicolas Buscoducensis. Des deux procès contre Praepositus, le premier se termina par une rétractation, le deuxième par la fuite de l'inculpé. Les procès contre Grapheus et Buscoducensis aboutirent à des rétractations.

Le 6 octobre 1522 l'inquisition fit arrêter tous les augustins du cloître d'Anvers. Leur procès se déroula à Vilvorde. La plupart des augustins désavouèrent leurs opinions, mais trois d'entre eux résistèrent à toutes les tentatives des inquisiteurs et de leurs conseillers théologiques pour les amener à se rétracter. Le 1 juillet 1523 deux de ces trois obstinés, Henri Voes et Jean van Esschen, moururent sur le bûcher sur la Grande Place à Bruxelles et devinrent les premiers martyrs du Protestantisme. Le troisième obstiné, Lambert de Thorn, resta en prison jusqu'à sa mort en 1528.[2]

Le martyre des deux augustins luthériens fut célébré dans quelques pamphlets.[3] Le plus repandu était *Der Actus und hendlung der Degradation und verprennung der Christlichen dreien Ritter und merterer Augustiner ordens geschehen zu Brussel*, qui connut au moins seize impressions. Cette plaquette raconte que trois augustins qui furent détenus à Vilvorde refusèrent de se rétracter. Deux d'entre eux furent dégradés par l'évêque, livrés à la justice de Bruxelles et conduits vers le lieu du supplice. Jusqu'à leur mort au bûcher ils restèrent inébranlables dans leurs convictions. Trois jours après on brûla dans les mêmes circonstances le troisième augustin qui avait demandé un délai pour réfléchir.

Nous savons maintenant que l'information concernant la mort du troisième augustin, Lambert de Thorn, est fausse.

Selon l'*Actus und hendlung*, les articles que Henri Voes et Jean van Esschen ne voulurent pas abjurer étaient: «que le pape n'a pas le pouvoir de remettre les péchés à quelqu'un, que Dieu seul peut lier et délier, que pouvant pécher comme les autres hommes, le pape n'a pas plus de pouvoirs qu'un prêtre ordinaire».

Deux autres pamphlets qui commémorent les martyrs bruxellois sont dus à Martin Luther: *Die artickel warumb die zwen Christliche Augustiner münch zu Brussel verprandt sind, sampt eynem sendbrieff an die Christen ym Holland und Braband* et le cantique *Ein neues Lied wir heben an*. En effet, ce cantique fut imprimé séparément une fois, à Nürnberg, vers 1530. La brochure *Die artickel*, qui fut imprimée deux fois à Wittenberg, consiste dans une lettre de Luther aux chrétiens des Pays-Bas et la reconstruction d'un dialogue entre les inquisiteurs et les deux martyrs. Ces derniers restèrent inébranlés dans leur foi et moururent en priant et en louant Dieu, mais sans qu'on ait lu la sentence du tribunal comme il aurait fallu.

Selon le pamphlet *Die artickel*, les articles auxquels Voes et van Esschen s'obstinaient à adhérer déclaraient que les lois de l'Eglise doivent correspondre aux préceptes de l'Ecriture et que ceux qui transgressent les lois purement ecclésiastiques ne pèchent pas.

Le plus important des pamphlets sur le martyre des deux augustins anversois est la *Historia de duobus Augustinensibus, ob evangelii doctrinam exustis Bruxellae*. Cette brochure, qui ne connut probablement que deux éditions, nous fournit la description du martyre la plus conforme à la réalité ainsi que la liste la plus étendue des articles incriminés. La *Historia* consiste en deux lettres datées du 10 et du 14 juillet qui relatent la dégradation et le martyre des augustins, comme l'*Actus*, mais avec plus de détails. La *Historia* ne parle que de deux augustins morts sur le bûcher. A propos du troisième augustin, elle dit ne pouvoir reproduire que des racontars: qu'il aurait été tué clandestinement ou qu'il aurait rétracté ses erreurs.

Selon l'*Historia*, les articles incriminés de Voes et van Esschen concernent l'importance de Luther et de ses livres pour la propagation du véritable évangile (art. 5–6, 21, 57), l'injustice de la condamnation de Luther (art. 11) et de la défense de lire ses livres (art. 1–3, 10), l'autorité de l'Eglise (art. 7–9, 19–20, 33, 48–50, 59) et du pape (art. 35), les sacrements (art. 28–30, 32), l'Eucharistie (art. 16–18, 39, 43, 46–47, 53–55), la Pénitence (art. 27, 40, 44, 52), le sacrement de l'Ordre (art. 25, 31) et le sacerdoce de tous les croyants (art. 12, 24) avec ses implications pour l'Eucharistie (art. 22, 25 – 26) et la Pénitence (art. 13 – 15), la justification (art. 34, 38), le purgatoire (art. 41, 45), la vénération des Saints (art. 56), les voeux (art. 36 – 37), les privilèges du clergé (art. 58). Quelques articles constituent des affronts pour les inquisiteurs ou témoignent du mépris des inculpés pour leurs juges (art. 4, 23, 42, 51, 60 – 62).

Voes et van Esschen expriment plusieurs fois leur conviction que la hiérarchie ecclésiastique est liée à l'Ecriture et que les dogmes et les préceptes de l'Eglise ne peuvent qu'énoncer ce qui est contenu dans l'Ecriture. Le Christ n'a pas fait du pape son vicaire, mais son ministre. Il n'y a que trois sacrements: le Baptême, l'Eucharistie et la Pénitence. L'Eucharistie n'est pas un sacrifice. Voes et van Esschen doutent de la transsubstantiation mais sont catégoriques en exigeant le calice pour les laïcs. Il n'y a pas d'obligation de confesser tous les péchés mortels ou de faire pénitence après avoir reçu l'absolution.

Parce que tous les croyants sont prêtres, l'ordination ne confère que le mandat d'exercer un ministère et n'octroie pas des pouvoirs spéciaux, que les autres chrétiens ne possèderaient pas. Tous les chrétiens possèdent le pouvoir de consacrer le corps du Christ et même les femmes ont celui de donner l'absolution.

Les bonnes oeuvres des croyants sont opérées par le Christ. La charité est liée inséparablement à la foi.

Voes et van Esschen doutent de l'existence du purgatoire et de la possibilité d'aider les défunts par des prières. Il ne veulent pas s'expliquer sur la vénération des Saints. Les voeux ne sont pas obligatoires.

Un certain Martinus Reckenhofer a donné une adaptation de l'*Historia de duobus Augustinensibus* en Allemand. Dans cette version les articles sont pourvus d'un ample commentaire. Sur le frontispice de l'*Histori so zwen Augustiner Ordens gemartert seyn tzü Bruxel* se trouve une gravure représentant les deux martyrs bruxellois en saints. L'*Histori* ne fut imprimée qu'une seule fois.

A Bâle, Érasme suivit avec beaucoup d'intérêt les activités de l'inquisition d'état aux Pays-Bas, parce que, selon lui, la persécution n'était pas dirigée contre les luthériens mais contre les adeptes des *bonae litterae*.[4] Il vit son interprétation confirmée par les procès que l'inquisition intendit à ses amis anversois, Grapheus et Buscoducensis, et à l'humaniste hollandais Hoen.

Au sujet de la condamnation à mort de Voes et van Esschen, il ne savait pas très bien ce qu'il fallait en penser. Le 31 août 1523, Érasme écrivit à Zwingli que trois augustins étaient morts á Bruxelles, le 1 et 3 juillet, dans une constance inouïe, non pour des articles de la foi, mais pour les paradoxes de Luther.[5] Il douta qu'ils soient de vrais martyrs.

Vraisemblablement Érasme connaissait le récit de l'*Actus*, comme son ami Jean Botzheim. Celui-ci lui avait annoncé, le 24 août 1523, la nouvelle de l'exécution de trois moines à Bruxelles.[6] Mais il est aussi probable qu'Érasme, qui était bien au courant de ce qui se passait aux Pays-Bas par ses *amanuenses*, avait encore d'autres sources d'information.

Dans la lettre à Zwingli, Érasme dit que mourir pour le Christ est glorieux mais que, quant à lui, il ne voulait pas mourir pour les paradoxes de Luther. Il énumera quelques-unes de ces propositions énigmatiques du réformateur: «toutes les oeuvres des saints sont des péchés, qui appellent le pardon de Dieu et sa miséricorde; le libre arbitre est un mot vide de sens; seule la foi justifie l'homme, ses oeuvres ne font rien à l'affaire».[7]

Il avait dit à peu près la même chose dans la *Spongia adversus aspergines Hutteni*, qu'il avait écrite vers la fin de juillet et que Froben était en train d'imprimer à l'époque où Érasme écrivit sa lettre à Zwingli:[8] «Hutten avance qu'il faut subir la mort pour la vérité évangélique. Je ne le refuse pas, le cas échéant. Mais on n'en est pas encore arrivé à subir la mort pour Luther et les paradoxes de Luther. Il ne s'agit pas des articles de foi, mais de savoir si la primauté du pontife romain vient du Christ, si le collège des cardinaux est un organe indispensable de l'Eglise, si la confession a le Christ pour auteur, si les évêques peuvent par leurs constitutions obliger sous peine de péché mortel, si le libre arbitre conduit au salut, si la foi seule contribue au salut, si on peut dire que l'homme est capable d'oeuvres méritoires, si la messe peut être en quelque manière considérée comme un sacrifice. Pour ces choses, qui constituent des thèmes habituels des joutes scolastiques, je n'oserais prendre la vie à personne, si j'étais juge, de même que je ne voudrais point me mettre en danger de mort pour elles. Je veux être le martyr du Christ s'Il me donne la force nécessaire; être le martyr de Luther, je ne le veux pas».[9]

Ici Érasme ne parle pas explicitement des martyrs bruxellois, mais la plupart des questions qu'il énumère ont été débattues aussi entre les martyrs bruxellois et leurs juges: les lois ecclésiastiques purement humaines, le pouvoir papal, l'Eucharistie et la Pénitence, la justification. Il est donc possible qu'Érasme, quand il écrivit ce passage dans la *Spongia*, ait pensé aux augustins anversois morts quelques semaines auparavant pour leurs convictions luthériennes.

Un des théologiens qui avaient collaboré avec l'inquisition d'état, Jacques Latomus, a vraisemblablement interprété le passage cité de la *Spongia* comme une condamnation de la façon d'agir du tribunal dans le cas de Voes et van Esschen. En 1525, il publia chez Michel Hillen à Anvers, outre le *De Confessione* et le *De ecclesia*, le traité *De quaestionum generibus quibus ecclesia certat intus et foris*.[10] Dans ce dernier écrit il s'en prend à ce qu'Érasme dit au sujet des paradoxes de Luther dans la *Spongia*, toutefois sans appeler le grand humaniste par son nom.[11]

Selon Latomus, il y a deux genres de discussions théologiques: d'une part, les discussions que les théologiens catholiques mènent avec des païens, des juifs, des hérétiques et des schismatiques; d'autre part, les discussions que les théologiens catholiques ont entre eux, dans les écoles, sous forme d'exercices. Ensuite le théologien louvaniste démontre qu'il faut classer dans le premier genre les discussions sur «des articles que certaines personnes qualifient de paradoxes de Luther en disant qu'il ne s'agit pas d'articles de foi mais de savoir si la primauté du pontife romain vient du Christ, etc. . . . .»[12] Latomus cite ici tous les paradoxes qu'Érasme a énumérés dans la *Spongia*. Il reprend ensuite une à une toutes ces propositions et démontre pour chacune d'elles que Luther en parle comme un hérétique. Latomus discute plus amplement la dernière question: la messe est-elle un sacrifice. Il donne aussi la raison pour laquelle la réponse doit être négative, bien qu'Érasme n'en ait pas parlé: la messe doit être dite en mémoire de la passion du Seigneur. C'est ce qu'avaient dit les martyrs bruxellois.

Aux paradoxes de Luther qu'Érasme avait énumérés, Latomus en ajoute un: à l'origine des voeux se trouve l'ignorance de la liberté chrétienne, ce qui est encore une réminiscence des assertions des martyrs bruxellois.

Selon Latomus, dans tous ces paradoxes il s'agit d'articles de foi pour lesquels il faut tuer ou mourir.

Dans la deuxième partie de son traité, Latomus parle de la relation entre la doctrine de l'Eglise et la théologie. Les articles de foi sont les principes de la théologie. Le théologien catholique doit approuver explicitement la doctrine de l'Eglise, surtout les articles controversés. Une position intermédiaire entre l'Eglise et l'hérésie n'est pas possible. La troisième partie du *De quaestionum generibus* concerne la relation Ecriture-Eglise. Il faut que l'Ecriture soit interprétée selon la doctrine de l'Eglise. Il faut aussi accepter les vérités, que l'Eglise tient en sus de ce que l'Ecriture contient.

En guise de conclusion nous voulons faire quelques remarques sur les positions qu'ont prises Érasme et Latomus dans cette controverse sur l'étendue et l'importance du dépôt de la foi.

La position d'Érasme doit être interpretée à la lumière de ce qu'il dit dans la préface à l'édition des écrits d'Hilaire, qui date du début de 1523: «La somme de notre religion, c'est paix et unisson des âmes. Elle pourra difficilement se maintenir si nous ne bornons pas nos définitions à un nombre de points aussi restreint que possible, et si, pour beaucoup de ces points, nous ne laissons pas à chacun son libre jugement . . . Jadis la foi se révélait dans la façon de vivre plus que dans l'énoncé d'articles. Bientôt la nécessité fit comprendre qu'il fallait rédiger des articles, mais en petit nombre et d'une concision digne des Apôtres. Ce fut ensuite l'effronterie des hérétiques qui a conduit à une explication plus précise des Livres divins, ce fut l'opiniâtreté qui a contraint à faire préciser certains points par l'autorité des synodes. Finalement la foi a commencé à se manifester dans les écrits plutôt que dans les coeurs et il y eut à peu près autant de croyances que d'hommes. Les articles s'accrurent, mais la sincérité décrut; la discussion s'échauffa, l'amour se glaça».[13]

Érasme veut reduire les articles de foi à un petit nombre,—ceux qu'on a définis dans l'ère patristique,—parce que pour lui l'essence du christianisme, c'est la loi d'amour, bien que normalement on ne puisse l'accomplir que dans la foi, par la grâce du Christ. Les dogmes, même les dogmes fondamentaux des premiers siècles de l'Eglise, n'ont qu'une valeur toute relative.

Chez Latomus par contre, les dogmes ont une valeur absolue. De même, le nombre d'articles auxquels il faut croire est beaucoup plus élevé que chez Érasme. Selon Latomus le dépôt de la foi englobe en plus la *communis opinio* des théologiens scolastiques concernant l'ecclésiologie, la sacramentologie et la doctrine de la justification.

Sa conception du dépôt de la foi, Latomus l'a déjà exposée en 1519 dans ses *De trium linguarum et theologici studii ratione dialogus*, deux dialogues sur les tentatives des humanistes, surtout d'Érasme, de réformer les études théologiques.[14] Latomus n'est pas de l'avis des humanistes, qui, dans la formation du théologien, veulent accentuer beaucoup plus la grammaire et la rhétorique que la dialectique. Les deux principes sur lesquels il s'appuie pour repousser les revendications des humanistes sont: «*conceptus esse vocibus priores*»[15] et «*in evangelicis quaestionibus ultimam resolutionem esse ad evangelium scriptum in tabulis cordis fidelium*».[16] Pour le théologien louvaniste, comme pour Saint Augustin et les scolastiques, le *verbum in corde* ou l'*oratio mentalis*,—c'est à dire le discours conceptuel—, est antérieur au mot ou au langage. Or la révélation est d'abord une *oratio mentalis*, notamment l'*evangelium in corde* ou la *lex Christi mentalis*,[17] qui est antérieure à l'Ecriture. Pour les controversistes du seizième siècle, l'évangile écrit dans le coeur des fidèles, c'est la Tradition ou le dépôt de la foi, qui depuis les apôtres est transmise d'âge en âge dans l'Eglise du Seigneur.[18] La Tradition de l'Eglise est donc antérieure à l'Ecriture. Cela veut dire que celui qui veut connaître le message du Christ doit plutôt écouter la prédication de l'Eglise que lire l'Ecriture.

De la même manière que les pratiquants des sciences profanes perçoivent, sous la lumière naturelle de l'intelligence, les principes de leur science, le théologien perçoit, sous la lumière surnaturelle de la grâce dans la doctrine que l'Eglise nous présente à croire, les articles de foi qui sont les principes de sa science: la théologie. Cette conception de la théologie qu'expose ici Latomus se trouve aussi chez Saint Thomas par exemple.

Dans la préface à ses dialogues sur la réforme de la théologie, Latomus avait dit qu'il avait l'intention d'en ajouter un troisième: «*tertium addere de dogmatum ecclesiasticorum, quae non iure vellicantur, ratione*».[19] Ce troisième dialogue n'a pas été édité, mais il fut remanié et devint le traité *De quaestionum generibus* sur les paradoxes de Luther, qui sont en réalité des «*ecclesiastica dogmata*» que le réformateur «*quantum in se est, convellit*».[20]

Mais, selon Latomus, Luther n'est pas seul à ébranler les dogmes ecclésiastiques. Dans la deuxième partie de son *De quaestionum generibus*, Latomus attaque ceux qui ne sont pas d'avis que ce que Luther a dit sur ses paradoxes, soit hérétique. Il est clair qu'il vise ici en premier lieu Érasme, qui a formulé dans sa *Spongia* ces paradoxes de Luther. Selon Latomus, Érasme, en mettant l'accent sur la charité et l'unité, ébranle des dogmes de l'Eglise qu'il faut maintenir à tout prix.

NOTES

1 Les sources sur l'inquisition d'état (1521–1523) ont été éditées dans le *Corpus documentorum inquisitionis haereticae pravitatis neerlandicae*, ed. Paul Fredericq, t. IV–V, Gent–'s-Gravenhage, 1900–1902. Cf. Paul Kalkoff, *Die Anfänge der Gegenreformation in den Niederlanden*, 2 vols., Halle, 1903–1904.

2 Johan Decavele, "De opkomst van het protestantisme te Brussel",—*Noordgouw*, t. 19–20 (1979–1983), p. 29–30.

3 *Bibliotheca Belgica. Bibliographie générale des Pays-Bas*, fondée par Ferdinand van der Haeghen, rééditée sous la direction de Marie-Thérèse Lenger, Bruxelles, 1964, t. I, p. 3–7 et p. 106; t. III, p. 401, p. 411–412, p. 476–477 et p. 1171–1172; t. IV, p. 298–299 et p. 302; Hildegard Hebenstreit-Wilfert, "Märtyrerflugschriften der Reformationszeit",—*Flugschriften als Massenmedium der Reformationszeit*, ed. Hans-Joachim Köhler, Stuttgart, 1981, p. 397–406 et 432–439. Les pamphlets concernant les martyrs bruxellois ont été édités dans: *Corpus*, ed. Fredericq, t. IV, p. 193–204, p. 207–214 et p. 223–228; *Bibliotheca Reformatoria Neerlandica*, t. VIII, ed. F. Pijper, 's-Gravenhage, 1911, p. 1–114; Martin Luther, *Werke*, t. XII, Weimar, 1891, p. 73–80 et t. XXXV, Weimar, 1923, p. 376 et p. 411–415. De diverses impressions de ces pamphlets sont ou seront éditées sous forme de microfiches: *Flugschriften des frühen 16. Jahrhundert*, ed. H.–J. Köhler, H. Hebenstreit, Chr. Weismann, Zug: IDC, depuis 1978.

4 *Allen* 1299. 9–12, 35–36, 96–98; 1300. 8–9, 10–12; 1301. 81n–84n; 1302. 78–81; 1311. 31–35; 1330. 49–56; 1345. 38–39. Cf. aussi les lettres du début de 1524: *Allen* 1408. 18–19; 1411. 13–16; 1417. 17–20; 1432. 64–66 et 1434. 38–41.

5 *Allen* 1384. 2–9.

6 *Allen* 1382. 46–49: Botzheim avait vu l'*Actus* imprimé à Nürnberg (= Hebenstreit-Wilfert, 'Märtyrerflugschriften', p. 432, no. I.2) et savait qu'on allait imprimer l'*Historia*.

Dans ses lettres Érasme parle encore quelques fois des martyrs bruxellois de 1523. Il doute de l'efficacité des méthodes inquisitoriales: après le martyre des deux ou trois augustins à Bruxelles, cette ville commença à prendre parti pour Luther; l'inquisition sème le germe de l'hérésie (*Allen* 1526. 155–169 et 2445. 72–76). Il ne croit pas les racontars sur des rétractations de martyrs sur le bûcher comme on en a répandus aussi après le martyre des augustins le 1 juillet 1523 (*Allen* 2188. 54–71). Beaucoup d'éléments du récit d'Érasme dans cette lettre correspondent à l'*Historia*, mais il y a aussi quelques différences (la négation d'Egmondanus que les augustins ont révoqué, l'apparition de l'un des deux martyrs). Il n'est pas impossible qu'Érasme, quand il écrit cette lettre le 1 juillet 1529, sache quelque chose sur les circonstances de la mort de Lambert de Thorn en 1528.

 7 *Allen* 1384. 6–7, 9–13; traduction française: *La correspondance d'Érasme*, ed. Aloïs Gerlo, Bruxelles, 1967–1984, L. 1384. 7–8, 12–16.
 8 Voir *Allen* 1376. 27–28; 1383. 13–14; 1389. 69–70, 75–76.
 9 Desiderius Erasmus, *Spongia adversus aspergines Hutteni,—LB*, X, 1663A–B et *ASD*, IX–1, p. 190, l. 635–646. Sur ce texte de la *Spongia*: Jean Delumeau, *Le Christianisme va-t-il mourir?* Paris, 1977, p. 131. D'autres énumerations de paradoxes de Luther dans la *Spongia*: *ASD*, IX–1, p. 164, l. 40—p. 165, l. 42 et p. 208, l. 89—p. 209, l. 91.
10 *Bibliotheca Belgica*, t. III, p. 750–751; W. Nijhoff et M.E. Kronenberg, *Nederlandsche bibliographie van 1500 tot 1540*, 's-Gravenhage, 1923–1966, no. 1325. Cf. *Allen* 1581. 407–410; 1582. 74–77; 1585. 79–81; 1603. 46–48; 1621. 28–31; 1624. 38–41; 1674. 29–30; 1686. 47–48; 1719. 55–60; 1747. 49–50.
11 Jacobus Latomus, *De quaestionum generibus, quibus ecclesia certat intus et foris,—Opera*, Louvain, 1550, f. 86–93.
12 Latomus, *De quaestionum generibus*, f. 86v°D. Cf. *Allen*, ep. 1621. 30: "... citabat verba mea."
13 *Allen* 1334. 217–219, 362–369; traduction française: *Correspondance*, L. 1334. 302–306, 502–512.
14 Jacobus Latomus, *De trium linguarum et studii theologici ratione dialogus,—Bibliotheca Reformatoria Neerlandica*, t. III, ed. F. Pijper, 's-Gravenhage, 1905, p. 41–85.
15 Latomus, *Dialogus*, p. 62.
16 Latomus, *Dialogus*, p. 64.
17 Latomus, *Dialogus*, p. 77.
18 Yves M.-J. Congar, *La Tradition et les traditions*, t. II, Paris, 1963, p. 245–254.
19 Latomus, *Dialogus*, p. 45.
20 Latomus, *De quaestionum generibus*, f. 87v°C.

E. RUMMEL

ERASMUS AND THE VALLADOLID ARTICLES: INTRIGUE, INNUENDO, AND STRATEGIC DEFENSE

In 1526 friends warned Erasmus that he had many enemies among the Spanish orders, and Erasmus acknowledged the danger: 'Spain has its new Stunicas'.[1] The ensuing battle of minds passed through three stages: a period of manoeuvring behind the scenes during which Erasmus found it difficult to distinguish friend from foe; a period of confrontation culminating in the Valladolid conference when the protagonists showed their true colours; and the period following the conference when Erasmus went public, replying to the charges brought against him in a printed *apologia*.

The first phase is well documented in Erasmus' correspondence of 1526/7 which is full of references to a Spanish plot.[2] His suspicions, for the most part justified by subsequent events, were occassionally misdirected. Thus he was convinced that his old enemy, Edward Lee, who had gone to Spain on a diplomatic mission in 1525,[3] was the chief instigator of the plot. He first voiced concerns in August 1526 in a letter to the French court physician Guillaume Cop and soon afterwards lodged a complaint with the imperial chancellor Mercurio Gattinara.[4] Unconvinced by the chancellor's assurances that Lee would not be permitted to publish anything damaging to Erasmus' reputation, he also lobbied William Warham, archbishop of Canterbury.[5] Oblique references to Lee appear moreover in contemporary letters to Willibald Pirckheimer in which the Englishman is depicted as the driving force behind the machinations of the monks, and indeed as their ghostwriter.[6] Despite the frequency and persistence of Erasmus' allegations, there is, however, little external evidence to substantiate the claim that Lee played a personal role in these matters. Erasmus cited the reports of friends, naming among his informants Cuthbert Tunstall[7] who had good diplomatic connections, but there is only one independent reference extant which explicitly links Lee with the Spanish inquisition. It occurs in a letter by Juan Vergara who mentions rumours that the Valladolid Articles "were largely put together in Lee's workshop" (*Allen* 1814, 284–285). The phrase *magna ex parte in Leica officina conflatum* may however mean nothing more than that Lee's *Annotations* (published in 1520) had supplied the source material for the censures.

Lee was not the only culprit in Erasmus' eyes. He saw conspirators everywhere. In Olmedos, Alonso Ruiz de Virués had drawn up *Colla-*

tiones, passages from Erasmus' works which, he felt, exposed the author to suspicion.[8] He dispatched a copy to the humanist, asking for clarification. Erasmus, however, misread Virués' intentions and denounced him as an underhanded critic in letters to Pirckheimer, More, Maldonado, and Alfonso Valdés.[9] Unfortunately Valdés received his letter while in the company of Virués and, unprepared for its contents, shared it with his visitor. On reading Erasmus' allegations, Virués was much taken aback and exclaimed in dismay: "Is this the thanks my Erasmus, whom I have praised so many times, returns for my good services?" (*Allen* 1839, 24–26). The confusion spread when Erasmus accused Juan Vergara of having inspired the *Collationes* whereas the latter protested that he had never even heard of Virués.[10] Both men eventually succeeded in convincing Erasmus of their loyalty and goodwill. In the end Erasmus himself suggested that they let the matter rest and "join in Christian friendship under better auspices" (*Allen* 1875, 31–32). By this time he had probably been informed about Virués' defense of his writings at the Valladolid conference.[11]

Alonso Fernándes, who had published a Spanish translation of the *Enchiridion* in 1526, was another follower whose efforts were not entirely welcome to Erasmus. The translation, which made the book accessible to a large audience, contributed significantly to Erasmus' unpopularity with the regular clergy. It aroused resentment among the monks, Vives wrote, because it exposed their machinations and took away much of their tyrannical hold on the people. Vergara concurred with him: "More enemies arose instantly out of the published translation of your book," he wrote, "than from Cadmus' sowing of dragon-teeth".[12] Such reports made Erasmus wonder aloud whether the translator had acted out of good or ill will toward him.[13] Fernándes, who was an ardent admirer of Erasmus, immediately wrote to exonerate himself. Erasmus accepted his declaration of good faith but insisted that the publicity resulting from the translation was a mixed blessing: "I would rather be the least known of all men than have fame tempered with the leaven of envy" (*Allen* 1969, 20–21).

The first phase—one of confusion and suspicion—came to a close in 1527 when secular and ecclesiastical authorities called for a formal investigation of Erasmus' works.[14] This measure was designed to end the intrigues and settle the dispute regarding Erasmus' orthodoxy. In March of 1527 the Inquisitor General, Alonso Manrique, instructed representatives of the monastic orders to report in writing on any points in Erasmus' work that appeared questionable to them, reminding them at the same time that the final verdict rested with a panel of qualified judges to be assembled at Valladolid.[15] Letters from Vergara and Vives describe the frenetic activity that ensued in the wake of these instructions. Rumour had it that the brethren had no time even to hear confession, working feverishly "to catch the heretic" (*Allen* 1814, 223). Within a short time they had collected twenty-one articles or *propositiones*, of which Pedro Juan Olivar dispatched a copy to Erasmus on March 13.[16] After some revision the articles were submitted to a consortium of scholars and regular clergy at Valladolid in July.[17] The votes registered and the written opinions submitted show that those present were evenly divided in their judgment.[18] The process of discussing the articles and polling the participants was a slow one. By the middle of August, when an outbreak of the plague forced an adjournment, only four articles had been dealt with. No final verdict was rendered as the meetings were never reconvened.[19]

The Erasmian party sounded the victory trumpet, but the war was far from over.[20] Although the meetings had been held behind closed doors, the contents of the Articles were soon public knowledge. Against the advice of friends,[21] and indeed of Manrique himself, Erasmus proceeded to make a formal reply. The dispute therefore moved into a third phase: a rebuttal of the charges.

First indications that Erasmus was planning a reply came in a letter of 23 August 1527 to Robert Aldridge, a scholarly friend in Cambridge.[22] Soon afterwards a *Gustus responsionis* (*Allen* 1877) was sent to Manrique. The *apologia* was printed but kept back for a time while Erasmus prevaricated. It finally reached the bookstalls in March 1528.[23]

In his *Apologia ad monachos Hispanos* (*LB* IX 1015 – 1094) Erasmus answered the Valladolid Articles point by point. His accusers had questioned, among other things, his pronouncements on the Trinity and on the divine nature of Christ, on the sacraments, on the authority of the apostles, Fathers, and scholastic exegetes, on ceremonies, celibacy, and indulgences. They had gathered their material mainly from Erasmus' *Annotations*, but also attacked passages in the *Paraphrases*, the *Colloquies*, the *Enchiridion*, the *Ratio*, and other works. Defending his orthodoxy, Erasmus relied primarily on four tactics: he invalidated his critics' charges by claiming that they had not observed correct procedure; he diluted their criticism by claiming that his statements had been proposals rather than firm pronouncements; he strenghtened his own case by citing irrefutable authorities in his support; and he attacked his critics in turn by questioning their qualifications and intentions.

Replying to his censors, Erasmus repeatedly insisted on correct procedure. Any critic must first quote the passage he faults, then give reasons for his dissatisfaction: "It is the first duty of a legitimate inquisitor to quote *verbatim* the words that, in his opinion, contain some impiety, then to add briefly what it is in these words that gives offense" (*LB* IX,

1030B). This principle, Erasmus said, had been disregarded by his accusers in many instances. In citing his words, they arbitrarily combined
passages, gave incorrect references or no references at all, omitted or added words thereby significantly altering the meaning, paraphrased the
contents obscuring the point, or quoted Erasmus second-hand out of the
books of his critics. In sum, they "either misunderstood or maliciously
corrupted" his meaning.[24] Moreover, they attributed to him views that
were not his own. In the *Colloquies*, for example, he had Luther speak under the name of Barbatius, himself under the name of Aulus. "Here they
confuse the person and quite impudently change Barbatius to Erasmus",
he complained (1060C). He could not be held responsible, he argued, for
the words of each and every character introduced in the *Colloquies*,
"whether spoken in jest or earnest" (1069C). The same argument applied to works written for *epideixis*, such as his *Encomium matrimonii*, for
"in a declamation one does not look for factual truths but for ingenuity
and rhetorical skill" (1089E).

In replying to his critics Erasmus also pointed out frequently that the
issue under dispute had not yet been settled by the church. He therefore
had a right to give his opinion, and he stressed that it was strictly an opinion in no way prejudicial to the final verdict of the church. Nowhere in
his writings had he questioned articles of faith, he insisted. Here it is
worthwhile to quote Erasmus' definition: Articles of faith, he says, are
based not on the casual pronouncements of scholastic teachers but on
clear scriptural evidence, established creed, or the decisions of universal
synods: *de quibus certo pronunciant vel Scripturae evidentes, vel symbola publicitus
recepta, vel synodi universales* (1091C). He described himself as a kind of researcher who "presented material for discussion to those who inquire into
such things" (1067C). Thus he did not advocate a renewal of baptismal
vows, as alleged by his critics, but merely 'submitted the idea for consideration by bishops and priests': *nec doceo . . . sed propono* (1062B). Similarly
his critics were mistaken if they supposed that he had "defended corrupt
manuscripts" in his *Annotations*. He had merely presented variant readings, deferring in each case to the judgment of those in authority (1030C).
With regard to the words used by Jesus to consecrate bread and wine, he
declared his willingness "to submit immediately, if someone can tell me
what the church has pronounced in this matter" (1065C). On the question of divorce, too, he insisted that he was not disputing *contra Ecclesiam,
sed sub Ecclesiae judicio*, not against the church but pending its judgment.[25]

Another method of defense involved corroborating his views by appealing to higher authority.[26] In a number of cases Erasmus dealt with his accusers by aligning himself with impeccable sources, often gleefully pointing out that if blame was to be attached to his words, it must be shared by the luminaries of the church: "If this is false, let them bring before the law Chrysostom, Jerome, and Augustine whose authority I have followed" (1046B). Censured for declaring that Mary's perpetual virginity could not be proven on the basis of scriptural passages, he countered: "Why should I not state what Jerome has stated?" (1084B). Defending his negative remarks on the powers of the inquisition, he insisted that his views were supported by Augustine, "the fountainhead and parent of all scholastic theology on which those who raise this hubbub particularly pride themselves" (1058D – E). Similarly he argued: "If it is unlawful to investigate the rationale behind papal decrees, they must condemn Thomas, Scotus, Durandus, and innumberable other theologians" (1066E). In one case he had the satisfaction of pointing out that the censured opinion was that of Augustine (1073C); in another that the words of Jerome were on trial: "Since this note of mine quotes Jerome's words, I wonder why they would deal with me rather than with him" (1075A). Similarly he rebutted the charge of having spoken irreverently of the apostles: "Why should I be said to weaken the authority of the gospels when a great man like Augustine [has expressed himself in the same vein]?" (1073A)

Finally Erasmus fought back by accusing his critics in turn. Among the faults he attributed to them were carelessness, ignorance, and malice. They had failed to read, or were ignoring, his earlier explanations. He could not be expected to give fresh replies "every time some slanderer or other accuses me of the same things all over again" (1040B). He referred readers to his earlier controversies with Lee, Stunica, and Béda, inviting them to read his responses to them: "No better reply can be made, nor one that makes more evident the impudence of their calumny".[27] The ignorance of his critics also galled Erasmus: he was dealing "with men who had become theologians without the benefit of philology" (1037C). He solicits the reader's sympathy for having to put up with men "who know neither Greek nor Latin and cavil at what they don't understand" (1050A). "O sacred inquisition," he exclaims at one point, "carried out by such great pillars of the church!" (1075A)

Erasmus questions not only the competence but also the intentions of his critics. "There is a great difference between sacred inquisition and slanderous persecution," he writes, comparing his enemies with the biblical Satan "roaring like a lion, going about seeking whom he may devour—from this sort of search the inquisition of the church should be as far removed as possible" (1054C). Although Erasmus declared in his preface to the *apologia* that he would not trade insults,[28] the text does not always bear him out. He describes the substance of the Valladolid Articles as "drivel and slander" (1082E) and the authors' judgment as "stupid, ignorant, boorish, and malicious" (1092A).

Perhaps Erasmus' reaction to the Valladolid Articles should be sought, not only in the words of his *apologia*, but also in his actions, that is, in the revisions (or retention, as the case may be) of censured passages. That Erasmus was willing in principle to make such revisions is apparent from an appendix to the second edition of his *apologia* which bore the title *Loca quaedam in aliquot Erasmi lucubrationibus per ipsum emendata*.[29] In a prefatory letter he reports premonitions of his impending death and declares his readiness to "make good my earlier negligence . . . and list individually a number of errors which I have discovered in my works after their publication" (*Allen* 2095, 10 – 13). At the same time he emphasizes that this appendix does not constitute a recantation. "Here someone will perhaps expect me to change everything ever criticized by anybody. But that would be corruption, not correction" (*ibidem*, lines 63 – 64). His list of *errata* pertained to typographical errors, slips of the pen, in short mistakes caused by ignorance or negligence, "for nowhere shall I admit the charge of impiety" (*ibidem*, lines 68 – 69).

The fact that the *Loca* were published as an appendix to the second edition of the *Apologia contra monachos* does not mean that they are to be construed as a delayed response to the Valladolid Articles. Indeed a perusal of the changes suggested by Erasmus shows that there is little correspondence between the Articles and Erasmus' emendations. Erasmus had chosen this form of publishing his *errata* because he did not expect to live long enough to publish revised editions of the works in question. As it happened, the *Annotations*, the work most heavily censured in the Articles, did appear in a revised form in 1535. This last authorized edition will illustrate Erasmus' *de facto* response to his Spanish critics.

An examination of the annotations on the Gospels reveals that Erasmus was not prepared to recant and surrender. Among the passages censured in the Articles was the textual change *verbum/sermo* at John 1: 1 (*LB* IX, 1048A – F). The note *ad locum* (*LB* VI, 335A – 337C) had been revised and enlarged in the third and fourth editions of 1522 and 1527 respectively, but remained unchanged in 1535.[30] A note concerning Luke 2: 52 ("And Jesus increased in wisdom", *LB* VI, 239F – 240B) was censured because it was allegedly at variance with the concept of Jesus' perfect state of grace (*LB* IX, 1049A). In this case, too, Erasmus left his note intact in 1535. In the Articles, Erasmus had been reproached (*LB* IX, 1085B) for labelling the popular belief that Mary's hymen had remained intact during delivery "pious credulity". The note in question (*LB* VI, 234F – 235D) also remained unchanged. The Spaniards had criticized Erasmus (*LB* IX, 1084E) for describing the angel's greeting as "loving". In this case the offending term had already been removed in 1527 in response to similar complaints by Lee and Sutor.[31]

A few of the 1535 revisions in the Gospels may be interpreted as oblique reactions to the Valladolid Articles. In a note on Matt 2: 6 (*LB* VI, 12E), Erasmus suggested that the evangelist had misremembered a passage from the prophets. The Spaniards accused Erasmus of questioning the principle of divine inspiration (*LB* IX, 1070C). Although Erasmus did not remove the offending interpretation, he did elaborate on two alternative explanations in 1535, namely that the error was contained in the answer of the Pharisees or that the reference in question was an interpretation rather than a literal quotation. The Spaniards had also expressed concern about the removal of the words *ex te* from the text of Luke 1: 35 ("he will be born out of you", *LB* IX, 1049B–C) since this excision would weaken the scholastic argument against the Sabellian heresy. Erasmus refused to restore the words in question, but added an explanatory phrase in 1535 which appears to address his critics' concerns: "The point here is not the person conceiving," Erasmus wrote, "but the novel method of conception and the excellence of the fetus" (*LB* VI, 225C).

Cases in which Erasmus bowed to the Spanish censors are infrequent. They had charged him with casting doubts on the resurrection because he had stated that neither Chrysostom nor Origen commented on the last chapter of Matthew (*LB* VI, 148D). This, the Spaniards reasoned, somehow suggested that the chapter, which dealt with the resurrection of the Lord, was not genuine. Although Erasmus rejected this interpretation of his words in the *apologia* (*LB* IX, 1079A) he nevertheless modified the note in 1535, explaining that there was indeed evidence for Chrysostom's exegesis, but that the work was not extant. Another note on Mark 1 (*LB* VI, 151E–153C) was thought by the Spaniards to smack of Arianism. Erasmus had stated that "the evangelists hardly ever [changed in 1522 to 'quite rarely'] attributed the epithet 'God' to Jesus". Although Erasmus denied the validity of the charges in his *apologia* (*LB* IX, 1047F), he nevertheless deleted the offending phrase in 1535.[32] He made a similar gesture of appeasement in a note on Matt 6: 1 (*LB* VI, 171E–172C) where the Spaniards had been offended by the term *vitrius*, stepfather, as applied to Joseph (*LB* IX, 1049A). Erasmus changed the word to *patri legali*, father before the law, in 1535.

The strategies employed by Erasmus in his 'war' against the Spanish orders are both complex and subtle. At the preliminary stage he tried to have his critics suppressed by soliciting help from friends in high places and invoking the support of the scholarly community. Through contacts with Spanish humanists he tried to keep abreast of the developments though his information seems to have been at times confusing and misleading. When the hostilities came to a head and his works were investigated by official authority, he decided to take his case to the public with an apologia, a step which his friends regretted in view of the fact that the Valladolid Articles remained unpublished. In his apology Erasmus employed a number of effective strategies, corroborating his position by citing patristic writings in his own support and clearing his name by expressly submitting to the authority of the church. At the same time he weakened his opponents' case by questioning their procedure and casting doubts on their qualifications and intentions. In the apologia as well as in the subsequently revised *Annotations* Erasmus appears unrepentant, if not recalcitrant. The changes he introduced in the wake of the Articles are often semantic rather than substantive, and his attitude toward his critics is frequently one of contempt and disdain. He justified the publication of his apologia by explaining that his orthodoxy was on trial. If his scholarly reputation alone had been at stake, he might have remained silent, but 'no one ought to tolerate the charge of impiety unless he is prepared to admit it' (*Allen* 1879, 49–50).

NOTES

1 *Allen* 1744, 135; for first indications of the plot in Spain thickening see Juan Maldonado's letter *Allen* 1742, especially 80ff.
2 In Erasmus' opinion, Edward Lee, who had been the first to attack his *Annotationes* in print, had started the trouble in Spain (on his controversy with the Englishman see R. Coogan "The Pharisee Against the Hellenist: Edward Lee versus Erasmus", *Renaissance Quarterly* 39 (1986) 476–505. At court the emperor's confessor García de Loaysa was agitating against him; certain Franciscans at Alcalá were also making difficulties for him; and at Burgos Pedro Vitorio was preaching against him. This standard account appears in *Allen* 1903, 1–21; 1909, 10–44; 2094 passim (in more oblique terms), and *LB* X, 1479A.
3 Cf. Brewer *Letters and papers, foreign and domestic, of the reign of Henry VIII, 1509–46* (London, 1862–1910) IV 1789.
4 *Allen* 1735, 21–23 (*Leus, ut suspicantur, ... his furiis perstrenuam navat operam*); 1747, 76–79 (see also below note 7). In *Allen* 1861, 9–10 (to Warham) Erasmus says that Lee also agitated against him in Paris.
5 *Allen* 1785, 31–34 (from Gattinara: *quidquid erit, nequaquam illi in Hispania edere licebit*); 1828, 11; 1831, 13–14 (to Warham).
6 *Allen* 1864, 10–13 (*clanculum monachos instruens in me*), cf. also lines 181–182 (*colligunt ... ex libro Eduardi Lei vel ex ipsius indice potius*); 1893, 28–33; 1903, 27–29; 1977, 27–29, *LB* IX, 1038F (*ex indice sycophantico descripserunt*), similarly ibidem 1030A.
7 *Allen* 1815, 39–41 (to Gattinara: *fragmentum epistolae Cutberti Tonstalli ... his inserui quo magis credas meis verbis*); 1909, 10. He also reports that Lee is working on another book: *librum apparet aedere ... in me* (*Allen* 1747, 76; 1893, 28–29; 1877, 27). Luis Carvajal, another of Erasmus' conservative critics, confirmed the existence of such a book (perhaps the basis of the Spanish *propositiones*) but insisted that Erasmus was mistaken about its author: *Edoardo Laeo tribuit libellum elegantissimum iuxta ac catholicum Francisci Castelli et Francisci Menesii* (*Dulcoratio*, Paris 1530, fol 78r).

8 Cf. 1717: 41–2, 1786: 1–7, 1838: 6–16.

9 *Allen* 1804, 260–77; 1839, 21–26; the letter to Maldonado (*Allen* 1805) is extant only in its expurgated form and no longer contains the remarks critical of Virués.

10 Cf. *Allen* 1684, 1–4 (to Vergara: *tuo quidem suasu scripsisse testatur*); 1814, 1–2 (from Vergara: *nec de facie aut nomine quidem tum noram cum mihi litterae tuae redditae sunt*); compare Appendix in Allen VI, Letter 6: 12–13, Ep 2163: 81.

11 Cf. Vives' letter of 13 June 1527 to Erasmus: *Misit mihi [Virués] acta diei unius apud inquisitorem fidei*. For Virués' written opinion see V. Beltrán de Heredia *Cartulario de la Universidad de Salamanca* (Salamanca 1973) VI 113–115.

12 *Allen* 1814, 126–127, cf. *Allen* 1836, 45 (from Vives: *Existimo tumultus hos ex Enchiridio tuo verso natos esse*).

13 Cf. *Allen* 1904, 11–12: *an mei studio id faciant nescio*.

14 Clement VII formally instructed Manrique to conduct an investigation (*Allen* 1846, July 1527); the emperor Charles V also favoured the proceedings, reassuring Erasmus of his support in *Allen* 1920, 19–28 (December 1527); cf. *Allen* 1847, 102–103 (July 1527, from Vergara to Vives): *Res ad magistratus relata est*.

15 Cf. *Allen* 1814, 150–152: *eius rei iudicium ad ipsos non pertinere*.

16 Cf. *Allen* 1791, 1–2; 1814, 208–222, 283; 1847, 89–90. The propositions have been published in facsimile by M. Avilés *Erasmo y la Inquisición* (Alcalá 1980) 17–49.

17 For an extract of the minutes of the meetings see D.A. Paz y Meliá and D.M. Serrano y Sanz "Actas originales de las congregaciones celebradas en Valladolid ...", *Revista de archivos, bibliotecas y museos* 6 (1902) 60–73; the proceedings are also discussed by M. Bataillon *Erasmo y España* (Mexico 1966) 242–18 and Avilés *op.cit.* (previous note).

18 The written opinions are analyzed by M. Avilés "Erasmo y los teólogos españoles" in *El Erasmismo en España* eds. M. Revuelta Sañudo y C. Morón Arroyo (Santander 1986), 175–93.

19 Erasmus claimed that Manrique "gladly refrained from reconvening the panel" (*Allen* 2094, 66, preface to the second edition of his apologia).

20 Cf. *Allen* 1899, 98–99; 1897, 5–6; 1908, 73–74; Erasmus himself was more cautious in his assessment, cf. Ep 1903: 35–6: *malim* τὴν ἥττην *quam sic vincere*.

21 Cf. *Allen* 1893, 14–17 (to Pirckheimer: *me revocas ab apologiis*); 1907, 24–29 (from Valdés: *optarim ut tuam responsionem ad monachorum articulos premeres*).

22 Cf. *Allen* 1858: 573–4. The letter itself is a mini-apologia.

23 See the apologetic letter, *Allen* 1967, to Manrique. Erasmus said he had intended for Froben to put the printed copies of his *apologia* away and not let them fall into anyone's hands (line 30), but in the confusion surrounding Froben's death in October 1527 a copy had come into the possession of a Cologne printer (lines 37–38). Publishing the *apologia* himself had merely been a preemptive strike (lines 40–44).

24 *LB* IX, 1038 D–E (combining passages: *contexuisse duo fragmenta*); 1049A, F (citing the wrong chapter), 1075E, 1077E, 1078E, 1090D (missing reference). In the following Erasmus pointed out that he had been misquoted: 1050E (*verba praetermissa*), 1051B (*truncatim referunt*), 1051E (*si totus fuisset recitatus ...*), 1077C (*in meis scriptis non habetur*), 1082B (*si totum pronunciassent ...*), 1083B–D (*nusquam est in mea annotatione*), 1096E (*nec integre nec recte citarunt*), 1083B, 1085C.

25 *LB* IX, 1069D. For this strategy, which he adopted throughout his *Annotations* to fend off criticism, see E. Rummel *Erasmus' Annotations on the New Testament* (Toronto 1986), 29–31.

26 This technique is prominently used in the later editions of the *Annotations*, where we find numerous patristic references added, often expressly to defend a point against criticism. See Rummel *op.cit.* (note 25) 71–2.

27 *LB* IX, 1047A–B; for Erasmus' replies to Lee see W. Ferguson *Erasmi opuscula* (The Hague 1933) 236–303, *LB* IX, 123–284 and Coogan *op.cit.* (note 2); for his principal apologies against Stunica see *LB* IX, 283–356, 355–75 and H.J. DeJonge in his introduction to *ASD* IX–2 (containing the critical edition of Erasmus' *apologia* of 1520); for the *apologiae* against Béda see *LB* IX, 441–702 and J. Farge *Orthodoxy and Reform in Early Reformation France: The Faculty of Theology of Paris 1500–1543* (Leiden 1985)

186–196 and on the controversies in general E. Rummel "A Reader's Guide to Erasmus' Controversies", *Erasmus in English* 12 (1983) 13–19.

28 *Allen* 1879: 81–82: *Verum hic par pro pari non referam, quo videlicet non minus moderatione vincam quam causa.*

29 On pp. 226–[253] in the Basel edition of 1529. Not reprinted in *LB*, presumably because it was superseded by revised editions of the works to which the list of *errata* refers.

30 Erasmus had answered the arguments of his critics at length in a separate *apologia* (*Apologia refellens quorundam seditiosos clamores* ... Louvain 1520, text in *LB* IX, 111–122). For the dispute see C.A.L. Jarrott "Erasmus' *In principio erat sermo*: A Controversial Translation", *Studies in Philology* 61 (1964) 35–40; M. O'Rourke Boyle *Erasmus on Language and Method in Theology* (Toronto 1971) 3–31.

31 Cf. his replies to Lee and Sutor in *LB* IX, 151A–153D, 807B. The changes in his *Annotations* are discussed by Rummel *op.cit.* (note 25) 167–71. Determining what changes have been made has been greatly facilitated by the recent publication of a fascimile of the 1535 text with variants marked, eds. A. Reeves and M.A. Screech (London 1986).

32 Cf. Erasmus' justification in the *Loca* 241: He removed the words, *non quod insit aliquid impium sed quod parum suo loco dicta videantur.*

CHRIS L. HEESAKKERS

ARGUMENTATIO A PERSONA IN ERASMUS' SECOND APOLOGY AGAINST ALBERTO PIO

When, in September 1523, Erasmus was looking forward to his *Spongia* against Ulrich von Hutten coming from the press, his anticipation was painfully disturbed by the news that his adversary had died on August 29. Though compared to Hutten's extremely agressive *Expostulatio*, the *Spongia* could be considered moderate in tone, the author was greatly embarrassed by the death of his victim. Erasmus foresaw the reproach that it was all too easy to take up arms against a silenced opponent. At the time nothing could be done, but a month later, when his printer was preparing a second edition of the *Spongia*, Erasmus tried to cover himself by substituting a "Candido Lectori" for his former dedicatory letter to Zwingli, in which he said that had he foreseen Hutten's death, he would perhaps not have written the *Spongia* or at least would have written it differently: "Nam si praescissem, aut non respondissem aut respondissem aliter".[1] Consequently Erasmus did not reply when others took up the gauntlet on Hutten's behalf.[2]

About seven years later Erasmus found himself in a similar situation. This time he was waiting for the publication of an opponent's work, when he was informed of the death of the author two months prior to the publication date. Therefore he had time enough to think about what his attitude should be and to decide whether it was wiser not to take the odious step of counter-attacking the dead. After the Hutten affair a decision along these lines could have been expected. However Erasmus' reaction was quite the opposite. Obviously, not even for a moment, did he consider the possibility of simply refraining from making a reply. On the contrary, not only did he not restrict himself to a formal, objective refutation of the hostile publication, but he went so far as to ridicule his victim's final hours by the addition of a mordant satire to the following edition of his Colloquies.

The polemics in question, that is, Eramus' controversy with the Italian humanist and diplomat Alberto Pio, Principe di Carpi (c. 1475–1531), had a fairly long history.[3] The personal acquaintance of the participants dated from 1507–08, when Erasmus lived in Venice in the house of his printer Aldus Manutius who, incidentally, called himself Aldus Pius Manutius after his Maecenas and former pupil, our Pio. Early on in the polemics Pio had referred to this acquaintanceship,[4] but Erasmus did not acknowledge it. Pio's name first turned up in Erasmus' correspondence in 1525. To an Italian friend, Celio Calcagnini, Erasmus ventilated his annoyance at the denigratory insinuations and imputations that Pio, at the time living in Rome as an envoy of the king of France, is said to have made on all possible occasions.[5] In his answer Calcagnini, who had known Pio since their study days and knew him to be an honest and high-minded person, advised Erasmus not to heed this kind or rumour.[6] However, his letter did not reassure Erasmus. On October 10, 1525 Erasmus addressed himself directly to Pio. His letter accused Pio, the confidant of the "Purpled Fathers", of openly and overall stating his view that Erasmus was no philosopher, nor was he a theologian, nor a scholar of solid doctrine.[7] Erasmus admitted with a touch of irony that he himself would not gladly claim the title of philosopher or theologian: however the assertions of the Prince, that Erasmus was entirely responsible for the ecclesiastical troubles of the time and that Luther drew his inspiration from the writings of Erasmus,[8] were more serious. Erasmus in his turn explained the real situation and requested Pio to change his opinion and to stop arousing sentiment against him, assuming that the rumours contained a germ of truth. He asked for forgiveness for his credulity in the case of the rumours being false.[9]

It was the identification with the Lutheran cause, particularly in Roman pontifical circles, that had stung and alarmed Erasmus. It was this very aspect that was emphasized in a suggestive way by Pio in his answer to Erasmus' letter: the title of this answer, dated May 15, 1526, at least in its version printed three years later (Rome 1529), couples the names of Erasmus and Luther: *Ad Erasmi Roterodami expostulationem Responsio accurata et paraenetica, Martini Lutheri et asseclarum eius haeresim vesanam magnis argumentis, et iustis rationibus confutans*.[10] Despite the amiable tone of the long answer Erasmus felt himself gravely compromised: "summa quidem humanitate, et laudibus leniens omnia, sed interim miscens Luteri negocium cum meo". Nevertheless he assumed that in Rome action against him would not be easy to undertake: "Rome tamen non audent quicquam excudere in Erasmum".[11] Therefore he did not hasten to reply to Pio's manuscript treatise. He thought it wise, however, to safeguard himself against this kind of campaign by addressing himself directly to Pope Clement.[12]

Towards the end of 1528 Erasmus learned that Pio's *Responsio* was to be printed in Paris, Pio's actual place of residence. In a short letter, which also explained that he had made no answer to the *Responsio* because of the fact that he had been uncertain of what had become of Pio at the Sacco di Roma, he warned against precipitate publication of the treatise, at least in its orginal form.[13] This did not, of course, stop the printing.

Now that the compromising text had been widely spread, Erasmus felt forced to a refutation which he wrote within a mere five days.[14] "Ludus exit in rabiem",[15] the game became a fury. However the tone remained as yet civil and courteous and Erasmus cherished hopes that the polemics had come to an end.[16]

The extent of the fury came to light only two years later, but long before that Erasmus had understood that his hopes for an end to the polemics had been idle. Moreover, he knew that this time Pio would bring on the heavy artillery and for a time he wondered whether he ought to reply now that the situation had arisen.[17] Friends advised him to maintain a wise silence.[18]

Towards Christmas 1530 Erasmus knew that Badius' presses in Paris were in action against him.[19] Three weeks later, January 10, 1531, Pio died. Erasmus' first comment on this event is to be found in a letter dated March 6. This comment was definitely not very sensitive. Erasmus compares Pio's demise with the proverbial behaviour of an insect that leaves its sting in the flesh and flees. "I hope", Erasmus adds, "that now his soul may play among the seraphical minds". For three days before Pio's death his body had been adorned with the Franciscan habit and thus adorned after his death it was carried through the centre of the city to the monastery, borne on the shoulders of Franciscans in solemn procession. Nothing remained undone that was usually done for the actual adherents of St. Francis. The tenor of the comment, in several letters, was that of irony and sarcasm[20] and, not surprisingly, Erasmus was blamed for exceeding the limits of good taste by holding Pio responsible for the crime of his own death.[21] The extent of Erasmus' persistence in his irony is shown by his first published response, a colloquy in invective vein, *Exsequiae Seraphicae*, Franciscan Funeral, included in the following edition of his Colloquies, September 1531.

After the appearance of the *ingens opus* there is no trace of dilemma or even hesitation, as in the Hutten affair, as to whether or not to compose a retort. In fact, Pio's work was an *ingens opus*, not only in its immense size (23 books), but also in the totality of its range. All Erasmus' works that were open to possible criticism, were taken to task, all his statements about disputed religious doctrines and ecclesiastical rites were scrutinized. In this new text Pio had preceeded the body of the work by the complete dossier of the polemics carried on thus far. After a kind of Subject Index of 25 columns (evidently missing from the copy Erasmus had first seen, see below n. 32), is Erasmus' letter of October 10, 1525, followed by Pio's *Responsio paraenetica* of May 15, 1526 and Erasmus' tardy answer to its published version, 13 February 1529. This answer was not simply reproduced, but was accompanied by extensive marginal commentary often

continued at the bottom, right across the width of the page, refuting
Erasmus' text in minute detail.

After these preliminary 132 pages comes a *Praefatio* (in fact this is Book
II), which once again summarizes the history of the controversy. Then follows an indictment of Erasmus' *Moria* (Book III), a ''recitatio et examinatio'' of all that is erroneous in it. It seems that this title indicates the actual
division of the twenty books that were to follow: first an enumeration of
reprehensible quotations on a particular subject, gathered willy-nilly
from various works of Erasmus (*recitatio*) and then repeated one by one
and accompanied by Pio's comments and refutations (*examinatio*). The
origins of the quotations are sometimes exactly, sometimes vaguely indicated, but often not indicated at all. The paragraphs in the books are very
large and only indicated by the alphabetical characters in the margin. Because of this the text, compactly printed on large pages and swarming
with abbreviations, has a massive, amorphous and impenetrable appearance. This, added to the mass of quotations and repetitions, makes of
Pio's work an unappetizing and scarcely readable book.

It is not surprising that Erasmus' first revealed reactions were annoyance, disgust and wrath. The size of the work, its composition and even
its Latin nauseated him. The way his texts were handled smacked to him
of shameless lies and slander, in absolute contradiction to the pretended
good intentions of the author. Therefore Erasmus was not receptive to
the reproach of a correspondent: that his anger showed evidence of his
irritability and hypersensitivity.[22] Erasmus might have considered for-
bearing from making a reply to his deceased opponent, but he did not
refrain because of the fact that Pio was not only Pio: ''Non eram illi
responsurus, nisi me vehementer gravaret, primum autoris celebritas, ad
haec liber Lutetiae editus, postremo foedus cum gente Seraphica''.[23] Of
these three reasons, Pio's celebrity, particularly in ecclesiastical circles,
the fact the book had been published in Paris, city of the Sorbonne, of Sutor and Beda,[24] and Pio's alliance with the Franciscans, the last was the
decisive factor. Erasmus spoke of a pact, a conspiracy. Pio's death was
not the end of the hostile campaigns against him and he therefore was
forced to keep on defending himself: ''quid facias, si in te scribant mor-
tui?''[25] This induced him to react by immediately writing his satirical *Exsequiae Seraphicae*. The title leaves one in no doubt as to its target. His formal riposte, *Apologia adversus rhapsodias calumniosarum querimoniarum Alberti
Pii*, was to be based on the same assumption of a plot. In Pio he fought
Pio's instigators, his assistants, his accomplices. To Erasmus, Pio was
only a pawn in the hands of other hostile forces.

Erasmus' assumption that Pio did not fly with his own wings and did
not even take up arms on his own initiative, was not new and did not date

from the later phase of the controversy. Right from the first Erasmus talked about two enemies in Rome, who in his estimation were pure pagans, ill-disposed towards everything connected with *Germania*. These enemies were, in this order, Aleander and Pio. Erasmus always coupled Pio's first text with an anonymous piece of writing "Racha", which Erasmus had promptly attributed to Aleander.[26] To Budé and even to the Pope he directly stated that Aleander was behind Pio's activities.[27] Even when Pio had left Rome for Paris and was working there on his *ingens opus*, Erasmus assumed that Aleander was still the driving force behind Pio whom he provided with arguments against Erasmus and for which he systematically combed Erasmus' oeuvre.[28]

When we make a close examination of Erasmus' Apology with regard to its *modus argumentandi*, it immediately strikes us that, right from the title of the treatise, Erasmus is determined to undermine Pio's authority by making him out to be a senile and sick plaything of other men whose intentions can rightly be questioned because their relations with Erasmus are coloured by animosity. Erasmus presents his answer as a "Defense against the hodgepodge of slanderous charges by Alberto Pio, once the Prince of Carpi, who, although being aged and sick and better equipped to do almost anything else, was hoisted into his armour by certain ill-disposed fellows to do this ignoble job". Following the title-page are two pages of index (p. 3 – 4), giving "some of the innumerous passages that are to illustrate the extent of Pio's impious calumnies". It notes many lies (*mendacia*). Then Erasmus indicates some passages, in which Pio makes false (*falso*), distorted (*depravate*) or mutilated (*truncatim*) quotations. These comments return as marginal notes in the text of the Apology. This index too is used to emphasize that Pio is not the sole author. The stylistic variety (*phrasis varietas*), Erasmus says, immediately betrays the fact that we are dealing with a stack of contributions from many collaborators (*multorum opera conflatum congestumque*). In the book itself this thesis of there being several authors is maintained and underlined time and again by such comments as *sub defuncti titulo* (p. 5) and many others. At one time Erasmus ironically observes, that it is the way of princes not to write their own texts (p. 13) and he repeatedly uses the plural to indicate the opponent. The alien contributions are called *fragmenta* (p. 121), and *schedae* (p. 8). Many are the terms, singular or plural, by which Pio's instigators and accomplices, hidden in this Trojan horse (p. 6), are indicated. I cite *impulsor* (p. 10), and for the accomplices, besides the more innocent *famuli* (p. 8), there are much more suggestive expressions like *collector* (p. 114), *pharmacologi* (collectors of poisons, p. 180). Occasionally it is insinuated that Pio, with all his sincerty (p. 10), has been manipulated

(p. 5), but more often the wording implies the reproach that Pio had, inexcusably, not even made the effort to read Erasmus' works himself (p. 18). Eventually the comments indicate it was Pio himself who had hired his accomplices (p. 123) and the responsibility is his, as he pretends that everything is his own creation (p. 13). Many depreciatory expressions, like *calumniator* (p. 61), are therefore as equally applicable to Pio as to his assistants. Once Erasmus had decided not to keep silent, Pio became the target of his irony no less than did his companions in arms. The introductory pages ridicule Pio's death once again by comparing his way of behaving with that of an insect's stinging and then flying off (p. 6) or with the delivery of a Parthian shot (p. 5). Several times Erasmus assures the reader that his answer would have been much more vehement had Pio still been alive (*parco defuncto*, p. 213). This implies that Pio merited more serious reproaches than Erasmus puts forward, that things are even worse than he puts them. His often repeated assertion that he prays for Pio's repose (p. 136–137) is not devoid of the ring of irony: Pio might have escaped from Erasmus' clutches, he has not escaped from the judgement of the Lord (p. 202).

Throughout the Apology Pio is presented as a quarrel-monger. *Rixator* is Erasmus' most frequent epithet for Pio. With his *carpendi libido*[29] Pio is a credit to his name (p. 12). *Carpere, decerpere, carptim* are words gladly used (p. 7; cf. the pun Pius-impius in the title of the index). Pio's assertions are constantly called *convicia* (p. 7). The idea is put forward, that Pio might have stepped into the ring in the hope of winning the fame of having contested with no less an adversary than an Erasmus (p. 227). This lust for fame might also explain the extravagant size of Pio's book (p. 115). Pio resembles a *mulier morosa rixosaque*, a capricious and quarrelsome woman (p. 206). Erasmus purposely uses *morosus*, for he had noted Pio's incorrect use of the phrase *morosus esse* instead of *immorari* (p. 4): Pio is *morosus* in the sense of long-winded and verbose (p. 188). This is, by the way, not the only mistake in Latin Erasmus says to have stumbled on (cf. p. 129).

The contents of the Apology mainly consist, of course, of theological, dogmatic and liturgical subjects, frequently accompanied by the remark that they had been put forward and refuted long ago but that Pio had neglected to read the works concerned. The actual argumentation, however, is based throughout on the doubt as to the opponent's moral trustworthiness and intentions. The Apology is primarily an *argumentatio a persona adversarii*, or rather *adversariorum*. The whole approach of the polemics is one which is out to undermine Pio's moral authority by making him out to have been the plaything of others who had skillfully misused his lust for fame. Erasmus, to put it in current jargon, plays the man and not the ball.

It remains to be seen if Erasmus' view of Pio and his intentions and of the way his book came into being was correct. In an extensive, civil and friendly letter Aleander absolutely rejected having had any part in the twenty-three books, stating that throughout the last decade he had spoken to Pio only three or four times.[30] Sepulveda, whom Erasmus suspected of having been Pio's right hand (p. 13), also denied having been in any way responsible. He does so in his *Antapologia pro Alberto Pio principe Carpensi, in Erasmum Roterodamum*, published expressly to clear Pio's memory of the stain Erasmus' Apology had cast on him. Sepulveda defends Pio's upright intentions and repudiates Erasmus' view that he had made use of the services of a third party. The only assistance Pio had made use of in Paris was that of his young Italian amanuensis.[31]

Erasmus did not counter the *Antapologia* and the relationship between Sepulveda and Erasmus remained correct. He was, however, unable to refrain from making a final thrust. Some time later he seems as well to have received a copy of Pio's long Subject Index mentioned in the Apology (p. 3). Erasmus is uncertain as to its authorship, but not, he assures us, as to the latter's disingenuousness. In his last anti-Pian writing, *In Elenchum Alberti Pii Brevissima Scholia*, added to the *Dilutio* against Jodocus Clichtoveus (1532), Erasmus once more condemns the nasty trick of putting his name on the title page of a book against Luther (32) and he gives a succinct answer to 122 items of the index.

NOTES

* For the correction of my English I am indebted to Mrs. Jane Zaat-Jones (Oegstgeest).
1 *ASD*, IX–1, 118, 35–37.
2 *Ibid.*, 111sq.
3 The main dates and documents concerning the development of the polemics are the following:
  A) 1525, October 10: Erasmus' letter to Pio, *Allen* 1634;
  B) 1526, May 15: Pio's answer to Erasmus, edited only in 1529, January 9: *Alberti Pii Carporum Comitis illustrissimi, ad Erasmi Roterodami expostulationem responsio accurata & paraenetica, Martini Lutheri & asseclarum eius haeresim vesanam magnis argumentis & iustis rationibus confutans*, Paris, Badius, 1529;
  C) 1529, February 13: Erasmus' answer to the publication of Pio's letter of May 15, 1526: *Ad exhortationem Clarissimi doctissimique Comitis Alberti Pii Carporum Principis Des. Erasmi Roterodami Responsio*, Basel, Froben, 1529;
  D) 1531, March 9: *Alberti Pii Carporum Comitis illustrissimi & viri longe doctissimi, praeter praefationem & operis conclusionem, tres & viginti libri in locos lucubrationum variarum D. Erasmi Roterodami, quos censet ab eo recognoscendos & retractandos*, Paris, Badius, 1531;

E) 1531, autumn: *Des. Erasmi Roterodami Apologia adversus rhapsodias calumniosarum querimoniarum Alberti Pii quondam Carporum principis, quem & senem & moribundum & ad quidvis potius accomodum homines quidam male auspicati, ad hanc illiberalem fabulam agendam subornarunt*, Basel, Froben—Episcopius 1531;

F) 1532: *In Elenchum Alberti Pii brevissima scholia per eundem Erasmum Roterodamum*, added to *D. Erasmi Roterodami Dilutio eorum quae Iodocus Clithoveus scripsit adversus Declamationem suasoriam matrimonii*, Basel, Froben 1532;

G) 1532: *Io. Genesii Sepulvedae Cordubensis Antapologia pro Alberto Pio Comite Carpensi in Erasmum Roterodamum*, Rome, Bladus, 1532; Paris, Augurellus, 1532.

– Some recent contributions to the history of the controversy are to be found among the articles by Myron P. Gilmore: "Erasmus and Alberto Pio, Prince of Carpi", in: T.K. Rabb, J.E. Seigel, eds., *Action and Conviction in Early Modern Europe. Essays in Memory of E.H. Harbison*, Princeton 1969, p. 299–318; "De modis disputandi: The apologetic works of Erasmus", in: *Florilegium Historiale. Essays presented to Wallace K. Ferguson*, Toronto 1971, p. 63–88; "Erasmus' Defense of Folly", in R.L. DeMolen, ed., *Essays on the Works of Erasmus*, New Haven—London 1978, p. 111–123.

4 Doc. D (above n. 3), fol. 2v.
5 *Allen* 1576, 39–40 (May 13, 1525).
6 *Allen* 1587, 229sqq. (July 6, 1525).
7 *Allen* 1634, 10–14: consentientibus vocibus narrant Romae quendam esse Principem Carpensem, doctum magnaeque apud purpuratos patres autoritatis, qui passim ac palam depraedicet Erasmum nec esse philosophum nec theologum, nec vllius solidae doctrinae.
8 *Ib.* 39–42: Magis me commouent illae voces quas audio subinde repeti ab eodem Principe in conuiuiis cardinalium, in conciliabulis eruditorum, quicquid est huius tumultus, ex Erasmo natum esse; 69: Sed 'occasionem Lutherus hausit e libris meis'.
9 *Ib.* 105–109: Nunc si verum est quod ad me delatum est, quaeso vt istam persuasionem abiicias, et istiusmodi voces mihi periculosas contineas; sin vanum est, ignosce quod huiusmodi naeniis obtuderim celsitudinem tuam, cui precor omnia laeta feliciaque.
10 Doc. B (above n. 3).
11 *Allen* 1804, 250–252 and 257–258 (March 30, 1527).
12 *Allen* 1987 (April 3, 1528).
13 *Allen* 2080, 1–5 and 20–21 (December 23, 1528): Quod superest, moneo ne praecipites aeditionem libelli; aut si non vis istuc operae perdere, mitiga partem qua mecum agis.
14 *Allen* 2118, 25 (March 10, 1529).
15 *Allen* 2108, 15 (February 25, 1529).
16 *Allen* 2328, 41–42 (June 24, 1530): Iam Lutetiae libellum vnum euulgauit, cui respondimus ciuiliter.
17 *Allen* 2261, 69–71 (January 31, 1530): Albertus tuus ... magno molimine parat Responsionem aduersus meam Apologiam; *Allen* 2375, 81: Alberto fortasse respondebo.
18 Alciati to Erasmus, *Allen* 2394, 101–104 (October 7, 1530): Ostendisti eruditis quid potueris cum tale argumentum tibi tractandum censuisti; ostende nunc quae sit animi tui magnitudo, quantus iniuriarum neglectus, quanta aequanimitas: impones, mihi crede, Zoilis omnibus pudorem.
19 *Allen* 2414, 13 (December 22, 1530).
20 *Allen* 2441, 71–72 (March 6, 1531): Hoc nimirum est, iuxta prouerbium, infixo aculeo fugere. Spero tamen animam illius inter Seraphicas mentes ludere. Nam corpus triduo ante mortem Franciscano cultu decoratum est, ac mortuum eodem ornatu Franciscanorum humeris per mediam vrbem religiosa pompa deportatum in monasterio, nec quicquam omnino ceremoniarum praetermissum est qua solent γνησίοις Francisci τέκνοις impendi; cf. 2443, 336–346 (March 7, 1531) and 2466, 101–115 (March 28, 1531); for the proverb, repeated in 2443, 346 and 2466, 102, cf. Erasmus, *Adag.* 6.
21 Augustinus Steuchus to Erasmus, *Allen* 2513, 685 sqq. (July 25, 1531).

22 *Ib*. 294–296.
23 *Allen* 2522, 77–79 (August 20, 1531).
24 *Allen* 1744, 120 sqq. (September 2 c., 1526).
25 Doc. E (above n. 3), p. 6.
26 *Allen* 1717, 5–6 (June 6, 1526): sunt duo praecipue mihi peculiariter infensi, qui nunc extrema moliuntur denuo, quum id facere nunquam cessarint; 1719, 34–36 (June 6 c., 1526): Romae paganum illud eruditorum sodalitium iam pridem fremit in me, ducibus, vt ferunt, Aleandro et Alberto quodam Principe Carpensi; 1744, 130–131 (September 2 c., 1526): Vnum libellum ad me misit is qui scripsit Albertus Pius, alter sine titulo missus est per amicos.
27 *Allen* 1840, 81–83 (June 22, 1527): Non hoc imputo Alberto, sed illi qui nec deum nec hominem quenquam laudari patitur praeter seipsum. Nam hunc Albertus, vt audio, facit plurimi.
28 *Allen* 2375, 78–79 (September 1, 1530): nisi quod suspicor illum hoc agere instinctu mitrati cuiusdam, cui foederatissimus est; 2329, 106 (June 24 c., 1530): Aleander huic et addit animum et loca suppeditat; 2371, 34–36 (August 29, 1530): Aleander agit Venetiis, diciturque quicquid est operum meorum diligentissime euoluere; in hoc, vt suspicor, quo Alberto suo suppeditet calumniandi materiam.
29 *Allen* 2466, 106 (March 28, 1531).
30 *Allen* 2638, 1–5 (April 1, 1532): Albertum Pium toto hoc decennio ter quaterue non amplius sum adlocutus et tunc quauis alia potius de causa quam tua; scripsi vero ad eum post septem annos ne semel quidem, quantum meminisse possum. Illud certo scio, proximo quinquennio me non vidisse hominem.
31 Doc. G (above n. 3), in Sepulveda's *Opera, quae reperiri potuerunt omnia*, Cologne 1602, p. 606; the Italian amanuensis was Franciscus Floridus Sabinus.
32 Doc. F (above n. 3), sign. m2v: Quum magna voluminis pars pugnet cum Lutero tamen primus titulus in frontispicio libri tantum praefert nomen Erasmi. Habes primum specimen Christianae mentis. In the Venetian edition of Pio's work, also published in 1531, the title-page contains the following significant remark, printed below the printer's vignet: Cuncta haec candide lector diligenter considera, nam vniuersum ferme Lutheri dogma in his confutatum inuenies. Eme & fruere bonis auibus.—As we have seen above, the extensive Index preceding Pio's voluminous work came separately into the hands of Erasmus, as he communicates in his *In Elenchum*, sign. m2r: Verum index post ad me missus est: qui cuius sit, nec scio, nec scire refert.

P.P.J.L. VAN PETEGHEM

ERASMUS' LAST WILL, THE HOLY ROMAN EMPIRE AND THE LOW COUNTRIES

Introduction

Erasmus of Rotterdam died on July 12th, 1536, as is well known. Only five months before, he had made in the city of Basel his last will (February 12th, 1536).[1] Nine years before, in the same city, he made his first will (January 22th, 1527).[2] In the mean-time, another revocation of his first will had taken place in his home at Freiburg (November 26th, 1533).[3] Only the former two wills[4] have survived; the latter was only attested by the Freiburg notary, Mathias Rasch Isninus.[5]

Hitherto little attention has been given to the study of these wills.[6] There can be no doubt that Erasmus himself was very concerned about this issue. The importance of this matter results from a great number of aspects, which are related to his deepest feelings and to his material world, about which not enough can be said in this paper.[7]

As a matter of fact not only historians, but jurists, theologians, literary scholars and scholars in many other disciplines could be interested in the study of Erasmus' testaments. These could well be considered one of the most important sources for the study of the last years of his life. The purpose of this paper is thus to provide arguments and to suggest ideas towards a deeper understanding of a subject too much neglected.

All things considered, without getting involved with the implications of his last wills, one is doomed to be unsuccessful when forming an opinion about Erasmus. The celebrations to mark the 450th anniversary of the last will and the death of Erasmus could be the starting point for a large number of investigations, which must result in a new understanding of significant problems in his life and in the reappraisal of some minor related issues.[8]

To cut a long story short, his testaments deal with his innermost feelings and they foreshadow a lot of problems that were to defy solution to those who were appointed by its maker to carry out the terms of his will. In this respect we must recall Carl Roth, who fifty years ago wrote an article on "Das legatum Erasmianum".[9]

Erasmus' Basel Foundation was endowed with money to acquire three kinds of objects: "in usus pauperum, aetate aut valetudine infirmorum, item in puellas nupturas, in adolescentes bonae spei, breviter quoscunque subsidio dignos iudicarint".[10] Erasmus had appointed as heir or *fideicommissarius* the Basel jurist Bonifacius Amerbach, who in 1525 was appointed to one of the chairs of law in the University of that city and remained there from then on until his death in 1562.[11] With regard to our present point of view the names of the two executors (Hieronymus Frobenius[12] and Nicolaus Episcopius[13]) are of minor importance. It should be noted that the history of these trusts proves Erasmus' survival after death.

An anniversary like this tempts one to reach a new understanding of Erasmus. Today we would like to explain, by giving a few examples, some aspects of the donation to Goclenius, that previously have passed unnoticed. Although this donation immediately precedes the already quoted words from Erasmus' last will, nobody paid enough attention to this question. That's why the following quotation deserves to be cited here: "Pecuniam apud Conradum Goclenium depositam illi in Brabantia dispensandam relinquet, quemadmodum ei mandavi".[14]

Conrad Wackers, mostly called Goclenius, was born at Mengering-hausen, near Arolsen, in Waldeck: *in montosa Westphalia*.[15] Little is known about him before his appearance at Louvain in 1519. At the end of this year Busleyden's executors proposed him as a candidate to hold the chair of the late Adrian Barlandus in the Collegium Trilingue. From December 1st, 1519 until his death on January 25th, 1539 Goclenius was a professor at the Faculty of Arts (chair of Latin).[16] From the time of his appointment as a professor, Goclenius and Erasmus got on such intimate terms with each other, that Goclenius was the only one among Erasmus' many friends in the Netherlands to be mentioned in the plans for the publication of his *Opera Omnia*, in the preserved testaments and in the documents referring to the confidential donation mentioned.[17] From the above evidence, we can draw the following conclusion: this article will also deal with a particular agreement mentioned in the last will of Erasmus and related to Goclenius, whose birth-place was situated in the Holy Roman Empire and whose professorship in Louvain gave him a chance to be acquainted with the leading scholars of his time, especially in the Low Countries.

Erasmus' last will and Ius Commune

A couple of decades ago, Professor G. Kisch published his work on Erasmus and the jurisprudence of his time. He had only one aim, to show how humanists thought about equity and the importance of justice.[18] He didn't leave that book behind without a purpose but wanted us to read about Erasmus and some juridical problems he had come across. Consequently, the problem of the last wills is not dealt with.

Erasmus' position on juridical matters has not been studied before. Nevertheless political and juridical inheritances were constantly changing. Erasmus himself made a particular contribution to the history of the political ideas, providing us with his conception of the new State (*Institutio Principis Christiani*).[19] But much work still remains to be done before we know which was Erasmus' position on *Ius Commune, Usus Modernus, Mos Gallicus* and *Mos Italicus*.[20] In any way, we can't afford an ostrich-like behaviour, when we want to examine in detail the juridical relationships of Erasmus and his last wills to e.g. the reception of Roman law.

Within the scope of this short paper the listing of certain questions related to the above statement is by no means complete. Knowing the closeness of Erasmus' relations with the jurists of his time—think e.g. about Bonifacius Amerbach, Udalricus Zasius[21] or Viglius of Aytta[22]—we should not be surprised to learn much of variants of their ideas. How should the last will of Erasmus be considered: as a *mixtum compositum* of various juridical articles and advices or as a personal reflection of Erasmus on a theme with which he was not so familiar? Giving a good answer to this important question could easily bring us further a couple of years.

Legal history is not a popular topic among historians and philologists. Erasmus himself paid relatively little attention to what advocates, attorneys and judges did, his principal concern was *bonae litterae*, theology, education, morality and philosophy. Thus, the present inquiry is an attempt to shed some light on the importance of a certain legal revolution in the life of Erasmus. A particular combination of law, economy and state-building contributed to the development of an extensive corpus of private law that found its way into Roman law, canon law and the law codes of the growing national states.[23]

In Erasmus' time traditional law schools were mainly based on the Italian method[24] and the mediaeval professors of the Bolognese school (Bartolus, Baldus, Joannes Andreae). This meant that legal education was largely influenced by scholasticism and by the use of dialectics and that the corpus of Roman law was studied as a timeless subject. In the sixteenth century, however, another method of legal teaching emerged: the *mos gallicus*.[25] The protagonists of this approach were Andrea Alciato and Jacques Cujas, who considered that jurists should devote themselves to explaining apparent contradictions in Justinian's *Corpus Juris Civilis* through an historical approach to law. In this respect, those humanistic jurists used methods very similar to the method adopted by Erasmus himself: a certain return *ad fontes*. This new, more critical way of teaching flourished in the sixteenth century. The rapid growth in the size and sophistication of the legal profession, a population growth and an increase in litigation and legislation regularly went together. Going to court or making one's will gradually became unthinkable without expert advice.[26]

The labyrinthine state of law and legislation had its institutional counterpart. The administration of justice was plagued by a bewildering array of competing jurisdictions. Such matters as judging testaments could be complicated by the fact that ecclesiastical courts, royal tribunals and municipal justices would increase their own prestige by claiming exclusive jurisdiction. Together, ambiguous laws, conflicting customs and special juridical privileges and institutions helped to fashion a legal order which was for a layman and immigrant like Erasmus rather confusing. Moreover the religious problems such as the *Reformationsordnung* in Basel still could complicate the making of his will.[27]

Coing has pointed out that those problems related to the law of succession in the *Ius Commune* period were defined by the following three factors: the legislation of Justinian (i.e. the Novellae), mediaeval law and influences (the glossators) and finally the impact of the Church and the canon law. The legists have attempted to unify the disparate articles of the Roman legacy concerning the law of succession. Nevertheless, despite the growing effectiveness of national law, local and regional legislation continued to be used. Subsequently, in no country the Roman legacy found full acceptance. Finally, the law of succession was largely adopted from canonical usage as regards form and content.[28]

The donation to Goclenius to be reconsidered

Fifty years ago, Carl Roth quoted the following citation: "Item anno [15]39 uf Martini, als Academia Lovaniensis ein Notarium und Potten pro actione adversus heredes Goclenii ratione pecuniae depositae cedenda zugeschickt, hab ich den Botten uß der Herberg gelöst mit 10 Schillingen".[29] This citation led him to the conclusion, that Erasmus' Basel Foundation sometimes was used to fill in the gaps for the execution of charitable purposes. In any case, Boniface Amerbach, who had spent this money, must have intervened several times in the dispute about the Louvain donation. As an executor of the last will of Erasmus, Amerbach had to give his final support for the solution to any problem.[30] Even the difficulties with the moneys to be dispended in Brabant could not be settled without agreement from the Basel jurist. As a result, one may conclude that the citation above emphasized the key position of Amerbach, whose permission was essential to the work of the Louvain negotiators.

In 1941 the publication of tome X of the *Opus epistolarum Desiderii Erasmi Roterodami* unveiled much of this problem. Referring to a letter from Erasmus to Goclenius (Ep. 2863: Freiburg 28 August 1533) the editors discussed the problems to which this letter gave rise. It still remains interesting to repete and to remember what was at stake forty years ago: "Ep. 2863 professes to be a deed of gift, conveying to Goclenius, *pleno iure*, all the monies deposited with him by Erasmus up to the date of the letter (28 Aug. 1533). Erasmus had left, or made, deposits with Goclenius on three occasions.(1) In 1521, when he quitted Brabant, he had left with Goclenius the sum of 450 gold florins (Epp. 1437. 122–40, 2352. 38–40).(2) In May 1522 he had made, through Hilary Bertulphus, a deposit of monies amounting in their total value to 330 Rhenish florins (Ep. 2352. 41–61). At a later date, unspecified, he had deposited through Quirinus Talesius 909 gold Philippics (Ep. 2352. 62–71, and A2 of this Appendix). In 1539 Amerbach reckoned the value of the monies for which he held Goclenius' receipts at about 1960 *aurei*. Upon the death of Goclenius these monies became the subject of a protracted litigation, the history of which is in many of its details obscure. The obscurities which involve it are partially illustrated by documents preserved in the library of the University of Basel. These documents, fourteen in number, consist of the correspondence between Boniface Amerbach and the University of Louvain, the correspondence between Amerbach and John Altenanus and Conrad Heresbach (representing Goclenius' family), the correspondence between Amerbach and Goclenius in 1536, memoranda by Amerbach of documents forwarded by himself to the University of Louvain and to Altenanus, and, finally, a deed of Goclenius (17 Sept. 1533) acknowledging monies received from Erasmus, together with a memorandum by Erasmus (8 April 1534) of monies placed in trust with Goclenius".[31]

From this quotation and from the related documents it results that P.S. Allen (already in 1924), H. de Vocht[32] and A. Hartmann[33] were hard at work upon the donation to Goclenius before World War II. As a matter of fact all these scholars must have experienced the obscurities mentioned above. They also must have experienced the hardships caused by the long-distance discomfort. The journey from Basel to Louvain, comprising only a few hundreds of kilometers, raised difficulties to the XVIth century negotiators as well as to the XXth century scholars. None of them has seen all the documents still in existence and at present a few texts still remain unpublished. Unless the other historical records relating to the donation to Goclenius were known, previous scholars had to have failed. A reconstruction of the whole problem not being possible within an hour nor within the framework of the forthcoming publication of these papers, we felt rather restricted to explaining why the problem of the donation was not yet solved and to the suggestion that our solution reaches to the end of the chapter. Neither the later works of Henry de Vocht[34] nor the very important publication of the correspondence of Boniface Amerbach[35] by

Alfred Hartmann has helped us to solve definitely a question left unsolved from the XVIth century onwards.

Non reddendam pecuniam germanis? ...

After the general statements about Erasmus' last wills and after making the acquaintance of the special case of the donation, this rather strange quotation could hold our attention, in order to become aware of the possibilities of deepening and widening our subject-matter. Why explain how some Louvain doctors of law had to be consulted and why they believed that the moneys of Goclenius should in no way be given to residents of Germany? In this way it should be possible to connect more firmly the three elements of our present title, as will be shown.

After the death of Karel van Egmond, three parties claimed the duchy of Gelderland and the county of Zutphen: Antoine, duke of Lorraine,[36] William V of Cleves[37] and Charles V.[38] According to an agreement with the Estates of the duchy of Gelderland William V succeeded Karel van Egmond as duke. Within a few months he became Duke of Cleves-Mark-Jülich-Berg-Gelderland and Zutphen and thus the most important prince of the Rhineland i.e. the most dangerous opponent of Charles V to the east of his beloved "Burgundian Circle".[39]

This led to conflict with the Emperor, who laid claim to Gelderland and Zutphen according to a secular conflict with his Burgundian ancestors, in particular with Charles the Bold. This also meant that the political and diplomatic relations between William V's court and the allies of Charles V grew hostile.[40] On October 28th 1539, when Johannes Altenanus, the legal agent of the Goclenius' family, wrote from Louvain to Boniface Amerbach the alledged strange line,[41] the usurpation of the duchy of Gelderland and of the county of Zutphen presented the Hapsburg government with one of its major difficulties. Cleves and Charles V were virtually in a state of war.

It's curious enough that several friends of the late Erasmus lived at that time in the entourage of William V. Karl Harst[42] was to be used on a mission of great importance to Charles V in Spain. Konrad Heresbach[43] is to be mentioned as representing Goclenius' family. Others, such as Johann von Vlatten, Johann Gogreve and Henrich Olisleger, happened to be the most important councillors of William V, thus forming an influential circle of confirmed Erasmians.[44] Moreover the home country of Goclenius was supposedly an ally of William V, while the princes of Waldeck, where Goclenius was born (Mengeringhausen), were closely related to the Cleves house.[45]

Conclusion

In general, what emerges clearly from the examination of the three testaments is a discrepancy between Erasmus' original motives for writing his first will and the causes for which his last will was called on to support. To examine his testament in the light of the historical, political, religious and juridical issues of his time is to understand the reasons why this study is so important for new and renewed studies.

In reading Erasmus one is aware of how often the presence of death came to him during his lifetime. The short paper makes an appeal for the study of his last wills. We have argued that different parties may benefit from studies like this. As can be seen from the major topics in this study, we have presented some reflections on a subject that has been neglected too long.

Our analysis has provided some examples which raise a number of wider questions. As is shown in this paper, we were limited. It is perhaps uncertain what progress has been made. We were only able to open a few new avenues and suggest that other studies may widen horizons and bring about some changes in the course of various debates.[46]

Key statements

1) Within the scope of this short paper we can only suggest some reflections on a subject that has been neglected too long: the last wills of Erasmus. Although several scholars have made comments on particular aspects of these wills, an autonomous report on Erasmus' wills is still to be published.[47] 2) Until now people have never looked upon the testaments in the light of the reception of Roman law. This paper is an attempt to show how closely the last will depended on specific juridical conditions, whose implications have been underestimated. 3) The donation to Conradus Goclenius, a Louvain professor and an intimate friend of Erasmus, only forms one line in the Erasmian testament. Here again it should be noticed that the first monograph or article is still to be written. On the other hand, it is certain that the study of this donation is as interesting as the study of the Erasmus' Basel Foundation. The title of our paper comes from the combination of this donation with the man, who was born in the Holy Roman Empire and lived in the Low Countries. 4) The present inquiry, restricted to the examination of the last wills, should shed some light on the period between 1527 and 1536. The result of the combination with the donation to Conrad Goclenius brings back our chronology to the period when Erasmus was leaving Louvain in October 1521. In Appendix XXIII (A1–A14) Allen collected and published most of the documents relating to this question, but he did not know of all of them. 5)

Under these circumstances, we could only attempt to explore the beginnings of a story, which might be described as "unfinished". It was impossible to call your attention to a great number of other related problems. Put simply, this survey gives a general approach and one particular case. In order to give general information about the last wills of Erasmus we could suggest that different factors operating with varying force in different systems increased the need for testamentary (Erasmus) as opposite to intestate (Goclenius) succession.[48] Even such important items as the testamentary incapacity of the testator or the formal requirements of a valid will, the revocation of wills or the appointment of executors could not be looked at. As for the particular problem of the donation to Goclenius, it has been observed that the difficulties arose from the moment of the death of Goclenius. Goclenius' family from Westphalia, the University of Louvain, the treasury and the Council of Brabant, but also the so-called Collateral Councils (especially Lodewijk Van Schore[49]) were engaged in a protracted litigation.

NOTES

1 *Allen* XI, 362–365.
2 *Allen* VI, Appendix XIX: 503–506.
3 *Allen* XI, 362.
4 With respect to the city of Basel, one has to bear in mind that Basel was a free imperial city, see: G. Landwehr, "Freie Stadt", in: *Handwörterbuch zur deutschen Rechtsgeschichte*, Berlin 1971, I, 1222 and P. Eitel, "Reichsstädte", *ibidem*, IV, 755. As for the city of Freiburg, it is to be noted that Udalricus Zasius, a friend of Erasmus, had been invited to reform the laws and statutes of that city in the year 1520, H. Mitteis- H. Lieberich, *Deutsche Rechtsgeschichte. Ein Studienbuch*, München 1985[17], 315 Chapter 40, I, 5 a.
5 *Allen* XI, 362.
6 L. Sieber, *Das Testament des Erasmus vom 22. Januar 1527*, Basel 1889. In several works can be found reproductions of Erasmus' last will; I refer e.g. to the Rotterdam catalogue *Erasmus en zijn tijd*, Rotterdam 1969, Part 2, nr. 530, 150–151.
7 I should like to write a monograph on this subject.
8 I am thinking about J.K. McConica, "The Riddle of 'Terminus'", in: *Erasmus in English* 2 (1971) 2–7. The discussion about the publication of the *Opera Omnia* could take on a different appearance; and so on ...
9 C. Roth, "Das Legatum Erasmianum," in: *Gedenkschrift zum 400. Todestage des Erasmus von Rotterdam*, herausgegeben von der Historischen und Antiquarischen Gesellschaft zu Basel, Basel 1936, 282–298. Note also that this author is mentioning another Basel will (June 5th 1535).
10 *Allen* XI, 365.
11 P.G. Bietenholz and T.B. Deutscher, *Contemporaries of Erasmus: A Biographical Register of the Renaissance and Reformation*, Toronto 1985, Vol. I, 42–46.
12 *Ibidem*, II, 58–60.
13 *Ibidem*, I, 437–438.
14 *Allen* XI, 365.

15 *Allen* X, 418.
16 Cfr. note 10, Vol. II, 109–111.
17 See e.g. C. Reedijk, "Tandem bona causa triumphat. Zur Geschichte des Gesamt-werkes des Erasmus von Rotterdam" *Vorträge der Aeneas-Stiftung an der Universität Basel* XVI, Basel und Stuttgart 1980, passim and C. Reedijk, "Das Lebensende des Eras-mus", *Basler Zeitschrift für Geschichte und Altertumskunde* 57 (1958) 23–66.
18 G. Kisch, *Erasmus und die Jurisprudenz seiner Zeit. Studien zum humanistischen Rechtsdenken*, Basel 1961.
19 *ASD* IV–1, 142–155.
20 For a recent survey H. Coing, *Europäisches Privatrecht*. Bd. 1 *Älteres Gemeines Recht (1500 bis 1800)*, München 1985, 559–599.
21 Udalricus Zasius (Ulrich Zäsy), *Opera omnia*, Aalen 1964–1966, 7 tomes.
22 F. Postma, *Viglius van Aytta als humanist en diplomaat 1507–1549*, Zutphen 1983. For his importance as a jurist one has to consult now: R.M. Sprenger, *Viglius von Aytta und seine Notizen über Beratungen am Reichskammergericht 1535–1537*, Nijmegen 1988 (Gerard Noodt Instituut. Rechtshistorische reeks nr. 13).
23 *Ibidem*, 7–82.
24 H.G. Coing, "Die juristische Fakultät und ihr Lehrprogramm", in: *Handbuch der Quellen und Literatur der neueren europäischen Privatrechtsgeschichte*, München 1973, I, 39–128.
25 H.E. Troje, "Die Literatur des gemeinen Rechts unter dem Einfluß des Humanis-mus" , in: *Handbuch, ibidem*, München 1977, II, 1, 615–795.
26 "Rechtsprechungs- und Konsiliensammlungen", in: *Handbuch, ibidem*. München 1976, II, 2, 1113–1445.
27 P. Roth, *Aktensammlung zur Geschichte der Basler Reformation in den Jahren 1519 bis Anfang 1534*, Basel 1937, III, 383–410 (nr. 473). See also M. Alioth, *Basler Stadtgeschichte*. II: Vom Brückenschlag 1225 bis zur Gegenwart, Basel 1981.
28 See above, note 19, 559–561.
29 Cfr. note 8, 290.
30 The juridical position of Amerbach as *heres seu fideicommissarius* needs further expla-nation.
31 *Allen* X, 296 and 406–424 (Appendix XXIII).
32 H. de Vocht, "Literae virorum eruditorum ad Franciscum Craneveldium 1522–1528", Humanistica Lovaniensia 1 (1928), 245–249.
33 The editors of *Allen* X thanked him for transcripts of the 14 documents, and for per-mission to print them.
34 H. de Vocht, *History of the Foundation and the Rise of the Collegium Trilingue Lovaniense, 1517–1550*. Louvain 1951–1955.
35 A. Hartmann and B.R. Jenny, *Die Amerbachkorrespondenz*, Basel 1942–.
36 Cf. note 10, vol. 2, 349.
37 *Ibidem*. vol. 1, 315–317.
38 *Ibidem*. vol. 1, 295–299.
39 As regards the problems of centralization and state-building in the Low Countries, see my dissertation: *Centralisatie in Vlaanderen onder Keizer Karel (1515–1555). Een onderzoek naar de plaats van de Raad van Vlaanderen in de Habsburgse Nederlanden*. Gent 1979, 3 tomes.
40 See my article: "Die Vorstufen der Eroberung Gelderns im Jahre 1543 aus euro-päischer Sicht" (Referate der 4. Niederrhein-Tagung des Arbeitskreises niederrheini-scher Kommunalarchivare, Wesel 1985), *Studien und Quellen zur Geschichte von Wesel* 8 (1986) 64–113.
41 *Allen* X, 418.
42 Cf. note 10, vol. 2, 165–166.
43 *Ibidem*. 183–184.
44 *Ibidem*. 112–113 (Gogreve); In 1987 appeared Vol. 3 of the biographical register: Johann von Vlatten 414–416 by A.J. Gail, where Olisleger 415 is only mentioned.
45 F. Meuser, "Conrad Goclenius aus Mengeringhausen (1489–1539)"; *Geschichtsblätter für Waldeck* 60 (1968) 10–23.

46 See my second article on this subject, "Le testament d'Érasme et l'histoire du droit privé. Remarques préliminaires", in: *Studies presented in memory of Fernando Valls-Taberner* (University of Malaga, forthcoming).

47 B.R. Jenny, "Erasmus' Rückkehr nach Basel, Lebensende, Grab und Testament", in: *Erasmus von Rotterdam. Vorkämpfer für Frieden und Toleranz.* Ausstellung zum 450. Todestag des Erasmus von Rotterdam veranstaltet vom Historischen Museum Basel. Basel 1986, 63–65.

48 It will be necessary to continue the following studies: H.R. Hagemann, "Basler Stadtrecht im Spätmittelalter. Studien zur Rezeptionsgeschichte", in: *Zeitschrift der Savigny-Stiftung für Rechtsgeschichte (Germ. Abt.)* 78 (1961) 140–297 and P.–J. Schuler, *Geschichte des Südwestdeutschen Notariats. Von seinen Anfängen bis zur Reichsnotariatsordnung von 1512.* Bühl/Baden 1976, 10: "Auf den Rechtsinhalt der Notariatsurkunden wurde bewußt nicht eingegangen, weil hierzu noch umfangreiche rechtswissenschaftliche Einzelforschungen erforderlich sind".

49 P. Van Peteghem, *Lodewijk Van Schore. President van de Raad van State en van de Geheime Raad (1540–1548).* Gent 1972, 2 tomes.

PART TWO

EDUCATION AND THE WORLD OF LEARNING

WILLEM FRIJHOFF

ÉRASME, L'ÉDUCATION ET LE MONDE SCIENTIFIQUE DE SON TEMPS—RAPPORT INTRODUCTIF

Parmi les nombreux qualificatifs qui s'appliquent à Érasme, ceux d'éducateur et de savant occupent une place de choix dans la mesure où—plus que les épithètes d'humaniste, de philologue, etc.—ils insèrent l'homme dans un réseau de fonctions socio-culturelles précises. Ils permettent, par conséquent, de l'étudier non seulement en interaction avec les personnes ou les idées d'autres savants et éducateurs, mais aussi sous l'angle de sa conformité ou non avec ces fonctions, telles qu'elles étaient perçues et vécues par ses contemporains. L'Érasme «tel qu'en lui-même», qui domine très largement la biographie érasmienne jusqu'à ce jour, pourrait ainsi être enrichi d'un Érasme au travail qui dévoilerait mieux son originalité véritable en nous livrant les coordonnées précises de sa place parmi ses concitoyens. Afin de permettre à la réflexion et la discussion communes de prendre la mesure de cette originalité, il paraît important de situer brièvement le travail du savant et de l'éducateur que fut Érasme dans la société de son temps.

Érasme naquit et grandit dans un monde en plein bouleversement éducatif et scientifique. Nous analyserons cette mutation sous trois angles:
- un bouleversement dans les *objectifs* et les *idéaux* éducatifs;
- un bouleversement dans les *structures* et les *institutions* de la science;
- un bouleversement dans les *moyens* d'éducation et de divulgation scientifique.

1. *Bouleversement dans les objectifs et idéaux éducatifs*

Du point de vue de l'éducation, le passage du monde médiéval au monde moderne se caractérise par le transfert du pouvoir éducatif, qui passe de l'Église à la société civile, et par la mutation de la clientèle scolaire qui, plus que d'ecclésiastiques, est désormais composée de laïcs. Si l'Église continue de fournir l'essentiel du personnel éducatif—Érasme lui-même était religieux de Saint-Augustin et prêtre—, les décisions en matière éducative sont de plus en plus souvent prises par les pouvoirs civils, qui deviennent les premiers demandeurs d'éducation. En formulant des exigences propres, ceux-ci contribuent puissamment à la définition de nouvelles priorités et, partant, de nouveaux idéaux éducatifs. La fonction intellectuelle se laïcise, tout comme la 'bonne' éducation devient un distinctif des élites civiles qui se veulent reconnues comme telles. Un nouvel idéal se dessine: celui de l'homme bien formé, mû par une éthique, un sens de justice qui se fonde sur l'examen oculaire des textes sacrés eux-mêmes, et par une piété (*pietas*) qui permette d'appliquer dans le concret de sa vie quotidienne les préceptes découverts dans ces sources.

La conscience aiguë que manifeste Érasme à l'égard de ces nouvelles exigences tient pour une large part au fait qu'il reçut sa propre formation dans une région d'Europe qui fut un des noyaux mêmes de cette mutation. Érasme grandit et acquit ses facultés intellectuelles, son mode de pensée, ses catégories de raisonnement—tout cet ensemble que le sociologue Pierre Bourdieu a appelé l'*habitus* mental, base inconsciente et banque de perceptions intériorisée nourrissant toute activité ultérieure—dans les villes de trois ou quatre provinces néerlandaises en pleine prospérité: Rotterdam, Gouda, Deventer, Bois-le-Duc, Utrecht peut-être. C'est le fait urbain qui domine sa vie, en particulier au cours de ses années de mûrissement psychologique et de formation mentale. Hors de la ville, et exception faite de quelques couvents ou maisons de campagne qui la prolongent, il n'y a pour lui guère que des rustres. Or, en s'agrandissant ces villes—dont l'Europe prospère de son temps était parsemée—devenaient plus complexes, plus difficiles à gérer, exigeant pour leur bon fonctionnement un partage des rôles, la naissance de petites bureaucraties de fonctionnaires compétents (c'est-à-dire instruits ou du moins formés par un maître) possédant une véritable culture juridique, puisée aux sources communes du droit enseigné à l'université. Il en était de même pour le gouvernement des provinces et des États. Le prince ne pouvait plus se contenter des conseils bien intentionnés prodigués par ses compagnons d'armes ou les ecclésiastiques de son entourage. Dorénavant il avait besoin de légistes professionnels et de fonctionnaires, instruits au minimum dans ces arts triviaux qui façonnaient précisément l'habitus mental en inculquant la façon de raisonner ou l'art d'aborder et de résoudre les problèmes. L'administration des cités et des États se profile peu à peu comme une affaire de culture. Les couches sociales qui rivalisent pour partager le pouvoir—la bourgeoisie, mais aussi la noblesse—investissent écoles et universités ou engagent des précepteurs privés, comme l'atteste la vie même d'Érasme.

Voilà donc comment arrivent de toutes parts ce que nous appellerions aujourd'hui des flux de demandes d'éducation:

a) D'une part, des demandes d'éducation *formelle*, d'un accroissement du volume des connaissances. Elles se traduisent concrètement en une demande scolaire de maîtres, de textes, de livres d'une qualité toujours meilleure et répondant à des critères valables au delà des frontières des

États ou des zones d'influence des différentes écoles. Ceci explique le sou-
ci primordial manifesté par les humanistes de fournir des textes scientifi-
quement irréprochables de toutes les autorités qui étaient supposées se
trouver aux sources du savoir. En outre, dans le Nord de l'Europe, le
mouvement vers le droit codifié, qui était en fait un mouvement vers le
droit romain, exigeait désormais des magistrats une culture latine que le
droit coutumier en langue vulgaire n'avait pas impliquée. Il inaugurait
ainsi un retour à grande échelle aux sources de l'Antiquité.

b) On assiste, d'autre part, à une demande d'éducation *informelle*,
autrement dit à une demande d'amélioration du niveau de culture générale et de savoir-faire, en fonction des exigences sociales formulées par les
nouvelles élites. Le sociologue Norbert Elias a magistralement analysé
cette dernière demande, dans la perspective de ce qui s'appelle désormais
le 'processus civilisateur'. Dans le cadre de la domestication de la
noblesse guerrière, le prince construit patiemment un nouveau système
de rivalité qui ne privilégie plus la force exprimée, mais la force retenue:
c'est l'étiquette de la société de cour qui introduit peu à peu dans la société toute entière le code social de la bienséance. La diffusion de ce système dans les nouvelles élites qui, aspirant au partage du pouvoir, sont
forcées d'adopter les valeurs et conduites des puissants en place, im-
prègne des couches toujours plus larges de la société de cette civilisation
du paraître et de la maîtrise de soi. L'extrême sensibilité d'Érasme pour
cette demande d'éducation informelle renvoie sans aucun doute aux men-
talités collectives des milieux ambiants fréquentés par lui dans ses phases
de formation.

Dernière conséquence de ce besoin accru d'une double culture dans les
élites nobles et bourgeoises de la société: une plus grande mobilité sur la
route des écoles, des universités, des cours princières et autres hauts-lieux
de culture formelle ou informelle. En agrandissant leur horizon, en en-
richissant leur vision du monde, les voyageurs se rendent complices
d'une culture laïque qui s'internationalise, en contrepoint à la culture
supranationale de l'Église. Ce double réseau constitue la trame qui pré-
pare la République des Lettres. Il est la condition même de la réussite de
l'humanisme en tant que mouvement européen. Comme ses milliers de
lettres en témoignent, Érasme doit beaucoup de son efficacité à l'existence de ce réseau et à sa virtuosité dans l'emploi de ses ressources.

2. *Bouleversement dans les structures et les institutions de la science*

Le bouleversement des structures éducatives et scientifiques découle en
grande partie de ce qui vient d'être dit. L'augmentation quantitative du
nombre des écoles et des universités au cours des XVe et XVIe siècles,

souvent sous l'impulsion des autorités civiles, désormais soucieuses d'être bien éduquées, se doubla d'une mutation plus qualitative. La nécessité de disposer d'outils adéquats permettant d'aborder à fond l'étude des textes conduisit, souvent en marge des universités classiques, à la création de nouveaux centres d'enseignement, en particulier les collèges trilingues, véritables laboratoires destinés à parfaire le nouveau paradigme scientifique que constituait la philologie historique. L'on sait la part qu'Érasme y prit lui-même. Ou aurait tort de sous-estimer l'importance tant réelle que symbolique de ce dédoublement du réseau universitaire, qui battit en brèche le monopole des universités et l'unicité du cadre de l'activité scientifique. Sur l'autre versant de cette évolution, les universités furent attaquées par en bas, au niveau plus strictement éducatif. En effet, la nouvelle exigence d'une culture à portée des élites dominantes des villes et adaptée à leur niveau conduisit simultanément au surgissement d'un réseau de plus en plus important d'écoles urbaines, les collèges d'arts triviaux—à commencer dans ces régions précisément où l'essor des élites urbaines tournées vers une culture laïque fut le plus marqué et où les universités firent le plus cruellement défaut: les Pays-Bas septentrionaux. Ce n'est point un hasard si le grignotage de la clientèle universitaire par les écoles urbaines commence, au tournant du XIVe et du XVe siècle, à Zwolle et à Deventer, cités hanséatiques prospères, aux bourgeoisies exigeantes. Mais, bercé par l'esprit de la Dévotion moderne, l'humanisme y restait chrétien, et de préférence biblique. C'est là qu'Érasme forma son horizon intellectuel; l'humanisme quelque peu paganisant des méridionaux devait toujours lui rester foncièrement étranger.

3. *Bouleversement dans les moyens d'éducation et de divulgation scientifique*

La multiplication des écoles urbaines dans un désordre apparent posa de façon aiguë le problème des livres de textes: il en fallait toujours plus, répondant, en outre, à un minimum de qualité. Or, le développement des techniques d'imprimerie, peu avant l'époque de la naissance d'Érasme, permit de jeter sur le marché des textes scolaires en grand nombre et d'un contenu standardisé, faciles à vérifier ou à améliorer par des retouches cumulées. Dorénavant, culture et savoir ne dépendent plus du seul maître, mais peuvent se référer à une sorte d'étalon 'objectif' qui est la vérité du verbe imprimé. L'humanisme biblique, loin d'apparaître comme un soubresaut de la chrétienté médiévale dans un monde qui se sécularise, prend ici, au contraire, tout le relief de son désir de modernité. Car l'exigence de vérité du Verbe (le Christ) amène une exigence égale de vérité du verbe (le texte qui l'atteste), comme facteur d'éthique. La foi sanctionne la mondanité: elle moralise le travail parce qu'elle en légitime les exigences.

Érasme entre de plain pied dans cette évolution, déjà suffisamment avancée pour qu'il puisse en cueillir les premiers fruits. Il y participe de tous les ressorts de son corps et de son esprit, en intériorisant les enjeux fondamentaux de cette mutation. Saisi d'une véritable frénésie du texte authentique, il publie édition sur édition sans toujours prendre le temps d'achever le fond de sa pensée ou le suivi des commentaires, quitte à apporter dans l'édition suivante les améliorations qui s'imposent. Ce vertige de retouches cumulées, ce perfectionnisme à intervalles, est tout à fait caractéristique de l'humaniste qui prend au sérieux non seulement le contenu des textes, mais également les moyens de les divulguer, et qui sait en optimiser l'usage. L'imprimerie bouleversa, en effet, non seulement les chaînes de transmission du savoir, en datant et personnalisant ses étapes, mais tout autant les formes mêmes de la sociabilité des savants. Ceux-ci multiplient les moyens de communication et de vérification, n'hésitant pas à confondre sphère publique et domaine privé—comme le fit intentionnellement Érasme, en publiant ses lettres. Le réseau scientifique, la trame de la République des Lettres, se structure désormais essentiellement par l'imprimé: c'est le texte imprimé, non plus la leçon orale ou la lettre manuscrite, qui crée la réputation et qui décide à l'avenir de ce qui compte dans le monde des savants. Aussi celui qui veut jouer un rôle structurant sur la scène de la science internationale—et telle était bien l'ambition d'Érasme—se fait-il imprimer sans relâche, souvent et vite: textes, manuels, recueils, occasionnels, lettres, éloges de collègues ... sans oublier celui de sa propre vie.

Cette analyse de la place qu'a occupée Érasme dans la société de son temps, en tant que savant et éducateur, pourrait permettre d'élargir le débat sur les textes présentés au colloque. La mutation tripartite de la société globale évoquée plus haut définit, en effet, à son tour trois éclairages complémentaires qui nous font aborder sous un jour nouveau le travail de l'humaniste:

a) les idées et les idéaux d'Érasme en ce qui concerne la pratique éducative;

b) la position d'Érasme à l'égard de l'organigramme des sciences et des curricula scolaires;

c) son habitus de savant.

Pour ce qui est des idées et idéaux d'Érasme à propos de la pratique éducative, plusieurs contributeurs ont insisté sur son regard essentiellement éthique. C'est en particulier le cas de J. *Chomarat* (La philosophie de l'histoire d'Érasme d'après ses réflexions sur l'histoire romaine*), qui ana-

---

* Ce texte n'est pas repris dans ce recueil.

lyse le plan tripartite caché de la vision de l'histoire que l'on peut distiller
de l'oeuvre d'Érasme. Il y voit une analogie avec sa vision de l'homme,
qui est corps, esprit et âme. L'éthique et plus concrètement la politique
(au sens fort du terme) dominent toujours l'esthétique chez Érasme. Aussi *J.C. Olin* (Erasmus and Saint Jerome: An appraisal of the bond)
souligne-t-il que la réforme de l'Église passe toujours, pour Érasme, par
la réforme de la parole: l'esthétique de l'édifice théologique ancien et l'é-
thique religieuse moderne se rejoignent; culture est pour Érasme corréla-
tive de sainteté ou, mieux peut-être, de piété. Lorsque *J. van Herwaarden*
(Erasmus and pilgrimages*) affirme que la critique religieuse d'Érasme
ne porte que sur ce que celui-ci identifie comme des excès, sans jamais attaquer les valeurs vraies et les pratiques authentiques, nous en arrivons
à une conclusion semblable: la norme religieuse, qui est la toise de la
réforme, épouse chez Érasme un idéal culturel et esthétique qui explique
sans doute autant ses conflits avec les autres réformateurs de son époque
que l'appel qui jusqu'à nos jours continue d'émaner de ses textes nor-
matifs. Mais *G. Chantraine* (Quelle intelligence de son temps Érasme nous
donne-t-il?) n'a certainement pas tort lorsque, dans une analyse péné-
trante, il nous montre en même temps l'enracinement d'Érasme dans
une vision ancienne du monde et son pari nouveau sur l'historicité de
l'homme. Son originalité ne réside-t-elle pas avant tout dans l'articulation particulière de ces deux coordonnées de sa façon de penser?

A son tour, *M. Marin* (L'«Institution du Prince» d'Érasme et de Guillaume Budé) fait remarquer que la sagesse est la valeur qui domine chez
Érasme: elle s'appuie obligatoirement sur le savoir, sur les arts, sur ces
studia humanitatis qui fourniront les conditons cognitives nécessaires à la
bonne éclosion de la parole sage. En cela, comme le fait valoir *Ch. Béné*
(Piété thérésienne et piété érasmienne*) dans une communication suggestive, Érasme ne devait pas rester un prophète isolé: unissant une ferme
volonté de réforme de la piété à une nette préférence pour les 'letrados',
Sainte Thérèse d'Avila relevait clairement d'un même univers mental.
L'importance du texte dans l'éducation est encore soulignée par *J.K.
Sowards* (Erasmus as a practical educational reformer) qui, dans la pratique éducative d'Érasme, relève sa conviction que l'homme commence
par la parole; l'éducation consiste en quelque sorte en un réajustement
continuel entre la croissance de l'homme et sa maîtrise de la parole dans
toute la richesse que son niveau personnel de développement lui permet
d'en tirer.

Ces conclusions amènent des conséquences bien marquées pour la position d'Érasme à l'égard de la place des arts et des sciences dans l'éducation, et à l'égard des curricula scolaires en particulier. *J. Chomarat*

---

* Ce texte n'est pas repris dans ce recueil.

souligne le rôle des historiens dans la formation des gouvernants. De même, *M. Marin* montre que pour Érasme la présence du précepteur constitue une condition indispensable à une bonne éducation. Ne s'agit-il pas d'aller au delà d'une transmission pour ainsi dire objectivée des connaissances, afin de conduire le disciple à la sagesse de la vie collective régie par une 'politique' qui n'est autre qu'une fonction de l'éthique chrétienne? Érasme eut certainement le désir intime d'être un tel maître de sagesse, non seulement pour les jeunes gens dont il a pu avoir la charge, mais—comme le souligne *R. Stupperich* (Erasmus von Rotterdam in seiner persönlichen und wissenschaftlichen Entwicklung*)—pour la collectivité toute entière, à l'échelle européenne. N'a-t-il pas multiplié les gestes attestant ce désir? On en trouvera une preuve supplémentaire dans son identification avec Saint Jérôme, mise en avant par *J. C. Olin.* La connaissance intime de son héros, savant 'trilingual' par excellence et précepteur de la chrétienté, a conduit Érasme à lui consacrer sa plus belle étude biographique.

En ce qui concerne le curriculum scolaire, *J. K. Sowards* souligne le peu d'originalité qu'Érasme a manifesté à son égard. Il voit l'apport pédagogique propre d'Érasme plutôt dans sa nouvelle conception, plus psychologique, du rôle de l'enseignant. Mais ne faut-il pas regarder plus loin? On peut, en tout cas, déduire de la communication de *J. Chomarat* que l'histoire, en tant que discipline, dépasse pour Érasme le niveau traditionnel du trivium: elle devient la clef de voûte de ce qu'on pourrait appeler, dans la terminologie d'aujourd'hui, les sciences socio-culturelles. Érasme a-t-il voulu préluder ainsi à l'introduction de nouvelles disciplines dans le curriculum universitaire? On ne peut qu'être frappé, en tout cas, du parallélisme que fournit la contribution de *E. J. Ebels* et *B. Ebels-Hoving* (Erasmus and Galen): les auteurs nous montrent un Érasme rehaussant le blason de la médecine théorique. L'appel à ces 'nouveaux' historiens et ces médicins philosophes manifeste l'envergure de la vision d'Érasme, plus peut-être que sa profondeur. A moins que l'histoire et la médecine n'aient été pour lui les exemples mêmes de sciences tout court, pratiques et théoriques à la fois.

Les auteurs des différentes contributions atteignent un large consensus pour ce qui est de l'habitus d'Érasme en tant que savant. *R. Stupperich* montre avec insistance à quel point les attitudes scientifiques et morales d'Érasme s'appuient sur l'habitus du «pauvre honteux»—le terme est de l'auteur de ces lignes—qu'il a intériorisé tout au long de ses années de formation. *B. I. Knott* (Erasmus' working methods in ''De Copia'') souligne la boulimie de la parole chez Érasme: son fétichisme du texte l'empêche de trier ou de couper. Cette incapacité traduit à coup sûr le sen-

---

* Ce texte n'est pas repris dans ce recueil.

timent d'écrasement qu'éprouvèrent alors les savants, Érasme compris, sous la masse de textes dont le nouvel art d'imprimer les inondait et qu'ils n'avaient pas encore appris à digérer avec des méthodes appropriées. Il en résulta pour les savants du XVIe siècle une pratique scientifique différente de la nôtre. Il serait important d'en définir les caractéristiques.

En attendant, l'on peut affirmer avec *D.F.S. Thomson* (Erasmus and textual scholarship in the light of sixteenth-century practice) que la place propre d'Érasme tenait à deux traits personnels dans le maniement de la masse des textes: d'une part sa rapidité d'écriture, liée à sa fascination du texte imprimé qui le poussait à suivre, sinon à devancer le rythme des imprimeurs; d'autre part sa methode de critique textuelle qui reposait moins sur une collation de l'ensemble des manuscrits disponibles que sur une pratique de l'éloquence, fondement d'un jugement intuitif d'une extrême sûreté. Érasme n'a pas réalisé que, de la sorte, son travail de restitution fut lui-même oeuvre historique, inscrite dans l'épaisseur de la tradition. Il a pourtant sciemment privilégié certaines plages de temps, dans les choix qu'il fit parmi les textes. Ainsi, *J. den Boeft* (Illic aureum quoddam ire flumen: Erasmus' enthusiasm for the Patres) montre qu'Érasme réussit à maîtriser et à canaliser la masse des sources en se construisant un corpus préférentiel de témoins, les écrits des Pères de l'Église: des sources (*fontes*) définies comme telles selon ses propres critères mais qui présentent comme caractéristique essentielle que les *sacrae litterae* et les *bonae litterae* s'y rejoignent. Cependant, lorsque l'occasion l'exigeait, Érasme savait restreindre ce corpus. Livrant dans son Commentaire sur le Psaume 86 (85) l'essentiel de sa «philosophia Christi», il limite le réseau des citations aux sources profondes de cette vision de la foi et de la vie: les livres bibliques. Dans ce commentaire programmatique il devait d'ailleurs, comme le montre *C.S.M. Rademaker* [Erasmus and the Psalms: his Commentary on Psalm 86 (85)], s'avérer d'une extrême précision dans sa manière de citer, sans les à-peu-près qu'on a pu glaner dans d'autres oeuvres.

Deux contributions enfin ont abordé l'étude du réseau de relations scientifiques qui était à la base de l'humanisme en tant que pratique scientifique et mouvement d'idées. *L. Voet* (Erasmus and his correspondents) étudie les caractéristiques socio-culturelles du réseau des correspondants d'Érasme: ceux-ci s'avèrent appartenir bien plus à l'ordre des lettrés de condition modeste et des officiers civils qu'à la classe des nantis, même si ces derniers ne manquent point. Il suffit d'évoquer le nom de Thomas More, dont *G. Marc'hadour* (Thomas More in emulation and defense of Erasmus) étudie les rapports avec Érasme, placés sous le signe même de cette émulation ludique que ce dernier prône avec tant d'insistance dans l'éducation des jeunes gens. Il y voit un bon exemple de la constitution de ces réseaux de solidarités, ou 'tissus conjonctifs', qui se forment en suivant des options intellectuelles, des manières de voir le monde, bref, l'habitus mental, plutôt que des idées.

G. CHANTRAINE S.J.

QUELLE INTELLIGENCE DE SON TEMPS ÉRASME NOUS DONNE-T-IL?

Se souvenir du passé ne consiste pas seulement à se raconter des événements passés, mais aussi à découvrir un sens à ces événements en vue d'ouvrir un sens à l'histoire présente. La mémoire, en effet, s'inscrit dans l'effort fait pour construire l'avenir. Il entre dès lors toujours une part de projection dans le récit historique et l'histoire doit être à chaque époque réécrite. C'est certes le signe de la fragilité humaine, de sa contingence, mais aussi c'est le signe d'une espérance plus forte que cette fragilité; de la transcendance de l'homme, car, comme l'a dit Pascal, l'homme surpasse l'homme.

C'est à l'intérieur d'une telle perspective que je voudrais mieux apercevoir quelle intelligence de son temps nous donne Érasme. Il ne s'agit nullement de se demander de qui il fut le précurseur: de Voltaire,[1] des modernistes du XXe siècle[2] ou de Vatican II,[3] de telles vues ne concernent pas ce que j'ai appelé de manière vague sa pertinence théologique pour notre temps.[4] Il s'agit de comprendre autant que possible l'effort fait par Érasme pour se situer dans l'histoire, c'est-à-dire pour garder à l'histoire toutes les dimensions requises en vue d'être chrétien. Les moyens qu'il mit en oeuvre à cet effet ne seront pas tous employés par la suite et l'esprit dans lequel il travaillait eut en un sens peu d'adeptes. Mais son effort lui-même, tel assurément que nous le comprenons,[5] atteste à nos yeux ce que fut la situation historique de l'occidental aux débuts du XVIe siècle.

Rappelons d'abord trois axes de l'histoire au tournant du XVe et du XVIe siècle. Puis examinons l'effort d'Érasme pour se situer dans cette histoire. Enfin reportons cet effort sur les trois axes afin d'en apprécier la qualité.

1. *Trois axes de l'histoire au tournant du XVe et du XVIe siècle*

On a souvent observé qu'autour de 1500 la représentation de l'espace s'est modifiée. Avec les grandes découvertes le Nouveau Monde est venu s'inscrire sur les cartes et des relations régulières se sont établies avec l'Extrême-Orient. D'autre part, le regard s'est modifié par l'introduction de la perspective. Enfin Copernic a remodelé la cosmologie physique en abandonnant le géocentrisme, que Nicolas de Cuse et Pic de la Mirandole[6] avaient déjà abandonné pour d'autres raisons (philosophiques ou théologiques). On n'ignore pas qu'à la même époque la représentation du temps s'est également modifiée. L'allongement du temps de l'histoire naturelle et humaine se fera plus tard. Peut-être la multiplication des échanges grâce aux nouveaux moyens bancaires et celle de l'information grâce à l'imprimerie produisirent-elles une «accélération» de l'histoire. Corrélativement on constate un peu partout la conscience d'un «âge nouveau». L'homme y accède à une conscience nouvelle de son humanité. Il peut se libérer d'une conception de lui-même, modelée par la théologie et incarnée dans des pratiques chrétiennes. Il tend les bras à l'antiquité païenne qui lui apprend ce qu'est l'homme. A certaines heures, il rêve—malgré les guerres continuelles—d'un nouvel âge d'or, de quelque paradis enfoui dans les Antilles ou d'une cité idéale: projection de lui-même marquée par la nostalgie des païens mais aussi par des aspirations apocalyptiques, teintées ou non de joachimisme. L'antiquité avait déjà été redécouverte lors de la «renaissance» carolingienne, puis à nouveau lors des «renaissances» du XIIe et du XIIIe siècle. Au XVe siècle, la «redécouverte» de l'Antiquité s'accompagna d'une interrogation de l'homme sur lui-même: les humanistes s'intéressent aux Anciens pour eux-mêmes; ils les interrogent sur ce que c'est d'être homme. Une telle interrogation suppose une mise en perspective: pas moyen de s'interroger sur soi-même sans se donner une perspective. Et puisque l'interrogation passe par la médiation antique, l'histoire est mise en perspective elle aussi. L'antiquité est mise à distance, tenue pour passée et pour différente.

Autant qu'un «monde nouveau», géographique, cosmologique et vécu, l'homme de cette époque découvre donc un «âge nouveau». C'est que l'anime un «esprit nouveau». Celui-ci s'affirme déjà dans la conscience nouvelle que l'homme veut prendre de soi. La mise en perspective historique à la fois suppose et suscite une situation spirituelle nouvelle: on prétend connaître les anciens purement par leurs textes, sans se servir d'une tradition interprétatrice, en l'occurrence la Tradition chrétienne (dans laquelle leurs doctrines et leurs vies prenaient sens au XIIIe siècle par exemple). Luther, de son côté, prétendra de manière analogue comprendre la Parole de Dieu purement dans le texte en écartant la Tradition de l'Eglise qui, selon lui, souille cette Parole.[7] Humanistes et Luther n'ont pas seulement des réactions homologues, chacun dans leur domaine.[8] Ils sont mûs par un esprit commun: la conscience nouvelle que l'homme veut prendre de soi acceptera-t-elle non point seulement telle ou telle médiation, mais *toute* médiation? La question se pose aussi bien aux catholiques qu'aux protestants. En termes assurément différents, certains catholiques écartent la médiation de même que Luther. Dès la fin du XVe siècle, avec Denys le Chartreux, compilateur insigne notamment de saint Thomas, puis durant le XVe siècle avec le dominicain Cajetan, célèbre commentateur de S. Thomas, puis avec le jésuite Bellarmin, le dominicain Baniès et le jésuite Suarez, on imagine une nature «pure», c'est-à-dire une nature humaine qui pourrait se réaliser selon une fin purement naturelle. Assurément ces grands théologiens ne nient pas la nécessité de la grâce surnaturelle; au contraire, leur théorie vise à mieux l'affirmer, mais c'est en supposant un état dans lequel la nature humaine pourrait s'accomplir sans le secours de cette grâce.[9] Dans une perspective toute différente, Luther permet l'usage du libre arbitre dans le domaine mondain ou civil tandis qu'il le rejette dans la relation avec Dieu. De façon analogue aux tenants catholiques de la «nature pure», Luther accorde ainsi une indépendance à l'homme «mondain». Mais comme nul autre, il pose le problème de la médiation: l'homme peut-il devenir lui-même grâce à la médiation de la nature et à celle de la grâce? La réponse est deux fois négative.[10]

2. L'effort d'Érasme

Tâchons maintenant de comprendre l'effort d'Érasme pour se situer dans une telle histoire. Quelles en furent les orientations essentielles? Quel en fut d'abord le but?

1. C'est la *Réforme*. La Croix attire tout à elle: tout l'homme et tous les hommes. Érasme se fixe comme but d'offrir tout l'homme à Dieu par le Christ. Ce but est visé par un esprit qui a pris conscience de l'humanité de l'homme et qui dès lors considère le christianisme dans cette *perspective* historique. Les abus de la société chrétienne proviennent, à son sens, de la piété formaliste, judaïque des moines, qui l'inculquent à un peuple superstitieux, et d'une théologie «froide», c'est-à-dire abstraite et disputeuse, insensible, souvent par principe, à la beauté littéraire et à ce qu'elle contient d'humanité, enfin de la collusion des moines et des théologiens, prétendant régenter la société chrétienne par volonté de puissance et goût du lucre. Ces abus proviennent d'autre part de ce que les évêques n'exercent pas purement leur ministère spirituel et de ce que les princes ne recherchent pas la paix. Cette critique, dont l'*Eloge de la Folie*[11] présente l'énoncé complet, n'est pas cependant appuyée sur un pur évangélisme. Elle est modérée: Érasme ne rejette ni la vie monastique, ni la scolastique, ni le ministère épiscopal, ni l'autorité civile. Il souhaite contribuer à leur réforme en les soumettant à l'emprise du Christ mort pour nous. Le Christ est connu par le Nouveau Testament que nous devons apprendre à lire dans l'Eglise comme les Pères l'ont lu (*vetus theologia*), eux qui étaient proches de la Source et dont le grec était la langue maternelle. Ce Christ accueille la sagesse antique et la purifie

de ses erreurs pour inculquer à travers sa Croix (folie) la sagesse véritable
(*Philosophia Christi*) qui, chez Érasme, reste trop marquée peut-être de
platonisme.

2. Percevant les plans historiques, Érasme suppose leur unité: sa critique sert surtout à montrer le surplus de la Révélation chrétienne par
rapport à ses réalisations historiques de son temps avec l'espérance in-
altérable que la Source coule encore aujourd'hui.

Cette espérance fut éprouvée par la «tragédie luthérienne».[12] La
réforme d'Érasme, largement diffusée en 1517, ressemble à celle de
Luther par certaines critiques. Cette ressemblance fera confondre
Érasme avec Luther; Érasme se défendra jusqu'à sa mort contre une telle
confusion. Sa réforme en effet appelle la paix comme son but et comme
son moyen, car les coeurs doivent être persuadés (par la douceur), non
déchirés par des tensions intolérables. Et ses critiques ne sont pas
radicales comme celles de Luther.

Ce que Luther met en cause par là, c'est l'Alliance de Dieu et de
l'homme, dont la réalité finale est la paix et dont le principe se trouve
dans le libre arbitre donné par Dieu à sa créature et dans la grâce qui le
restaure. Sans vigueur spéculative, avec une tendance à la partition entre
ce qui revient à l'homme et ce qui revient à Dieu, Erasme défend ce principe en s'efforçant de le sortir d'un augustinisme raidi ou étriqué, qui fut
selon lui celui d'Augustin dans sa polémique avec Pélage.

Luther, d'autre part, l'amena à abandonner ce que son exégèse gardait
de trop littéraire, et à élaborer la notion de *fabula Christi* (ou action drama-
tique du Christ). Grâce à celle-ci l'exégèse traditionnelle, qu'il connaît et
pratique avec discernement, pourrait recevoir un fondement «moderne».
Mais ce moyen ne sera pas reconnu, parce que Luther a persuadé même
les théologiens catholiques qu'Érasme n'est qu'un philologue (un 'gram-
mairien'), et qu'il n'a pas le sens de Dieu. (Le Concile de Trente con-
damnera une proposition d'Érasme concernant la profession de foi bap-
tismale en la comprenant de travers).[13]

3. Au moment où s'achève la polémique avec Luther, Érasme ouvre
délibérément un troisième front: il critique le 'cicéronianisme',[14] c'est-
à-dire la maladie de singer Cicéron. Son *Ciceronianus* (1528) n'est pas
seulement un opuscule de critique littéraire, où un nordique s'amuse à
damer le pion aux italiens, c'est aussi une défense de la langue chrétienne: impossible de dire la nouveauté du Christ dans la langue de Cicéron. Par là, son goût pour la beauté littéraire achève de se transformer:
le langage est modelé de l'intérieur par le contenu, lui-même vivant (tradition). Les *bonae litterae* sont ouvertes á la Révélation *en elles-mêmes*,
précisément parce qu'elles sont bonnes. Seulement cette raison toute formelle ne saurait suffire. Elle aurait même un effet nuisible, si par leurs

moyens l'homme ne faisait que se découvrir lui-même. Il faut donc encore que les *bonae litterae* soient ouvertes à la Révélation *par-delà elles-mêmes* en acceptant de la dire dans sa langue propre, et cela jusqu'à l'apparente inélégance et le solécisme.

4. Par sa réforme Érasme a voulu rendre vivante la Tradition. Plus qu'il ne l'a assimilée, sa pensée s'est laissée assimiler par elle. Sa critique, tout en supposant l'unité, ne la considéra cependant ni selon toute sa force logique (Luther, mais pour la mettre en pièce) ni selon toute sa puissance spirituelle (S. Ignace). Malgré cette limite (il n'est ni un théologien génial, ni un grand saint), Érasme a élaboré la notion de *fabula Christi* à l'intérieur de laquelle l'Alliance de Dieu et de l'homme s'achève et grâce à laquelle l'exégèse ne doit pas choisir entre la lettre et l'esprit. Corrélativement, il tient que la paix fournit un critère (spirituel) de la vérité, étant par là plus proche d'Ignace que celui-ci n'a pu le savoir. Par ces deux moyens il s'est opposé à la *tragedia lutherana* et à la déchirure de la Tradition, qu'elle provoquait. Autant qu'à cette critique judaïque de la Tradition, il s'est délibérément opposé à sa critique païenne: on ne peut cultiver pour elle-même la langue de Cicéron sans cesser de penser en chrétien.

Érasme nous apparaît dès lors comme un chrétien à l'esprit perspicace. Un manque de vigueur spéculative et d'intensité spirituelle ne lui permit pas de donner à ces éléments l'ampleur et la profondeur requises par la crise. S'il l'avait fait, aurait-il été entendu et suivi? Il est certain que même ces éléments ne servirent pas la reconstruction.

3. *La qualité d'un effort*

1. Reporté sur les trois axes qui nous paraissent définir l'histoire au tournant de 1500, l'effort d'Érasme manifeste ses limites. L'humaniste semble ignorer les découvertes de son époque. Pas davantage il ne s'intéresse à la conception du monde; la révolution copernicienne inquiétera Luther; pas lui. Jean Pic mourut trop jeune pour connaître le Nouveau Monde, mais la grandeur de l'homme réclamait pour lui un univers qui ne fut pas centré sur la terre. Nicolas de Cuse l'avait conçu ainsi pour des raisons analogues. C'est qu'ils étaient eux aussi possédés par le sens de l'homme, mais leur humanisme avait créé un nouvel espace pour l'homme, espace dans lequel prendront place les découvertes et la recherche scientifique.

A Pic, au Cusain comme á Érasme, les trois langues paraissent un instrument nécessaire du renouveau, Pic y ajoute d'autres langues orientales. Mais les deux illustres devanciers du Roterodamois parlent et écrivent l'italien ou l'allemand; Érasme n'écrit pas dans sa langue maternelle ni dans aucune langue moderne. Il a certes reconnu l'importance du langage dans le *Ciceronianus*, mais cela ne l'amène pas à voiloir imprégner une langue moderne de la sagesse du Christ. Il n'a pas créé une langue comme Luther a créé l'allemand; il n'a pas été un créateur comme Rabelais le fut en français. Il le fut sans aucun doute en latin. L'esprit qu'il sert n'est donc plus relié à tout le corps social; déjà il se construit un monde—qui n'est pas encore celui de l'érudition; déjà il prend quelque distance à l'égard du corps—social ou individuel. C'est, à mes yeux, la raison secrète et décisive pour laquelle sa réforme a quelque chose d'éthéré et ne pouvait pas aboutir: son intention est juste, mais les moyens qu'il propose ne sont pas adéquats.

Enfin l'oecuménisme qu'il partage avec le Cusain et le jeune comte de la Concorde n'a pas gardé chez lui l'ampleur et la profondeur métaphysique et spirituelle qu'il a chez eux. C'est sans doute la raison première pour laquelle, dans sa controverse avec Luther, il apparaît—en partie à tort—comme le vaincu.

Nicolas de Cuse et Jean Pic de la Mirandole avaient, chacun à sa manière, annoncé dans une synthèse prophétique un «monde nouveau», un «âge nouveau», un «esprit nouveau»; ils avaient voulu non opposer du neuf à de l'ancien, mais élargir le monde ancien à la dimension de l'homme, magnifier la dignité de l'homme créé par Dieu et racheté par son Fils et restaurer l'unité de l'être et de l'esprit.

Érasme ne reprend qu'une partie de ce vaste dessein: magnifier la dignité de l'homme créé et racheté: par sa conception du monde, par son choix du latin, par sa défense du libre arbitre, il appartient au monde ancien. D'autre part, il n'est plus en situation de sauvegarder l'oecuménisme de Cusain et de Pic: avec Luther l'esprit s'est intérieurement déchiré.

Tant par son choix que par sa situation, Érasme atteste ce que devient l'Occidental à partir du XVIe siècle.

2. Mais il atteste aussi ce que demande l'âge nouveau à l'homme pour devenir—ou demeurer—chrétien. Quand l'homme se met lui-même en perspective, quand il se donne sa perspective, il devient inévitable de soumettre la Tradition humaine et divine, la culture et la Révélation, à la critique. Mais il ne sert à rien de radicaliser la critique en la retournant finalement contre l'homme avec un Luther, ni de la refuser par principe avec certains scolastiques. C'est, dans l'un et l'autre cas, ne pas faire confiance au Dieu créateur et sauveur en n'admettant pas dans la pratique que Dieu a remis les moyens de le connaître entre les mains de l'homme parce que finalement il s'est incarné en son Fils: la notion de *fabula Christi* est dès lors la notion centrale sans laquelle l'homme ne saurait achever son histoire[15] et sans laquelle la critique ou la non-critique seraient l'une et l'autre destructrices de l'homme et du christianisme.

Devenue inévitable, la critique est aussi indispensable pour recevoir les réalités vitales, essentielles selon l'esprit. La superstition est à proscrire tant de la religion que de la culture. Les cicéroniens sont aussi blâmables que les moines. Mais comment la critique peut-elle devenir positive? Comment ne pas écarter de l'essentiel avec l'accidentel? On voit bien que le superstitieux écarte l'essentiel—l'esprit—par attachement à l'accessoire. Mais comment ne pas succomber à la tentation inverse, qui est de ne garder que l'esprit sans la lettre et le corps? Sans réussir à écarter toute tentation de purisme, comme je l'ai indiqué plus haut, Érasme a dû, pour la surmonter, réinventer et renourrir de l'intérieur la relation de la lettre et de l'esprit (ou de l'histoire et de l'Esprit). Apprise auprès des Pères de l'Eglise, d'abord conçue de manière plus littéraire qu'historique, cette relation est déterminée par le mystère du Christ et réglée par la double relation d'opposition et d'harmonie entre l'Ancien et le Nouveau Testament. Aussi rend-elle Érasme attentif aux développements de l'esprit dans l'histoire: d'une part, lors de la «tragédie luthérienne», comme il dit, il prend la paix comme critère de vérité: une doctrine, oeuvre d'esprit, ne peut être vraie si elle ne réconcilie pas les esprits entre eux; d'autre part, dans l'affaire cicéronienne, le critère de vérité est la capacité qu'a la langue des cicéroniens de parler du mystère chrétien.

Grâce à la *fabula Christi* et à la relation qu'elle détermine entre l'histoire ou la lettre et l'esprit, le problème de la médiation, primordial pour l'homme du XVIe siècle, se trouve déjà résolu. Érasme l'aborde expressément dans sa controverse avec Luther. Il eut le mérite—peu reconnu—de fonder cette relation de la lettre et de l'esprit sur la liberté divine et humaine, sur l'Alliance du Dieu Trinité avec l'homme, sa créature rachetée. La relation immédiate de Dieu et de l'homme n'exclut pas, mais au contraire implique le don que Dieu fait à l'homme de sa grâce et le don que l'homme fait librement de lui-même à Dieu. La relation immédiate de Dieu et de l'homme implique donc sa propre médiation. C'est ainsi qu'est affirmée et fondée l'histoire comme histoire de Dieu et de l'homme.

Le génie d'Érasme me paraît être de s'être tenu fermement dans la même perspective, celle de l'historicité de l'homme.[16] Il a défini avec précision ce que l'homme doit faire pour devenir chrétien une fois qu'il se met dans une perspective historique, qu'il se pense comme sujet, non pas seulement agent de l'histoire. Par là il nous met sous les yeux cet aspect de la situation historique et spirituelle de l'homme à partir du XVIe siècle.

NOTES

1 J. – B. Pineau, *Érasme, sa pensée religieuse*, Paris, 1924, p. VII.
2 A. Renaudet, *Érasme et l'Italie* (*Travaux d'humanisme et Renaissance*, 15), Genève, 1954.
3 J. Coppens, "Erasmus kritisch doch gelovig theoloog", dans *De Spectator*, 28 – 29 juin 1969, p. 3; M. Bataillon, «La situation présente du message érasmien», *Colloquium Erasmianum*, Mons, 1968, p. 3 – 10.
4 Cette perspective a été ouverte par Hutten et Luther, comme le montre C. Augustijn, "Vir duplex: German interpretations, of Erasmus", p. 219 – 227, elle fut développée par l'*Aufklärung*, comme le fait voir avec pénétration B. Mansfield, "Erasmus in the age of revolutions", p. 228 – 239.
5 On se reportera à mon «*Mystère*» et «*Philosophie du Christ*» *selon Érasme* (Bibliothèque de la Faculté de Philosophie et Lettres de Namur, 49) Gembloux, 1971, et à mon *Érasme et Luther. Libre et Serf arbitre* (Coll. Le Sycomore), Paris, 1981.
6 H. de Lubac, *Pic de la Mirandole*, Paris, 1974, p. 332 ss.
7 M. Lienhard, *Martin Luther. Un temps, une vie, un message*, Paris, Genève, 1983, p. 324 – 328.
8 Cf. W.J. Bouwsma, "Renaissance and Reformation: An Essay in their Affinities and Connections", dans *Luther and the Dawn of the Modern Era*, Leiden, Brill, 1974, p. 127 – 149 et B. Haegglund, "Renaissance and Reformation" dans *Ibid.*, p. 150 – 157.
9 H. de Lubac, *Le mystère du Surnaturel* (Coll. Théologie 64), Paris 1965.
10 *Érasme et Luther*, surtout le ch. IX.
11 M.A. Screech, *Ecstasy and the Praise of Folly*, London, 1980.
12 *Érasme et Luther*, 3 – 76, 102 – 119, 307 – 358.
13 Concile de Trente, session VII, 3 mars 1547, canons sur le sacrement de baptême, n° 14: H. Denzinger-A. Schoenmetzer, (ed.) *Enchiridion Symbolorum*, Herder, 1967, n° 1627.
14 Cf. mon «Langage et philosophie du Christ selon le Ciceronianus (1528) d'Érasme», dans Actes du Colloque de Bologne.
15 Jacques Chomarat, *La Philosophie de l'histoire*, a montré qu'au niveau politique l'histoire humaine ne saurait s'achever. Même la sagesse humaine, à laquelle les *bonae litterae* éduquent, est folie au regard de la sagesse divine. Inachèvement moral autant que politique.
16 Peut-être comme le suggère dans ce volume D.F.S. Thomson, "*Erasmus and textual scholarship in the light of 16th century practice*", p. 158 – 171, Érasme n'a-t-il pas conscience de la dimension historique de son travail? Nous verrions dans cette sorte d'ignorance une marque du vrai génie.

MAXIM MARIN

L'«INSTITUTION DU PRINCE» D'ÉRASME ET DE GUILLAUME BUDÉ

L'exposé qui suit ne traitera pas un thème politique. Au premier plan il y aura l'homme. Nous étudierons brièvement la conception de l'homme d'Érasme et de Budé, l'idée que les deux humanistes se font de la nature humaine, le problème du bien et du mal.

La plus grande partie de cet exposé sera réservée à l''institution', c'est-à-dire à l'éducation et à la formation de l'homme destiné à devenir prince, appelé tout court 'Homme-Prince', terme dont nous userons plus d'une fois. En nous appuyant sur les arguments d'Érasme et de Budé, nous présenterons le type de l'idéal de l'homme que nous proposent deux des plus célèbres humanistes du XVIe siècle.

L'idée que les deux humanistes se font de l'être humain est, comme on le sait, aristotélicienne et correspond à l'image de l'homme à la Renaissance: l'homme est un être doué de la faculté de raisonner et de parler, et en cela supérieur aux autres êtres.

La conception de l'homme est, chez Érasme, «celle de la tradition humaniste, issue de la pensée latino-grecque, celle de la pensée judéo-chrétienne. L'homme est un être raisonnable, séparé des autres créatures par sa faculté de penser. L'homme est une créature que Dieu a faite à son image, sollicité par le péché, sauvé par le Christ''.[1]

Budé partage la même conception de l'homme, en révélant l'exellence de la nature humaine: «La nature humaine ayant preeminence sur les aultres animaulx et don singulier et divin d'intelligence et sermocination''.[2]

Une autre source antique, la platonicienne, complète cette conception optimiste de l'être humain: «Dieu luy (à l'homme) a donné prerogative d'entendement pour regarder au ciel et dresser la face contremont''.[3]

Etroitement liée à la conception de l'homme qu'ont les deux humanistes est la question de savoir si la nature humaine est bonne ou mauvaise. Nous allons y répondre avec les arguments d'Érasme et de Budé.

Érasme nous transmet une image optimiste de l'espèce humaine. Le bien, ce but vers lequel tendent toutes les actions humaines—pour parler avec Aristote—réside dans l'âme de la créature, constitue un attribut inhérent à son être. Bien qu'il fasse la distinction entre l'origine noble du prince, dont nous verrons plus loin l'éducation et la formation, et le vulgaire, Érasme conçoit la nature humaine comme bonne et généreuse.

L'avenir de l'homme dépendra selon Érasme de l'éducation qu'on lui donnera.

Tout conscient de l'impossibilité que tous les hommes soient bons, il envisage pourtant de choisir parmi des milliers d'hommes celui qui dépasse les autres en vertu et en sagesse:[4] ce sera l'Homme-Prince dont nous nous occuperons plus loin.

De son côté, Budé adopte une attitude plutôt réservée à l'égard de l'être humain. Il admet la supériorité de l'homme face aux autres êtres, mais, à son avis, nombreux sont ceux qui s'écartent du bon chemin de la raison et de la sagesse pour succomber aux passions et à la folie mondaines: «La pluspart des hommes prennent le chemin à gauche. Il se trouve peu d'hommes douez d'entendement et jugement naturel qu'on les puisse ou doive appeller sages».[5] Ainsi, les mots sage, sagesse définissent l'idéal auquel devra aboutir toute 'institution' de l'Homme-Prince.

Etant convaincus qu'il ne peut pas y avoir une *multitudo philosophorum*—comme dit O. Herding[6]—Érasme et Budé considèrent l'existence de l'Homme-Prince comme une nécessité requise par la loi divine, car c'est lui qui régnera selon les lois de la bonté et de l'équité, c'est lui qui veillera sur l'ordre et sur le destin de la Cité.

Comment éduquer et former l'Homme-Prince, quels sont les préceptes de son «éducation morale et religieuse» ainsi que de sa «formation intellectuelle et politique» (termes empruntés à Pierre Mesnard) et comment réaliser l'idéal du prince-philosophe, tels seront les sujects de la 'doctrine' d'Érasme et de Guillaume Budé que nous allons traiter dans les pages suivantes.

L'éducation morale et religieuse de l'homme, le futur prince, doit commencer selon Érasme dès les premières années de sa vie, à l'âge où il ne se rend pas compte qu'il sera un jour prince: »Die richtige Erziehung muß schon in der frühesten Zeit beginnen. Der Prinz muß zum Herrscher erzogen werden, wenn er gar nicht weiß, daß er einst ein Fürst sein wird«.[7]

La période la plus propice à l'éducation serait celle qui est comprise entre trois et six ans: «Sur cette période de la vie de l'enfant, Érasme exprime ses intentions pédagogiques les plus personnelles, même s'il met ici encore ses pas dans ceux de Quintilien ou de Plutarque»[8]—et de Sénèque—dirais-je.

Érasme établit des principes pédagogiques rigoureux, correspondant à sa morale et visant à l'accomplissement de l'idéal humain de bonté et de sagesse. Les idées de son système pédagogique reposent sur les commandements de la philosophie chrétienne. Ainsi, le moine Érasme conçoit-il le prince comme un homme fait à l'image de Dieu, réunissant dans son être divines et humaines facultés, un prince terrestre régnant dans l'observance des lois célestes.

L'éducation morale et religieuse de l'enfant ainsi que la formation intellectuelle et politique du prince n'auront d'autre but que d'éveiller en celui-ci avant toute autre chose l'amour pour Dieu,[9] la passion pour l'étude des *bonae literae*, grâce à laquelle il pourra acquérir sagesse et prudence, et de tenir en haute estime le bien commun et la félicité publique.[10] A cet endroit, les idées de la philosophie chrétienne cohabitent avec celles de la philosophie païenne pour accomplir ensemble l'oeuvre parfaite: l'homme bon, juste, vertueux, sage.

Budé s'avère être moins rigoroux pédagogue qu'Érasme, son *Institution* révèle moins d'ordre que celle de son ami. Cependant, l'idéal de l'Homme-Prince envisagé par Budé correspond exactement à celui que nous propose Érasme. L'éducation de l'enfant commencera dès son plus jeune âge, car, comme parle Budé par parabole en imitant le sage Salomon, il faut semer sa semence le matin pour qu'elle apporte les fruits souhaités.[11] Avant tout, il faudra inculquer dans l'âme de l'enfant l'amour pour Dieu. La jeunesse du prince sera consacrée, comme propose Budé, à l'étude des bonnes lettres et á l'acquisition de la 'sapience' et de la 'prudence': «La fleur de jeunesse est la saison d'acquerir sens et doctrine».[12] La «sapience» aide l'homme à se détourner des ténèbres de la vie terrestre et le conduit vers le chemin de la lumière et de la vérité. Ce n'est qu'en exerçant son esprit que l'homme pécheur réussira à se sauver du mal mondain que le guette à chaque pas, et à s'élever vers les choses célestes. La sagesse seule aidera la créature à échapper aux plaisirs éphémères de la vanité humaine, et lui permettra de lever les yeux vers le Créateur, vers la félicité divine.[13]

Le futur prince devra aussi boire aux sources de la sagesse antique, qui lui apprendront à régner selon les lois de l'équité, à priser plus haut la chose publique que l'intérêt privé, la félicité commune que la félicité personnelle.

On peut constater que chez Budé comme chez Érasme les idées chrétiennes viennent parfaire les idées païennes, le profane rejoint le sacré pour former un tout harmonieux, pour parachever l'image idéale de l'homme de la Renaissance, pour prouver peut-être que l'être humain est une somme de sagesse chrétienne et d'instruction païenne.

Il se pose aussi la question de la noblesse de l'Homme-Prince. Est-ce qu'un enfant qui plus tard sera prince est noble et vertueux de par sa naissance, grâce à ses ancêtres illustres et à la renommée de sa famille?

Érasme adopte à cet égard une position sévère, conforme à la morale chrétienne: la noblesse de l'homme ne réside ni dans l'éclat de la naissance, ni dans la richesse ou dans la beauté physique, mais dans la noblesse de l'âme et du caractère: »Denn nicht Reichtum, plebeische Vergnügungen, Adel und Ahnenbilder machen die Würde des Fürsten aus, sondern Wahrheit, Sittenreinheit und moralisches Handeln«.[14]

Érasme distingue trois genres de noblesse,[15] à l'intérieur desquels la première place revient aux actions vertueuses; la seconde est occupée par la connaissance des disciplines élevées, et ce n'est qu'à la troisième place, la dernière, qu'est mentionnée la noblesse dérivant de la renommée de la famille. La noblesse naturelle doit pourtant s'accompagner d'actes bons et justes, autrement elle devient nulle.[16]

Budé, qui n'insiste pas tant sur l'éducation de l'enfant que sur la formation du prince, attribue à celui-ci une supériorité face aux autres hommes: «Il est à presumer qu'ilz (le princes) sont si parfaictz en prudence, si eminens en noblesse, si imbuz de justice et d'equité qu'il ne leur fault point de reigle ... comme ... aux autres subiectz».[17] La supériorité du prince dérive de sa vertu et de sa sagesse, ce qui autorise et justifie sa présence à la tête de la république.

Le problème des biens auxquels doit aspirer l'Homme-Prince est fondamental aus sein de l'Institutio d'Érasme. Ne pourra pas être appelé vrai philosophe le prince qui se sera approprié les disciplines du *trivium* et du *quadrivium*, mais celui qui tendra aux vrais biens et les concrétisera par des oeuvres charitables et vertueuses: «La véritable sagesse ne consiste pas en effet dans la possession de la physique et de la dialectique, mais dans la compréhension et l'acquisition des véritables biens. C'est dire à quel point la vraie philosophie est identique au christianisme».[18]

Le rôle du préceptuer dans l'éducation de l'enfant est déterminant en ce qui concerne les connaissances que celui-ci fera siennes. Aussi Érasme accorde-t-il un intérêt particulier au choix de celui qui sera responsable de l'éducation du futur prince. Le précepteur d'Érasme éduquera selon les principes de l'éducation libérale de Sénèque:[19] gronder sans offenser, louer sans aduler.[20]

Le précepteur de Budé aura le devoir de guider l'adolescent dans ses études, de lui faire découvrir les sources instructives de la 'sapience' et, à l'aide de hauts faits, tirés de l'histoire des hommes illustres, l'exhorter à agir pour être à la hauteur de leur vertu. La présence du précepteur auprès du jeune prince sera indispensable selon Budé: «A ceux qui ont desir de sçavoir et apprendre, il est besoing d'avoir bon maistre».[21] «Un homme estant en adolescence ne se peult bonnement conduire sans curateur».[21] «Commandement ne se peult pratiquer sans ayde, car il faut au prince un inquisiteur pour le moins ... pour entreprendre, conduire les affaires et mener a chef».[21]

Selon l'importance qu'Érasme y attache, nous distinguons trois domaines dans les sources de la formation intellectuelle et politique du prince:

1. Premièrement, les sources de la tradition judéo-chrétienne: les Proverbes de Salomon, l'Ecclésiaste, le Livre de la Sagesse, «textes profitables, car ils portent la marque du sceptre».[22]

2. Deuxièmement, l'Evangile qui inculquera dans l'âme du prince l'amour pour Jésus-Christ.

3. Troisièmement, les *Apophtegmes*, les *Moralia* de Plutarque,[23] car «on ne peut trouver rien de plus saint»,[24] sans oublier ses *Vitae*.[24]

Après Plutarque, le prince lira Sénèque dont la philosophie «excite et enflamme à l'étude du bien, élève vers les choses sublimes l'esprit du lecteur empli de vils soucis».[25]

La *Politique* d'Aristote et les *Offices* de Cicéron offriront des passages dignes d'être connus. Pourtant, comme dit Pierre Mesnard, «en la matière la palme revient à Platon»,[26] dont le rêve de la république heureuse est si cher à Érasme.

La place qui vient immédiatement après la philosophie revient à l'histoire. Elle peut fournir au prince des actions dignes d'être imitées, mais les héros païens ont causé beaucoup de mal. C'est pourquoi, avertit Érasme le prince chrétien, il faut être réservé à l'égard des exploits d'Alexandre le Grand ou de Jules César.

Chez Budé nous trouvons à peu près les mêmes sources que celles que nous venons de voir chez Érasme, mais, et il faut le souligner, on y cherche en vain l'ordre, la précision et la profondeur de l'humaniste de Rotterdam.

L'humaniste parisien, par contre, traite plus amplement dans son «Institution» de l'histoire qui, selon lui, pourrait remplacer le précepteur, et surtout de l'éloquence et de la poésie, en mettant en évidence leur rôle primordial dans la formation du prince. Parmi toutes ces disciplines l'éloquence mérite la première place: «Sans laquelle (éloquence) sapience est un glaive qui ne peult estre tiré de son fourreau; et par ce elle est de nulle defence sans éloquence».[27] Le prince, devenu orateur, «homme de bien qui a acquis la science de bien dire»,[28], saura plaire, instruire et persuader grâce au seul art de la parole. En somme, l'éloquence et la poésie et «avec elles la sagesse et la beauté»[29] seront indispensables à l'accomplissement de l'idéal de l'homme.

Après avoir vu dans leurs grandes lignes les préceptes de l'éducation et de la formation de l'Homme-Prince, on pourrait dire en conclusion qu'Érasme autant que Budé nous met devant les yeux l'image parfaite de l'homme, où sagesse et prudence sont équivalentes aux notions de capacité et d'esprit humains. Érasme surtout se veut le réalisateur du rêve de Platon de la république heureuse dont la félicité est due uniquement au prince-philosophe. Il crée ainsi une cité semblable à celle de son ami

Thomas More, située entre le ciel et la terre, où il régnera une harmonie parfaite.

Rappelés aux besoins matériels de notre vie terrestre, nous, les hommes, nous pourrions nous demander en quelle mesure cet idéal correspond aux possibilités réelles et à la vérité d'ici-bas. Nous devrions nous répondre à nous-mêmes que le sort de l'homme—et du philosophe—est non pas de trouver, mais d'aimer et de chercher la vérité.

NOTES

1 Érasme, *De pueris statim ac liberaliter instituendis*, ed. J. – C. Margolin, Genève 1966, p. 63.

2 G. Budé, *L'Institution du Prince*, Paris 1548, fol. 8 v°; cf. Aristote, *Pol.* 1253 a9 – 18.

3 *ibid.* fol. 52 v°; voir aussi Platon, *Resp.* 586 A; Sall., *Cat.* I, 1; Cic., *de leg.* I, 9, 26 – 27; Juv., *Sat.* XV, 142 – 147.

4 *LB* IV, 563 C.

5 *Inst.* fol. 6 r°, 7 r°.

6 *ASD* IV – 1, p. 124.

7 F. Geldner, *Die Staatsauffassung und Fürstenlehre des Erasmus von Rotterdam*, Berlin 1930, p. 120; cf. *LB* IV, 562 A.

8 J. – C. Margolin, o.c. p. 51.

9 *LB* IV, 565 B.

10 *LB* IV, 562; voir aussi Aristote, *Pol.* IV, 1295 a 10; III, 1279 a 18 et suiv.

11 *Inst.* fol. 52 v°; voir aussi *LB* IV, 561 E.

12 *Inst.* fol. 56 v°.

13 *ibid.* fol. 19.

14 F. Geldner, o.c. p. 104.

15 *LB* IV, 566 D.

16 *ibid.* 566 E.

17 *Inst.* fol. 11 r°.

18 P. Mesnard, «Érasme ou l'évangélisme politique», *L'essor de la philosophie politique au XVIe siècle*, Paris 1977, p. 94; *LB* IV, 566 A.

19 cf. Sen. *de brev. vitae*, 15,2.

20 *LB* IV, 562 E.

21 *Inst.* fol. 22 v°, 29 r°, 54 r°.

22 P. Mesnard, o.c. p. 97.

23 voir à ce sujet R. Aulotte, *Amyot et Plutarque. La tradition des «Moralia» au XVIe siècle*, Genève, 1965.

24 *LB* IV, 587 F.

25 *id.* trad. P. Mesnard, o.c. p. 97.

26 P. Mesnard, o.c. p. 97; cf. *LB* IV, 588 A.

27 *Inst.* fol. 41 r°.

28 *ibid.* fol. 40 v°; cf. Quint. *Inst. or.* XII, 1,1.

29 A. Michel, «Avant-propos à Rhétorique, pédagogie et culture», *Bulletin Budé*, 1986 – 1, p. 51.

J.K. SOWARDS

ERASMUS AS A PRACTICAL EDUCATIONAL REFORMER

Erasmus was the most important literary figure of the early sixteenth century, the "Prince of Humanists", the leading spokesman for the principal intellectual fashion of his age. He was a reformer second only to his great rival Luther in influence and following. He was the greatest biblical scholar, the virtual architect of the first age of modern biblical scholarship. And he was the most important educational writer and theorist of the century.[1]

His interest in education began in the 1490s while he was still a theological student at the University of Paris and took private tutorial pupils to supplement his income. Many of his later books began as guides and manuals that he prepared for these pupils—the *Adagia, De copia, De conscribendis epistolis, Colloquia, De ratione studii*.[2] All these were later revised, expanded, and published. Two of them, *De copia* and *De conscribendis epistolis*, took the form of textbooks and were among the most widely used school texts of the sixteenth century and beyond.[3] Another work, *De civilitate morum puerilium*, though it was intended only as a book of manners for boys, was equally widely used as a drill-book for pupils in the lower grades.[4] *De ratione studii*, in its final published form, was a curriculum manual for Dean Colet's reformed St. Paul's School in London.[5] *De pueris statim ac liberaliter instituendis*, which was intended as a demonstration piece in *De copia*, outgrew this intention and was separately published, taking the form of a powerful and popular declamation on the subject of early childhood education and parental responsibility.[6] *De recta latini graecique sermonis pronuntiatione*, like its companion piece *Ciceronianus*, was a dialogue addressing the serious problem of the reform of the classical languages, a problem as fundamental for the Latin-speaking society generally as for pedagogy.[7] The *Adagia*, having begun as a modest collection of classical aphorisms for his tutorial pupils, became through edition after edition, following the great Aldine edition of 1508, the most widely used reference book of the sixteenth century.[8] And the *Colloquia*, also in edition after edition, became one of the most broadly influential books ever written.[9]

Erasmus' reputation and influence as an educational theorist rested, in part of course, upon his exalted standing in the contemporary world of letters and upon his mastery of the Latin language in an age that prized such classical eloquence even above substance. But the enduring popularity and influence of Erasmus' educational writings rest in considerable part as well upon the practical good sense of much of what he wrote about education and the educative process. For in education, as in most of the fields on which he touched, Erasmus was an intensely practical reformer.

This will, I think, become clear as we turn to examine the several categories of education with which he was principally concerned.

Probably the least original area of Erasmus' educational theory was curriculum. He endorsed wholeheartedly the classical *litterae humaniores* that his earlier Italian Renaissance predecessors had revived from antiquity. Like them he advocated, virtually without change, the instructional program found in Cicero, Plutarch, and especially Quintilian. Like them, too, he considered this an intensely practical program, in two respects. First, it was a program that would prepare the sons of the aristocracy and the well-to-do to take their place in the world, as he writes in *De pronuntiatione*, as "senators, magistrates, doctors, abbots, bishops, popes, and emperors."[10] But, secondly, it was a program that prepared those same children to be responsible and knowledgeable Christians. This aim had been implicit in the earlier humanists' theorizing but seldom ever more than implicit. With Erasmus it took on a greater importance. Yet, as a practical matter, it was scarcely reflected in his notions about curriculum. In *De pronuntiatione*, again, he writes, "the Book of Psalms may be more holy than the Odes of Horace, but for all that Horace is the better to learn Latin from."[11] It is, in short, the end of the curriculum that is Christian, not its content: the aim of education may be the informed Christian man, but the method is grammar.

Erasmus' most substantial and most original ideas about education had to do with the subject of the teacher. In a letter to a discouraged schoolmaster at Sélestat, Johannes Sapidus, in 1516, Erasmus wrote, "Do you think it a mean task to take your fellow citizens in their earliest years, to instill into them from the beginning sound learning and Christ himself, and to return them to your country as so many honorable upright men? Fools may think this is a humble office; in reality it is very splendid."[12] And, in an earlier letter to Christian Northoff, one of his former tutorial pupils, in 1497, he advises him not only to choose the most learned teacher he can find but to cultivate a relationship with him like that of a son to his father, "since we are no less indebted to those from whom we have acquired the rules of right living than to those from whom we acquired life itself."[13]

This latter sentiment, by the time of Erasmus, was a *topos* of humanist educational theory. To an extent too, such pedagogical ideas as the desirability of fathers' overseeing their sons' education, the lamentable tendency of parents "to pay their grooms better than their sons' teachers,"[14] and the outrage over the excesses of school discipline and "flogging schoolmasters,"[15] all had become educational commonplaces. But Erasmus enlivened these venerable *topoi* with his own shrewd observations and sensible practicality. For example, while he says "it is much easier to specify the qualities of an ideal schoolmaster than to find any who actually corresponds to that ideal,"[16] Erasmus is very realistic and specific with his own prescriptions for the schoolmaster. He wants a man of mature years, preferably a layman—even one with children of his own—industrious, reliable, of good family, and with as much experience as possible, ideally one who has spent the greater part of his life in literary pursuits. He must have "a certain friendliness and flexibility" and a willingness to "make allowances for what a child does not know."[17] But also, Erasmus shrewdly advises, before hiring him as a teacher inquire "how his previous pupils have turned out."[18] Equally shrewdly, while Erasmus is properly outraged at the tendency to underpay good teachers, he is averse to the notion of a teacher's salary as a sinecure. His salary should not be fixed or the man himself tenured lest incompetents be attracted: "An upright man who is above all temptations is what that office needed, a man devoted to his duties even if he is paid nothing. A big salary and the prospect of high social standing might attract every criminal to the post."[19]

Erasmus was more offended by the brutality that obtained in the common practice of education than had been most of his humanist predecessors.[20] There is no theme in all his educational writings to which he returns more often than his hatred of the abuse of children by brutal schoolmasters. This theme, for example, becomes the principal subject through which Erasmus illustrates the device of rhetorical amplification (*copia*) in his treatise *De pueris instituendis*. But what makes the passage particularly arresting is that the detailed examples Erasmus uses are taken from his own experience and knowledge.[21] But more is involved, for Erasmus, in the brutality of the typical schoolmaster than simply brutality on the one side and humaneness on the other. As a practical matter, he contends in a strikingly modern observation, brutality actually harms the pupil and impedes his learning. "I maintain", he writes, "that nothing is more damaging to young children than constant exposure to beatings. When corporal punishment is applied too harshly, the more spirited children are driven to rebellion while the more apathetic ones are numbed into despair."[22] Certainly neither rebellion nor despair is quite what we expect as the product of an educational system.

In the matter of educational methodology we find Erasmus recommending a blend of classical practice with his own practical experience and personal preferences. His insistence upon game-playing as a method of instruction is a good example. It is an idea that builds and evolves out of his own experience and thought on the subject. It is implicit in his *Familia-*

rium colloquiorum formulae, dating from the 1490s. In his letter to Christian Northoff of 1497 he writes that "a constant element of enjoyment must be mingled with our studies so that we think of learning as a game rather than a form of drudgery, for no activity can be continued for long if it does not to some extent afford pleasure to the participant."[23] He advocates it again, in passing, in *De ratione studii* in 1511,[24] and in the *De pronuntiatione* of 1528, where he talks of giving "children by way of a present letter-shapes to hold or to pin on their clothes. Looking at them, handling them, guessing their right names will all be fun. At that age they enjoy recognizing the picture of a man or an animal or anything else and telling its name."[25] But the most detailed statement of the method is contained in *De pueris instituendis* (1529). He notes, for example, Horace's advocacy of baking cookies in the shape of letters for children and Quintilian's of using carved ivory letters as toys.[26] But he goes on to describe how an English friend of his (unidentified) had a beautiful set of bow and arrows made for his son, decorated all over with the letters of the alphabet. As targets he used the shapes of letters in the Greek and Latin alphabets. When the boy hit a target and pronounced the letter correctly he was rewarded with applause and a small prize, a cherry or something else that children like. Erasmus went even further, advocating making a competitive game out of it with two or three boys playing. And he concludes, "It was by means of this stratagem that the boy in question learnt in a few days of fun and play to identify and pronounce his letters—something which the majority of teachers, with all their beatings, threatenings, and insults, could scarcely have accomplished in three years."[27]

Beyond the evolving concept of game-playing as a stratagem of instruction, we can discern in Erasmus' educational writings an entire regimen of instruction which came to philosophical maturity in the major educational works of the late 1520s. In a passage in *De pueris instituendis*, for example, Erasmus asserts that "there are elementary principles in acquiring knowledge just as there are in developing virtue: and the process of education, too, goes through the phases of childhood, adolescence, and adulthood."[28] There are two strikingly practical ideas here: not only the idea of a cycle of education to fit the cycle of human maturation, but the idea that the process of acquiring knowledge is parallel to the process of acquiring, or developing, virtue. The two processes are linked together in Erasmus' thought from beginning to end.

In line with this philosophic framework Erasmus' concern for education begins with the conception of the child—with the character and temperament of the parents and with the care of the mother during her pregnancy. Erasmus, again in an astonishingly modern manner, advocates the most intimate parental involvement with the baby from early infancy, the closest supervision in the choice of nurses and attendants, and as much control as possible over the little world of environment in which very young children first begin to learn about the larger world.[29] If a child misbehaves at the dinner table, he says, he is corrected, and thus learns proper behavior in that setting. He is taught how to behave in church, at play, with servants, with friends. And such principles of good behavior stay with children all their lives. This is the burden of his work *De civilitate*. It deals essentially with the formation of the habits of decent social and personal behavior in young children that must be the base on which more formal education rests.

As to the regimen of formal education itself, Erasmus advocates starting it at a much earlier point than was usual in his time. He never quite specifies the age but his guiding principle is that instruction should begin at the earliest point at which a child can benefit from it: ideally "as soon as a child is born, he is ready for instruction in right conduct and, as soon as he is able to speak, he is ready for learning his letters."[30] The precise age is not important; what is important is that instruction begins "while his mind is still uncorrupted and free from distractions, while he is in his most formative and impressionable years, and while his spirit is still open to each and every influence and at the same time highly retentive of what it has grasped."[31]

Erasmus said that the child is ready to begin learning as soon as he is able to speak. This is the essential point for him because the substance of what he proposes to teach children is the classics and this learning begins with speaking. As we have seen with the use of the bow and arrow to learn his letters, the child is to be drilled and practiced to teach him care and accuracy in grammar and vocabulary. There is, he points out, a natural urge in children to imitate, and it is as easy for them to imitate the proper use of the classical languages as anything else. After all, he observes, if such "a barbarous and irregular language as French" can be readily learned by children, why not Latin and Greek?[32] Moreover, the classics themselves should be the vehicles of instruction, starting with the ancient fables, which are inherently interesting and at the same time models of both good grammar and practical morality. Next, students should be exposed to brief, pointed aphorisms, proverbs, and the sayings of famous men, again not only as linguistic models but for their moral truths. Here the compiler of the *Adagiorum chiliades* was on the solid ground of his own accomplishment.

Additionally, in the course of their instruction, teachers should observe the individual inclination of students for mathematics, geography, music, and other subjects and encourage them. But with whatever subject, the teacher must be careful that the material he puts before his students be agreeable, relevant, and attractive. For, to return to an earlier Erasmian theme, if usefulness combines with pleasure and integrity with enjoyment, children acquire a whole range of beneficial learning quickly, readily, and without boredom.

In his other books Erasmus developed most of the themes we have dealt with here. It is, however, in *De conscribendis epistolis* that he goes on to deal with the subject of educating more mature students. For this work, in addition to being the most comprehensive of Renaissance manuals of epistolography, is also a comprehensive treatise on the mastery of literary form, of teaching, and of learning.

He is quite practical and specific, for example, in telling the teacher how to set out the form of a practice exercise. He should explain the story in as much detail as necessary, specifying its main turning pionts, the distinctive characteristics of the persons involved, and the like. He must be sure that sources are available from which the students may draw topics or supporting proofs and guide them to the passages in the classical authors where these topics are treated, at the same time pointing out the wealth of classical commonplaces that would be apt for the subject. But he warns that the teacher should not give so exhaustive a treatment of the subject that he leaves nothing for the students to do. He should point out the types of theme, explain the divisions generally belonging to the particular type, review the main arguments and point the moral. He should then show some methods of composing the exordium, various types of openings that may be used, and propositions that can be used in building the argumentation.

He also advocates the use of 'recantations', "arguing against what they have just proposed."[33] At times "to sharpen their wits (the teacher) should propose disagreeable subjects. One might be asked, for instance, to defend poverty, exile, ingratitude, illness, contempt of study, neglect of language, or tyranny, or to argue that an old man should marry an old woman or bring home a lewd wife. For nothing is so inherently good that it cannot be made to seem bad by a gifted speaker. By such practice both fluency and readiness in speaking on any topic will be acquired."[34]

Not only in the assignment of themes but at every stage of their preparation students' work must be painstakingly corrected, not only for obvious mistakes but for ungainly, vulgar, or wooden words, inelegant figures of speech, defective rhythms, and weak passages. Again, we see Erasmus as intensely practical in his prescription. For he warns that teachers should not censure everything at once but different things at different times so as not to discourage students or make them hate study. The good teacher should single out individual students for approval of what is cleverly stated or handled, and explain the basis of his approval. At other times he might have one pupil read his exercise aloud while the rest take note of the criticisms he makes. But students should always be praised for whatever attributes they have. ''Such apportioning of praise and blame will ensure that no one gives up hope in himself or looks down on someone else; in addition, a sense of rivalry is stirred up among them.''[35] Some will need private help, encouragement, and reward. At all cost they should be discouraged from rote memorization and encouraged rather to look for general meaning. They should also be encouraged to keep notebooks for vocabulary, apt illustrations, quotations, and points of grammar. And the teacher should constantly take them back over work already done to note points of vocabulary, grammar, phrasing, rhetorical embellishment, and harmony. In these ways the effect of rote learning will be achieved but the material will be more usefully fixed in their minds.[36]

It is no wonder that Erasmus' educational ideas were approved by such disparate figures as the Lutheran Philipp Melanchthon[37] and the Jesuit educator Father Jerome Nadal,[38] or that his theories were adopted by Johann Sturm, Juan Luis Vives, Sir Thomas Elyot, and the Elizabethan teacher-scholar Roger Ascham who, in the *Scholemaster*, called Erasmus ''the honor of learning of all our time.''[39] Nor is it a wonder that he can still speak with convincing authority to those today who have an interest in educational theory and practice.

NOTES

1 R.R. Bolgar, *The Classical Heritage and its Beneficiaries*, Cambridge 1954, p. 336, calls him ''the greatest man we come across in the history of education.''
2 See the account in the introductory essay to vols. 25–26 of *CWE*.
3 For *De copia* see *CWE* 24, pp. 280–83 and for *De conscribendis epistolis*, *CWE* 25, pp. li–ii.
4 *ibid.*, pp. lvii–ix.
5 *ibid.*, p. xxxix and *CWE* 24, p. 662.
6 *CWE* 25, p. lvi.
7 *ibid.*, pp. liv–vi.
8 See Margaret Mann Phillips, *The Adages of Erasmus, A Study with Translations*, Cambridge 1964, pp. 5, 84, 135, 148, 165. Mrs. Phillips identifies nine authorized editions in Erasmus' lifetime, each with substantial additions to the number of adages. But beyond these, Ferdinand vander Haeghen, *Bibliotheca Erasmiana, Répertoire des Oeuvres d'Erasme*, lre Série (Ghent 1893), lists 53 and an additional 76 editions over the remainder of the sixteenth century plus 24 more up to the Leclerc *Opera Omnia* of 1703–06.
9 See the account in either of the two excellent works of Franz Bierlaire, *Erasme et les Colloques: le livre d'une vie* (Geneva 1977) or *Les Colloques d'Erasme: réforme des études, réforme des moeurs et réforme de l'Eglise au XVIe siècle* (Paris 1978).
10 *CWE* 26, p. 383.

11 *ibid.*, p. 386.
12 *CWE* 3, Ep. 391A. The letter numbering in the *CWE* correspondence volumes follows that of *Allen*. In later references only the letter number will be cited. For other letters of encouragement to schoolmasters see Epp. 1232 and 1234.
13 Ep. 56, to Christian Northoff. The same sentiment is expressed in *De civilitate, CWE* 25, p. 286.
14 In *De pueris instituendis, CWE* 26, pp. 313–14. But see also *De pronuntiatione, CWE* 26, pp. 374–75, and *De conscribendis epistolis, CWE* 25, p. 23. The traditional nature of the sentiment is seen in Gerald Strauss' reporting almost exactly the same complaint of a Lutheran schoolmaster a generation later in *Luther's House of Learning: Indoctrination of the Young in the German Reformation*, Baltimore 1978, p. 184.
15 The specific citation is to *De pueris instituendis, CWE* 26, p. 334, but the theme is dealt with in great detail in the foregoing ten pages, as well as in parallel passages in his other major educational works.
16 *CWE* 26, p. 333.
17 *ibid.* p. 378. Interestingly, Dean Colet wrote some of these same requirements into his prescription for the headmaster for St. Paul's School, perhaps on Erasmus' advice. See, for example, Ep. 227 and the statutes of St. Paul's School in J.H. Lupton, *A Life of John Colet, D.D.*, new edition, London 1909, Appendix A, pp. 271–84.
18 *CWE* 26, p. 374
19 Ep. 391A. But see also *De conscribendis epistolis, CWE* 25, p. 23 and *De pronuntiatione, CWE* 26, pp. 376, 714–15.
20 The *topos* of the flogging schoolmaster certainly is as old as Petrarch in the commonplace tradition of Renaissance educational theory. See Petrarch, *Ad familiares* 12.3; or Guarino, *De ordine docendi et studendi*, in W.H. Woodward, *Vittorino da Feltre and Other Humanist Educators*, Cambridge 1897, p. 163
21 *CWE* 26, pp. 326 ff.
22 *ibid.*, p. 331.
23 Ep. 56.
24 *CWE* 24, p. 676.
25 *CWE* 26, p. 400.
26 Horace, *Satires* 1.i.25–6; Quintilian 1.i.26–7.
27 *CWE* 26, p. 339. Philippe Ariès, *Centuries of Childhood, A Social History of Family Life*, tr. Robert Baldick (New York 1962), pp. 83–4, suggests that Erasmus went well beyond his ancient models in his arguments for game-playing. He proposes that because of the contemporary custom of allowing children to play games indiscriminately with adults—sports and parlor-games, games of chance, even licentious games—this predeliction disposed both children and adults to accept the idea of learning as play. Again Erasmus is the practical educational reformer. And he was further concerned to substitute harmless or, better, constructive games for the usual ones like dice or chess, which he disapproves in *De pueris instituendis, CWE* 26, p. 339.
28 *CWE* 26, p. 317.
29 *ibid.*, pp. 317–18.
30 *ibid.*, p. 319.
31 *ibid.*, p. 297.
32 *ibid.*, p. 320.
33 *De conscribendis epistolis, CWE* 25, p. 43.
34 *ibid.*, pp. 245–46.
35 *ibid.*, p. 40, part of ch. 39 of the work, titled "Correction".
36 This is all dealt with in the chapter "The Method of Going Over a Lesson," *ibid.*, pp. 194 ff.
37 See *Corpus reformatorum* 5.567–72, 11.5, 15, 106, 3, 1119, 20, 700, 26, 92. See also Clyde Leonard Manschreck, "The Bible in Melanchthon's Philosophy of Religion", *Journal of Bible and Religion* 23 (1955), 203–5; Maria Grossman, *Humanism in Wittenberg 1485–1517*, Nieuwkoop 1975, *passim*; and Strauss, *Luther's House of Learning*, p. 53.

38 *Monumenta paedagogica societatis Iesu*, XCII, 97, 99–100, 168–9, 172; CVII, 130, 153–4, 589, 599, 715, 741; CVIII, 108, 140, 251, 573; René Hubert, *Histoire de la pédagogie*, Paris 1949, p. 228; Gabriel Godina Mir, S.J., *Aux sources de la pédagogie des Jésuites*, Rome 1968; and Mabel Lundberg, *Jesuitische Anthropologie und Erziehungslehre in der Frühzeit des Ordens*, Uppsala 1966.
39 In the *Scholemaster*, ed. Lawrence V. Ryan, Ithaca 1967, p. 51.

B. EBELS-HOVING and E.J. EBELS

ERASMUS AND GALEN

Introduction

Erasmus and science—an unlikely connection, as students of our great humanist have long been agreed. However broad his interests and his capacities, they do not seem to have encompassed the observation of Nature, the analysis of the material world. Erasmus' orientation was, to follow Huizinga's famous characterization, purely philological and moral.[1] This is not to say, of course, that he was indifferent to 'Nature', but to him this 'great book of the world' was—to quote Margolin—like a number of texts and signs to be deciphered, first and foremost, in order to be able to conquer oneself.[2] On the whole, Erasmus' interest in Nature means interest in *human* nature and its potentialities. He may have noticed the beauty of gardens, may have been caught by the peculiarities of human behaviour that he happened to observe—this testifies to the alertness of his mind, to his general sensitiveness and curiosity, not to an inclination to question and analyse what appears to our senses. The laws of nature, the *ultimae causae*, are to Erasmus matters of divine fact, to be admired, not to be scrutinized. This becomes clear when in one of his later works, the colloquium *Epicureus* (1533), Erasmus scorns the *opifici* who try to improve upon Nature, while praising the *homo pius* who simply rejoices in the happy conviction that all Creation is there for man's sake, to be used and enjoyed, not to be attacked by doubtful questions.[3]

Does this mean that here Erasmus launched a general 'attack on the scientists', as was recently suggested by Christ-von Wedel?[4] Probably not: he explicitly criticizes the *opifici*, not the (real) philosophers of Nature. His attitude to what we call 'science' was more complex. According to Margolin Erasmus was in certain respects not uninterested in scientific problems.[5] But then the question is: what was the type of interest: that of a cultivated man in general, without a really scientific bent, or was it more specific? An interesting and perhaps exemplary insight into Erasmus' attitude in this respect may be provided by his dealings with medicine, and especially by his work on Galen. Here we have an occasion not only to see what 'medicine' may have meant to an allround humanist, but perhaps also what the individual humanist Erasmus 'did with' medicine. This could provide us with some more insight into the apparently tricky question of 'Erasmus and science.'[6]

The Encomium artis medicinae

That Erasmus was preoccupied with medicine all his life is well known. His everlasting concern with his own health and physical well-being entailed a continuous interest in physicians and their craft. Though at times he could not prevent himself from making sceptical remarks on the power of doctors, on the whole he certainly believed in the salutary influence of medicine.[7] Whatever we may think of this early work (written ca 1499) in which he deals explicitly with the physician's craft, the *Encomium artis medicinae*,[8] it is important to notice that he decided to write a *praise*, in contrast to the humanist tradition of *invectives* that went back to Petrarch.[9] Dománski, the latest editor of this treatise, is right in emphasizing Erasmus' being in harmony with 'l'esprit et la lettre des disputes du XVme siècle sur les valeurs respectives des arts'[10]—but in this tradition it was quite well possible for medicine to be the loser, which she is not with Erasmus. The fact that he himself prepared the treatise for publication many years after its composition, viz. in 1517, shows that then he was at any rate not ashamed of it. Whereas so many un-authorized publications of his earlier works in those years raised his indignation and made him excuse himself for these raw works of his young years, in the case of this *Encomium* there is no question of expression of (false) modesty. We know that he had rather down-to-earth reasons for publishing his *praise* and dedicating it to the physician Van den Eynde: he was remarkably explicit in wanting his enumeration.[11] Still, this authorized edition proves that he thought this particular little exercise worth renewed attention.

In doing so, he took a stance: *for* the doctors and their dealings, their theories, their behaviour, their power. Though he credits Medicine with exploits that even in our days surpass its real potential and thus seems to exaggerate its powers beyond credibility, the fact remains that he chose to praise and defend Medicine. Nuyens' suggestion that the *Encomium* was in fact an attack, a praise of folly under cover, so to say, is certainly too far-fetched, as Baumann already remarked.[12] There must be a middle way between under- and overrating the rhetorical character of the treatise: it is definitely tinged with irony, but it also, on the whole, seems to express real feelings of esteem. To us the obvious exaggerations and the nature of the comparisons may seem questionable or not in good taste: that the doctor's work is of a semi-divine character, that Christ and St. Paul were doctors in their way[13]—all this does not make the case of the craft of medicine actually persuasive. Our knowledge of the abysmally low state of the medical art in Erasmus' time adds to our scepsis. But we must realize that the limitations of the actual power to heal formed no obstacle, neither then nor at other times, to a positive esteem for medicine and for doctors. Psychologically the attitude towards medicine has always been a complex one: appreciation, often unjustified, alternates with rejection, also often unjustified. If it is almost impossible to unravel the real feelings of our own contemporaries on this subject, we can certainly not expect a complex character like Erasmus to convey a simple clear message.

If we may take, then, this *Encomium* for what it says it is: a Praise, a look at Erasmus' sources becomes the more worthwhile. Are they only of a general literary kind—or do they also come from more specific medical works? And if from the latter, does this mean: from Galen? Does material from the three Galenic treatises that Erasmus himself will publish in Latin in 1526, or do other *Galeniana*, already figure in the *Encomium*? The sources that Erasmus himself enumerates are Pliny, Homer, Plato, the Bible.[14] Dománski's annotation confirms an extensive use of Pliny's *Historia naturalis*. He states that other sources are easily detectable and names Galen as an example; he does so on the authority of Elaut, but like Elaut fails to give any direct reference.[15] Yet it may well be that already early-on Erasmus actually had some knowledge of Galen, if only from the second hand. Before exploring this point in more detail we must see in what way Galen was actually available to humanists of the early XVIth century.

Galen-editions before 1525

For ages Galen had been, with Hippocrates, the greatest name in medicine. His voluminous output may be divided into three categories: 'technical'-medical works, like those treating on anatomy, physiology, practical medicine; works on more philosophical and deontological aspects of medicine; and general philosophical works, like an Introduction into Logic. Galen had remained influential in Byzance and was extensively translated into Arabic. Although in the early Middle Ages translations into Latin were made, mainly around Ravenna, these seem to have exerted no real influence on medicine in Western Europe. This became different when translations were made from the Arabic Galen-versions into Latin, by men like Constantine Africanus (died 1087), Gerard of Cremona (1114–1187) and Marc of Toledo. Translations were also made directly from the Greek, often very literally: already in the XIIth century by Burgundio of Pisa, and then by Pietro of Abano and William of Moerbeke in the XIIIth and by Niccolo of Reggio in the XIVth.[16] These several Arabic-Latin and Greek-Latin translations were the basis for the first printed Latin edition of the *opera omnia* published by Philippus Pincius at Venice in 1490, under the supervision of Diomedes Bonardus.[17] But this enterprise meant no *terminus*: in the late XVth and early XVIth centuries new translations, the so-called *translationes novae*, were made directly from Greek manuscripts by humanists who, in Durling's words, 'may well have imagined they were pioneers, in the sense of translating from the Greek for the first time a number of texts previously available in crabbed versions from the Arabic . . .'.[18] As we have seen, real pioneers they were not—they can be said to have worked in a tradition. Still, humanists like Giorgio Valla, Linacre, Kopp (Coppus) and Leoniceno, representing the emerging type of the humanist-physician, were convinced of their providing the world with something new.

Erasmus and the Galen-aldina

A major even in Galenism was the publication of the first printed edition of the then available works of Galen in the original Greek at the press of Aldus Manutius in Venice, 1525. This edition, made under the supervision of the humanist-physician Giovanni Batista Opizzoni from Pavia, has been called "a pure product of the philhellenic movement".[19] The growing conviction that the classical Greek heritage was of a superior kind had led to the eager acquisition and collection of Greek manuscripts and to the development of printing in Greek fount; this *Galen-aldina* was an impressive result of this kind of activities. Erasmus, at Basel, received a copy of the 5-volume edition through Francis Asulanus, presumably in the late autumn of 1525. He must have set out to translate the first three treatises of the edition very soon afterwards, as in May 1526 Froben could already print the Latin versions.[20]

In his introduction to these Galen-translations by Erasmus Waszink mainly emphasizes the clever emendatory work on the very faulty Greek version that was done in the process: 'the numerous emendations are by far the most important part of Erasmus' work as a scholar in these translations'.[21] The corrections in some cases remained valuable for more than three centuries: the world had to wait for XIXth-century scholarship to provide new Greek Galen-versions made on the basis of manuscripts unknown to Erasmus and other translators of his days. Waszink's assessment has recently been confirmed by Erika Rummel.[22] If it is obvious, then, that Erasmus' work on Galen was the work of a philologist, we like to raise the question here whether the *contents* of the three treatises were of any intrinsic interest to their translator. One at least has been called 'a surprising choice' (by Erika Rummel[23]); in our opinion this can also be said of the other two. This statement asks for an insight in their contents, of which we give the following summaries:

1. Galeni paraphrastae Menodoti exhortatio ad artium liberalium studia.
The intelligence of man places him above all animals. The animals practise no

arts, be it that they occasionally do so by instinct. Man however has mastered all the arts. Man even equals Gods, like Aesculapius in medicine and Apollo in music or prophecy. He cultivates all the arts of the Muses and even masters astronomy and geometry; yes by his love of study he has acquired the greatest good of all: philosophy. He is the rational being *par excellence*. Therefore he should not neglect the arts by simply following Fortune. To the contrary: he should follow Mercury, the master of reason and the universal artist. It is in Mercury's train that we find men like Socrates, like Plato, like Hippocrates. People should not pursue wealth, and neither should they boast their birth: a good education is of greater worth than a noble ancestry. Above all, young men should avoid senseless arts, especially professional athletics. For the condition of athletes is a miserable one, as attested by authors like Euripides and philosophers like Hippocrates. The athlete's mind is bogged down in flesh and blood, his body, in its overtrained condition, subject to all sorts of diseases. The athlete's strength only serves particular sports and thus becomes useless for serious matters like agriculture or defence. Therefore one should opt, when young, for a training in the liberal arts, that is to say for medicine, rhetoric, music, geometry, arithmetic, dialectics, astronomy, litterature, law—to which perhaps may be added sculpting and painting. But the best of them all is medicine!

2. Galeni de optimo docendi genere.
Favorinus, an Academician, states that the best teaching favours an equal estimation of opposing arguments, even to the point of *epoche*, suspension of a conclusion. This leads to absurdities, such as negating the existence of the sun. Favorinus contradicts himself when in one book he says that nothing can be known with certainty, whereas in another treatise he admits that some knowledge is possible. Academicians and Sceptics even hold that the judgment of insane people is as good as that of the sane, that sick people judge as well as the healthy, sleepers as well as those who are wide awake. If that were true, the Academician and his pupils would never be able to decide between various arguments.
It is, however, possible to train and to educate people in the acquisition of knowledge, not by making them uncertain, but by way of exercise and reasoning. For we do not have knowledge by nature, we acquire it through the various arts, like wrestling, building houses or ships, through rhetoric, reading, writing. Favorinus behaves like the craftsman who, while teaching his pupils, fails to provide them with the necessary tools and instruments.—We feel that such scepticism cannot be sustained. We *do* distinguish with our senses, we know the difference between a fig and an apple. But this natural power must be developed. I shall give you the instruments for building your own discourse and for judging the arguments of others. Where our senses do not suffice, we need other knowledge. It is foolish of Favorinus to grant the power of reasoning to his pupils while at the same time debunking reason itself. Vision is not equally acute for all of us, nor are our mental powers equally strong. To strengthen these as much as possible is the real task of the preceptor, as Plato says, with whom I fully agree.

3. Galeni quod optimus medicus idem sit et philosophus.
Most physicians resemble athletes who, though striving for Olympic victories, do not really prepare themselves. So most doctors praise Hippocrates, but actually do everything but try really to emulate him. They fail to acquire the necessary knowledge of astronomy, of geometry, of the nature of our body, of the various kinds of disease, of the art of prognosis. They do not perfect their language (in which Hippocrates excelled). They do not even read his writings, or—when they

do—they do not understand them. They are too lazy to travel around in order to learn about the natural differences in the locations and situations of towns, they do not examine the waters, their supply, their quality. But how could they? Due to their negligence and their preferring money to virtue we lack excellence these days: we no longer have a Phidias in sculpture, an Apelles in painting, a Hippocrates in medicine. Doctors should be well-versed in logic. They should despise money and practise temperance. If we were to be real followers of Hippocrates we must be philosophers, in order not only to equal him but even to surpass him and discover what he did not yet know.

These summaries of the contents of Erasmus' choice of *Galeniana* show that they do not contain messages that appear to bear relevance to the problems of his days. The issues in all three treatises were clearly of interest to Galen and his world of the 2nd century A.D.—but it is difficult to imagine that they were also interesting to Erasmus. While the main part of Galen's work, that on technical-medical problems, still had real importance for doctors of the early modern period, the three 'general' treatises Erasmus chose to translate seem to suffer from a certain obsolescence. This holds least for *Quod optimus medicus*: its arguments remain valid as long as there exist lazy, lascivious and greedy doctors, who can do with a serious reminder of their duty to practise the art of medicine well. And as long as the term 'philosopher' is used sufficiently loose to allow for a range of different qualities it remains useful to ask of the physician that he be such a philosopher. But in this wide sense the moral message became rather trivial in character, for Erasmus' times no less than before or after.—As to the second treatise, *De optimo docendi genere*, here the message had even less poignancy. Though the problem of the best way to teach is, on the face of it, a perennial one, this particular attack on Academic scepticism as it was being taught, apparently, in Galen's time cannot reasonably be connected to any of the educational issues that had the interest of Erasmus and his contemporaries.—Strangest of the three is the first, the longest of the treatises, the *Exhortatio*. Most of it is devoted to a warning against professional sports. In Galen's own time there may have been sound reasons for such a stand, and as a one-time physician to the school of gladiators at Pergamum Galen had firsthand knowledge of the perversion of sports, of the physical and mental harm they could do their practitioners. But in Erasmus' times professional athletic games were simply no social feature, so there was no need for defending the case of the liberal arts against professional physical training.

All this is not to say, of course, that Erasmus' undertaking of the translation of these three lesser *Galeniana* should call for a specific explanation. Simply the fact that another great Greek author had become available must have enticed him to try his powers. Yet it raises the question of his interest in and knowledge of Galen—before and after the publication of the Galen-aldina.

Galen in the Letters and in the Adagia

What were the sources of Erasmus' knowledge of Galen: did he know Latin translations[24], did he see any Greek text-versions before he got his Galen-aldina, and did the publication of the latter work result, for himself, in a raised interest? Trying to answer these questions we checked Erasmus' references to Galen in his letters and in the *Adages*—both covering the larger part of his working life.

First signs of knowledge of Galen emerge in 1515. In an addition (to *Adage* I iii 6) in the 1515-edition of the Adages Galen is quoted, but in Latin, and from an unidentified work.[25] In the same edition Erasmus lists Galen among his sources (under the heading 'philosophi').[26] In 1516 Budé, in a letter to Erasmus, discusses a passage from Galen.[27] As in the following year, 1517, another famous friend, Linacre, published a translation of Galen's *De sanitate tuenda*, we may assume that Erasmus got to know this particular work. The first time he himself refers to Galen in his correspondence is when he quotes from the same *De sanitate tuenda*, in Latin, writing to the physician John Francis around 1524.[28] Hereafter Galen is mentioned in letters dated 1525, 1526 (4 ×), 1527, 1528 (2 ×) and 1533 (2 ×). In most cases he is only cursorily referred to. But in a letter to Francis Asulanus, of the Aldine press at Venice, from 1526, Erasmus shows a particular appreciation of Galen: 'Author per se gratiosus est, mihi vero peculiari quodam sensu vel iudicio adamatus'.[29] As this was a few months after the publication of his translations it would appear that he had become positively attracted by Galen during this work. Much later he again testifies to his admiration: in a long letter of 1533 to John Agricola, professor in Greek and Medicine, printed in 1534 as an introduction to the latter's *Scholia copiosa in therapeuticam methodum, id est, absolutissimam Claudii Galeni Pergameni curandi artem*, he writes: 'Galenum vero in omni medicina summum esse tot eruditorum hominum iudicia ... honorificentissimis testimoniis comprobant'.[30] At that time he had already for some years been considered a connoisseur: a certain Caduceator, private tutor at Mainz, says in a letter from 1527 that to Erasmus 'Hippocrates, Galenus, Averrois, Celsus et si qui sunt alii medicae professionis principes scriptores ... sunt notissimi'.[31] Of course there is considerable exaggeration in this flattery, but that Erasmus had continued to busy himself with Galen around that time is evident from a letter dated 1528 in which he thanks his medical friend Joachim Martinius for sending him some quotations of Galen.[32] On this occasion he gives as his opinion that this author deserves serious attention.

In the Adages Galen is mentioned 36 times (*LB*-edition). In a minority of cases he is only briefly referred to by name, but no less than 26 times he is quoted, more or less extensively, in the original Greek. It is remarkable that Erasmus roams through a large part of Galen's many works, but cites from each separate work only once or twice[33]—with the notable exception of *De naturalibus facultatibus*, which is mentioned no fewer than 9 times. The quotations are found in all Chiliads, but especially in the IVth: 13 out of the 26, with a cluster of 9 in IV vii. The various works of Galen are randomly scattered over the Chiliads. It would be interesting, of course, to exactly date the inclusion of each separate quotation in the Adages, but as Erasmus went on adding material to earlier, already printed, proverbs we have, from the time of their first appearing in print, only *termini post quem*. On the basis of the grouping of the Adages as given by Phillips[34] we can conclude that 12 quotations in the IVth Chiliad (those in IV vi and vii) were not included before 1528. For the rest comparison between the various original editions allows for the detection of later additions: so far it has been shown, at any rate, that 3 quotations in the Ist, and also 3 in the IIId Chiliad have been added in the 1528 edition. Taken together, this means that at least 18 of the 26 Galen-quotations in the Adages were included after Erasmus' translation of the three treatises.[35]

From the Adages it emerges that Galen, though a second-rate source of material, was nevertheless not quite unimportant as a provider of quotations. As Erasmus cites him in the original Greek, he shows his dependence from the Galen-aldina (or other Greek Galeniana). That the famous Latin *Opera Omnia*-edition of 1490 should have served him as a source is very unlikely. The relatively large number of quotations in IV vii points to an increased interest in Galen after the publication of the Galen-aldina. This growing interest is also evident from the correspondence.

It is noteworthy, however, that from the three treatises he himself translated Erasmus drew no quotations for his Adages. The 26 we mentioned are all taken from other works by Galen. This makes us return to the translations.

It is obvious that in the humanist context the appearance of the Galen-aldina was a major event. For Erasmus its publication occurred at a time when he was in the midst of an outburst of work at new Latin translations of Greek texts: in May 1525 he published works of John Chrysostomus and of Plutarch, in February 1526 Chrysostomus again, in August of that year Irenaeus.[36] More than ever in his life he was bent on the 'great Greeks'. Since the *Paraphrases* on the New Testament were finished, he was approaching Greek texts of lesser renown but of a linguistically challenging kind, and among these Galen had a natural place.—But why these three treatises? The fact that they stand at the beginning of the Galen-aldina does not in itself provide a sufficient reason. More important seems to be their non-technical nature: as such they seemed more suitable to

Erasmus than the technical-medical ones—and perhaps a more likely source for gathering new proverbs. The speed with which the treatises were translated and printed (in October 1525 Erasmus complained of not yet having received the Greek Galen, and in May 1526 the translations were already published) may point to a commercial interest of the printer, Froben. In this respect it is probably relevant that two of the three treatises had not been translated into Latin before, whereas the third was available only in the Latin *Opera Omnia* of 1490, in the old version by Niccolo da Reggio.

But, as we said, Erasmus actually drew his Galen-quotations for the Adages *not* from the general treatises he was so familiar with, but (mostly) from the medical Galeniana one would expect him not to know well. It appears that, having done his translatory job and looking back, Erasmus did not think the treatises of much interest for further use.[37] His work at the translations had certainly raised his general interest in Galen, whom he now acknowledged as an important author and whom even he especially appreciated—but this appreciation seems mainly to have been one of Galen as the author of 'real' medical work. Thus, while using Galen as a scholar, and not as a 'scientist', Erasmus yet shows that it was Galen's scientific-medical side which had impressed him most.

NOTES

1 Huizinga, J., *Erasmus* (1924), *Verzamelde werken* VI, Haarlem 1950, p. 102.
2 Margolin, J.-C., "L'idée de Nature dans la pensée d'Erasme", *Recherches Erasmiennes* (Travaux d'Humanisme et Renaissance, CV), Genève 1969, p. 11–12.
3 *ASD* I–3 (1972), p. 27; cf. Huizinga, J., *Erasmus-Gedenkrede im Basler Münster* (1936), *Verzamelde werken* VI, p. 214–215.
4 Christ-von Wedel, C., *Das Nichtwissen bei Erasmus von Rotterdam* (Basler Beiträge zur Geschichtswissenschaft, Band 142), Basel etc. 1981, p. 88.
5 *Op. cit.* n. 2, p. 17.
6 'Erasmus and science' being one of the original headings under which scholars were invited to contribute to the Rotterdam colloquium, 1986. (In later stages it quietly disappeared from the program.)
7 Baumann, E.D., *Medisch-historische studiën over Des. Erasmus*, Arnhem s.a. p. 13.
8 Editions: *Encomium artis medicinae* in *Opuscula selecta neerlandicorum de arte medica*, I, Amsterdam 1907, p. 1–43; *Encomium medicinae* in *ASD* I–4 (1973).
9 See *Francesco Petrarca, Invective contra medicum*, ed. P.G. Ricci, Roma 1950; Kessler, E., *Das Problem des frühen Humanismus*, München 1986 (Humanistische Bibliothek, Reihe I Band 1), p. 130 ff. ('Petrarcas Invektive').
10 *ASD* I–4, p. 155.
11 Bauman, *Medisch-historische studiën* (see n. 7), p. 10–11.
12 *Ibidem*, p. 13–15.
13 For the *topos* 'Christus medicus' see Dománski, *ASD* I–4, p. 153, n. 20 and cf. the

image of Christ as *doctor medicinae* (woodcut in *Siecten der broosscer naturen*, Brussels ca 1510): C.G. van Leeuwen, "Opvattingen omtrent ziektes en zieken in de Nederlanden gedurende de late middeleeuwen. Een eerste aanzet", *In de schaduw van de eeuwigheid*. Tien studies over religie and samenleving . . . aangeboden aan prof. dr. A.H. Bredero, ed. N. Lettinck en J.J. van Moolenbroek, Utrecht 1986, p. 139.

14 *ASD* I–4, p. 154.

15 Dománski, *ibidem*. He refers to Elaut, L., "Erasme, traducteur de Galien", *Bibliothèque d'Humanisme et Renaissance*, XX, 1958, p. 37, where we find the following bland statement: 'Il (Erasme) avait été impressionné par l'édition latine des *Opera omnia* de Galien, parue en 1490 . . .' for which no proof is given.

16 Baader, G., "Galen im mittelalterlichen Abendland", in: *Galen, problems and prospects*, ed. V. Nutton, London 1981, p. 213–228, here p. 215. Also Durling, R.J., "A chronological census of Renaissance editions and translations of Galen", *Journal of the Courtauld and Warburg Institutes*, 24, 1961, p. 230–305, esp. p. 231–235.

17 Durling, *ibidem*, p. 250.

18 Durling, R.J., "Linacre and medical humanism", in: *Linacre studies. Essays on the life and work of Thomas Linacre*, ed. F. Maddison, M. Pelling and C. Webster, Oxford 1977. p. 83.

19 Mani, N., "Die griechische Editio princeps des Galenos (1525), ihre Entstehung und ihre Wirkung", *Gesnerus*, 13, 1956, p. 29–52, esp. p. 34–35.

20 *Allen* 1628. The modern edition of the treatises is *Galeni tractatus tres*, in *ASD* I–1 (1969), p. 631–669.

21 *Ibidem*, p. 632–633.

22 Rummel, E., *Erasmus as a translator of the classics*, Toronto etc. 1985, p. 111–117.

23 *Ibidem*, p. 110; it concerns *De optimo docendi genere*, see our summary under 2., hereafter. This was the only one of the treatises included in the Latin *Opera-Omnia*-edition of 1490.

24 For the easy assumptions in this respect cf. above n. 15.

25 *Collected Works of Erasmus*, Adages I 1 l to I v 100, translated by M. Mann Phillips, annotated by R.A.B. Mynors, Toronto etc. 1982, p. 239 en n. 16.

26 Phillips, M. Mann., *The 'Adages' of Erasmus. A study with translations*, Cambridge 1964, p. 94.—It is surprising to note that there is no mentioning at all of Galen as a source for the Adages in Appelt, Th.C., *Studies in the contents and sources of Erasmus' Adagia, with particular reference to the first edition, 1500, and the edition of 1526*, Chicago 1942. See "Frequency Table of Writers Mentioned in the *Chiliades*," p. 144–145. The solution to this problem of the omission of Galen is perhaps that Appelt had the opinion that Galen-quotations were taken from lexica like the much-used one from the Byzantine Suidas. To us this seems improbable; the years when Erasmus starts quoting Galen and the growing frequency of his citations after 1525 point, in our opinion, to a direct use.

27 *Allen* 403, dated 1 May (1516).

28 *Allen* 1532, dated 27 Dec 1524(?). Allen, n. 8, states that Erasmus derived his knowledge from *De sanitate*, "no doubt" through Linacre's translation.

29 *Allen* 1746, dated 3 Sept. ˙1526.

30 *Allen* 2803, dated 3 May 1533.

31 *Allen* 1811, dated 18 April 1527.

32 *Allen* 2049, (c. 16 Sept. 1528). To these quotations Allen adds the note "I cannot trace any reference to contributions by Joachim from Galen in the next edition of the *Adagia*, 1533".

33 Mentioned once are: *De simplicium medicamentorum temperamentis et facultatibus*, *De semine*, *De usu partium*, *De temperamentis*, *In Hippocratis aphorismos commentarii*, *De praenotione*, *Methodus medendi*, *De placitis Hippocratis et Platonis*, *De libris propriis*, *De compositione medicamentorum*.

Mentioned twice are: *Adversus Julianum*, *De pulsuum differentiis*, *Thrasybulus*. For the various and varying titles of Galen's writings see Fichtner, G., *Corpus Galenicum— Verzeichnis der galenischen und pseudogalenischen Schriften*, Tübingen 1985.

34 Phillips, M. Mann, 'Adages' (see n. 26), p. xii.

35 For the IIId Chiliad it is possible to consult the *ASD*-edition: *Adagiorum Chilias Tertia*,
ed. by F. Heinimann and E. Kienzle, II, 5 en 6, (1981): the Adagia referred to are
III iii 3 (2203), III vi 18 (2518) en III vii 76 (2676).—For the first Chiliad we have M.
Mann Phillips' translation in the *Collected Works* (see n. 25) which however only reaches
Adage I v 100. The three Galen-references here are in I iii 62 (p. 286), I iii 85 (p. 304)
and I iii 92 (p. 311)—Thus far we have not been in the position to carry out an overall
check of the remaining quotations in various original editions.

36 Chomarat, J., *Grammaire et rhétorique chez Erasme*, 2 vols., Paris 1981, I, p. 476 ff. (table
chronologique).

37 At least, not for the Adages. Some influence from one of the treatises, the *Exhortatio*,
can however be found in other works: in *De recta pronunciatione* (1528) where he describes
the main difference between man and animal: man has a *vox enunciativa*. See Chomarat,
n. 36, I, p. 53, p. 66.

BETTY I. KNOTT

ERASMUS' WORKING METHODS IN DE COPIA

Erasmus wrote at great speed, with ideas, illustrations, parallels, quotations, tumbling out onto the page, and he was believed to be reluctant, having written, to submit to the self-discipline of re-reading, checking, polishing, re-writing. His enemies taunted him with this, and he himself ruefully or laughingly admits to it; see e.g. *Ciceronianus*, *ASD* I‒2, 681: "(Erasmus) abiicit ac praecipitat omnia, nec parit, sed abortit; interdum iustum volumen scribit 'stans pede in vno', nec vnquam potest imperare animo suo vt semel relegat quod scripsit"; *Allen* 1352, 92: "Praecipitaui fateor pleraque omnia—nam hoc mihi vicium est genuinum"; *"Allen* 1885, 46: "Nunc adeo non vacat expolire quod scribo (sc. to achieve the meticulous perfection of Ciceronianism), vt crebro nec relegere liceat".

De copia was written in a hurry when it came to the point. Erasmus had been collecting material and working on bits of it since c. 1495, but the process of turning the material into a book for publication in 1512 was carried out at speed. Two circumstances spurred Erasmus into activity at that juncture: the obligation to produce something in answer to Colet's request for a work dedicated to the newly-founded St. Paul's school, and the fear of being forestalled by an unauthorised publication of some of the material he had assembled—material contained in papers left in Italy in 1509, which had got into unscrupulous hands.

See the introductory epistle to Colet (*Allen* 260): "Quanquam et fateor et doleo huic operi iustam curam defuisse. Siquidem olim rudem materiam in futurum opus temere congesseramus, ad quam expoliendam plurimis vigiliis, plurimorum autorum lectione videbam opus fore; itaque non admodum erat in animo aedere. Verum cum intellexissem quosdam his commentariis insidiari, parumque abfuisse quin incastigatissimos etiam aediderint, coactus sum vtcunque emendatos in lucem emittere. Nam id malum visum est leuius."

This may be in part ascribed to the conventional 'author's apology for his short-comings', but *De copia* does show signs of hasty putting together, fast writing and inadequate revision, and this reflects the author's personality as well as the circumstances of production.

A large part of Book I is made up of lists of examples of various Latin figures, constructions and idioms which can be deployed in the interests of *varietas*, the essential pre-requisite of *copia*. Up to ch. 53 these examples are offered with a small amount of linking material and some comment, but many sections in the 1512 version seem little more than jottings, and often the examples are left to speak for themselves. Chs. 54ff. are bare lists of examples. When speaking in Book II of the need to organise the material gathered in one's voluminous reading of the classics, Erasmus recommends the making of lists under appropriate headings. These later sections in Book I (e.g. 75 Accusandi formulae, 84 Referendi beneficium, 130 Laudandi ac vituperandi) have every appearance of being Erasmus' own lists in which he has noted down interesting usages as he came across them. They would provide material both for writing Latin himself and for teaching resource of expression to others, and may have originated in his early teaching activities. Many of the examples are derived from classical texts, usually without any indication of source in the 1512 version of the text, but quite a number appear to have been invented by Erasmus himself to illustrate classical usage, a normal teaching procedure. The content of the various sections is mixed, and often jumbled. The heading often refers directly only to the first two or three examples, the others being somewhat remotely connected. This might be because Erasmus found in his notes extraneous material which he had jotted down *pro tempore* at the time of reading, or because he scribbled in more material as he looked over his lists at the time of incorporation into *De copia*.

To give some various examples: ch. 122 (Pollicendi) contains *Littoribus nostris ancora pacta tua est* (i.e. Ov. *Her.* 2, 4), suggested by the preceding *Ita mihi stipulanti pactus est*. In ch. 157 (Studii) *Dedit se ad leges* is followed by *Seruos ad remum dedit* and *Ad terram dedit pro deiecit* (from Suetonius). Ch. 159 (Solitudinis) surprisingly ends *Vix asse emeris si totum hominem per se aestimes*, an example presumably dependent on *per se*. Ch. 102 (Inter coenam) includes several ways of saying 'during dinner', but also lists *inter alia: per iocum, inter iocandum, inter conventum, inter poenam, per iocum, inter pocula, inter potandum*, i.e. it seems to be more about *inter*. Its pair, ch. 103 (Post coenam) includes other ways of saying 'after'. Ch. 92 (Verba finis seu propositi) includes *Omnes spes meas in te vno fixi, Admirationem Aristoteles maxime petendam putat*.

Furthermore, the order of the sections seems almost completely haphazard, with little or no attempt at classification except for some pairs of chapters (e.g. 58–9 Finales, Causales Formulae: 61 Assentiendi, Dissentiendi) which may have been on the same page, in accordance with Erasmus' recommendation that related or opposite ideas should be listed together (*LB* I, 100). The removal of whole groups of chapters to different places in the 1514 edition seems no improvement, if indeed it was done by Erasmus' wish.

The juxtaposition of disparate material causes *De copia* to separate into three very different sections: i) Book I, chs. 1–54, introductory material and exposition of different methods of varying expression in the interests of *copia*, including the virtuoso practical demonstration of ch. 33; ii) the lists exemplifying Latin usage; iii) Book II, on developing subject matter. The introductory matter and Book II have mostly been filled out and are presented in very readable form, in Erasmus' characteristic fluent style. The rest of i) has been given some kind of form, even if it is still rather incohate, but the bare lists of the second section are stark and at first sight a puzzling component. Even at the time this section was unappreciated, and often neglected when other parts were reprinted. Also this material seems disproportionate: the 1512 edition has 119 such sections, i.e. about 40% of the work.

One wonders at what point Erasmus decided to incorporate it: whether it had always been part of his plan to include a comprehensive phrase-book, or whether he had the sudden idea of putting it in; it would at the same time expand *De copia* into a substantial work and a worthy offering. Having decided, for good or ill, to include it, he did not, it seems, have time or inclination to go through his considerable bundle of phrase-lists carefully, excising, tidying and checking, but copied them out more or less as they stood. Far from reducing this material later, he added for the 1526 edition another 17 sections in similar vein, and another 35 for 1534.

There are places in the other sections where Erasmus seems to have copied out or written up his notes in considerable haste, with the result that the text is barely comprehensible unless one can elucidate what was at the back of his mind. E.g. (*LB* 16C–D): *Tempus* (a species of heterosis) is illustrated not merely by straightforward examples such as *memini legere et memini legisse, vicimus pro vincemus*, but by *laurus erat pro laurus esset*. In this well-known example from Vergil (*Georg.* 2, 133) *erat* is substituted for *esset* (a 'vivid' use of the indicative); *esset*, if used, would refer to *present* time in an unreal conditional clause. The example could therefore illustrate change of tense, but in a very oblique manner; no doubt it would be comprehensible to teachers used to explaining this sort of thing, for whom *De copia* was presumably written. The explanation however seems rather to be that Erasmus had been somewhat hastily re-reading Valla at *Eleg.* 3. 49, where the discussion moves from change of tense to conditional sentences with mixed moods. Erasmus has compressed this material, substituting the Virgilian tag for Valla's equally well-known examples of this usage, and has produced a puzzle.

Book II, like the introductory sections of Book I , was written in running prose with much in the way of comment and explanation. An investigation of the sources apparently being used suggests that Erasmus, like Livy, tended to follow one main source at a time, with appropriate insertions from or reminiscences of other authors. For Book II the main source is usually Quintilian, with added material from *Rhet. Her.* and Cicero's rhetorical works. Erasmus appears to write with the appropriate text open in front of him; he reads it over, then paraphrases it, not always accurately, sometimes reproducing the material in a different order or picking out salient points in hasty compression. The examples in the source may be re-used, sometimes to illustrate a different point, or Erasmus may add or substitute comparable examples. Sometimes the summary is so compressed as to be almost incomprehensible without reference to the original. This is especially the case with some of the more detailed and technical parts of rhetorical theory.

An example of his method may be provided by Book II (*LB* 85B – 89A), in the section dealing with the development of multiple arguments in support of a rhetorical proposition. The whole passage depends on Quintilian 5, chs. 5, 9 and 10, where types of argument are discussed, including arguments of a general nature and those derived from the circumstances peculiar to the case in question. In the last section of ch. 10 Quintilian demonstrates how such arguments may be developed by means of a practical example: the question of whether the Thessalians are obliged to repay a certain debt to the Thebans. This obviously appealed more to Erasmus than the definitions of types of argument that precede: he starts with this section, and quotes or paraphrases Quintilian 5.10.110 – 18 in some detail, indicating the application of specific or general arguments, although his own text has not yet explained these. He then adds several further demonstrative examples, some well-known ones derived from ancient sources, some he has invented himself: Should the pope make war on the Venetians?; Should one get married?; Should one learn Greek? His fertile brain found it easy to develop these topics, and writing this section was obviously congenial: it reads very easily.

Only after this does he give a version of the earlier sections in Quintilian: a muddled account of *probationes artificiales* and *probationes ab arte semotae*, followed by a perfunctory list of Quintilian's main categories of *signa* and *argumenta* (see the passage *LB* 88F, quoted below, p. 148). This brings him back to the point at which he had started in Quintilian's text.

Quintilian next (in 5.11) deals with *exempla*. This again was congenial to Erasmus—it is the kind of material he used in *Adagia* and *Parabolae*—and he happily devoted most of the next twenty-two pages to discussing all the different types of *exemplum*, showing how they could be applied in the most unlikely contexts, and displaying his own prodigious knowledge and ingenuity. As the illustrative material pours out onto the page, one finds the same well-known examples recurring—Verres, Sardanapalus, Cicero's *Pro Milone*. The same point may be made again in similar words, and this is sometimes acknowledged by a hasty *vt dixi, vt superius demon-strauimus*. Erasmus is perhaps writing under too much pressure to pause and find alternative illustrations, to remove the repetition, but he was never averse to repeating himself, and it is in the nature of teachers to have their own stock examples; Erasmus has his favourite examples which recur from work to work.

In the final section of *De copia*, Erasmus takes as a source of *copia* the development of the standard sections of a speech (*narratio* etc.). Here again his pen runs away with him. On close investigation one discovers that there is sort of structure: he does actually proceed through the sections in order, but this is obscured by illustrations, repetitions, uneven development, and a neglect to name each section precisely as he comes to it.

These fluent and rather undisciplined sections are in marked contrast to perfunctory and inadequate summaries such as are found at *LB* 88D: "Demonstratiuum (genus) item suos (locos) habet, nempe bonorum ordines et quae his comprehenduntur"; 95F: "notum est exemplum (inductionis) de Aspasia ex Aeschine"; 97F: "sunt noua sententiarum genera: ex inopinato, et ex alio translatis, ex geminatione, ex contrariis. Quorum exempla si quis desiderat, ex Quintiliano petat licebit." All this makes the texture of *De copia* very uneven.

Even in its 1512 version, it is a sizeable work. Erasmus frequently says in it that he is only writing notes, showing the way, picking out what is relevant, and this indicates that he himself was aware of the abrupt and scrappy nature of some sections. He had obviously collected a huge amount of material, none of which he wanted to sacrifice. With such a vast heap before him, it is not surprising that he had to work at speed. The impression one receives is that he put his collection of notes into some sort of order (possibly three heaps), and just worked through them. Perhaps the written-up sections were already in usable form; perhaps they were developed at this point. Other less tractable material that required a different approach, a different style, and detailed checking, was left in note form. It was probably less congenial to Erasmus in any case.

According to the title-pages, Erasmus revised the text for subsequent editions in 1514, 1526 and 1534, but these revisions did not change the text in any fundamental way. It remained essentially what it had been in 1512, rich, uneven, confused, obscure. In fact, as hardly anything was removed and a great deal of new material was written in, especially for the 1534 edition, it became even richer and longer, within the same basic structure.

Many of these later insertions elucidate the original text, expanding it quite naturally, and can only be detected by comparing the different editions. To give two typical examples: the first taken from Book I in which

Erasmus is illustrating how the grammatical and lexical resources of the Latin language can be employed in the interests of *varietas*: *LB* 32A: (Formulae augendi positiuum): 1512: "Adiungunt Iureconsulti praepositionem 'in' tamquam idem pollentem." He added in 1534: "sed errant mea sententia. Quod enim illi legunt 'indifficile est' pro valde difficile, legendum est 'in difficili est' pro difficile est: quemadmodum dicimus 'in procliui est' pro eo quod erat, procliue est; et 'in promptu est' pro promptum est. In tuto est, in causa est, in vitio est. Augetur positiuum et . . ." The last three words provide the link with the existing text.

Or from Book II, which deals with expansion and enrichment of material: (*LB* 78C – D): 1512: "Praecipue vero narrationes nunciorum in tragoediiis, quoniam vice spectaculi subiiciuntur, hac virtute (sc. euidentia) abundant". The 1534 version reads: "Praecipue vero narrationes nunciorum in tragoediis, quoniam vice spectaculi subiiciuntur, dum ea referunt quae repraesentari in theatro aut non possunt aut non conuenit, hac virtute insigniter abundant. Veluti quum in Euripidis Hecuba Talthybius narrat . . ." (Erasmus proceeds to give several examples).

Other insertions however disrupt the text in a disconcerting way, e.g. Book I, ch. 34 (Quibus modis tribuimus plura ex aequo) *LB* 29F: "Est vir tum eruditus, tum probus. Est iuuenis et formosus et bene ingeniatus. *Atque* repetitum poetarum est: Vergilius 'Atque deos atque astra vocat crudelia mater'. Est vir doctus pariter ac probus. Est vir tam doctus quam bonus . . .", and numerous other variants on this basic theme. The words *Atque . . . mater* were inserted in 1534. Or from Book II, *LB* 88F, a passage dealing with *loci* where *argumenta* may be found: ". . . a relatiuis, a causis, ab euentis, a comparatione quae trifariam sumitur (a maiore, a minore, a pari), a iugatis, et si qui sunt alii. Nam neque de ordine, neque de numero, neque de vocabulis satis conuenit inter scriptores. Scripserunt autem de his copiosissime Aristoteles ac Boetius, satis accurate M. Tullius sed subobscure, breuissime Quintilianus. Oportebit autem eum qui semet exercet ad eloquentiam singulos excutere locos ac veluti ostiatim pulsare si quid possit elici. Vsus efficiet vt deinceps sponte ocurrant. Item ab ea quae rursum pluribus locis est communis, fictione, a causae propriis." Here the words *et si . . . Item*, inserted in 1534, with an echo of Quintilian 5.10.122, strangely separate the last two *loci* from the rest.

Some later insertions produce duplications of material, e.g. Book I ch. 11, where Greek borrowings are eventually treated twice.

Erasmus was addicted to scribbling in margins. See *Allen* 1596 (anno 1525), where he says of Augustine's commentary on the Sermon on the Mount: "vbi coepissem tuo hortatu relegere, comperi margines omnes notulis manus meae plenas." Possibly a good many of the insertions in *De copia* had originally been jotted in the margins of the book simply as ideas, as fresh material, not designed to fit in anywhere specifically, nor intended at first as corrections for a revised edition. When a new edition was being prepared, either Erasmus incorporated them, some more successfully than others, or possibly for the 1526 and 1534 editions he simply sent Froben his own text with its marginal scribblings, which the printer incorporated as best he could. Many corrections such as emendation of misprints and naming of sources for stylistic examples could have been made by any intelligent and informed reader, and do not necessarily imply any editorial activity by Erasmus.

Some awkwardly inserted material seems intended to correct passages that gave a misleading or wrong impression. Here Erasmus did not recast the paragraph or sentence in question, which was what was really required, but repaired it by insertions into the existing text, making minor adjustments to fit the new material to the old. The result is often puzzling until the different layers are separated.

For example, in Book I ch. 11 (*LB* 12B) Erasmus wrote in 1512: "Nouata: vt ductare exercitum, vt patrare bellum Sallustianum. Catonianum est vitili[ti]gator ..." (followed by six further examples of new formations). As another reference in ch. 79 makes clear, Erasmus derived the Sallustian usages from Quintilian (8.3.44), where they are given as examples of *in obscoenum intellectum sermo detortus*. Erasmus himself may have been well aware that he was referring to linguistic innovation as manifested in change of meaning, or at least of register, but this is not made clear by Erasmus' cryptic remarks to the reader unfamiliar with Sallust or Quintilian, who might deduce that Sallust invented the two words in question.

Erasmus realised in rereading the passage that his compressed note gave a misleading impression, and he tried to put things right by insertions: in 1534 the text reads: "Nouata trifariam accipi possunt: vel quae finguntur noua, vel quae in alium vsum deflectuntur, vel quae compositione nouantur. Primi generis exemplum fuerit, quod Nero *morari* dixit ... Secundi, quod Salustius *ductare exercitum* dixit, quum ductare apud Terentius aliosque veteres sensum habet obscoenum: vt meam ductes gratis; item: *patrare bellum* pro gerere bellum, quum patrare prius diceretur qui daret operam creandis liberis. Tertii generis sunt vitilitigator ..." We now have a clearer exposition of linguistic neologism, but one feels it might have been better if he had at the same time freed himself from the original text and substituted a new and more self-evident example of change of meaning, that did not entail the cumbersome explanation. The point is perhaps not entirely clear even in the end.

Again at Book I, ch. 11 (*LB* 10B), in a section on 'poetic' words, Erasmus quoted Verg. *Aen.* 4.419 to illustrate the poetic usage of *sperare*

to mean 'foresee': "Hunc ego si tantum potui sperare dolorem/ Et per-
ferre soror potero." In 1534 we find inserted a note to the effect that 'poetic' words should be sparingly used in prose, and also two more examples
of *sperare*: one from Terence (the exemplar of good Latin usage), and one
from Cicero's correspondence, introduced by: "a qua tamen sermonis
forma non abhorruit M. Tullius in epistolis familiaribus". It is not clear
from this whether Erasmus now means to correct the original idea that *sperare* in this sense is a 'poetic' usage, or whether he had collected two more
examples of *sperare* which he incorporates regardless of any inconsistency.

Again at Book I, ch. 148, 'Dierum notatio', we have 1512: "Calendis
Ianuariis. Ad calendas Ianuarii. Calendarum die. Nonis Ianuarii. Ad
nonas. Die nonarum" etc. One suspects from the context that in 1512
Erasmus thought *ad calendas* meant 'on the calends'. Again he modified
the text by an awkward insertion rather than a change: 1526: "Ad calendas Ianuarii, id est, circiter eum diem. *Sub idem tempus* pro circiter idem
tempus dixit Suetonius. Statis temporibus. *Stata vice* pro certis vicibus dixit
Q.Curtius. Calendarum die etc."

An investigation of the four authorised editions of *De copia*, especially
the last of 1534 in which a good deal of new material was incorporated,
suggests that Erasmus went on making jottings in his own personal copy
for years. In spite of improvements on many points of detail that this produced, even in the final edition there are a good number of passages that
still strike the reader as unsatisfactory in some way—bald, compressed,
unclear—e.g. the section at *LB* 36F–37F on indefinite pronouns and ad-
verbs (such as *quisquis, vbicunque, vbiubi, vtut* and many more). Such passages presumably could not be easily repaired, or dealt with subjects that
Erasmus had always found boring and could not bring himself to deal
with. Some of the insertions produce fresh puzzles. Nothing probably
could be done to improve the clumsy structure which was given *De copia*
at its first publication. The work remains uneven and untidy, and many
of the faults due to the original hasty composition are still there. Erasmus
had always had too much material, and never got it under control.

To deal adequately with all the blemishes would have required a fundamental rewriting of various sections. Though Erasmus made superficial
modifications by tinkering with the text, he was not prepared to take a
thorough revision in hand. It would be a daunting task in any case to put
such a huge and unwieldy work into good order, and Erasmus was maybe
not inclined temperamentally for that kind of systematic revision. In any
case, by 1534 at least the impulses that produced *De copia* were long past,
and there was no real incentive.

H.J. DE JONGE

WANN IST ERASMUS' ÜBERSETZUNG DES NEUEN TESTAMENTS ENTSTANDEN?

Nur wenige von Erasmus' Werken haben seine Zeitgenossen so beeindruckt, wie seine Übersetzung des Neuen Testaments. Nur wenige Werke bedeuteten auch Erasmus selbst soviel wie diese neue Übersetzung. Genau genommen war sie eher eine Revision der Vulgata in klassischerem Latein.[1] Mit diesem neuen lateinischen Text des Neuen Testaments hoffte Erasmus sein Programm zur Reform von Kirche und Gesellschaft nach der Norm der *philosophia Christi* verwirklichen zu können. Die erste Veröffentlichung der Übersetzung erfolgte 1516 in Erasmus' *Novum Instrumentum*. Bis in das 17. Jahrhundert erschienen ungefähr 250 Editionen.

Mit dieser Übersetzung ist ein historisches Problem verbunden: es steht nicht genau fest, wann sie entstanden ist. In diesem Beitrag soll das Entstehungsdatum von Erasmus' Übersetzung näher untersucht werden. Es soll dargelegt werden, dass Erasmus spätestens 1512 mit dieser Arbeit begonnen hat.

Bis vor kurzem ging man aufgrund der Autorität von P.S. Allen davon aus, dass Erasmus seine Übersetzung des Neuen Testaments 1505 – 1506, während seines Aufenthaltes in England, angefertigt hat.[2] Diese Datierung stützte sich auf die Jahreszahlen ''1506'' und ''1509'', die in den Kolophonen der Handschriften genannt werden, in denen eine Abschrift der Übersetzung zu finden ist. A.J. Brown hat 1985 jedoch unumstösslich aufgezeigt, dass die Jahreszahlen sich lediglich auf den Text der Vulgata beziehen, der ebenfalls in den Handschriften anzutreffen ist.[3] Brown hat bewiesen, dass die Übersetzung von Erasmus erst später, d.h. nach der Vulgata, in die Handschriften übernommen wurde, und zwar erst in den 20er Jahren des 16. Jahrhunderts. Der Text muss aus einer gedruckten Ausgabe von Erasmus' Übersetzung stammen. Dies hat 1985 auch Carlos Gilly vermerkt.[4]

Die Kolophone der Handschriften bilden also für eine frühe Datierung von Erasmus' Übersetzung auf 1505 – 1506 keine Grundlage mehr. Brown schlug daher vor, Erasmus' Arbeit an der Übersetzung des Neuen Testaments in Übereinstimmung mit den Mitteilungen zu datieren, die er selbst nach dem Erscheinen des *Novum Instrumentum* in seiner Korrespondenz und in Apologien darüber gemacht hat. Nach diesen eigenen Mitteilungen ist es bis zu seiner Ankunft in Basel, im August 1514, nie sein Ziel gewesen, eine neue Übersetzung zu machen. Die Idee einer neuen Übersetzung sei ihm erst in Basel von Freunden suggeriert worden, als Froben bereits im Begriff war mit dem Druck der *Annotationes* zu beginnen, d.h. 1515.[5]

Nun steht ausser Zweifel, dass Erasmus, der alles in seinem Leben in grösster Eile tat, seiner neuen Übersetzung nach seiner Ankunft in Basel noch ihre definitive Form geben musste. Es existieren jedoch Hinweise darauf, dass er nicht erst nach seiner Ankunft in Basel im August 1514, sondern bereits spätestens 1512, während seines Aufenthaltes in England (1511–1514), damit begonnen hat.

Für ein richtiges Verständnis der Sache ist es wichtig, sich zuerst über den Charakter von Erasmus' neuer Übersetzung im klaren zu sein. Sie ist, wie gesagt, keine radikal neue Übersetzung aus dem Griechischen, sondern eine Bearbeitung der alten Vulgata. Das altkirchliche Latein der Vulgata war nach Erasmus' Maßstäben rhetorisch unzweckmäßig. Darum änderte er unter Heranziehung griechischer Handschriften die Worte und Konstruktionen im Vulgatatext, die ihm zu unklassisch, zu unelegant oder zu undeutlich erschienen. Dies alles geschah mit dem Ziel, die Botschaft des Neuen Testaments besser und effektiver zum Ausdruck zu bringen. Erasmus brachte außerdem die Textform der Vulgata textkritisch mit der byzantinischen Textform der von ihm herangezogenen griechischen Handschriften in Übereinstimmung. All' diese Änderungen erfolgten allerdings in einem bereits existierenden Text der Vulgata, d.h. in einem Exemplar einer gedruckten Ausgabe der Vulgata. Darin strich Erasmus bestimmte Worte und ersetzte sie durch andere. Das setzte er in den Ausgaben seines eigenen Neuen Testaments fort. Die fünfte Edition seines *Novum Testamentum* (1535) bestand schließlich zu 40 Prozent aus geändertem Text der Vulgata, während 60 Prozent beibehalten worden war.

Nun kann man eine Vulgata, in der 40 Prozent geändert worden ist, nicht mehr die Vulgata nennen. Erasmus' Übersetzung ist demnach tatsächlich etwas anderes als die Vulgata. Sie ist allerdings auch keine völlig neue Übersetzung: sie bleibt eine humanistisch-rhetorische Revision der Vulgata. Um sie zu charakterisieren, sprach Erasmus selbst von seiner ''Verbesserung'' der bestehenden lateinischen Übersetzung: seiner *correctio*, seiner *emendatio* oder seiner *castigatio*.

Besonders der letztgenannte Ausdruck ist für uns von Bedeutung. Erasmus verwendete ihn 1516 in der *Apologia*, mit der er seine neue Übersetzung gegen die drohende Kritik konservativer Gegner verteidigte. Er fürchtete, daß man ihm vorwerfen würde, er wolle seine neue Übersetzung die Stelle der Vulgata einnehmen lassen. Das ist nicht der Fall, sagt Erasmus: ''Denen diese Ausgabe (die Vulgata) gefällt—weder verurteile ich sie, noch ändere ich sie—, diesen soll ihre Ausgabe bleiben. Sie wird ja durch unsere Übersetzung (*nostra castigatio*) nicht verletzt ...''.[6]

Mit dem Ausdruck *castigatio* meint Erasmus hier nichts anderes als seine neue lateinische Übersetzung, *nicht* auch noch die *Annotationes*. Das geht aus der Art hervor, in der er hier seine *castigatio* der Vulgata gegenüberstellt. Es erweist sich außerdem aus dem folgenden Satz in der *Apologia*: ''Die Vulgata möge in den Schulen gelesen, in den Kirchen gesungen, bei den Predigten zitiert werden; das verhindert niemand. Folgendes möchte ich mich jedoch zu versprechen getrauen: Wer die unsere (*sc.* unsere *castigatio*) zu Hause liest, wird die seine (die Vulgata) besser erkennen''. Daß Erasmus sich hier mit *castigatio* auf eine Übersetzung und nicht auf seine *Annotationes* bezieht, geht schließlich auch aus der Anwendung von *castigare* in einer späteren Passage der Apologie aus dem Jahre 1527 hervor. Dort klagt Erasmus über konservative Theologen, die über seine Übersetzungsarbeit ausrufen: ''Daß es eine nicht zu tolerierende Untat sei, die Evangelien zu verbessern, das Magnificat (Lk. 1: 46ff.) zu säubern (*castigare*), das Gebet des Herrn zu ändern.''[7]

Daher zielt der Gebrauch von *castigatio* und *castigare* bei Erasmus im Zusammenhang mit seiner Arbeit am Neuen Testament auf eine Revision der Vulgata, deren Resultat seine eigene Übersetzung ist. *Castigatio* und *castigare* können bei Erasmus auch die folgenden Bedeutungen haben:

2) die pädagogische Zurechtweisung und Bestrafung von Kindern;[8]

3) die textkritische Emendation und Edition eines Textes;[9]

4) die stilistische Verbesserung einer noch nicht vollendeten Prosakomposition oder eines Gedichtes;[10]

5) Korrektur lesen.[11]

Die häufigste Bedeutung ist jedoch: das Revidieren, Verbessern und Ergänzen eines literarischen Werkes im Hinblick auf eine sowohl stilistisch, als auch rhetorisch und inhaltlich verbesserte Ausgabe. In dieser letzten Bedeutung verwendet Erasmus *castigare* und *castigatio* in bezug auf seine lateinische Übersetzung des Neuen Testaments: diese Übersetzung soll eine Verbesserung, *castigatio*, der Vulgata sein.

Hierauf bezog sich Erasmus auch in seinem Brief an Servatius Rogerus vom 8. Juli 1514, als er schrieb: *castigavi totum Novum Testamentum*. Dies kann nicht auf die Festlegung eines griechischen Textes zielen, da Erasmus erst nach seiner Ankunft in Basel, Ende August 1514, auf Drängen von Frobens Mitarbeiter Nikolaus Gerbel, den Entschluß faßte, den griechischen Text herauszugeben. Ein Bezug auf das Schreiben der *Annotationes* ist ebenfalls nicht möglich. Erstens nennt Erasmus die *Annotationes* im direkt folgenden: *et supra mille loca annotavi*.[12] Zweitens ist seine neue Übersetzung zweieinhalb Monate später fertig. Das geht aus seinem Brief an Jakob Wimpfeling vom 21. September 1514 hervor. Darin spricht Erasmus von seinem Vorhaben, das *Novum Testamentum a me versum*

in Druck zu geben.[13] Sollte die Übersetzung in irgendeiner Form, wie
vorläufig auch immer, im September 1514 fertig gewesen sein, dann müs-
sen sich Erasmus' Worte *castigavi totum Novum Testamentum* vom Juli 1514
ebenfalls auf seine Übersetzung beziehen.

Es existiert jedoch noch eine frühere Passage in Erasmus' Korrespondenz, in der er von seiner *castigatio Novi Testamenti* als etwas spricht, woran
er arbeitet. Im Herbst des Jahres 1512 schrieb er aus London an Peter Gillis: *Absolvam castigationem Novi Testamenti*, ''Ich werde meine Revision des
Neuen Testaments vollenden'' (Ep. 264, 13–14). Wie wir sahen benutzte
Erasmus 1516 und 1514 *castigare* und *castigatio* im Zusammenhang mit
dem Neuen Testament für die verbesserte Ausgabe der lateinischen Übersetzung. Es gibt keinen Grund anzunehmen, daß *castigatio* hier, im Jahre
1512, etwas anderes bedeutet. Allerdings implizierte diese *castigatio* auch
das Vergleichen von griechischen und lateinischen Handschriften mit der
gedruckten Vulgata. Das zeigt sich in einem Brief, den Erasmus am
11. Juli 1513 an Colet schrieb (Ep. 270, 58–61). Hierin spricht Erasmus
von seinen *castigationes* des Neuen Testaments und der Werke von Hieronymus. Er präzisiert, daß die *castigatio* des Neuen Testaments den Vergleich (*collatio*) von Handschriften umfaßt. Aber der Vergleich mit Handschriften ergab zwei Dinge: a) interessante Lesarten von griechischen
und lateinischen Handschriften, und b) darauf gestützte Änderungen im
Vulgatatext. Erasmus beschrieb seine Arbeitsmethode am 8. Juli 1514
genau: ''Aufgrund eines Vergleiches mit griechischen und alten Handschriften habe ich das gesamte Neue Testament korrigiert'', *Ex Graecorum
et antiquorum codicum collatione castigavi totum Novum Testamentum*. Erasmus
notierte also Varianten mit der Hand in den Margen eines Exemplares
einer gedruckten Vulgata. Gleichzeitig brachte er mit der Hand Änderungen im gedruckten Text der Vulgata an. Dieses handschriftliche
Material erweiterte er im Laufe mehrerer Jahre. Mit diesem Material
(einer Vulgata mit handschriftlichen Korrekturen im Text und handschriftlichen Varianten und anderen Aufzeichnungen in der Marge)
reiste Erasmus im August 1514 nach Basel. Einen vollendeten Text seiner
Übersetzung in einer separaten Abschrift hatte er zu dem Zeitpunkt noch
nicht. Das einzige, was er besaß, war ein Vulgatadruck mit seinen handschriftlichen Verbesserungen und Aufzeichnungen. Wesentlich ist jedoch, daß Erasmus spätestens 1512 mit den Verbesserungen begonnen
hat. Denn es gibt keinen Grund anzunehmen, daß seine *castigatio* des
Neuen Testaments (*absolvam castigationem Novi Testamenti*) 1512 etwas anderes ist, als in den Jahren 1514 und 1516.

Es gibt noch andere Angaben, die darauf hinweisen, daß Erasmus nicht
erst nach seiner Reise nach Basel auf die Idee kam, eine neue lateinische
Übersetzung des Neuen Testaments anzufertigen, sondern daß er bereits

vor August 1514 an einer solchen Übersetzung gearbeitet hat. Zwei dieser Hinweise verdienen es, hier noch erwähnt zu werden.

Erstens sah Erasmus sich selbst bereits im Juli 1514, sofern es seine Arbeit am Neuen Testament betraf, als einen zweiten Hieronymus. Das wird aus seiner Mitteilung deutlich: *Ex graecorum et antiquorum codicum collatione castigavi totum Novum Testamentum.*[14] Die Kombination *graeci et antiqui* in diesem Satz ist merkwürdig und auffallend. Man hätte eher *graeci et latini* oder *recentes et antiqui* erwartet. Die befremdliche Kombination, die Erasmus verwendet, ist jedoch eine Reminiszenz an eine ähnliche Mitteilung von Hieronymus im Prolog zu seiner lateinischen Revision der vier Evangelien. Hierin sagt er, daß er die existierende lateinische Übersetzung (die Vetus Latina) mit Hilfe eines ''Vergleiches mit griechischen Manuskripten, allerdings alten'': *codicum graecorum . . . collatione, sed veterum*, revidiert und bearbeitet hat.[15] Erasmus' Worte *Ex graecorum et antiquorum codicum collatione castigavi Novum Testamentum* vom 8. Juli 1514 sind eine Imitation dieses Satzes. Bereits zu dem Zeitpunkt betrachtete Erasmus sich also als eine Art ''zweiten Hieronymus''. Das kann jedoch nur dann der Fall gewesen sein, wenn er bereits damals an einer Revision der lateinischen Bibelübersetzung gearbeitet hat. Erasmus muß daher vor Juli 1514 mit seiner Übersetzungsarbeit am Neuen Testament begonnen haben.

Zweitens schrieb Erasmus, als er 1515 oder Anfang 1516 seine *Apologia* schrieb, die vorn im *Novum Instrumentum* abgedruckt werden sollte, daß seine neue lateinische Übersetzung des Neuen Testaments das Resultat von zwei *recognitiones* sei, d.h. zwei Revisionen der Vulgata. Erasmus unterscheidet hier eine *prima recognitio* und eine *posterior recognitio*.[16] Für die *prima recognitio* soll er vier, für die *posterior recognitio* fünf griechische Manuskripte herangezogen haben. Es steht auf jeden Fall fest, daß Erasmus in Basel ab August 1514 griechische Handschriften verglichen hat. Es steht ebenfalls fest, daß er in England, d.h. zuletzt in den Jahren 1511–1514, griechische Handschriften, u.a. Minuskel 69, verglichen hat.[17] Es ist darum äußerst wahrscheinlich, daß die *prima recognitio* des lateinischen Textes des Neuen Testaments, die Erasmus in seiner *Apologia* von 1516 erwähnt, 1511–1514 in England stattgefunden hat. Die erste *recognitio* fällt dann in die Periode zwischen 1511 und 1514, die zweite zwischen 1514 und 1516. Der Unterschied, den Erasmus zwischen den beiden *recognitiones* macht, macht es auf jeden Fall plausibel, daß er bereits während seiner Jahre in England an seiner lateinischen Übersetzung des Neuen Testaments gearbeitet hat.

Zusammenfassend können wir sagen, daß Erasmus mit der Revision der lateinischen Übersetzung des Neuen Testaments, d.h. mit der Arbeit an seiner eigenen Übersetzung, während seines Aufenthaltes in England zwischen 1511 und 1514, aber spätestens 1512, begonnen haben muß.

Nach der Veröffentlichung vom *Novum Instrumentum* im März 1516 behauptete Erasmus immer wieder, daß er ursprünglich nicht seine eigene neue Übersetzung drucken lassen wollte, sondern die Vulgata, und daß er erst den Entschluß zur Publikation seiner eigenen Übersetzung gefaßt habe, als Froben bereits im Begriff war, mit dem Drucken vom *Novum Instrumentum* zu beginnen.[18]

Diese Darstellung entspricht offensichtlich nicht der Wahrheit, da Erasmus bereits am 21. September 1514 sein Vorhaben, seine eigene Übersetzung drucken zu lassen, zum Ausdruck gebracht hatte (Ep. 305, 222–224). Mit dem Druck des griechischen und lateinischen Bibeltextes im *Novum Instrumentum* hatte man am 11. September 1515, ein Jahr später, noch nicht begonnen, da Nikolaus Gerbel damals noch das gesamte Layout der Edition bei Erasmus zur Diskussion stellen konnte (Ep. 352, 7ff.). Mit dem Druck der *Annotationes* wurde noch später begonnen.[19] Erasmus' Vorstellung der Tatsachen, die er ab Juni 1516 gab, ist daher nachweisbar falsch. Der Grund für diese spätere, verkehrte Darstellung war, daß er sich entschuldigen wollte, als die Kritik an seiner Übersetzung über ihn hereinbrach. Erasmus wollte es im nachhinein so erscheinen lassen, als ob er ursprünglich gar nicht die Absicht gehabt hätte, eine eigene Übersetzung zu veröffentlichen. Freunde hätten ihn erst im allerletzten Moment dazu überredet. Es sei nicht seine eigene Idee gewesen und die Übersetzungsarbeit sei nur in aller Eile geschehen.

Man kann Erasmus' spätere Äußerungen möglicherweise so interpretieren, daß er bis September 1514 wenigstens nicht die Absicht gehabt hat, eine neue Übersetzung zu publizieren, wohl aber daran gearbeitet hat. Selbst wenn man auf diese Art und Weise die Ehrlichkeit von Erasmus retten wollte, entkommt man der Schlußfolgerung nicht, daß er seit spätestens 1512 an einer neuen Übersetzung gearbeitet hat. Er mag dann vielleicht nicht unmittelbar das Vornehmen gehabt haben, diese zu publizieren, er hat in jedem Fall seit 1512 daran gearbeitet.[20]

ANMERKUNGEN

1   H.J. de Jonge, ''The Character of Erasmus' Translation of the New Testament,'' *Journal of Medieval and Renaissance Studies* 14 (1984), S. 81–87.
2   Allen, II, 164.
3   A.J. Brown, ''The Date of Erasmus' Latin Translation of the New Testament,'' *Transactions of the Cambridge Bibliographical Society* 8 (1984), S. 351–380.
4   Carlos Gilly, *Spanien und der Basler Buchdruck bis 1600*, Basel 1985, S. 153, Anm. 79 i.

5 *Responsio ad Iuvenem gerontodidascalum, LB* IX, 987A: "Sed amici quidam improbis instinctibus huc perpulere reclamantem, et cum iam adornaretur editio Annotationum,
   novaretur et contextus."
6 H. Holborn, ed., *Desiderius Erasmus Roterodamus: Ausgewählte Werke*, München 1933,
   S. 168: "Quibus haec placet editio, quam ego nec damno nec muto, huic sua manet
   editio. Siquidem ea nostra castigatione non laeditur." Vgl. Gerhard B. Winkler,
   Erasmus von Rotterdam. In Novum Testamentum Praefationes, Darmstadt 1967, S. 94–95.
7 Holborn, S. 169; Winkler, S. 100–101.
8 Z.B., *Allen* 154, Z. 11; *Apologia ad ea quae Iac. Lopis Stunica taxaverat, ASD* IX-2, S. 62,
   krit. App. zu Z. 38.
9 Z.B., *Allen* 308, 2; *Allen* 298, 11–12.
10 Z.B., *Allen* 475, 15–16; *Apologia ad ea quae Iac. Lopis Stunica taxaverat, ASD* IX–2,
   S. 68, 2, 'kritisieren'; *Allen* 211, 90; 241, 29; *Allen* 95, 40; 139, 109; *ASD* IX–2,
   S. 70, 182.
11 Z.B., *Allen* 356, 12; *ASD* IX–2, 66, 132; *Allen* 396, 376. An diesen drei Stellen
   gebraucht Erasmus *castigator* mit der Bedeutung 'Korrektor'.
12 *Allen* 296, 156–157.
13 *Allen* 305, 222–223.
14 *Allen* 296, 155–156.
15 R. Weber, ed., *Biblia Sacra iuxta Vulgatam versionem*, Stuttgart 1975², S. 1515.
16 Holborn, S. 166, Z. 4–5. In der vierten Ausgabe des *Novum Testamentum* (1527) hat
   Erasmus *posteriore* in *secunda* geändert und eine Mitteilung über die dritte und vierte
   Ausgabe eingefügt. Offenbar hat er damals (1527) selber den ursprünglichen Sinn
   von *prima* und *posterior recognitio* nicht mehr recht verstanden. Jetzt handelt es sich bei
   der zweiten *recognitio* nicht mehr um die Vorbereitungen für die erste Ausgabe, sondern um die zweite Ausgabe. Ursprünglich aber bezogen sich *prima* und *posterior* beide
   auf die Vorbereitungen für die erste Ausgabe von 1516.
17 Siehe Brown, "The Date", S. 367–368; Erasmus, *Apologia respondens ad ea quae Iac.
   Lopis Stunica taxaverat, ASD* IX–2, S. 192: "At ego illi Rhodiensi oppono tot vetusta
   exemplaria, quae nos vidimus partim in Anglia, partim in Brabantia, partim Basi-
   leae." *Responsio ad Iuvenem gerontodidascalum, LB* IX, 986: "collationis negotium
   peregeram in Anglia et in Brabantia".
18 Brown, "The Date", S. 372–374. Siehe z.B. die *Responsio ad Iuvenem gerontodidascalum, LB* IX, 987A: "Sed amici quidam improbis instinctibus huc perpulere
   reclamantem, ut cum iam adornaretur editio Annotationum, novaretur et contextus".
19 H. Holeczek, *Erasmus von Rotterdam. Novum Instrumentum. Basel 1516. Faksimile-
   Neudruck*, Stuttgart-Bad Cannstatt 1986, S. XIII.
20 Frau Andrea Fuhrmann (Leiden) danke ich für die Übersetzung dieses Beitrags aus
   dem Niederländischen.

D.F.S. THOMSON

ERASMUS AND TEXTUAL SCHOLARSHIP IN THE LIGHT OF SIXTEENTH-CENTURY PRACTICE

In the pregnant words *nos vetera instauramus: nova non prodimus*,[1] Erasmus identifies his function as that of a restorer of ancient things—ancient *texts*, since we are in the sphere of Good Letters, and by implication the wisdom contained in them. Often, he describes himself as a "grammarian", which in the tradition of Quintilian refers to literary criticism as well as language. Applied to existing texts the word "grammarian" converts into "editor"; that in principle Erasmus saw himself overwhelmingly as an editor, albeit with an ideal of edification to guide him in his choice of tasks, is attested by his practice. We must therefore ask how he discharged a function he considered so important, and whether, concentrating upon it his high intelligence, he substantially advanced this branch of study.

Seneca

Erasmus tells us that in early youth he preferred Seneca to Cicero. But there was a more immediate reason why in 1515 he set about editing Seneca's works. Beatus Rhenanus had just finished publishing the so-called *Apocolocyntosis* or *Ludus de morte Claudii*, attributed to Seneca. He had done so without any MS, simply reprinting "with minor modifications" the abysmally bad *editio princeps* of only two years earlier by "Caius Sylvanus", which in its turn was based on a single bad MS. But Rhenanus was Erasmus' friend and *protégé*, and needed encouragement. (Later, in 1529, he was able to redeem himself by the timely acquisition of the now lost *codex Wissenburgensis*, the readings of which were similar to those of the cardinal manuscript *L*; an enormous step forward in editing at once resulted.) Though Erasmus desired to incorporate Rhenanus' work in his 1515 Seneca, he was called to England in May and stayed there for a year. The oversight of the Seneca was given to the still inexperienced Rhenanus and the enthusiastic but incompetent Wilhelm Nesen, who botched the job of correcting; this left Erasmus with an acute sense of failure, which drove him to re-edit all of Seneca in 1529. Did Erasmus too search energetically for better MSS, to be the foundation of his own recovery of editorial self-respect? Yes, he did, though some of those whose readings he sought through friends in England had already disappeared. But different parts of the Senecan corpus are carried by different MS traditions, so that the hunt could not be uniformly successful. One tradition where Erasmus drew readings from an early Carolingian MS, now known to be the extant archetype, is that of the *De beneficiis* and *De clementia*. We can illustrate this from *De clem.* 2.6.4, where the archetype (N)[2] has *estitationem*. From his knowledge that in Carolingian minuscule the letters *e* and *o*, *t* and *c*, are easily interchanged, Erasmus was able to restore the correct reading *oscitationem*, a good example of his divinatory skill. In the corrupt later MSS derived ultimately from the pure N text, the word appears as *(a)estimata*, the result of the scribes' unfamiliarity with Carolingian errors and their attempts to manufacture "sense". In the preface to the 1529 edition[3] Erasmus claims to have removed countless *portenta* with the aid of various codices "inter quos erant aliquot mirae vetustatis". How many *aliquot* signifies is unclear, but in one passage (*De benef.* 6.11.2) we find, besides a citation of the reading *error* in N (which Erasmus calls *Longobardicus*, a word he applies to Carolingian minuscule) a statement that he himself conjectured *erro*, a less familiar noun, and presently found it in the *codex Basiliensis*, a now lost but apparently good MS which only Erasmus mentions. The same preface tells us that for the *Naturales Quaestiones* Erasmus was lent what he calls a *codex* (but, as often, he means by this a printed edition) formerly belonging to, and containing emendations by, R. Agricola, "sed in multis, ut apparebat, divinationem ingenii secutus magis quam exemplaris vetusti fidem"; that is, Agricola did not draw his corrections from a MS but produced them by intelligent guesswork. Erasmus' own attitude to this activity is made clear in the words of the preface: "Divinationi non temere indulsimus, experimento docti quam id tutum non sit. Et tamen alicubi divinandum fuit, nec raro feliciter cessit coniectura, nisi me fallunt omnia." That this was no idle boast may be illustrated by citing a very few of the improvements first made in the text by Erasmus. In the *Letters to Lucilius*, at 15.4 Erasmus suggested *saltus Saliaris* for the meaningless *saltus saltaris*, drawing on his knowledge of Roman antiquities; at 73.7 his linguistic *flair* enabled him to replace *ita communia* with *ista communia*; at 86.18 he was the first to print *teneras* in place of the *ceteras* offered by all MSS, which is meaningless in its context (*teneras* has been found as a marginal variant in some of the *deteriores*)). At Ep. 56.2, confronted with the non-word *sordalum* (all the MSS have it), Erasmus drew from his vast memory the rare word *scordalum*, and substituted it (rightly).

In his preface,[4] Erasmus gives for the benefit of *studiosa iuventus* a list of the peculiarities, or some of them, of Seneca's style. Among these is the habitual use of *tamquam* in the sense of *velut*; he makes use of this at least once in emending the text. In the first letter, Seneca uses the phrase *aliud agere* in its normal Latin sense of "inattention": Erasmus points out what contortions ignorant critics have got into when they tried to explain it without a knowledge of Latin idiom, and comments: "Quam est fecunda

inscitia! Atque haec quaestio magnis voluminibus agitata est . . .'' There
are, he explains, two special causes of error in the MSS of Seneca. One
is the Senecan style itself, which is both affected and obscure. The other
is rooted in the credulity of those Christians in late antiquity who believed
that Seneca himself was a Christian. To the resulting veneration of Seneca's memory among the semi-literate we owe, Erasmus acknowledges, the
survival of so much of the Senecan corpus—"si tamen hoc est
superesse"—that is, in the hopelessly garbled state of the tradition as it
existed in Erasmus' youth, which left this author both unprofitable and
unpleasing to read. We have now seen how Erasmus addressed himself to
these problems, and why his two editions of Seneca are important. It
should be stressed, as a mark of Erasmus' standing in criticism, that he
made unusually effective use of external historical data such as the *testimo-
nia* to be found in ancient sources. (He learned this from Lorenzo Valla,[5]
and applied it widely in the second edition, though hardly at all in the
first.) The author must be seen in his context, stylistically as well as historically; and both these tests must be applied to the question of authenticity.
It is easy, of course, to settle this question in regard to a collection of moral
maxims, masquerading as Seneca's, which *inter alia* referred to the Devil;
but there are more complicated problems, of the same general sort. Similar problems of authenticity infested the corpus of St. Jerome's works, to
the editing of which Erasmus was later to address himself; and here too,
as we shall see, the historical approach proved triumphantly successful.
Yet there was another and a very important respect in which the historical
way of considering a problem failed to come to Erasmus' rescue when it
might have helped him once again to transcend the standards prevailing
in his time. To put it briefly, he failed (as Politian who grasped the principle of *eliminatio codicum descriptorum* had not entirely failed) to view the
reconstruction of a text as itself a historical enterprise. Perhaps the moment when he came nearest to understanding this was when he compared
two English MSS and found such a lack of agreement in their *errors* that
he at once realized that he was in the presence of two separate branches
of a text-tradition, and made the comment that it should be possible for
a scholar to get at what lay behind such divergences, just as a judge may
arrive at the truth by sifting the evidence produced by a number of lying
witnesses. But he did not follow this up. He did not draw the inference
that manuscripts should be systematically *collated* (though others had done
so before his time, Politian for instance), but merely *consulted* them—
intermittently, e.g. when his instinct for language suggested to him that
there might be grounds for suspecting corruption.

Suetonius

The year 1518 saw the publication by Froben, in a single volume, of three Roman historical texts to all of which Erasmus lent his name as editor. These texts were of widely differing quality. That of Ammianus Marcellinus was no more than a pirated copy of the edition by Petrus Castellus, "who disfigured the already poor and truncated text (of Sabinus, 1474, who merely reproduced the worst among the later MSS) with his own monstrously bad conjectures."[6] For the *Historia Augusta*, Erasmus was able to use the *codex Murbacensis* (now lost, except for a recently-found fragment) of the 9th century, which may well have been copied directly from P, the parent of the tradition.[7] As for Suetonius, Erasmus unfortunately missed the best codex of all, the *Memmianus*—Turnebus seems to have been the first scholar to see its merits—and had to be satisfied with an inferior one, the *Torniacensis*, which came to him by the fortuitous circumstance that his patron, William Mountjoy, was appointed governor of Tournai during the English occupation under Henry VIII, and there found in the monastery[8] of St. Martin a codex he thought likely to interest his friend Erasmus. Several aspects of Erasmus' way of editing Latin texts can be conveniently illustrated by means of his Suetonius: 1. Emendation based on a knowledge of Greek; at *Divus Julius* 32 – 33, where the reading was *Iacta alea est*, Erasmus counsels us to read *Iacta esto alea* since, as he points out, the Greek of Plutarch's narrative uses the imperative in the famous phrase (*"Let* the die be cast"). 2. Use of previous commentaries by scholars of whom Erasmus approved; in this case, P. Beroaldus, whose valuable notes are frequently quoted by Erasmus, e.g. at I.50. 3. Attention is drawn to unusual words, and to syntactical irregularities, such as *fungi munera* (for *muneribus*). 4. Parallels are cited from other authors in matters of language (*"decollare* etiam apud Senecam"").[9] 5. Explanatory comments are derived from Erasmus' wide knowledge of Roman antiquities (*"Latinitas* ius Latii, ut *civitas* ius urbis"). 6. Metres are identified where verse is printed, both in Latin and (as at *Claud.* 1) in Greek. 7. The provision of an Index to the notes; in this instance for *new* expressions, and also for *Greek* words and expressions. 8. At *Otho* 7, Erasmus gives a Greek quotation, τί γάρ μοι καὶ μακροῖς αὐλοῖς;—noting that a few MSS have the corrupt reading ἀσύλοις instead of αὐλοῖς. He opts for αὐλοῖς, recognizing here a Greek proverb, for a fuller discussion of which he refers the reader to *Adagiorum Chiliades*.

Cicero, De officiis

In a prefatory letter, Erasmus claims to have examined many divergent MSS and, by comparing these, to have come closer to the "archetype", by which he must mean the text as it left Cicero's hands, than anyone be fore him. In fact this means only that he has found, as he says in the same context, some faults never detected before; it does not mean that he anticipated the "method of Lachmann",[10] or evolved any other consistent method of comparing and evaluating MSS. He again stresses linguistic knowledge as a tool of textual criticism; in particular the importance of avoiding rigid criteria of Latinity in restoring readings—for there is some unusual Latin even in Cicero. The other great strength of Erasmus as a critic, his grasp of antiquities, emerges e.g. in an unusually long note near the end of Book II.[11] Here he dismisses the vulgate *ad medium ianue* and rightly restores *ad medium Ianum*, explaining it from Horace *Satires* 2.3.18. He goes on to show his sound grasp of palaeography and the habits of scribes:[12] "Fortassis notula superposita, *um*, erat obscurior. Ea sublata, *ianu* (i.e. ianū after the accidental dropping of the too-faint virgula) nihil significabat; itaque scriba fecit *ianuae*; aut aliquis semidoctus, qui non legerat Horatium, eoque non intelligens quid esset medius Ianus, vertit in mediū ianuae . . . Nec id miror accidisse vel scribae, vel erudituli cuiuspiam et audaculi vitio; magis miror in opere tam celebri . . . tam insignem mendam hactenus a nemine fuisse animadversam." A good example of the note based on Latinity is this, from Book III: "Praefracte defendere] Cicero *praefractos* vocat qui a sententia non possunt abduci, quos (nisi fallor) Graeci vocant αὐθάδεις. *Praefracte* pertinaciter. Hoc annotavi, quod eruditi quidam contendunt has voces non esse Latinas."

Terence

This edition illustrates several characteristics of Erasmus' method: 1. Use of an indifferent text-base; 2. Spasmodic conjecture, often with considerable acumen; 3. "Practical" aims in annotation (to educate or edify); 4. Textual emendation based on a knowledge of metre; 5. Use, for critical purposes, of a related text (in this case the commentary on Terence by Aelius Donatus); 6. Reduced scale of annotation in the later parts of the work.

1. Erasmus took for his base the recent edition by R. Stephanus (Paris 1529). Not only are there many significant agreements in readings between them, such as the accidental omission of *affuisse* at *Adelphoe* 356, but these two alone place *Phormio* after *Hecyra*, thus undoing the change made in the 1476 edition by Calphurnius who had reversed the MS order of these plays (and been blindly followed by editors of the next two generations, thus showing how easily an influential humanistic edition could create a "monogenous" tradition among its successors).[13] It was perhaps more through good luck than good judgment on Erasmus' part that this exposed him to the indirect influence of a really old MS, namely that given

to Stephanus by his father-in-law Jodocus Badius; not only did this MS put the *Phormio* last, it included the Greek words which the XVc MSS either wholly or partially omitted. We may well ask why Erasmus made no use of a still earlier MS, the superb Codex Bembinus (IV/Vc), one of the few Latin MSS surviving from late antiquity. True, it was still in the hands of the Bembo family; but Politian had been allowed to inspect it in 1491, and had made a collation. Nor is it proper to object that, with much other work, the collation remained in the notebooks of Politian, and so unavailable, until after the latter's death; for Benedictus Philologus, in his Florence edition of 1505, clearly records his obligations to it.

2. A more cheerful picture of Erasmus as a Terentian critic is presented by an examination of his positive suggestions for healing the text. These are often directed towards the production of metre out of non-metre (see 4 below), but are particularly interesting when they invoke (as Stephanus had done before: see 1 above), the evidence furnished by Donatus, as at *Andria* 817, where Erasmus admits that one way to repair the metre of the line given as *optume hospes pol Crito antiquom obtines* would be to add *morem* at the beginning, but rejects this solution since the word does not appear in Donatus. (To the credit of Calphurnius it must be said that he was the first editor to print the commentary of Donatus round the text of Terence.) Erasmus suggests *opportune*; the reading of the *Bembinus* is *o optume*, but either will give a metrical line, which is what Erasmus aimed at.

3. The dedicatory letter is, unusually, addressed to children: two brothers, the elder 13 years of age,[14] the younger a mere 7. Not altogether surprisingly, however; for as Beatus Rhenanus tells us (and Erasmus himself confirms it), Erasmus as *puer* was as familiar with all of Terence as with his own fingers; and to this he attributed, as well as to a similar mastery of Horace, his grasp of Latin idiom in later life. At all events he commends the reading of Terence as an unsurpassed way of acquiring *Romani sermonis puritas* in addition to the civilizing and morally beneficial effects of the *disciplinae liberales*. Moreover, the letter continues, it is important to understand the metres of Terence, both to increase the enjoyment and benefit one derives from reading him, and also because a faulty text escapes the notice of those who do not understand metre; and similarly for other poetical authors. So Erasmus adds to his introduction a section *de metris*, giving a description of each metre, together with examples; and the metres are also named in the margins of the text. Erasmus recognizes the special difficulties of Terence's metre for the young, with its complications and numerous resolutions, and expresses the belief that his annotations will bring some light *parum exercitatis*.

4. Something has already been said about this in 2 and 3 above; but the following example, drawn to my attention by Professor J.N. Grant,[15]

shows not only Erasmus' skill in metrical matters but also his knowledge of the habits of scribes and resulting causes of error. At *Andria* 384, Erasmus' text as printed has this: P. egone dicam. D. cur non? P. nunquam faciam. D (for *Dave*). ne nega. This line will not scan either in the metre of the preceding lines or in that of the following lines. We now know, from the Bembine codex, that it should be read *egon* . . . and attached to the following section. Erasmus, however, lacking this information, regarded it as metrically continuing the *septenarii* of the preceding lines, and comments as follows: "Two syllables are missing. What may have been written was *faciam, Dave*: and because the speaker's name (*Dave*) follows, a reader thought the same word had been written twice"; i.e., Erasmus attributes the unmetrical state of the line to haplography. Notice that Erasmus here does not intrude his own reconstruction of the line into the body of the text. At another place (*Eunuchus* 624), where the MSS have the classical form of the vocative, *puer*, Erasmus points out that this gives a metrically defective text (one syllable short) and suggests *puere*—thus invoking his own wide knowledge, this time of archaic Latin forms. One final example: at *Andria* 449, Erasmus prints the line with the unmetrical *puerile est . . . quid est?*, and suggests repairing the metre by reading either *quid id est* or *quidnam est*, either of which would produce a metrical line. In fact *quid id est* is right: it has since Erasmus' time been found in the important MS known as p, which (as Professor M.D. Reeve has recently written) "quite often agrees with the Bembinus against Γ and the others, and sometimes has the truth on its own."[16]

5. See 2 above, on *Andria* 817. At *Eunuchus* 810, Erasmus cites the reading of Donatus and follows Donatus in identifying a haplography of the name *Thais*, due to the insertion of the speaker's name within the line, in exactly the same fashion we have noted under *Andria* 384 (see 4 above). At two places in the *Adelphoe* (37 *ac*; 125 *aliis*), where Erasmus' text agrees with Donatus, the readings in question, though not shared with the tradition in general, are also to be found in Stephanus' edition (see 1 above) and so probably came to Erasmus indirectly, *via* that edition. At *Eunuchus* 257, Erasmus has two reasons for rejecting the added word *aucupes*: (i) it spoils the metre, (ii) it is absent from Donatus; therefore, he concludes, it must be a later addition. In fact it is not in the text of the Bembinus, and the claim in the apparatus criticus of the Kauer-Lindsay *OCT* that it appears among the *scholia* there seems at least to be highly dubious.[17] Similarly at *Eun.* 401, Erasmus applies the same two tests—Donatus and metre—in deciding to retain *quod*: "Donatus legit quod, sed eliditur d" is his note.

6. The first two plays in the collection (*Andria* and *Eunuchus*, at that time) are richly annotated; in *Eun.* alone about seventy lines are furnished

with notes, including many on metre (see 4 above), or suggesting emendations. A good example is at line 10, where Erasmus prints *a thesauro*, adding that others have *a thesauris*, and opines that Terence wrote *a thesauro
is*; thus he seeks to account for the variant readings. After *Eun.*, however,
the number of annotations declines steeply. Apart from the names of
metres which are still added in the margin, the *Heautontimoroumenos* yields
on a rough count only some twenty notes; and half of these merely indicate
the existence of a variant, the source of which Erasmus does not indicate.
(This is true also of the notes to the *Eunuchus*, except when the source is
Donatus.) As for the *Adelphoe*, a quick check reveals a mere seven indications of variants, and little other annotation; in the *Hecyra*, four variants.
The *Phormio*, which comes last in Erasmus' edition, reverses this down-
ward trend to some extent; it has some eighteen recordings of variants,
and two suggestions for restoring the metre of the line by emendation.
Erasmus says he did not think it necessary to give his young readers so
many or such elaborate metrical explanations in the latter part of his edition, deeming that the rules set forth and illustrated in his preface might
by now be thought to have been absorbed by them; but it is not impossible
that, here as elsewhere, excessive haste to finish may have played its
part.[18]

St Jerome

Of all his "Herculean" labours (the word is his own), next to the New
Testament Erasmus valued most highly his own contribution, four
volumes of the Letters, to the Froben Jerome (*Opera Omnia*). Since he had
long complained of a corrupt Latin text in this author's works, we are not
surprised to find that he made many changes. On what were those
changes based? In a book published as recently as 1970 it is claimed that
no MS at all, but an earlier printed edition, was taken as a base-text and
that this was "probably" the Mainz edition of 1470.[19] But in 1935 Fritz
Husner demonstrated that of all previous editions the Mainz edition lay
furthest from Erasmus' text; there is only one identifiable borrowing by
Erasmus from it. As Husner showed, the facts are as follows.[20]

The textual tradition of all known MSS in the parts of Jerome that were
studied and compared for this purpose deviates completely from the text
offered by Erasmus. Now this of course *might* be merely a tribute to his
scholarly acumen; but Husner's relentless investigation of comparative
readings shows beyond a doubt that Erasmus used, as a base-text and also
as printer's copy, one of the two Lyon editions, namely that of 1508,
which in its turn was based, *via* earlier printed editions, on the Rome *princeps* of 1468. This, in all probability, drew its readings from *one* of the later

and worse Renaissance codices, available in Rome itself. Since Erasmus' text agrees with the principal subsequent editions down to Vallarsi and hence to Migne's *Patrologia*, we have, it seems, to consider him responsible for placing the *textus receptus*, or the modern vulgate text, on very shaky foundations indeed. The parallel with the well-known instance of his Greek New Testament will at once spring to mind. In other words, he altogether fails to improve the Humanistic practice—and not, it must be stressed, the *best* Humanistic practice—of the half-century preceding his own; this, too, in an author to whose study he attached more importance than to that of any, next to the Bible. Nevertheless, in spite of faulty principles of editing and a mass of errors, we are indebted to his Jerome for at least two major improvements, for both of which we have found parallels in his classical texts: the exquisite sense of a writer's personal Latin style which enabled Erasmus authoritatively to reject *spuria*, and the historical sense which allowed him to add a Life of Jerome that placed the Saint for the first time in his context of thought, letters and general culture.

Other texts

For *Irenaeus* (1526) Erasmus used three MSS. One, quite recently identified, came from Rome; two were from monasteries, and, as José Ruysschaert showed,[21] Erasmus—who had, incidentally, plenty of time—used one of these, employing the Roman codex to correct the other merely, and not as a base-text; since the gaps in the Roman MS are absent from Erasmus' edition. This MS itself had been affected by conjectures added by Andrea de' Bussi, editor of the 1468 and 1469 Irenaeus. As usual, Bussi's work was imperfect because hurried; but these emendations were largely accepted as they stood by Erasmus, just as if they had what we now call stemmatic authority.

From 1518 to 1527, on and off, Erasmus was busy with an edition of *St. Augustine*'s works. Where did he get his MSS? As usual, he is vague: "I got one (he says) from a monastery in Flanders, the name of which I can't recall at present." What seems clear is that whereas the MSS that Amerbach had hunted up for the 1506 Froben edition, which Froben urged Erasmus to replace with something better, were French and German, of good tradition on the whole, the Low Countries yielded to Erasmus indifferent or poor ones. We have a general statement that in volume 5 Erasmus added "non pauca" from a MS in "Longobardic" (i.e. uncial or minuscule) writing; but there is no list of corrections, and Erasmus fails to warn us when he alters a reading. Like other Humanists, not only does he neglect to name or describe his sources, but he does not make it clear which corrections are his own emendations and which have MS support. In spite of all this the Augustine, too, represents an outstanding example of the value of a profound knowledge of Latin and of personal stylistic usage in detecting spurious work; and again, of the historical method applied to annotation (which is interesting, sometimes consisting of brief and mordant remarks addressed apparently by Erasmus to himself concerning Augustine: βίαιον, "good argument"; ὡς φλυαρεῖ, "what nonsense he talks!"; *soloecismus*, "a solecism", for Erasmus freely criticizes Augustine's Latin).

Similarly trenchant notes can be found in the edition of *Cyprian* (1519), a writer whose Latin *eloquentia*, unlike Augustine's, appealed to Erasmus; e.g., this note: "'Homicide' is here equivalent to 'war'; Cyprian seems not to distinguish these, except that one of them is public, and more are killed; but we are to understand this of an *unjust* war, i.e. the kind to which most, perhaps all, modern wars belong (*ut nunc quidem geruntur*)".[22] For Cyprian at least, Erasmus did his best to find 'new' and better MSS, and says in his correspondence, though oddly enough not in the edition itself, where some of them came from.[23]

Concerning his *Hilary* (1523), the repair of whose text cost him more sweat than even Jerome—not by the fault of scribes but of previous emendators—a point or two may be made. First, Erasmus deserves praise for his alertness to intrusive glosses which, originally intended as marginal or supralinear comment, have slipped into the body of the transmitted text. Arguing historically, Erasmus stresses how tempting it was to add and incorporate comments and additions where a theological doctrine looked for supporting texts; at this point, his principles as an editor and theologian come together and he enters a plea against *periculosa curiositas*, against defining too much, for which he blames the philosophical habit of mind.[24] (Quintilian lists it as one of the virtues of a grammarian—which is what Erasmus called himself—not to know everything.)[25] Turning to Hilary's Latin style, Erasmus calls for a thorough familiarity with its oddities, and argues for their retention in the text. Editors of his day, he says, were far too prone to alter readings if their language did not conform to what the grammars, or "Ciceronian" usage, prescribed—and this was true even, on occasion, with Cicero. (When he dealt with "odd" words in New Testament Greek, the same principle was insisted upon.)

With *Arnobius* (Commentary on the Psalms, 1522) Erasmus similarly stresses the importance of the language. In Ps. 77 the scribe, not understanding Greek as it turns out, had written *quod aures infaciens*, which is meaningless; Erasmus, divining two things at once, that a Greek word lay concealed, and that false word-division had occurred, suggested *quod auxesin faciens*, a palmary emendation which greatly pleased Erasmus himself.

He adds, and here he shows another kind of palaeographical expertise, that "in most kinds of script (as he puts it) the shape of *x* is very similar to that of *r*." In another correction, at Ps. 105, Erasmus expands the word (or abbreviation) *Nova* to "Novato, sive Novatiano"; for "both of them professed the same heresy and left no room for penitence".

As for Erasmus' *New Testament*, which so amply illustrates his virtues and failings as a critic, the most striking facts are well known.[26] In the peripheral essays published along with it, Erasmus outlines for editors his approach to text-criticism and interpretation. Erasmus' first requirement is a knowledge of the original tongues, "without which it is impossible to arrive at a sound understanding of Holy Writ." Next comes the acquisition of information concerning the practical disciplines that have to do with all kinds of human activity. After that, the aspiring philologist may turn his attention to MSS. He must first lay hands on all the *bonae fidei codices* he can reach. Then he must compare what seems to be the oldest and best reading with quotations (of scripture, say) found in the ancient authors. Of course, the text of these external witnesses must also be scrutinized selectively. It may be that the traditional text has become distorted, either through scribal error, or, what is much worse, in a conscious effort at improvement (worse because an ignorant slip may at least leave traces of the true reading, from which that can be reconstructed, whereas deliberate change blots it out). Intrusive glosses on theological grounds are to be especially watched for. When all this has been assessed and put right, we must next make the text clear and also stylistically elegant; if we return to the sources as we do in purging a text of accumulated error, then truth and clarity will guarantee each other at the same time as the language reassumes its classical purity and charm, and hence its power of persuasion. When Erasmus says, in the *Methodus*, "abunde magnus doctor est qui pure docet," he is emphatically not saying "be good, sweet maid, and let who will be clever", or anything remotely similar; he is not advocating the *renunciation* of learning, but on the contrary its *consummation*.[27]

Erasmus goes on to say that the interpretation of a text must closely follow its reconstruction. For interpretation of Holy Writ we ought to use the Fathers alone, especially Origen, who "is to Holy Writ as Donatus is to Terence." In discussing a passage we are to consider who said *what*, to *whom*, in what *period*, on what *occasion* and in *what forms of words*.[28] We are also to keep in mind the whole context, especially the immediately preceding and following passages. We must remember the forms of Biblical expression; a knowledge of the idiom of the Semitic languages may often be helpful. The next stage is to use your text thus improved, and your commentary thus constructed, to reconstitute the *whole* world of the Biblical age, and fit the details into that framework. This is the meaning of Erasmus' injunction *audi sermonem divinum, sed totum audi*. Any obscurities that remain must be explained consistently with the picture so obtained. Finally, turning to his own role as critic and teacher, Erasmus reminds us that he is only an *interpres*, not a *vates* ("prophet"), but it is only from the position of a humble *interpres* that one may hope to reach the gate of Evangelical truth.

"Good literature makes human beings human" (*bonae litterae reddunt hominem*). Taking this as an axiom, Erasmus deduces the importance, in terms of service to humanity, of the editorial function. Since the texts that held the key to wisdom and indeed to salvation were notoriously corrupt, nothing mattered more than to purge these of error and spurious additions. In this sense the activity of the editor of texts becomes the pattern of all research and the ultimate generator of standards in the pursuit of truth. Such are Erasmus' principles, and such is the end he set himself. The quality of his textual criticism is found to be marked by one outstanding virtue, rarely encountered today: an exquisitely sensitive linguistic attunement both to the *nuances* of the Latin written (and spoken) at various periods, and to the personal style of the author against the background of contemporary usage. This enabled him rapidly and with authority to reject spurious and interpolated passages. It also provided the basis for a number of emendations *ingenii ope* bequeathed by Erasmus to modern editions, quite often supported by MSS discovered after his time. Second in importance as a tool of criticism came Erasmus' wide *historical* grasp. Like his stylistic sense, this arose from long immersion in classical and post-classical reading; and not only did it enrich his annotations, but, as we have seen, at times it enabled him to restore the text with certainty where previous Humanists had feebly "corrected" it, thereby showing ignorance of some underlying antique fact.

On the other hand, Erasmus as a scholar suffered from one very serious disability, excessive haste. *Praecipitat omnia*, he says of himself;[29] and in another place, he speaks of his own New Testament as *praecipitatum . . . verius quam editum*.[30] When pressed, he took little trouble to find, or consult, the best MS (thus he missed the chance to base his *NT* on exhaustive reports of the readings of the *Vaticanus*), although he was in principle aware of the importance of doing so; and his critical use of those that chance, or a moderate amount of searching, put in his way was too often cavalier and spasmodic.[31] Moreover, like other Humanists, he habitually devolved on less qualified assistants the drudgery of preparing and correcting the editions to which he put his name. It is quite true that Erasmus "possessed a critical equipment that must have been, at the least, well above the average of his day",[32] if by "equipment" we mean—in addition to intelligence, common sense and wide general knowledge—such assets as an exceptional mastery of Latin, a good memory and an understanding of the habits of scribes and the usual sources of scribal error. Nonetheless, his editions are not, except for Seneca, among the best, as works of *scholarship*. Industrious and painstaking as in many respects he was, he had neither the scholar's perfectionism nor the latter's professional contentiousness, the desire to triumph by establishing a point of fact, or a reading. Budé, the pioneer of investigative research into certain aspects of antiquity, described Erasmus' *De Copia* as "trifling", and therein missed the point of it, which was the enrichment of stylistic competence, itself a marvellous instrument of textual criticism, but one in which Budé himself was markedly defective.[33] As for Erasmus, what *he* stigmatizes as "trifling" is the "Ciceronian" movement which would remove all possibility of an effective individual style in writing Latin. Infected by this movement, editors had tried to banish, from the text of certain writers, readings that seemed to them to embody "irregular" locutions; Erasmus points out, more clearly before and perhaps even than anyone after him, that "correction" such as this is worse for the text than inherited error. In this, as in other ways, he makes a contribution of a highly personal kind.[34]

NOTES

1   *Allen* 1153, 185–186.
2   On N (an *extant* archetype, ca. 800) see L.D. Reynolds (ed.), *Texts and Transmissions* (Oxford: 1983), hereinafter referred to as *T & T*, p. 363.
3   *Allen* 2091, 97–99.
4   *Allen* 2091, 259ff.
5   On Erasmus' debt to Valla (and to Politian) see also E.J. Kenney, "The Character of Humanist Philology," in R.R. Bolgar (ed.), *Classical Influences on European Culture 500–1500* (Cambridge: 1971), pp. 124–126: "(Politian) recognized the problem as essentially one of the control of sources." Cf. also H. Lloyd-Jones, (*Times Literary Supplement*, June 25, 1976): "Men like Erasmus and Valla cared about style not merely for aesthetic reasons but because they wished to improve the clarity of thinking together with the clarity of writing."
6   *T & T*, p. 7.
7   *T & T*, p. 354.
8   H. Glareanus, in the preface to his edition of Suetonius (Basle: 1560), so calls it; in fact it was an abbey. See C.G. Cruickshank, *The English Occupation of Tournai 1513–1519* (Oxford: 1971).
9   Note on *Caligula*, c. 32.
10 A method promoted, rather than invented, by Lachmann. See S. Timpanaro, *La genesi del metodo di Lachmann* (Florence: 1963), amplified and revised in *Die Entstehung der Lachmannschen Methode* (Hamburg: 1971); also E.J. Kenney, *The Classical Text* (Berkeley: 1974), pp. 102ff.
11 II. 90.
12 Sound, that is, by contemporary standards. The same qualification must be applied to his knowledge of metre, mentioned in the section on Terence.
13 For the word "monogenous" (or "unilinear", if that is to be preferred), see Kenney, *op. cit.*, p. 18.
14 *Allen* 2584, 96–97: "Nondum ... annum decimumquartum excessisti."

15 I owe to him the identification of Erasmus' Terentian base-text, and also much other information about specific passages, to which this section of my paper is deeply indebted.

16 *T & T*, p. 413.

17 See J.F. Mountford, *The Scholia Bembina* (Liverpool; 1934), p. 31.

18 See p. 169 for Erasmus' own recognition of this rapidity as a personal fault. It is the more surprising because in youth he learned the business of editing (and acquired many of the prevailing attitudes and techniques appropriate to it) at the press of Aldus, whose motto was *Festina Lente*. R. Peters (*Desiderius Erasmus: Prefaces to the Fathers*, 1970) is wide of the mark when he writes, à *propos* of the *Cyprian*, "Such speed is decidedly un-Erasmian!" It is, of course, nowhere contended in this paper that Erasmus never *revised* his work; the very fact that she dwells on his re-editing of Seneca in 1529, to take only one among a multitude of instances, should suffice to prove the contrary, even for the most careless reader.

19 R. Peters, *op. cit.* (n. 17).

20 Fritz Husner, "Die Handschrift der Scholien des Erasmus von Rotterdam zu den Hieronymusbriefen" in *Festschrift Gustav Binz* (Basel: 1935), pp. 132–146.

21 In *Scrinium Erasmianum* I (Leiden: 1969), pp. 263–276.

22 Book II, fol. 46.

23 *Allen* 975, dated 1519, requests from the abbot of Gembloux the loan of two *codices pervetusti* of Cyprian which Erasmus has found mentioned in the catalogue of the abbey library.

24 R. Peters, *op. cit.*, p. 31 top.

25 Quintilian 1.8.21: *inter virtutes grammatici habebitur aliqua nescire*. Cf. *Allen* 337, 419 (to Dorp): *et scientiae pars est quaedam nescire*. R. Pfeiffer, *Gnomon* 12 (1936), pp. 625–634, quotes this passage (on p. 630) as evidence that Erasmus should not be charged with narrow "Verbalkritik."

26 In English at any rate, a sound introduction can be obtained from books such as Bruce M. Metzger's *The text of the New Testament: its transmission, corruption and restoration* (2nd edition, Oxford: 1968).

27 Erasmus endorses (at least by implication) the words of Jerome, in a letter to Paulinus which forms the prefatory epistle to the Vulgate: *sancta . . . rusticitas solum sibi prodest*. See B. Botfield (ed.), *Prefaces to the first editions of the Greek and Roman classics and of the sacred Scriptures* (London: 1861), p. 3.

28 R. Pfeiffer, *op. cit.*, pp. 629ff.

29 In the *Ciceronianus* (LB 1. 1013E = *ASD* I-2, 681, line 11).

30 *Allen* 402, 2 (also *Allen* 694, 18).

31 For his good fortune in obtaining the sole surviving MS of Arnobius' commentary on the Psalms, see the introduction to *Allen* 1304.

32 E.J. Kenney, *The Classical Text*, p. 50.

33 I do not wish to imply that Budé's interests lay solely in the field of *Realien*. It is perhaps particularly in Budé's more "literary" works (on Greek language; on philology and its place in Christian culture) that in fact the difference between him and Erasmus emerges most clearly; Budé is always at the task of investigating in what might be called a "modern" and "scientific" spirit, whereas Erasmus' judgments in matters of language are for the most part those of an artist (which he was; in earlier years he was apt to call himself a poet) and contain a large subjective element. Erasmus remained in this way firmly anchored within the rhetorical, pre-scientific, tradition. By his writings he stirred the world of literate Europe into action; yet these writings in themselves—in their "encyclopaedic" aspect, as repositories of fresh and solid information—were on the whole, for the reason we have just given, more ephemeral than Budé's. On the defects of Budé's Latin style I have written in *Crossroads and Perspectives: French Literature of the Renaissance. Studies in Honour of Victor E. Graham*, edited by C.M. Grisé and C.D.E. Tolton (Geneva: Droz, 1986), pp. 84–90.

34 Still highly valuable is the article by P. Petitmengin, "Comment étudier l'activité d'Erasme éditeur de textes antiques?" in *Colloquia Erasmiana Turonensia* I (1972), pp. 217–222. For Seneca, the first part of Winifried Trillitzsch, "Erasmus und Seneca" (*Philologus*, volume 109, 1965, pp. 270–293) should also be consulted.

J. DEN BOEFT

"ILLIC AUREUM QUODDAM IRE FLUMEN" ERASMUS' ENTHUSIASM FOR THE PATRES

To anyone looking only cursorily through the pages of Erasmus' writings it will come as a surprise that up to a few decades ago the author's great interest in the works and, for that matter, the persons of the Church Fathers did not receive due attention in Erasmian studies. In Huizinga's famous monograph the Fathers are hardly mentioned, in fact, the only name which crops up some ten times is Jerome's, usually when Erasmus' edition of his opera is referred to. And yet in the dedicatory preface of his book, addressing himself to P.S. and H.M. Allen, Huizinga stated that he had been "walking along the paths of your *Opus Epistolarum Erasmi*". Obviously during these walks his eyes were caught by other sights than the often returning momentoes of patristic literature. A wholly different tour will probably be made by those who have inculcated upon themselves the enthusiastic page in the *Ratio*, in which the ancient theologians are compared with their more recent colleagues. He who makes such a comparison, "will see a kind of golden river streaming there, but some meagre brooklets here, and those not very pure nor corresponding to their source at that. There the oracles of evangelical truth are thundering, here one hears the poor fictions of men, which the closer you look at them the more they disappear like dreams ... There everything is full of majesty, here splendour is lacking in such a degree that most aspects are squalid and insufficiently worthy of theology's grandeur, to abstain for the moment from a comparison of morals."[1]

These words do not form the rare utterance of a momentary rapture. As John C. Olin put it, "this stress on going back to the ancient theologians, that is to the Fathers of the Early Church, and on their vast superiority over the 'modern' ones, that is, the late medieval schoolmen, is a constant theme in Erasmus."[2] A passage in the Life of John Colet, in which the protagonist's vast reading during his years of study as an adolescent is briefly touched upon, could easily function as a stroke in the writer's self-portrait: "He devoted himself entirely to the reading of the sacred authors; but having first travelled with great zeal through all sorts of literature he took especially delight in those old writers, Dionysius, Origen, Cyprian, Ambrose, Jerome."[3] The 'Areopagite' is less important to Erasmus, but the other four names belong to a canon of Fathers which in Erasmus' writings gradually developed from the pair in the earliest stages of his career, viz. Jerome and Augustine.[4] The term 'canon' was used on purpose. Erasmus was not a modern patristic scholar with a broad interest in all the authors and writings listed in the surveys of Altaner or Quasten. His horizon was determined by a selective group of prominent authors from the third and fourth centuries: Origen, Athanasius, the Cappadocians, John Chrysostom on the Greek side, and the Latins Tertullian[5], Cyprian, Hilary, Ambrose, Jerome and Augustine. By these canonical Fathers the standards for faith and theology have been set and providing a reliable text of their writings is therefore an almost holy task. Erasmus' labours in this field are not merely those of a conscientious philologist endeavouring to publish sound editions, his *furor philologicus* is kindled by a fire of another type. In a letter to John Longlond, which is the preface to a translation of some of Athanasius' works, he tells about his discovery of some glaring cases of pseudepigraphy. Some samples have been added to make clear "with how much impiety even the Greek writers of manuscripts have raged against the monuments of such men, although the mere alteration of a syllable in their works is a profanation."[6] All theological reflections are bound to be led astray when the theologians cannot dispose of trustworthy editions or, for that matter, translations. The use of the term 'source' should not be underrated. The writings of the Fathers can be drunk from directly, like Scripture, and the availability of a correct text is of vital importance: "Therefore I regard it as necessary for every profession, and above all for the theological one, that its votaries either draw from sources rather than from pools or are convinced of the reliability of the translators."[7]

The above may suffice to call to mind the well-nigh religious delight, the enthusiasm in the full sense of the word, which Erasmus experienced in reading, studying, explaining and editing the Fathers. Nowadays this aspect of his work and his person is no longer neglected. Several shorter articles testify to this[8], but above all it is the great merit of Ch. Béné and A. Godin[9] to have put it firmly on the map of Erasmian studies. The former's detailed investigation has brought to light the inspiration Erasmus received from Augustine's *De doctrina christiana*, whilst the latter in a vast survey describes the growing influence of Origen from the moment of his 'discovery' during the friendship with Jean Vitrier.

In spite of the valuable work done until now, the time has not yet come to compose an all-embracing methodical synopsis of Erasmus' dealings with the Fathers. The fine studies just mentioned certainly do not restrict themselves painstakingly to the specific Father they are concentrating on, but all the same these studies, as is quite natural, suffer a little from a "défaut de leur qualité". In turning the spot-light of their attention to the influence of one particular author, they inevitably leave the others in the shadow. It needs at least a comparable study of the Father who, not without reason, is regarded by many as Erasmus' favourite example and paragon, viz. Jerome[10], before an adequate summary could be attempted. But even then those calling for a thorough examination of the influence of e.g. John Crysostom—a *Life* of whom was included in one of the prefaces—Basilius or Ambrose could not be blamed.

A methodical survey recapitulating Erasmus' vast and varied dealings with the Fathers would have to spend ample space on an aspect which is quite characteristic of him, viz. the comparison between the Fathers and the careful weighing of the importance to be attached to each of them. In fact, Erasmus has a great liking for drawing up shorter or longer lists in which particular qualities are subjected to brief comparisons. Such lists stress the fact that the authors in question are above all regarded as examples which can be imitated directly. One of the longest ones figures in a section of *Ecclesiastes sive de ratione concionandi*, which calls to mind the first chapter of Quintilian's *Institutio Oratoria*, book 10, where the author presents a long survey of Greek and Roman literature in order to provide the future orator with models for his style. Likewise Erasmus offers a catalogue of pagan and ecclesiastical doctores, whose books should be studied with special care by a future preacher.[11] The Christian authors are far more numerous than the pagan ones, although in view of the subject Lactantius is a surprising absentee. The accent in this catalogue is all on the stylistic and rhetorical qualities by which the audience can be captivated. The numerical predominance of the Christian authors will not catch the assiduous reader of Erasmus' works unprepared, for their stylistic competence is often referred to, in fact it is one of the features of patristic literature which Erasmus found very attractive. In this domain there was indeed no opposition between *sacrae litterae* and *bonae litterae*. This view is not restricted to his old age, when he was writing the *Ecclesiastes*: it is also the purport of a praising remark about Jerome's Letters in his youth, in a letter dating from 1489[12], and it can be regarded as a continuing theme in his oeuvre.

Erasmus' consistency in the more general trends of his way of thinking about the Fathers cannot be denied, but in the details there is a certain degree of wavering and even capriciousness. In a passage of the *Life* Jerome receives ample, indeed lavish praise for the great variety of his rhetorical accomplishments (1400 – 1428, Ferguson), but some ten years afterwards, in a comparison with Athanasius, he is indirectly criticized as too much in love with outward display and the applause of the audience is indicated as his aim in another passage.[13] In the course of time Augustine comes in for different sorts of criticism, but in 1529 his portrait is sketched in well-nigh hieratic colours: ''I cannot imagine another teacher over whom the Spirit, Whose riches is matched by His benevolence, has poured out His gifts more liberally".[14] This phrase contrasts rather sharply with the regret expressed ten years before on Augustine's failure to emulate the eloquent style of Cyprian, whose praises are sounded in *De doctrina Christiana*, book 4. Erasmus even wonders whether he should not prefer Cyprian to Jerome. These waverings are not spectacular, but nevertheless it is not wholly without interest to notice such varieties. Superficially it seems that the order of preference has much to do with the intensity of his attention to a particular Father at a given moment. But of course this impression has to be verified by a thorough examination of the facts.

Erasmus' great interest in patristic literature can be perceived throughout his oeuvre, though in different gradations. The Fathers loom large in writings concerning faith, piety and theology, but they have to be content with much less room in e.g. the *Adages*. In Mrs. Mann Phillips' survey of the frequency of sources the classical Greek and Latin authors surpass the Fathers by far. Against 892 references to Cicero, 666 to Homer, 475 to Plautus, 428 to Plato, etc. only Jerome just holds his own with 121, whereas such favourites of Erasmus as Augustine, Basil and Chrysostom have only 32, 23 and 21 references respectively.[15] Of course, the columns and essays of the *Adages* serve a different purpose, for which patristic texts had less to offer, and this is true for other writings too. Nevertheless, for a solid review of Erasmus' use of the Fathers his whole oeuvre should be scrutinized.

There is one group of writings which is of prime importance for this subject, viz. the Prefaces of Erasmus' patristic editions[16], the three Lives, of Jerome, Chrysostom and Origen, included because here the meaning of the Fathers for contemporary society in the broadest sense of the term is explicitly dealt with. These dedicatory letters have something in common with the *Adages*. They too vary greatly in length, from the letter, over 900 lines long, to Jean de Carondelet, which serves as an introduction to the edition of Hilary, to the brief note added to Lactantius' *De opificio Dei*. This, however, is a mere outward similarity. More important is the resemblance in the structure of the contents. As in the case of the *Adages*, the reader is confronted with essays in which scholarly learning, literary taste and protreptic argument are combined. As can be expected, Erasmus usually pays ample attention to philological problems concerning the manuscripts and the constitution of the text, but, as was already touched upon in the above, the author's stylistic accomplishments also come up for discussion and, above all, in persuasive terms the great profit which can be derived from studying the writings in question and from following in the track of the writer is set forth. These texts, like the *Adages*, excellently demonstrate that learning for Erasmus and his readers was never an end in itself, but first and foremost should help to improve men's character, morals, piety and so on. The Fathers are not historical figures from a venerable but distant past, but living examples, whose writings are suited for immediate use in the tumultuous problems which Christianity finds itself confronted with.[17]

In the following some instances will be presented in which such an immediate benefit is implied. First, however, by way of digression, some cases of word-play with the names of the Fathers in question will be introduced. Jerome is called "ille sacri nominis heros", about Aurelius Augustinus it is said: "Quid enim habet orbis Christianus hoc scriptore vel magis aureum vel augustius", Ambrose is "dignus qui sit quod dicitur Ambrosius, hoc est immortalis", Athanasius deserved "ut iuxta nomen suum etiam apud mortales esset immortalis", Origen owes his name 'montigena' ("born from the mountains"), to the fact that he "nihil humile cogitavit".[18] Such puns, which follow a classical tradition, stress the direct importance of the texts which are quoted and dealt with. The names of the Fathers already signify their great value.

In September 1522 Erasmus published the *editio princeps* of Arnobius' commentary on the Psalms, which he dedicated as a congratulatory present to the newly elected pope Adrian VI. Not much is known about the author, who in modern manuals is usually called Arnobius the Younger to distinguish him from the ex-rhetor who during the reign of Diocletian wrote a defence of the Christian religion entitled *Adversus nationes*. Erasmus does not make this distinction, although he is aware of the possibility that the commentator and the apologist might not be one and the same person. That causes an interesting argument in which he tries to cope with the problem that the stylistic levels of the *Adversus nationes* and the commentary are very far apart. His solution is quite simple: it is the same author, but the readers are different: the first work was written for the educated, the second for the general public. The author's aim is to make all people understand what they are singing. His condescension from eloquence to popular language is inspired by Christian love, which wants to do good to as many as possible.[19] Even a completely mistaken scholarly assumption thus proves helpful for pious moralizing. Then a fascinating discussion follows about correct language and the use of solecisms, which cannot be defended by referring to Arnobius, who at the present time would write in pure Latin for the educated and in French for the general public. I would, however, rather look at the importance of Erasmus' scholarly gift from the point of view of the dedicatee.

Pope Adrian has taken office at a time of pernicious disagreement in the Church. The hopes of all good men are set on him: may he become the instrument through which the storms are abated and tranquillity is restored. In antiquity men like Pythagoras, Terpander and Arion have demonstrated the enormous possibilities of music to influence the human mind. If the *humana musica* had such a psychological impact, far greater efficacy should be ascribed to its heavenly counterpart. That music is represented most effectively by the Psalter. Against the infernal sound of worldly music, which tries to seduce men to anger, war, revenge, avidity, etc., in heavenly music one hears a melodious harmony composed of charity and the other Christian virtues. Unfortunately, this beautiful melody cannot be relished by those who fail to perceive the mystic sense of the Psalms. The nausea experienced by monks and priests when singing the Psalms is caused by their lack of understanding. Arnobius' succinct commentary can remedy this aversion by revealing the secrets of heavenly wisdom. Erasmus winds up his exposition by expressing the wish that the new Pope will be able to play a truly apostolic melody which can bring about a bond of Christian concord.[20] Thus even a relatively unimportant patristic work functions as an 'upbeat', to continue the musical terminology, for the heavenly music with which the new Pope will try to restore peace and concord.

Four years later Erasmus published another *editio princeps*, this time of Irenaeus. Of course, the name of this author lends itself excellently for word-play and Erasmus is quick in grasping the opportunity. God does not love strife but peace and the Lord calls the peacemakers blessed. If only some Irenaei would arise in order to bring the world back to concord by their Evangelical spirit![21] In the rest of the preface it becomes clear that this word-play is not restricted to a mere superficial pun. Irenaeus' work consists of the combating of heresies. The deeper sense of this activity should not be overlooked. God's inscrutable counsel strives to instruct and to strengthen the Church in wonderful ways. The Satan is allowed to attack God's sheep with all his varied guile and force, but God then turns all evil into blessing. The attacks on the Gospel by legalistic Judaism have convinced us even more that the shadows of the law have definitely passed. In a similar way the commotion caused by the subtle argument of the heretics has taught the Church to make better use of the equipment provided in Scripture.[22] This fact gives ample cause for an optimistic appraisal of the present situation: God will see to it that the tempest which is raging finally turns out to be beneficial and he will arouse some Irenaei to restore peace to the world.

Thus Irenaeus' *Adversus haereses*, the work of a polemic, within the framework of God's plan to save his Church is functioning as an instrument of peace, which fact is elegantly linked with the author's name and brought to the fore as a token of hope for the near future.

In 1527 Erasmus published an edition of Ambrose. In the preface, addressed to archbishop John Lasky, he deals with the stylistic qualities of the author and the characteristic tone of his writings, which he finds in the moderation with which all excesses of either harshness or fickleness are eschewed. Everywhere one can recognize his truly Roman or rather Christian spirit.[23] This excellent observation will be applauded by those who are well-acquainted with Ambrose's personality, in which the *gravitas* of a Roman aristocrat is so peculiarly blended with the humility of a pious Christian priest. For the present purpose, however, another part of this dedicatory letter should be looked at.

According to Erasmus the edition of Ambrose is very aptly dedicated to his addressee. The aristocratic and pious Milanese bishop, who strove after peace and tranquillity, is a most fitting visitor for the 16th century archbishop to receive. The Church could do with a replica for dealing with the disturbances in the world. With bishops of that type the present-day world would also have princes like Theodosius the Great. In order to explain this Erasmus recapitulates the history of the Thessalonice disaster and Theodosius' devout repentance. These events demonstrated the invincible firmness of the bishop an the readiness of the emperor to accept a less honourable place during the ecclesiastical ceremonies. Nowadays, however, a prince who visits some church is honoured with a tabernacle rising even above the altar. Ambrose never gave way, but such a consistent attitude is only possible when one is willing to die *pro pietate*. Erasmus does not explicitly draw the lesson from this, but the clarity of what is implied leaves nothing to be desired. He is confident that the edition of Ambrose's writings will meet the sympathy of readers everywhere, for the formidable bishop lived for the Insubrians, but wrote for the whole world.[24] Such a phrase is a clear illustration of the lasting value of the Fathers in the eyes of Erasmus. As in the two cases dealt with above, Ambrose's words and standards of conduct are directly applicable to the troubled world of 1527.

In the meantime Erasmus' attention had been drawn to John Chrysostom, some of whose treatises and homilies he published in the Greek text or in a Latin translation between 1525 and 1529, before he presented an edition of the *opera* in 1530. At the outset of the preface it becomes fully clear which quality of the author is most prominent in Erasmus' eyes, when Chrysostom is called "that most honey-voiced preacher and indefatigable herald of Christ".[25] The preface itself it not very long, but it contains an extensive *Life*, in which John's predicament in the last period of his life, during which he suffered continually sharpened forms of exile, is set forth in great detail. Erasmus does not even hesitate to call him a martyr. The reason for this is that indeed he was not executed with the axe, but hit many times by false accusations which are sharper than any axe.[26] Between the lines connoisseurs will easily find a reference to Erasmus' own difficulties here![27]

John was posthumously rehabilitated and his mortal remains were transported to Constantinople to the immense joy of the population. However, we possess an even more precious treasure in the living remains of his writings. This prompts Erasmus to a protracted eulogy of Crysostom's didactic and oratorical gifts and also of his constant attention to the level of understanding of his audience. Christ used his golden mouth to herald the Gospel. At this point the eulogy is accompanied by a sustained lament about the lack of good preachers and shepherds in Erasmus' own time. That, above all, has caused the decline of the Church. Although there is no question of the numerous distractions of the audience's attention which Crysostom had to cope with, such as sports and theatres, although the humble people lend their ears most willingly and religiously, really capable preachers are very scarce. Here is a field in which princes and bishops should be vigilant. They will deserve God's grace more readily by providing able shepherds than by founding monasteries. The emperor Arcadius found his beautiful residence incomplete before he had called John Chrysostom to the episcopal see. If only the present-day princes were willing to follow this example, if only the priests were willing to look at Chrysostom's standards, then wars and discord would end and pagan or semi-Christian nations would no longer be hampered by our morals to join Christ's sheepfold.

As in the other three cases, the scholarly edition of the works of one of the Fathers proves of direct use in the ecclesiastical situation. The reader can witness for himself the power of truly Christian preaching.

These brief glances at four of the prefaces may suffice to demonstrate that for Erasmus publishing reliable texts of the Church Fathers was a much needed service in the actual situation of Christianity. Arnobius' commentary reveals the mystic sense of the Psalms, the music of which will bring back peace and concord. The same ends are served by Irenaeus' polemics, which in harmony with the author's name will remove schisms and heresies. Studying Ambrose's life and works opens the eyes for a correct relation between the authorities of Church and state. John Chrysostom's honeyed voice demonstrates what the Church is in great need of, true and devout preaching of the Gospel. An examination of other prefaces would produce comparable results. The Church Fathers have a lasting and also an immediate value. "For what could we accomplish now in scriptural studies without the aid of the works left us by Origen, Tertullian, Chrysostom, Jerome, Hilary, and Augustine?"[28]

180 J. DEN BOEFT

NOTES

1 videbit illic aureum quoddam ire flumen, hic tenues quosdam rivulos, eosque nec puros admodum nec suo fonti respondentes. Illic tonant oracula veritatis aeternae, hic audis hominum commentula, quae quo propius inspicias, hoc magis similia insomniis evanescunt ... Illic maiestatis plena omnia, hic adeo nihil spendidum, ut pleraque sordida parumque digna dignitate theologica, ut interim a comparatione morum abstineam (*Rat. ver. theol.* 189.31–190.11, Holborn).

2 John C. Olin, *Six Essays on Erasmus.* New York: 1979. p. 34.

3 Ibi se totum evolvendis sacris autoribus dedit; sed prius per omnia literarum genera magno studio peregrinatus priscis illis potissimum delectabatur, Dionysio, Origene, Cypriano, Ambrosio, Hieronymo (*Allen* 1211, 270–273 = *Erasme, 'Vies de Jean Vitrier et de John Colet*: Traduction et présentation par André Godin. Angers: 1982. p. 48, 258–261). The immediate sequel to the quoted text certainly does not apply to Erasmus: Atque inter veteres nulli erat iniquior quam Augustino.

4 Their names are mentioned for the first time in a letter dating from 1489: *Allen* 20, 89.

5 In a most elegant short paper S.L. Greenslade has shown that Erasmus never studied Tertullian thoroughly and only read some of his works not long before 1527. S.L. Greenslade, "Erasmus and Tertullian", *Studia Patristica* XIV part III, Berlin: 1976, 37–40.

6 Ut hinc liqueat quanta impietate Graecorum quoque scribae debacchati sint in talium virorum monumenta, in quibus vel syllabam immutasse sacrilegium est (*Allen* 1790, 68–70); cf. also *Allen* 1334, 99–100: mutare suo quenque arbitratu quod scriptum est in veterum libris, temeritas est, ne dicam impietas.

7 Proinde quem omni professioni, tum in primis theologicae, necessarium arbitror ut aut e fontibus haurire malint quam e lacunis, aut eorum qui vertere fidem exploratam habeant (*Allen* 2611, 172–175).

8 E.g. D. Gorce, "La patristique dans la réforme d'Erasme", in: *Festgabe Joseph Lortz*, Baden-Baden: 1958, 233–276; R. Peters, "Erasmus and the Fathers: Their Practical Value", *Church History* 36 (1967); A. Etchegaray Cruz, "Erasmo, editor critico de la patrologia latina", *Boletin de la biblioteca Menendez y Pelayo* 44 (1968) 103–120; R. Stupperich, "Erasmus und Melanchton in ihrem Verhältnis zu den Kirchenvätern", *Vox Theologica* 39 (1969) 80–92; John C. Olin, "Erasmus and the Church Fathers", o.c. (n. 2) 33–47.

9 Ch. Béné, *Erasme et Saint Augustin, ou influence de Saint Augustin sur l'humanisme d'Erasme*, Geneva: 1969; A. Godin, *Erasme lecteur d'Origène*, Geneva: 1982.

10 Cf. incomparabilem Ecclesiae doctorem (*Vita Hier.* 195/6, Ferguson); quo viro nihil habet orbis latinus vel doctius vel sanctius (*Allen* 1334, 15). See also Eugene F. Rice jr., *Saint Jerome in the Renaissance*, Baltimore: 1985, 116–136 (ch. 5: "*Hieronymus redivivus*: Erasmus and St. Jerome").

11 Quorum libri potissimum sint evolvendi futuro concionatori (*LB* V, 856 D).

12 *Allen* 22, 18/9.

13 *Allen* 1790, 95/6; 1800, 192/3.

14 At non arbitror alium esse doctorem in quem opulentus ille iuxta ac benignus Spiritus dotes suas omnes largius effuderit quam in Augustinum (*Allen* 2157, 23–25).

15 M. Mann Phillips, *The Adages of Erasmus*, Cambridge: 1964, p. 393–403 ('Appendix III').

16 In the case of the Greek Fathers both editions proper and translations into Latin are concerned.

17 There are also quite a few hidden references to Erasmus' own career or situation. A particularly charming one can be found in *Allen* 2157, 245–248 (concerning Augustine): Porro, quoniam vir prudens perspiciebat librorum usum multo latius patere quam vocis, in hanc operam quicquid potuit temporis suffurabatur.

18 *Vita Hier.* 157/8, *Allen* 2157, 5/6; 1855, 31–33; 1790, 6–7; *LB* VIII, 425 B respectively.

19 Idem scripsit, sed non scripsit iisdem. Illud opus scripsit eruditis, hoc scripsit vulgo

(*Allen* 1304, 65 – 66); Proinde voluit Arnobius ab omnibus intelligi quod videbat cantari ab omnibus. Persuasit hoc illi Christiana charitas, quae studet prodesse quam plurimis. Maluit balbutiens utilitatem adferre multis, quam eloquentiae laudem auferre apud paucos (*Ib.* 97 – 100).

20   ... orat et expectat illud abs te cum primis populus Christianus, ut arrepto Psalterio Christi, melodiam aliquam vere Apostolicam incinas, quae principum ac populorum animos iungat Christiana concordia, quae perniciosas opinionum pugnas discutiat ... (*Allen* 1304, 471 – 475).

21   exoriantur aliquot Irenaei, qui spiritu Evangelico mundum redigant in concordiam (*Allen* 1738, 14 – 15). It is tempting to regard this phrase as a Christianized reminiscence of Virgil, *Aeneid* 4.625: exoriare aliquis nostris ex ossibus ultor.

22   dum haereticorum argutationibus agitatur, magis uti didicit armatura divinarum litterarum, et confirmata est impugnata veritas (*Allen* 1738, 240 – 242).

23   pectus vere Romanum, imo Christianum (*Allen* 1855, 206).

24   Vixit Insubribus, sed scripsit omnibus (*Allen* 1855, 299). Milan was the capital of the Insubres.

25   mellitissimus ille concionator Christique praeco indefatigabilis (*Allen* 2359.8).

26   Non percussus est securi, sed calumniis omni securi acutioribus non semel ictus est (*LB* III/2, 1342E).

27   Compare these two phrases: Hoc praemii vir optimus pro tam praeclaris in Ecclesiam meritis retulit, per episcopos orthodoxos et sub imperatore Christiano (*LB* III/2, 1342E); Quid autem ingratius quam pro tam immensis sudoribus vigiliisque, quas tantum iuvandi animo susceperis et quibus nulla par gratia referri queat, rependi calumniam idque potissimum ab iis, ad quos potissimum operis utilitas sit reditura? (*Apologia* 163, 29 – 33, Holborn).

28   Quid enim nunc possemus in sacris literis nisi Origenis, Tertulliani, Chrysostomi, Hieronymi, Hilarii, Augustini monumentis adiuti? (*Allen* 1334, 913 – 914). The translation is John C. Olin's.

JOHN C. OLIN

ERASMUS AND SAINT JEROME:
AN APPRAISAL OF THE BOND

We are well aware that Saint Jerome occupied a special place in the thought and work of Erasmus. P.S. Allen suggests that his interest in the saint stems from his early associaiton with the Brothers of the Common Life who were called *Hieronymiani* because of their devotion to Jerome.[1] We know that as a young monk at Steyn he had read and copied all the letters of Jerome and had drawn lessons from them that explain both his attachment to their author and his early formation as a humanist. In a letter to a fellow Augustinian Cornelis Gerard he wrote that if those who despise good literature "looked carefully at Jerome's letters, they would see that lack of culture is not holiness, nor cleverness impiety," and he treasured them as offering arguments against "the assaults of the barbarians."[2] Jerome was not his only model or inspiration. That revival of letters we associate with the Renaissance had captivated his youthful mind, and he credits Lorenzo Valla especially for helping to restore good literature and style.[3] But from the start Jerome held a place of prime importance in his studies and scholarly plans.

By 1500, soon after his return to the continent from a memorable trip to England, where he had met John Colet then lecturing at Oxford and the young Thomas More, Erasmus set to work on a project to restore and edit the letters of Jerome and write a commentary on them.[4] It is his first major enterprise. Inspired by Colet he now determined to devote himself to the study of sacred scripture and the reform of theology. The Jerome project was an essential part of that larger program. What prompts him to emend and elucidate Jerome, he tells us, "is the goodness of the saintly man who of all Christians was by common consent the best scholar and best writer."[5] Today inferior theologians hold sway, he declares, while Jerome "the supreme champion and expositor and ornament of our faith" is ill understood and sadly neglected.

That enterprise was not completed until 1516, when Johann Froben in Basel published the great edition of Jerome that Erasmus had long ago envisaged. In the intervening years, of course, other projects had also occupied him, and he had written some of his most famous and important books. He had especially continued to work on Holy Scripture, and 1516 also saw the publication of his Latin and Greek New Testament. Progress on these two landmark editions had gone hand in hand. From 1511 to 1514, while he was at Cambridge, he resumed work on both projects.[6]

The Paris printer Josse Bade had hoped to get the improved Jerome text, but when Erasmus left England in the summer of 1514 he made his way to Basel, where his famous collaboration with Johann Froben began. The Froben press had already underway an edition of Jerome, and this undoubtedly was one of the main attractions that drew Erasmus to Basel. Froben's recently deceased partner Johann Amerbach planned to publish complete editions of the four Doctors of the western Church. His sons Bruno and Basil tell us that "he had entertained the hope that, if the splendid theology of ancient times should come to life again, that prickly and frigid kind of sophistical theology would have less influence and our Christians would be more generous and genuine."[7] It was a view that Erasmus wholeheartedly shared.

Erasmus has given us several vivid accounts of his labors in emending and editing Jerome's text and of the importance of the great edition then in progress.[8] To Pope Leo X, to whom he had originally intended to dedicate the edition, he wrote that "the whole of Jerome is being born again," and he declared that he "is chief among the theologians of the Latin world" and that "Greece itself with all its learning can scarcely produce a man to be matched with him."[9] Erasmus' responsibility was the letters, treatises and other writings that went into the first four volumes of the edition although he helped and advised on the project throughout and wrote the dedicatory preface to Archbishop Warham of Canterbury and an introductory Life of Jerome that has been hailed as his "biographical masterpiece."[10] The nine volume edition was the first *opera omnia* of the saint and the first and most important of Erasmus' many patristic editions.

We have indicated that the Jerome project was an essential part of Erasmus' reform program. His chief aim was to reform theology by returning it to its scriptural and patristic sources, by restoring what Erasmus deemed the genuine theology of the early Church. Everything else would flow from that. In this return to the sources Holy Scripture, of course, came first, especially the Gospels and Epistles, but after this "literature of Christ" came the early Fathers. Their authority derived from their closeness in time as well as in spirit to the divine source, and their chief value lay in interpreting the sacred text and moving us to a fuller understanding and acceptance of it. They instructed and inspired us in living a Christian life.

Why did Jerome occupy so important a place in these reform plans? There is hardly any mystery about it. As Erasmus tells us over and over again, he believes Jerome is the greatest of the Latin Fathers and that even Greece could scarcely match him. The saint's erudition, his love of letters, his knowledge of languages, his superb style elevated him above all the others. He was the "Prince of theologians", the model of what the theologian ought to be. We can, of course, dig deeper into the reasons why Erasmus had so marked a predilection for Jerome. A good part of it, I believe, is already revealed in that early letter of Erasmus we referred to and quoted at the outset. He admired the letters of Jerome because of their literary quality, their elegance of style. They were decisive proof that there need not be a divorce between religion and culture. Jerome in fact embodied their union and could serve therefore as an exemplar for the young monk already captivated by that revival of classical letters which is the very essence of Renaissance humanism. And the saint's literary excellence and his eloquence and "stylistic power" pointed the way to that renewal of theology which soon became Erasmus' primary goal. Jacques Chomarat in his excellent *Grammaire et rhétorique chez Erasme* has shown us that Erasmus sought above all to unite eloquence and piety, that is, to forge what has been called, in the best sense, a "rhetorical theology." [11] In this Jerome was a model and an ideal.

Intimately connected with this literary excellence and eloquence was Jerome's classical learning. This in turn presupposed his knowledge of Greek, an accomplishment which gave him in Erasmus' estimation a distinct advantage over Saint Augustine. His formidable erudition along with his stylistic skill commended him naturally to the humanist, but more important was the bearing of this on his work as a theologian and its contribution to his scriptural studies. His training in rhetoric enabled him to endow theology with "dignity of style." His classical learning gave rich cultural context to his writing. His knowledge of languages, which included not only Latin and Greek but also Hebrew and Chaldee, made it possible for him to work with all the original texts of Holy Scripture. "What Roman eloquence, what mastery of tongues, what a range of knowledge in all antiquity and all history!", Erasmus exclaimed in his letter to Leo X which we mentioned above. This "mastery of tongues" certainly was one of the most important attractions of Jerome for Erasmus. The return to the sources and the careful study of the ancient texts in their original languages are the distinguishing marks of the humanist scholar. That Jerome did this so extensively and so notably with Holy Scripture gave Erasmus a precedent and justification for his own work on the New Testament and established perhaps the closest bond between them. The approach and method in this study of Scripture and in its exegesis has been called grammatical or philological, the emphasis being on the language of the sacred text and on the use and meaning of its words in their original context. As a theological method it stood in sharp contrast to the scholastic and was a subject of great controversy between Erasmus and his critics, but it joined him with Jerome in a single endeavor. [12] If the Pince of humanists sought to replace scholasticism with a "rhetorical theology," he strove also for one that would be basically and thoroughly "grammatical" as well.[13]

Erasmus' singular preference for Jerome has often been contrasted with his attitude toward Saint Augustine. In the Life of Jerome that he wrote for the edition, Erasmus discussing the correspondence that took place between the two saints remarked that Augustine was superior to Jerome only in his episcopal dignity and that he was inferior in all other respects (a sentence, by the way, he omitted when he revised his edition of the letters in 1524).[14] He also took issue in the Life with the Italian humanist Francesco Filelfo who had once said that Augustine was superior in dialectics but that Jerome surpassed him in eloquence. "It is not my purpose to diminish in any way the attainments of Augustine," Erasmus wrote, "but the facts themselves proclaim that Jerome surpassed Augustine no less in dialectics than he outstripped him in eloquence and that he was no less Augustine's superior in learning than he was in excellence of style."[15] Johann Eck, Luther's famous opponent, in a letter to Erasmus a few years later declared that he agreed with the judgment of Filelfo and bemoaned the fact that Erasmus was critical of Augustine.[16] He accused Erasmus of having failed to read Augustine. Erasmus replied at length defending his preference for Jerome.[17] He ridiculed the notion that he had not read Augustine. He "was the author I read first of them all," he declared, ". . . and the more I read him, the more I feel satisfied with my estimate of the two of them." He then launched into a comparison between the two, rehearsing Jerome's advantages at every point of the way—in birthplace, education, early Christian upbringing, long years devoted to the study of Holy Scripture. And he especially stressed that Jerome knew Greek. "All philosophy and all theology in those days belonged to the Greeks," Erasmus declared, yet "Augustine knew no Greek." This deficiency obviously was of decisive importance for the great humanist.

I might note parenthetically that Luther, somewhat paradoxically, shared the view of his arch-opponent Johann Eck concerning the superiority of Saint Augustine and disagreed sharply with Erasmus on this matter, as indeed he did on several others.[18] His reasons however were different from Eck's and dogmatically rooted. But that is another story and would take us quite beyond the scope of this brief paper.

A great deal more, of course, can be said about the close bond between Erasmus and Saint Jerome. It is of the utmost importance in understanding Erasmus. He identified with the early Father. His literary style closely resembles Jerome's. Certainly his humanism does, as do his scriptural focus and approach and achievement. And the model of Jerome and his precedent was guidance and assurance for Erasmus in his own endeavors.

We can also point to a broader significance. The affinity between the two great scholars is a classic example of that revival of antiquity—that return to the sources—we associate so basically with the Renaissance. The bond is a witness of a "discovery" but also of an assimilation, and this in turn generated intellectual ferment and religious reform. It is part of a larger picture, to be sure, but it is a very characteristic, integral, and important part. And it reveals, I think, something of the variety and richness of the western tradition and of its historic potential for personal and cultural renewal.

NOTES

1   *Erasmi epistolae*, 2, 210.
2   *CWE*, 1, Letter 22.
3   *CWE*, 1, Letter 23.
4   *CWE*, 1, Letters 138, 139, 141, and *CWE*, 2, Letter 149.
5   *CWE*, 1, Letter 141.
6   *CWE*, 2, Letters 245, 248, 264, 270, 273, 281, 296.
7   *Hieronymi opera* (9 vols, Basel: 1516), 5, title^v.
8   *CWE*, 3, Letters 333, 334, 335, 396.
9   *CWE*, 3, Letter 335.
10 On the edition see Denys Gorce, "La patristique dans la réforme d'Erasme," *Festgabe Joseph Lortz* (2 vols. Baden-Baden: 1958), 1, 233–276, and Eugene F. Rice, *Saint Jerome in the Renaissance* (Baltimore: 1985), chap. 5. On the Life see John C. Olin, "*Eloquentia, Eruditio, Fides*: Erasmus' *Life of Jerome*," *Acta conventus neo-latini Sanctandreani*, ed. I.D. McFarlane (Binghamton, N.Y.: 1986), pp. 269–274.
11 (2 vols. Paris: 1982). See Introduction, pp. 179–182, 540.
12 A. Humbert, *Les origines de la théologie moderne*, vol. 1 (Paris: 1911), pp. 228–238.
13 Chomarat, *op. cit.*, and André Godin, *Erasme, lecteur d'Origène* (Geneva: 1982), stress this double aim.
14 *Erasmi opuscula*, ed. W.K. Ferguson (The Hague: 1933), p. 167.
15 *Ibid.*, pp. 180–181.
16 *CWE*, 5, Letter 769.
17 *CWE*, 6, Letter 844.
18 See Rice, *op. cit.*, pp. 138–139.

For further reference see "Erasmus and the Church Fathers" in John C. Olin, *Six Essays on Erasmus* (New York: 1979).

    The forthcoming volume 61 of CWE is devoted to Erasmus' edition of Saint Jerome and will contain his Life of the saint in English translation as well as other parts of the edition.

    This subject of Erasmus and Saint Jerome and the bond between them has been treated more fully in my Folger Shakespeare Library lecture of October 27, 1986 which appears in the *Erasmus of Rotterdam Society Yearbook Seven (1987)*.

C.S.M. RADEMAKER ss.cc.

ERASMUS AND THE PSALMS
HIS COMMENTARY ON PSALM 86 (85)

Among Erasmus' biblical works there are 11 Commentaries on Psalms. They have been published recently again in the Amsterdam edition of the *Opera Omnia*.[1]

We can divide Erasmus' Psalmcommentaries into three groups:

A) The commentaries on Psalms 1 'Beatus vir' (1515), 2 'Quare fremuerunt gentes' (1522), 3 'Domine, quid multiplicati sunt qui tribulant me' (1523) and 4 'Cum inuocarem' (1525).

B) The commentaries on Psalms 86 (85) 'Inclina, Domine, aurem tuam' (1528), 23 (22) 'Deus, Deus meus, respice' (1530), 34 (33) 'Benedicam Dominum' (1531) and 39 (38) 'Dixi: Custodiam vias meas' (1532).

C) The three essays in the form of a commentary on Psalms 29 (28) *Vtilissima consultatio de bello Turcis inferendo* (1530), 84 (83) *Liber de sarcienda Ecclesiae concordia* (1533) and 15 (14) *De puritate tabernaculi siue Ecclesiae christianae* (1536).

Erasmus wrote and published the first group at the time when he was probably thinking of obliging the world with a modern commentary on all the 150 Psalms. He had been asked many times to do that and within the period 1515–1525 he published his commentaries on the first four Psalms. He was looking for the best form and so these commentaries were experiments: an *enarratio*, a *commentarius*, a *paraphrasis* and a *concio*. They were a great success, because they brought something new. New editions of the Latin texts, and also some translations in vernacular languages were published during and after his lifetime.

The second group Erasmus published after he had decided to give up his plan to comment on all the Psalms. In order to make this known, did he send his *In Psalmum LXXXV expositio concionalis* in 1528 to Bishop John Longlond of Lincoln, the man who had asked him so often to comment on the whole Psalter and who already had received Erasmus' edition of the *Commentarii in omnes psalmos* by Arnobius in 1522 and also Erasmus' Commentary on Psalm 4 in 1525? One of the reasons for giving up the original plan has probably been the changed interest of the public. As a matter of fact the four commentaries of this second group—now all of them written in the form of an *enarratio concionalis*—had not the same success as the first group of commentaries. They were published during the life of Erasmus just once, and only the Commentary on Psalm 34 (33) has been translated in a vernacular language, the Danish.

The third group, however, found greater response with the public, but these three publications were first of all essays on very up to date topics. They were far more commentaries on problems of the very moment, and the Psalms, used as points of departure, kept more or less in the background. That is why they are a very special group among the Psalmcommentaries and they are not so interesting for our knowledge of the way Erasmus studied and worked on the Psalms as biblical texts.[2]

One of the best examples of the manner Erasmus commented on the Psalms is his *Expositio concionalis* on Psalm 86 (85). He wrote this work relieved of the pressure to work out a commentary on the whole Psalter. If we may believe the author, he wrote this longest of his psalmstudies in seven days, to recreate himself from the heavy burden of many other tasks: "Isti commentario quem dignatus es legere", he wrote to Jacopo Sadoleto in 1530, "vix dati sunt dies septem, nec hi toti, nec ab integro, sed a defatigato. Vbi sex aut septem praela feruent, non licet vni vacare negocio. . . . Nos si quid istiusmodi damus, alieno fere damus affectui, idque obiter, velut a grauioribus operis redintegrantes animi vigores."[3] It is not clear why Erasmus had chosen this Psalm, but it is not impossible that he had been asked by Bishop John Longlond to make this choice. He had found now the best way to give form to his Psalmcommentaries, an *enarratio* in the form of a sermon, as Erasmus' great example, the churchfather Augustine, did so many times. He was entirely free to work out his text in the way he liked best and to deal with current and other religious and biblical topics he thought of interest for the moment.

To give an idea of the way Erasmus commented on the Psalms, I have chosen this Psalmcommentary, not only for the reasons given here, but also because I prepared this work for the Amsterdam edition. I want to deal with three aspects of the work and I can only hope this will be a way to give some information on Erasmus' working with and on the Psalms. First I am going to say something on the quotations from the Bible in this work of Erasmus. Secondly I like to point out how Erasmus used Psalmcommentaries by other authors, especially the *Enarrationes in Psalmos* by the churchfather Augustine. Finally I will try to give some information about the exegetical and religious contents of this Commentary on Psalm 86 (85) and I will end with some questions on the place of the Psalmcommentaries among the works of the great humanist.[4]

1. *Erasmus' quotations from the Bible*

The Latin text of Psalm 86 (85) used by Erasmus is the text of the *Vulgata*, the *Psalterium Gallicanum* of Hieronymus. However, from time to time Erasmus refers to the two other psalmtranslations by this churchfather, the *Psalterium Romanum* and the *Psalterium iuxta Hebraeos*. Sometimes he also gives the Latin text to be found in Augustine's *Enarrationes in Psalmos*. So in one place, speaking on verse 11 of Psalm 86 (85), Erasmus writes: "Caeterum Hebraica veritas hic nonnihil discrepat ab eo, quod et Latina et Graeca cantat ecclesia. Nam pro eo quod est: 'Laetetur cor meum', Hieronymus vertit: 'Vnicum fac cor meum', siue vt aliis placet: 'Vni cor meum'." Here Erasmus refers on the one hand to the *Vulgata* and to the *Septuagint* (reading in the Hebrew text 'chādāh', translated by ευφρανθήτω) and on the other hand to the *Psalterium iuxta Hebraeos* of Hieronymus (reading here correctly 'yachēd', it is 'Unite my heart').[5]

Following his exegetical principle, Erasmus often tries to explain the Bible with the Bible. In many places he refers to the biblical author or to the text he is quoting. In many more places he uses biblical texts, completely or partly, sometimes just some words, without giving the place or the author he is quoting. It is interesting to see in what number and proportion Erasmus quotes and uses the books of the Old Testament and the books of the New Testament. We took some samples at random and we came to the following percentages of biblical quotations in Erasmus' Commentary on Psalm 86 (85): from the Old Testament ca. 21% from the Psalms (not included the many quotations from Psalm 86 (85)) and ca. 20% from the other books; from the New Testament ca. 22% from the four Gospels, ca. 28% from the Letters of St. Paul and ca. 9% from the other books.

Many times, when quoting the Bible, Erasmus gives literal quotations, but he often quotes 'ad sensum' too. In general he uses the Latin text of the *Vulgata*. For the New Testament, however, in many places Erasmus prefers his own Latin translation of the Nouum Testamentum to the text of the *Vulgata*. So when a text differs from the *Vulgata*, one has to consult Erasmus' own translation and his Annotations on the New Testament, and sometimes also his Paraphrases. When we did that, we had to conclude that Erasmus, in his Commentary on Psalm 86 (85), quotes very carefully and that nearly all the differences from the *Vulgata* text can be explained with Erasmus' own Latin translation and his Annotations. Also the orthography of some words deserves our attention. I will give here three examples.

In one place Erasmus quotes the *Vulgata* text and also his own translation. Referring to *Phil.* 4,13 he first quotes in the Commentary the text from the *Vulgata*: "in eo qui me confortat", but some lines further he gives his own version, namely "in eo qui me corroborat", of which translation he had said in the Annotation on this passage: "*corroborat* erat Latinius."[6]

Quoting *Luc.* 24,13, Erasmus writes in the Commentary on Psalm

86 (85): "discipuli euntes in Emauntem". The *Vulgata*, however, gives "in castellum ... nomine Emmaus", with double *m*. Erasmus' New Testament has "Emaus" and in the Annotation on this place we read: "Graeci scribunt Ἐμμαοὺς per duplex *m*, vt sit dictio trisyllaba, et inflectitur *Emmauntos, ti, tem,* sicut *Pityus, Pityuntos.*"[7]

After having published his Commentary on Psalm 86 (85) in 1528, Erasmus published *Loca quaedam in aliquot Erasmi lucubrationibus per ipsum emendata* in 1529. There we also found three corrections on the Psalmcommentary of 1528. Quoting *Luc*. 22,43 ("Apparuit autem illi angelus de caelo, confortans eum") and *Matt*. 4,11 ("Et ecce angeli accesserunt, et ministrabant ei"; see also *Marc*. 1,13), Erasmus first wrote in the Commentary: "Venerunt enim angeli et ministrabant ei", but in the *Loca quaedam* he changed his text into: "et corroborabant eum".[8]

2. *Erasmus' using of Psalmcommentaries by other authors*

When in 1530 Erasmus sent his Commentary on Psalm 23 (22) to Jacopo Sadoleto, he wrote about the use of Psalmcommentaries written by other authors: "Hilarium habemus, sed mutilum; quem arbitror ex Origenis commentariis hausisse fere quae nobis tradit. Qui tum mihi quum enarrarem Psalmum LXXXV, nescio quo pacto non venit in mentem, quemadmodum nec Pomerianus: non quod omnino fidam huiusmodi scriptoribus, sed quod sapienti quaeuis occasio efficiat interdum vt fiat sapientior. Hieronymi commentarios in Psalmos opus habemus indigne contaminatos ab improbissimo quopiam impostore, cuius naeniae sunt et in eum Psalmum tuum. Augustinus non indiligenter tractauit hanc prouinciam; nisi quod permulta dare cogitur auribus populi quem instituebat, occupato doctoque lectori non admodum necessaria, nonnunquam et onerosa. In quosdam Psalmos non scripsit commentarium, sed breuissima modo scholia: quod accidit in hoc Psalmo quem nunc mitto. Cassiodorus maluit omnia scribere quomodocumque quam pauca exacte. Extant et Brunonis in Psalmos commentarioli, pietate verius quam eruditione commendabiles. Arnobii enarratio nonnunquam ipso breuior est Psalmo. Quin officit interdum scripturienti tam varia lectio. In hoc Psalmo praeter Hieronymum et Augustini scholia nihil a quoquam mutuati sumus."[9]

In his Commentary on Psalm 86 (85), Erasmus incorporated the whole *Enarratio in Psalmum LXXXV* of Augustine, despite his critical remarks on the Psalmcommentaries of the churchfather: too many things in it adapted to the common people and so much in it that is not necessary for a learned reader. In the period, however, in which Erasmus wrote his own Commentary, he was working on the new edition of the *Opera omnia* of Augustine.

In March 1529 he published Tomus VIII of these works with the *Enarrationes*. Moreover, John Longlond, to whom the Commentary on Psalm 86 (85) was dedicated, was a great admirer of Augustine. In fact, in Erasmus' *Expositio* we find all the topics, lines of thought, comparisons and biblical quotations that are found in the *Enarratio* of the churchfather. I could make an outline of Augustine's Commentary, dividing it into various parts which can all be found in Erasmus' work. I will give two examples.

In some places Erasmus uses the same biblical parable as Augustine does, but he gives it another tenor. Speaking of the rich man and the poor Lazarus (*Luc.* 16,9 – 31), Erasmus writes: "Euangelicus ille diues non inclinarat aurem Lazaro mendico et in die malo, quum cruciaretur apud inferos, non repperit qui ipsi opploranti inclinaret aurem." The churchfather writes: "In illo paupere humilitas intelligetur honorificata, in illo diuite superbia damnata." [10]

Sometimes Erasmus quotes Augustine's *Enarratio* literally, but gives the words another meaning. Augustine writes: "Caput autem nostrum ad dexteram Patris interpellat pro nobis; alia membra recipit, alia flagellat, alia mundat, alia consolatur, alia creat, alia vocat, alia reuocat, alia corrigit, alia redintegrat." And Erasmus writes: "Nec est simplex Domini misericordia, sed misericordiae illius multae, paratae omnibus clamantibus ad illum. Alia liberat, alia praeuenit, alia comitatur, alia sequitur, alia tuetur, alia consolatur, alia flagellat vt emendet, alia largitur vt ditet." [11]

It is curious that Erasmus wrote to Sadoleto that the Psalmcommentaries of Origenes did not come to his mind when writing the *Expositio* on Psalm 86 (85), because Origenes was his most beloved author from the early Christian period and in many other Psalmcommentaries he used his work. That he forgot Johann Bugenhagen's *Interpretatio* of the Psalms, Basle 1524, is not so amazing, because he did not like the work of the man with his Lutheran 'novelties'. [12] The Psalmcommentaries written by Ambrosius, Cassiodorus and the bishop of Würzburg Bruno of Carinthia, have left some traces in Erasmus' Commentary. The short *Breuiarium in Psalmos* of the Pseudo-Hieronymus, although, according to Erasmus, spoiled by an 'improbissimus impostor', can almost completely be found in the *Expositio concionalis* concerning the part on Psalm 86 (85), just like Arnobius' very short *Commentarius in Psalmum LXXXV*.

The references to all these commentaries are very precise in Erasmus' *Expositio concionalis* on Psalm 86 (85), just like the biblical references and quotations. This fact deserves our attention, because in other Psalmcommentaries Erasmus made some mistakes. In his *Enarratio Psalmi XXXVIII* from 1532, for example, Erasmus writes that he is quoting Prudentius ("Procedit e thalamo suo pudoris aula regia, etc."), but in fact this is a quotation from the well-known Christmas hymn of Ambrosius *Veni redemptor gentium* (also known as the hymn *Intende qui regis Israel*, translated by Martin Luther in his famous *Nun komm der Heiden Heiland*). Already Clericus, the editor of the Erasmus edition of 1703 – 1706, had to mention some errors of the same kind in the Commentary on Psalm 39 (38). In the *Expositio* on Psalm 86 (85), however, I didn't find such errors.[13]

3. *A summary of Erasmus' idea of the Philosophia Christiana*

On the titlepage Erasmus calls his Commentary on Psalm 86 (85) a 'Concionalis interpretatio, plena pietatis'. At the beginning of the text itself the work is entitled an 'Expositio concionalis', and at the end Erasmus writes 'Concionis finis'. In fact the readers are addressed many times as 'Fratres', 'Fratres charissimi' and 'Amici charissimi'. Often Erasmus gives adhortations such as: "Clamemus ad Dominum, fratres charissimi, et clamemus indesinenter!", or sayings as: "Huiusmodi spiritualibus deliciis liberet diutius immorari, sed non onerabo pluribus infirmiores."[14] The Commentary is built up as a real sermon, according to the rules of the 'Eloquentia sacra'. It starts with an 'exordium', followed by an extensive explanation of the title and the various verses of the Psalm, concluded with a short 'paraphrasis', a 'summarium' and a very short 'peroratio'.

In the explanation of the text of the Psalm, Erasmus not only refers to the literal sense of the words, but he also tries to find the mystical sense of the Psalm, referring to Christ, and the tropological sense, referring to the life of the Church and of the Christians. Many themes and topics are to be found in the sermon: the right way of praying; the necessity of good works and the free will (against Luther); the dissension among the Christians; the true joy of a good Christian and the light burden of the Gospel; God's goodness and love for all people (against the Jews); the knowledge of God men can find in creation and revelation; the redemption through the death and resurrection of Jesus Christ; the heresies from all times spoiling the true doctrine of the Church; the mission of all the Christians to fight for God and against the devil in the theatre of this world. In short, this commentary in the form of a sermon is a real summary of what is called Erasmus' 'Philosophia Christiana', with many references to questions and problems current in his days.

In his study *Ecstasy and the Praise of Folly*, London 1980, M.A. Screech, departing from the oldest editions of Erasmus' *Moriae Encomium*, tries to demonstrate, that in Erasmus' 'Philosophia Christiana' an important place has to be given to Christian ecstasy and ecstatic folly. At the end of his work the author gives a short survey of the works of Erasmus in which the great Christian humanist should be speaking of that ecstasy. Screech then concludes: "Closer still, where ecstatic folly is concerned, are those later commentaries on the Psalms, where Erasmus poured forth what he believed to be inspired prophetic insights into hidden mysteries. There we find expounded not the cunning 'vafritia' of 1514 but the pious ecstasy of 1511. These commentaries provided a wide field for Erasmus' emotions and for his imagination. His works on the New Testament were held on a tightish rein by the Greek texts he had to explain and by his patristic and philological scholarship. Not so the works on the Psalms. What these Psalms might have meant in the original Hebrew concerns him hardly at all. He sees them as a series of hidden truths, waiting to be revealed by divine inspiration working through a chosen vessel: an exegete inspired by the Spirit. When Erasmus expounds the Psalms he breaks away from the cramping restraints of philological scholarship, finding himself free to range over the limitless fields of allegory and enigmatic mysteries. What he finds in these Psalms is not so much David or Jeduthun but Christ the madman, Christ the self-emptying God, Christ the preacher and the example of the divine and ecstatic dementedness of truly spiritual philosophy."[15]

In the last chapter of his book, entitled 'The Inspired Exegesis of a Christian Prophet', Screech gives an analysis of Erasmus' Commentary on Psalm 34 (33), the Psalm with the title 'Psalmus Dauid quum Dauid mutauit vultum suum coram Abimelech'. This Psalm, Screech says, is full of hidden mysteries. It is not necessary to agree fully with all the conclusions of Screech and with the way he comes to them, but to his conclusions on Erasmus' Psalmcommentaries one can subscribe: In these commentaries Erasmus was free to say all he wanted to say about Christian religion, about the right understanding of the mysteries of God and men, about the way Christians have to live, in short all Erasmus is said to summarize in the words 'Philosophia Christiana'. Here we find the real and deepest significance of these works of Erasmus, which therefore deserve more attention than they have received up to now.

NOTES

1 *ASD*, V–2 (1985) "Introduction générale" by Ch. Béné; Commentaries on the Psalms 1 (ed. A. Godin), 2 (S. Dresden), 3 (S. Dresden), 4 (Ch. Béné), 15 (14) (Ch. Béné) and 23 (22) (Ch. Béné); *ASD*, V–3 (1986) Commentaries on Psalms 29 (28) (ed. A.G. Weiler), 34 (33) (R. Stupperich), 39 (38) (R. Stupperich), 84 (83) (R. Stupperich) and 86 (85) (C.S.M. Rademaker ss.cc.).

2 For the Psalmcommentaries in general, see Ch. Béné, "Introduction Générale", in *ASD*, V–2, pp. 1–17. See also Ch. Béné, "L'exégèse des Psaumes chez Erasme", *Fatio. Histoire de l'exégèse au XVIe siècle. Textes du Colloque International tenu à Genève en 1976*, (Etudes de philologie et d'histoire 34), Genève: 1978, pp. 118–132; G. Chantraine, "Erasme, lecteur des psaumes", in *Colloquia Erasmiana Turonensia*, T.II, Paris: 1972, pp. 700ff.

3 *Allen* 2315, 118–121 and 104–106.

4 The *Expositio concionalis in Psalmum LXXXV* has been published in *ASD*, V–3, pp. 315–427, and is also to be found in *LB*, V, 507–556.

5 *ASD*, V–3, 391, 696–698 with the notes; *LB* V, 539.

6 *ASD*, V–3, 343, 336–337 and 349–350 with the notes; *LB* V, 514.

7 *ASD*, V–3, 366, 15 with the note; *LB* V, 526.

8 *ASD*, V–3, 374–375, 252 with critical apparatus and note; *LB* V, 530.

9 *Allen* 2315, 149–168.

10 *ASD*, V–3, 346, 443–445; *LB* V, 515; Augustinus, *In Psalmum LXXXV enarratio, sermo*, in El. Dekkers and I. Fraipoint edd., *Sancti Aurelii Augustini Enarrationes in Psalmos*, *CCSL* 39, Turnholti: 1956, p. 1178, 22–24.

11 *ASD*, V–3, 362, 914–916; *LB* V, 524; Augustinus, *o.c.*, p. 1180, 14–17.

12 *Allen* 1539, 75–80.

13 *ASD*, V–3, 176, 183–187; *LB* V, 421. Cf. J. v. Biezen and J.W. Schulte Nordholt, *Hymnen, een bloemlezing*, Turnhout: 1967, pp. 22 and 254–257. See also Erasmus' Commentary on Psalm 39 (38), *ASD*, V–3, 190, 735–736 (*LB* V, 431), *ASD*, V–3, 192–193, 826–831 (*LB* V, 432) and *ASD*, V–3, 221, 902–903 (*LB* V, 452).

14 *ASD*, V–3, 363, 939, and 426, 640–641; *LB* V, 525 and 556.

15 Screech, *Ecstasy*, pp. 248–249.

L. VOET

ERASMUS AND HIS CORRESPONDENTS

Desiderius Erasmus Roterodamus dominated the world of learning of his age. Posterity has reciprocated by filling an impressive library with studies on his life, his activities, his works, his influence, his tribulations with friends and foes. Somewhat surprisingly, however, the large network of Erasmus' relations, which spanned practically the whole of Christian Europe, has escaped a thorough examination. Of course the circle of his friends has been examined in detail for some particular regions and cities[1], but a global study is missing.

It is out of the question to exhaust the problem within the limited number of pages of this paper. In fact, a more detailed approach is something which can keep a number of scholars quite happy for the rest of their lives, and it is an ideal subject for students in search of a thesis. Only a small introductory contribution will be given here, limited to Erasmus' correspondents—the people with whom he has exchanged letters; more specifically to the correspondents and letters cited in that monument of erudition, the *Opus epistolarum Des. Erasmi Roterodami* by P.S. Allen and his collaborators[2]. The—relatively few—additional epistles in the meantime found and published in other works have been left aside. These correspondents represent only a fraction of the relations whom Erasmus cultivated during his life.

The great humanist has seen to it that many of his letters were published. Already some 1.200 of the epistles he sent or received were available in print to the public at large at the time of his death[3], and Allen has saved many more from oblivion. It is, however, only from about 1515– 1516, when fame had come, that Erasmus became aware of the literary and scholarly importance of his correspondence and began to preserve more carefully, and to publish, his letters. This means that, notwithstanding the intense research by Allen, the gaps are large and many for Erasmus' youth in Holland, his sojourns in France and England and his visit to Italy. It is only beginning with the years spent in Brabant that the number of preserved epistles starts to rise[4]. This fact has to be taken into consideration when evaluating the relative importance of the English, French and Italian correspondents in Erasmus' circle.

Another fact may also not be overlooked: even a lifelong compulsory letter-writer as Erasmus considered it a bit odd to address epistles to people he could at any given time meet in his or their houses: the letters in his correspondence are addressed to or come from people who were, if often temporarily, 'out of sight'. This can explain why in the collected letters some strange omissions are to be noted[5].

On the other hand, by going through the letters and other documents, many names pop up of people who may not have been 'correspondents' in the narrow sense of the word (or whose letters have been lost), but, anyway, appear to have been close friends or relations. Digging up these personalities, however, does not enter into the scope of this paper.

The statistics in this contribution will thus only bear on the preserved epistles and their correspondents in Erasmus' collected letters as published by Allen. Even when taking into account the numerous omissions and gaps, they give a sizeable percentage of the people whom Erasmus has frequented, allowing already to draw a number of conclusions.

The letters published by Allen include a number of dedicatory epistles published in printed works and addressed to 'the (benevolent) reader', to 'all scholars', and the like; others were addressed to or received from institutions; of a number of correspondents nothing is known—not even the name. This leaves finally 3093 letters and 666 identifiable correspondents.

A last introductory remark: corresponding with Erasmus was by and large an affair of men. In the mass of 666 correspondents only seven women can be found: a queen (Catharina of Aragon), three princesses of royal blood (Margaret of Valois; the two Habsburg governors-general of the Netherlands, Margaret of Austria and Mary of Hungary), a noble woman from Zeeland, a nun from Holland and Margaret Roper, the daughter of Thomas More.

1. *Nationality of the correspondents*[6]

An interesting problem, but eventual conclusions have to a certain point to be relativated. The majority of Erasmus' correspondents were scholars who led an astonishingly ambulant life, to be followed, as in fact that of the great master himself, with an atlas at hand; first when as students wandering from one college and university to another; in their later years in eager search for patrons and interesting 'situations'. This means that a large percentage of the citizens of Germany, the Netherlands, Italy, etc. listed in the correspondence, have in fact contacted Erasmus outside their native country.

It may be noted that in Italy and in France correspondents from the Southern parts (Kingdom of Naples; Provence-Languedoc-Guyenne) are poorly represented, whilst in Germany correspondents from the Northern provinces remain far under the average.

Countries	Correspondents	Number of Letters
Germany[7]	217 (32,58%)	932 (30,13%)
Netherlands[8]	180 (27,03%)	748 (24,18%)
Italy[9]	77 (11,57%)	313 (10,12%)
England	54 (8,11%)	333 (10,77%)
France[10]	49 (7,36%)	197 (6.37%)
Switzerland	30 (4,50%)	304 (9,83%)
Spain	24 (3,60%)	116 (3,75%)
Poland	20 (3,00%)	73 (2,36%)
Hungary	6 (0,90%)	51 (1,65%)
Portugal	3 (0,45%)	16 (0,52%)
Scotland	2 (0,30%)	5 (0,16%)
Denmark	2 (0,30%)	3 (0,10%)
Greece[11]	2 (0,30%)	2 (0,06%)
	666	3093

In the Netherlands they were largely concentrated in the heartland of the Low Countries: in Flanders, Brabant, Holland and Zeeland (on a total of 180: 41 from Flanders, 38 from Brabant, 35 from Holland, 12 from Zeeland, i.e. 126; to whom may be added 3 from Loon, the actual Belgian Dutchspeaking province of Limburg then belonging to the bishopric of Liège). The other provinces were poorly represented. In the Eastern Netherlands: 7 from Friesland, 4 from Overijssel, 3 from Utrecht, 3 from Gelre, 2 from Groningen, i.e. 19. In the French (and German) speaking parts of the Netherlands: 8 from Luxemburg, 5 from Hainaut, 5 from Liège, 3 from Tournai, 3 from Artois, i.e. 24. Of 8 the native province is not known.

2. Social positions and functions

A fascinating but also a very confusing problem which it would be interesting to refine in a number of supplementary studies and of which we can only give a rough outline.

The great majority of the correspondents of Erasmus were men of learning: a list of their publications would fill quite a number of pages. But, then as now, scholarly research does not generally allow for a good living. If not from prominent families, scholars had to look for other means to remain in life whilst continuing their humanistic or theological hobbies on the sideline.

One ideal outcome was to go into an ecclesiastical career, in search of prebends which assured a livelihood—and, if possible, much leisure time; as was the case with Erasmus himself. But there were many other possibilities and an astonishing variety of combinations, which, in the limited scope of this paper, had to be contracted to the utmost, with the loss of many nuances[12].

A) *Ecclesiastics*

Pope: 5 (Ne.: 1; It.: 4)
Prelate: 58 (Ge.: 13; Ne.: 10; It.: 12; En.: 5; Fr.: 9; Sw.: 3; Pol.: 2; Sp.: 4)
Prelate + official: 20 (Ge.: 4; Ne.: 1; It.: 2; En.: 4; Fr.: 3; Pol.: 4; Sp.: 1; Hu.: 1)
Prelate + other combinations: 3 (2 professor: 1 It., 1 Gr.; 1 physician: It.)
Ecclesiastic: 120 (Ge.: 46; Ne.: 41; It.: 7; En.: 8; Fr.: 5; Sw.: 5; Pol.: 2; Sp.: 4; Hu.: 1; Por.: 1)
Ecclesiastic + professor: 28 (Ge.: 8; Ne.: 10; It.: 1; En.: 4; Fr.: 3; Sw.: 1; Sp.: 1)
Ecclesiastic + official: 35 (Ge.: 10; Ne.: 4; It.: 9; En.: 7; Fr.: 1; Sw.: 1; Sp.: 2; Hu.: 1)
Ecclesiastic + teacher: 15 (Ge.: 6; Ne.: 7; En.: 1; Sp.: 1)
Ecclesiastic + other combinations: 7 (Ge.: 1 professor + official, 1 physician; It.: 1 professor + official, 1 teacher + official; En.: 1 lawyer; Sw.: 1 professor + official; Sp.: 1 physician)

In all: 291 ecclesiastics

B) *Laics*

King or prince: 18 (Ge.: 8; Ne.: 1; It.: 2; En.: 1; Fr.: 2; Sp.: 1; Pol.: 1; Por.: 1; Sc.: 1)
Noble: 11 (Ge.: 2; Ne.: 7; Pol.: 2)
Notable: 10 (Ge.: 2; Ne.: 4; It.: 1; En.: 2; Sw.: 1)
Merchant/banker: 9 (Ge.: 5; Ne.: 2; It.: 1; Sw.: 1)
Official: 115 (Ge.: 33; Ne.: 41; It.: 10; En.: 8; Fr.: 10; Sw.: 1; Pol.: 4; Sp.: 5; Hu.: 2; Por.: 1)
Official + professor: 7 (Ge.: 5; Fr.: 2)
Official + teacher: 4 (Ne.: 3; It.: 1)
Professor: 33 (Ge.: 15; Ne.: 7; It.: 1; En.: 2; Fr.: 3; Sw.: 3; Sp.: 1; Sc.: 1)
Professor + printer: 2 (Ne.: 2)
Teacher: 38 (Ge.: 16; Ne.: 10; It.: 2; En.: 3; Fr.: 3; Sw.: 3; De.: 1)
Teacher + printer: 1 (Fr.: 1)
Physician: 31 (Ge.: 10; Ne.: 7; It.: 7; En.: 2; Fr.: 3; Pol.: 1; Hu.: 1)
Physician + official: 3 (Ge.: 1; It.: 1; Pol.: 1)
Physician + professor: 5 (Ge.: 3; Fr.: 1; Sw.: 1)
Lawyer: 8 (Ge.: 4; Ne.: 1; It.: 1; Fr.: 1; Pol.: 1)
Scholar: 16 (Ge.: 7; Ne.: 4; It.: 1; Fr.: 1; Sp.: 2; Gr.: 1)
Printing industry[13]: 19 (Ge.: 6; Ne.: 4; It.: 4; Sw.: 5)
Students[14]: 9 (Ge.: 5; It.: 1; En.: 1; Pol.: 2)
Servants[15]: 6 (Ge.: 1; Ne.: 1; En.: 2; Fr.: 1; Sw.: 1)
Family of Erasmus: 2 (Ne.: 2)

In all: 347 laics

C) *Unknown*

28 (Ge.: 5; Ne.: 10; It.: 5; En.: 3; Sw.: 3; Sp.: 1; De.: 1)

One can at a first glance already recognize the dominant position among ecclesiastics and laity alike, on one side of the 'patrons' (popes, prelates, prelates + officials, ecclesiastics + officials, kings and princes, nobles, notables, merchants and bankers etc.), on the other side of the scholars of all kinds. The other groups together form but a small minority. The printing industry is poorly represented but there are reasons for that[16]. Interesting to note is the rather large proportion of physicians. If, however, some of them may have attended to the bodily welfare of Erasmus, most of them appear in his circle as scholars interested in humanistic and classical studies[17].

Very noteworthy is the complete absence of artists, whilst composers are only represented by three practitioners of dubious quality, two of them mere amateurs[18].

3. *Frequency*

The letters exchanged between Erasmus and his correspondents have varied enormously:

One letter sent to or received from 283 correspondents, i.e. a total of 283 letters (Ge.: 94; Ne.: 85; It.: 34; En.: 16; Fr.: 19; Sw.: 12; Sp.: 8; Pol.: 8; Hu.: 2; Por.: 2; Gr.: 2; De.: 1).

Two letters—116 correspondents, i.e. 232 letters (Ge.: 36; Ne.: 27; It.: 15; En.: 10; Fr.: 14; Sw.: 4; Sp.: 4; Pol.: 4; Sc.: 1; De.: 1).

Three letters—58 correspondents, i.e. 174 letters (Ge.: 23; Ne.: 14; It.: 4; En.: 7; Fr.: 3; Sw.: 2; Sp.: 3; Pol.: 1; Sc.: 1).

Four letters—38 correspondents, i.e. 152 letters (Ge.: 6; Ne.: 15; It.: 7; En.: 3; Fr.: 1; Sw.: 2; Sp.: 1; Pol.: 2; Hu.: 1).

Five letters—25 correspondents, i.e. 125 letters (Ge.: 8; Ne.: 6; It.: 2; En.: 2; Fr.: 4; Sw.: 1; Sp.: 2).

Six letters—20 correspondents, i.e. 120 letters (Ge.: 7; Ne.: 7; It.: 2; En.: 1; Fr.: 2; Pol.: 1).

Seven letters—24 correspondents, i.e. 168 letters (Ge.: 11; Ne.: 4; It.: 1; En.: 3; Fr.: 1; Sw.: 1; Sp.: 1; Pol.: 1; Hu.: 1).

Eight letters—15 correspondents, i.e. 120 letters (Ge.: 5; Ne.: 3; En.: 2; Fr.: 1; Sw.: 1; Sp.: 2; Hu.: 1).

Nine letters—18 correspondents, i.e. 162 letters (Ge.: 7; Ne.: 3; It.: 3; Fr.: 1; Sw.: 2; Pol.: 2).

Ten letters—11 correspondents, i.e. 110 letters (Ge,: 6; Ne.: 1; It.: 2; En.: 1; Sp.: 1).

608 correspondents—1646 letters

More than 10 letters: 58 correspondents—1447 letters:
  11 letters to or from 5 correspondents (Ge.: 1; Ne.: 3; Fr.: 1);
  12 letters—8 correspondents (Ge.: 2; Ne.: 3; It.: 2; Sw.: 1);
  13 letters—2 correspondents (Ne.: 1; En.: 1);
  14 letters—2 correspondents (It.: 1; Por.: 1);
  15 letters—4 correspondents (It.: 2; En.: 1; Pol.: 1);
  16 letters—4 correspondents (Ne.: 1; It.: 1; Sw.: 1; Sp.: 1);
  17 letters—3 correspondents (En.: 3);
  18 letters—2 correspondents (Ge.: 1; Sw.: 1);
  19 letters—4 correspondents (Ge.: 3; Ne.: 1);
  20 letters—1 correspondent (Fr.: 1);
  22 letters—2 correspondents (Ne.: 1; En.: 1);
  23 letters—2 correspondents (Ne.: 1; En.: 1);
  26 letters—3 correspondents (Ge.: 2; En.: 1);
  28 letters—1 correspondent (Sp.: 1);
  29 letters—1 correspondent (Sw.: 1);
  30 letters—1 correspondent (Hu.: 1);
  31 letters—2 correspondents (Ge.: 1; Ne.: 1);
  32 letters—1 correspondent (Ge.: 1);
  35 letters—2 correspondents (Ge.: 1; Ne.: 1);
  36 letters—2 correspondents (Ge.: 1; Ne.: 1);
  49 letters—1 correspondent (It.: 1);
  50 letters—1 correspondent (Fr.: 1);
  51 letters—1 correspondent (En.: 1);
  55 letters—1 correspondent (Ge.: 1);
  82 letters—1 correspondent (Ne.: 1);
157 letters—1 correspondent (Sw.: 1).

This statistical survey tends to show that the larger part of Erasmus' correspondents were only—as far as they have exchanged letters (an important percentage of them must in fact have been rather close friends and relations who frequently met Erasmus in his or their residences)—what can be called 'occasional contacts': some 60% of the total number of correspondents are only listed for one or two letters.

On the other hand, the enumeration of the correspondents with whom Erasmus had a more intense epistolar relationship forms fascinating reading. As this paper is limited to statistics a more detailed approach has to be reserved for other contributions. However, the temptation is great to finish this article with a brief list of the correspondents with whom Erasmus exchanged twenty and more letters (together 955 or some 30% of the total correspondence); just to show how heterogenous the group of Erasmus' top-correspondents was.

A few were among the luminaries of their age: Luis Vives (Sp.: 28 letters), Guillaume Budé (Fr.: 50 letters), Thomas More (En.: 51 letters), Willibald Pirckheimer (Ge.: 55 letters). Others count among the enlightened patrons of the time: a reigning German prince (Duke George of Saxony: 31 letters), a prominent English noble (William Blount, lord Mount-joy: 22 letters), an even more prominent English prelate (William Warham, archbischop of Canterbury: 26 letters), an important Nether-landish official (Viglius ab Aytta: 31 letters), and, if not more exalted, anyway one of the richest men of his time, the Antwerp merchant-banker Erasmus Schets (82 letters). The larger number of these correspondents, however, were more modest—some of them very modest—scholars (eventually scholar + professor or scholar + official). In the Netherlands James Batt, a youth-friend of Erasmus (22 letters); Peter Aegidius (Gilles), an Antwerp town-clerk (35 letters); Martin Lipsius, professor at the Louvain university (36 letters). In Germany John Botzheim (Alsace; 26 letters); John Choler (26 letters); Conrad Goclenius, who spent the larger part of his life as professor at the Louvain university (32 letters); Ambrosius Storch (or Pelargus) (35 letters); Bernard of Cles (Trente; 36 letters). In France Germanus Brixius (20 letters). In Hungary Nicolas Olah (30 letters). In Italy Andrew Ammonius (49 letters). In Switzerland Ulrich Zasius (26 letters), and the man who tops the list with 157 letters, Bonifatius Amerbach.

NOTES

1 E.g.: for Alsace (*Catalogue of the exhibition Erasme et l'Alsace* at the Bibliothèque Natio-nale de Paris and the Bibliothèque Universitaire de Strasbourg, 1970), Louvain (*Catalogue of the exhibition Erasmus en Leuven*, Louvain, 1969; M.A. Nauwelaerts, "Ver-blijf en werk van Erasmus te Leuven", in *Mededelingen van de Geschied- en Oudheidkun-dige kring voor Leuven en omgeving*, 1969), Antwerp (M. Sabbe, "Erasmus en zijn Ant-werpsche vrienden", in *Verslagen en Mededeelingen van de Koninklijke Vlaamsche Academie voor Taal- en Letterkunde*, 1936; brief but worth reading: M.A. Nauwelaerts, "Erasmus en Antwerpen", in *Geschiedenis in het Onderwijs*, 1962).
2 French translation of the letters, under the direction of A. Gerlo and Paul Foriers, Brussels, 1967ff.
3 Cf. the very interesting study of L.E. Halkin, *Erasmus ex Erasmo*, Aubel, 1983.
4 1484–1494: 41 letters; 1495: 6 letters; 1496; 2 letters; 1497: 17 letters; 1498: 20 let-ters; 1499: 32 letters; 1500: 23 letters; 1501: 26 letters; 1502: 5 letters; 1503: 6 letters; 1504: 3 letters; 1505: 5 letters; 1506: 19 letters; 1507: 4 letters; 1508: 4 letters; 1509: 3 letters; 1510: —; 1511: 35 letters; 1512: 16 letters; 1513: 16 letters; 1514: 36 letters; 1515: 61 letters; 1516: 126 letters; 1517: 241 letters; 1518: 160 letters; 1519: 148 let-ters; 1520: 123 letters; 1521: 73 letters; 1522: 80 letters; 1523: 75 letters; 1524: 128 letters; 1525: 123 letters; 1526: 118 letters; 1527: 150 letters; 1528: 155 letters; 1529: 164 letters; 1530: 111 letters; 1531: 173 letters; 1532: 159 letters; 1533: 144 letters; 1534: 92 letters; 1535: 94 letters; 1536: 71 letters.
5 To give but one example: the many printers whom Erasmus has frequented are very poorly represented. Not a single letter e.g. has been preserved exchanged between Erasmus and his good friend Dirk Martens. the prominent typographer at Antwerp

and Louvain. It may be assumed that the dealings of Erasmus with printers were mostly discussed in personal meetings.

6   A problem somewhat complicated by the fact that the boundaries of the states in the time of Erasmus generally did not coïncide with those of contemporary Europe. For some specific remarks see following notes. Used abbreviations: Ge.: Germany; Ne.: Netherlands; It.: Italy; En.: England; Fr.: France; Sw.: Switzerland; Sp.: Spain; Pol.: Poland; Hu.: Hungary; Por.: Portugal; Sc.: Scotland; De.: Denmark; Gr.: Greece.

7   The massive body of states of all kinds and dimensions forming the German Empire included to the West entities which in the 17th century passed to France (Cambrai, Alsace, Lorraine, Franche Comté), to the East became in the 20th century sovereign states (Czechoslovakia), to the South went in that same 20th century to Italy (Trente). Of the 217 German correspondents of Erasmus 13 came from Franche Comté, 5 from Lorraine, 11 from Alsace, 1 from Cambrai, 6 from Bohemia, 1 from Moravia, 1 from Trente.

8   The Netherlands as defined here include the Eastern territories of the Northern Netherlands (actual Netherlands), which were only joined to the Habsburg Low Countries in the later years of Erasmus or even after his death, and Artois (ceded to France in the 17th century). Also included is the bishopric of Liège which, with the dependant county of Loon, remained in fact an autonomous principality within the Netherlands—and nominally part of the German Empire—till the end of the 18th century.

9   The numerous independent and less independent states of the Italian peninsula are here put together under the label 'Italy'. Not included is Trente (see Germany).

10 Not included are Artois (then part of the Netherlands) and Cambrai, Lorraine, Alsace and Franche Comté (then parts of Germany).

11 The two Greeks were living and working in Italy.

12 *Prelates*: cardinals, archbishops, bishops, abbots. *Ecclesiastics*: secular and regular clerics and monks below the dignities of bishop or abbot. *Professors*: attached to a university. *Teachers*: schoolmasters or teaching in colleges. *Officials*: agents in a central, regional or local administration, many of them licentiates or doctors in civil and/or canonic law. *Nobles*: when having no specific public functions; most of them have in fact been registered in other categories: as prelates, ecclesiastics, officials. *Notables* on the local level: burgomasters, aldermen and the like. *Lawyers*: when only practising as such; most of them, in fact, became officials. *Scholars*: when having no known specific functions.

13 Printers, booksellers, publishers, correctors.

14 Students at the time of their correspondence with Erasmus, their later life being unknown or obscure.

15 In the service or having served Erasmus; some of them pupils—servants.

16 See note 5.

17 Including the famous French author, François Rabelais, who called himself, in the subscription of his letter, *medicus*.

18 The Swiss physician + professor Jerome Artolbius and the Venetian official Nicolas Sagundinus. The third, the ecclesiastic John Mauburn, was *musicae cantor* at the cathedral church of Utrecht.

GERMAIN MARC'HADOUR

THOMAS MORE IN EMULATION
AND DEFENSE OF ERASMUS

The friendship between Erasmus and More has always been a matter of fact and a matter of speculation. That Erasmus held pride of place in More's *polyphilia* was taken for granted in their lifetime; they were *amicissimi* par excellence. When making the portrait of his London friend, Erasmus feels the need to quote other people's testimonies, lest he be suspected of partiality[1]. In his quarrel with Erasmus, the young Edward Lee is reluctant to accept the arbitration of a More who is notoriously biased in favor of the Dutchman.

Last Autumn, at Washington, I lectured on "Erasmus: first and best biographer of More."[2] My purpose today is to re-examine the other panel of the diptych, or, if you reckon a judicial metaphor more judicious in talking of a lawyer, to re-open the other half of the dossier by documenting More's attitude toward Erasmus over the thirty-six years of their acquaintance. The chronological order recommends itself the more strongly because not a few scholars have discovered—or imagined? asserted anyway, rather than ascertained—ups and downs in their friendship, and linked these vicissitudes with the divisive effects of the theological controversies raging from 1520 on.

More was only a student when, in the Summer of 1499, he first met an Erasmus who, though considerably older than himself, was still also a student holidaying in England. There appears to have been a teasing sharpness, a youthful belligerence in their early relationship: More delighted Erasmus by wrestling with him after Sparta's manner, with nails that bite into the flesh and draw blood[3]. More also boldly threw the bashful tourist into the deep water of a royal household, forcing him to swim for his life, as it were. Erasmus' annoyance[4] must have been, at least in retrospect, shot with gratitude: so as not to be outdistanced by More, who had brought a piece of verse for Henry VII's children, he wrote that *prosopopoeia ad Britanniam* which found its way into print within weeks, and was published many times, more often, I think, than any other composition of Erasmus. Of More's poem, on the contrary, we know nothing, not even the title; it may have been one of the pieces included in the Basel edition of his *Epigrammata* (1518).

In addition to a few letters, and to a *disputatiuncula* with Colet, published in 1503, the *prosopopoeia* is the only known product of Erasmus' first visit across the Channel, and it was prompted by emulation toward More. The same spirit, apparently reciprocal, inspired their joint labor on Lucian during Erasmus' second and longer sojourn in England (1505 – 1506). The result (published at Paris in November 1506)[5] is never so much as alluded to by More or his biographers; if Erasmus had not, on 1 May 1506, dedicated one of his translations to a common friend, we would know nothing of the competitive atmosphere which presided over the undertaking. More was to live another three decades without ever mentioning Lucian[6]: how grateful we should be to Erasmus, whose garrulity feeds our curiosity! As for More's early biographers, though the volume containing the *Lucianica* of Erasmus and More appeared fourteen times before the death of the authors, they ignore the very name of the Greek satirist.

Erasmus' third and longest taste of Britain began in the warm glow of Henry VIII's accession to the throne (1509), and lasted, across one brief visit to Paris in 1511 and the 1512 – 13 war between England and France, until 1514. Erasmus arrived big with at least the embryo of the *Moriae Encomium*, of which he was delivered under More's roof, and, so he tells us, not without some midwiving on the part of More[7]. He left heavy with manuscripts of daunting dimensions, all but ready for the printer: the Greek text of the New Testament, his own Latin translation of it with a set of Annotations thereon, and St. Jerome's copious Correspondence. The five heavy folios which issued from Froben's presses in the first semester of 1516 placed Erasmus in the forefront of Europe's scholars, while his *Praise of Folly*, coming on the heels of the *Adagia*, was beginning its career as a bestseller in world literature. More has entered the picture as the dedicatee of the *Moria*. In addition to explaining the pun on *Moros/Moria*, the prefatory letter was the first document to call More—a young lawyer barely past the age of thirty, and still new in his job as undersheriff of London—*omnibus omnium horarum hominem*, "a man for all seasons" in the now proverbial English rendering of 1519[8].

Morus Erasmi patronus

Before greeting Erasmus' *Novum Instrumentum* with three Latin poems of warm recommendation addressed to Cardinal Wolsey, Archbishop Warham, and the Christian reader[9], More defended the idea of it, while it was still in press, through his famous letter to the Dutch theologian Martin van Dorp, signed from Bruges on 21 October 1515. Though not printed in More's lifetime, this book-length epistle was highly influential: it converted Dorp to Greek studies, and its mark has been noted in Juan Luis Vives' *Pseudodialecticos*[10]. Coming sixteen years, almost to the day, after Erasmus' first extant letter to More, it contains, almost incredibly, ings. We cannot proceed without pausing for a good long look at it, and my only grief today is that I cannot use the first really critical edition of it, just out but not yet in my hands[11].

In its first printing (Basle, 1563, where it occupies 63 pages), the title, *Apologia pro Moria Erasmi, qua etiam docetur quam necessaria sit linguae Graecae cognitio*, represents only part of the contents. More begins by stressing how good Erasmus is at fostering friendship and how affectionately he speaks of his absent friends. Then he proceeds to defend both facets of Erasmus' genius, and the two complementary expressions of his concern to reform Christendom: the weapon of satire, which *castigat ridendo mores*, and the powerhouse of Christ's Revelation tapped directly *e fontibus* under the lead of its most authoritative exponent, the trilingual St. Jerome. Named in the very first sentence of the letter (Rogers, p. 28/6, and *CW15*, p. 2/1), Erasmus seldom exits from the stage. Because he thinks highly of you, More says to the budding thirty-year-old divine, Erasmus takes to heart your attacks on his *Praise of Folly* and your strictures on his project to emend the New Testament into conformity with the Greek original[12].

Moriae Encomium is the subject of a protracted defense, which goes much beyond a 'non-guilty' plea. More demonstrates the weight and wisdom of this light-hearted, light-tongued *Folly*: its quips may have ruffled some dour senior dons at Louvain, but many people have memorized whole sections of it (p. 30/67f.). I am surprised, More adds, that you "write to so important a friend with such acerbity, and so negligently to a man of such learning"[13]. Erasmus does not need my patronage, since he is considered, and *is* in fact, so great in the eyes of all. You haughty theologians dismiss him as a *grammaticus*; this label fits, like its Latin synonym *litteratus*, if you keep in mind that it designates, not the teacher of the letters A B C, but the scholar versed in all good letters: the secular disciplines, of course, but also, indeed more so, sacred literature[14]. Erasmus is familiar even with the petty questions which take up so much of your energy, and with that formal logic which has almost evicted true divinity from your schools: don't reckon that he, whose genius and learning are admired by all, will prove inferior to all of your logicians in disputation![15]

Nor is Erasmus a stranger to the academic world: he has studied and taught in more than one University: Paris, Padua, Bologna, not to mention Rome, queen of them all. Oxford and Cambridge cherish their connection with him and vie with each other in trying to secure him (p. 36/271–74). He does not attack the professors of Louvain; Dame Folly, insofar as she speaks for him, does ridicule those whose lore has not gone beyond sophistical trifles[16]. He wants to substitute rhetoric and poetry, not for theology, but for the host of thorny problems which have usurped the place of authentic theology, based on Holy Scripture.

Dorp has spoken of the Bible as if it were a pleasant meadow with no pitfalls, no hurdles. More sees it as the book sealed with seven seals[17]. Granted that the kind of chopping epitomized in Lombard's *Sentences* has its uses, nothing replaces direct recourse to the written Word of God and its best expositors—the oldest, holiest and learnedest Church fathers: hence the need for Erasmus' editorial labors. St. Jerome corrected whatever in the Latin New Testament of his day was untrue to the meaning of the Greek original[18]. Erasmus follows this example: the inspired text calls for emendation now just as it did then[19]. A variety of translations is a boon, even though none can rival the authority of the original. The task in which Erasmus is engaged, of leading the Christians *ad fontes*, will make that original available for the first time. More's wish that Dorp learn Greek for the sake of immediate access to such treasures (and to classics like Aristotle and his commentators) was fulfilled as early as 1516[20].

Before taking his leave, More returns to the *Moria* and the whole idea of criticism. Noviomagus (Geldenhauer of Nijmegen) uses biting sarcasm, in his 1515 *Satyrae*, with Dorp's approval; Erasmus achieves the same reforming goal by joking, under the mask of Folly, with greater prudence and lesser licence: "sumpta Moriae persona, et prudenter magis et minus licenter iocatur" (67/1383–5). Dorp had urged Erasmus to take the sting off his *Stultitiae Laus* by publishing a *Sapientiae Laus*. But, More answers, wisdom's darts would inflict deeper wounds, because they would hit those morons straight, without the courteous detour of irony. More's valediction betokens diplomacy as well as genuine love: "You are no less dear to me than you are to Erasmus; dearer you cannot be, not even to myself" (74/1610–11). Erasmus emerges from the letter not merely as an accomplished scholar and writer, but also as a paragon of friendship, and a lovable character.

More's Praise of Wisdom?

More put a stop to his first epistolary treatise when ordered back home by Henry VIII. As he crossed the Channel in that Autumn of 1515, his return freight included a rare exotic fruit, alone of its kind in Latin history, and in need of some further mellowing; it would be ripe in 1516, and appear under the name of *Utopia*. Belgium was its nursery. Conceived in the sea-harbors of Flanders, the "golden little book" saw the light of day at Louvain, where Erasmus now lived. In a way, it met Dorp's request of a *Praise of Wisdom*. It was like a "défense et illustration" of foolish reasonableness (*morosophia*) after Erasmus' exercise in reasonable folly (*sophomoria*): one of several reasons, perhaps, why Erasmus goes unmentioned in both the text of *Utopia* and its *parerga*, where other names abound—Busleiden, Gillis, de Schryver, Geldenhauer, Paludanus. And yet we know how active Erasmus was in sponsoring the production of the book, overseeing its publication, fostering its circulation, providing clues for its interpretation[21]. We know of Erasmus' role precisely because More's letters to him begin from 1516 to find their way into the permanence of print. Their total absence till then, after more than sixteen years of acquaintance with Erasmus, has never been construed as evidence of tepidity, any more than the total lack of references to Lucian and to Pico della Mirandola in the vast corpus of More's writings from 1506 to 1535 need betray a sense that he had outgrown these models of his early manhood.

The word "emulation" in the title of this paper implies no attempt on More's part at reproducing the social pattern of Erasmus' life. As in the pattern *imitatio Christi*—"the following of Christ" in More's English—the "holy ambition"[22] it indicates is fidelity to a spirit. Otherwise, More would not have become Undersheriff; he would have eschewed not only Court service, but also membership of Parliament, and even the bonds of wedlock, as did Plato and Christ, St. Paul and Erasmus, Pico and Raphaël Hythlodaeus. Because More, not content with extolling Erasmus, endeavored to secure a quiet canonry for him in the episcopal city of Doornik/Tournay, and performed menial jobs on his behalf (such as transferring his English pension and securing a horse), some biographers seem to have expected from him the greater compliment of remaining at the master's side in the free service of the muses. These historians imagine More's entrance into royal service as an affront to Erasmus. Did *Morus in bivio*, More at the crossroads, truly choose another path than his elder comrade? The contrast between their positions in this regard is less marked, in fact, than the differences between their education and their overall character. Erasmus was sorry that More should forfeit his chances of becoming a professional humanist, yet he also expressed pleasure and pride at More's political preferment. In 1519, he exhorted Hutten[23], and through him all the young intellectuals of Europe, to look up to More as a model by making their liberal education an asset in the service of their country, by winning a good name for the *bonae literae*, and by patronizing culture in the courts of their princes. In 1521 he chided Guillaume Budé for complaining that public duty is incompatible with literary pursuits[24]. This point needs stressing to discredit and deprecate the facile oppositions between two caricatures—that of Erasmus as an ivory tower abstentionist, and that of More as a gradual deserter of contemplation.

Further defense of Erasmian humanism

More's defense of Erasmus' personal vocation and his advocacy of Erasmus' reformist program continued after he himself, having entered the
King's Council, was endeavoring to demonstrate on the public stage the
indirect approach he had recommended in Book I of *Utopia*[25]. His campaign for Greek studies took the form of a long letter to his Alma Mater,
Oxford University, dated 29 March 1518 (*CW15*, pp. 129–49), and of
several epistles rebuking Erasmus' English foes. Unlike his response to
Dorp's attacks, More's answers to his countrymen Lee and Batmanson
were published in 1520 for all Europe to read[26]. *Europa*, a rather unusual
notion and term then, occurs at least three times in More's 1 May 1519
letter to Lee; nothing short of an international scale was appropriate for
a man of Erasmus' dimensions[27]. Having set the stage, he makes a loud
proclamation and justification of his predilection for Erasmus: "I confess
that I bear Erasmus a vehement love, and for hardly any other cause than
the one for which all of Christendom takes him to its heart, namely because all the people engaged in good studies everywhere have more profit-
ed from Erasmus' indefatigable labors alone than from the erudition,
whether sacred or profane, of hardly anybody else over a number of centuries before ours."[28]

Lee had begun to circulate *Annotationes* finding fault with not a few of
Erasmus' annotations on the New Testament, while the second edition of
that work was on the loom. What a pity, More writes to Lee, that your
special butt should be "that book of all books" which Erasmus composed,
at great cost to his own purse and health, for the common good of all mortals (p. 142/136f). The Holy Father has recommended it repeatedly: shall
we give more weight to Erasmus' detractors than to the Vicar of Christ
in this matter of Christ's doctrine? (p. 144/222). Lee may be learned and
intelligent, yet how can he dream of measuring up to a man who has
studied from childhood with "unsurpassable industry"? Nevertheless
Erasmus is far humbler and less dogmatic than most theologians; his suggestive, tentative statements contrast with the arrogant, apodictic assertions of schoolmen. Where they are eager to define, he merely lists opinions of earlier writers, "submitting himself on all points to the judgment
of the Church" (p. 146/301f). He also welcomes admonition, which
More, however, feels himself too small to offer even in the weighing of
"common matters," let alone in the field of literature (p. 147/327f). More
exhorts his younger compatriot not to publish the *Annotationes*. Approach-
ed by Lee "in the name of friendship"[29], More begs him to desist "for
the love of our country" (154/608), adding the threat that Erasmus, for
all his wonted gentleness and courtesy, might choose to wave his foe aside
with a mere push of his hand.

After the publication of the *Annotationes* (Paris, February 1520), More wrote to Lee again in sorrow, expressing fear lest "an Englishman's attack on a book which is so dear to all nations might bring on our motherland the ill-will of all the learned everywhere"[30]. In his view Erasmus has lost to the other side neither the holier nor the more learned readers. He again appeals to the authority of the Supreme Pontiff, who has twice given Erasmus his suffrage (p. 209/38f). More admits that he himself may be partial to the defendant (p. 211/113), but his voice is but one in a universal chorus of praise.

More's letter to a monk[31]

If More's defense of Erasmus remains general in his three letters to Lee, it becomes extremely specific in a much longer epistle which "refutes the furious backbiting of a certain monk, equally unlearned and arrogant" (*Rogers*, ep. 83)[32]. The unnamed correspondent, identified since as John Batmanson, belongs to that very Charterhouse of London which was a favorite haunt of More's early manhood. He has warned More against the subtle poison of Erasmus, using strong words such as "heretic" and even "forerunner of Antichrist". More's response is devastating: "What danger is there if I delight in reading books which all the most learned and the most pious people praise as though with one voice? Which the Supreme Pontiff—an excellent man too—has twice pronounced useful to all men of study?"[33]

You know Erasmus only by hearsay, More continues, whereas he is known personally to many great men of England: John Colet, dean of St. Paul's Cathedral, John Fisher, bishop of Rochester, William Warham, archbishop of Canterbury, not to mention Mountjoy, Tunstal, Pace, Grocin. With each one of these men Erasmus has stayed often and for considerable periods: has any of them, at any moment, heard him say anything which might throw suspicion on the rectitude of his Christian faith? The longer their acquaintance with him, the greater their affection toward him (p. 169/140f). One of Erasmus' crimes, in Batmanson's eyes, has been detecting and exposing errors in the great Church Fathers, those "illustrious organs of the Holy Spirit" (p. 170/194). More supports Erasmus' right to disagree with past masters by listing eleven instances of "diametrical dissent" between those two giants, Jerome and Augustine (p. 171/203f).

When the monk finds Erasmus difficult to read with that sprinkling of Greek terms, More laughs away the reproach; St. Jerome too, he points out, scatters Greek seeds among his Latin, and Budé taxes Erasmus' style of excessive facility (p. 172/255f). No apology is needed, anyway, for learning and teaching a language which is the vehicle of the New Testament and of its earliest interpreters, as well as of the liberal arts and philosophy (p. 173/293f). The Latin of the humanists, which emulates that of the Fathers, is obscure only to such passé readers as are steeped only in Gothic-Latin—*lingua Latino-Gothica* (p. 175/363).

The layman More does not recoil from rather technical comments on Scripture translators—the Septuagint, Jerome, Lefèvre d'Etaples—in his detailed defense of the Erasmian renderings which the monk has found offensive. Pride of place is given to the use of *Sermo* for the *Logos* in the Gospel of St. John, instead of the Vulgate's *Verbum*: the whole Catholic Church has used both, More retorts. Beginning with the Liturgy itself, he quotes from seven patristic sources, and lists seven instances from St. Cyprian alone: "How dare you call Erasmus a coiner of new words, when, as you hear, this most learned Father and most holy champion of Christ both read and used *Sermo* to designate the Word of God, for whom he shed his blood more than a thousand years before Erasmus was born?"[34]

Then, revisiting much of the ground he had covered four years earlier in trying to win Dorp over to Erasmus' side, but hitting even harder because this foe is older and seems to be past all hope of recovery, More urges that *Moria*, despite its name, has less folly in it, and more genuine piety, than most of the hymns by which some clergy court the favor of heaven (p. 188/848f). In a teasing passage, he argues that Erasmus never published the *Iulius exclusus*, rather deviously dodging the real issue—did Erasmus write that dialogue? (p. 188/877f). In a sentence which echoes Christ's protest before the High-Priest, More says: "If Erasmus' books are good, why do you condemn them? If they are bad, why do you read them?"[35] He is prepared to see the devil at work[36] among these cloistered busybodies who keep looking over the walls of their monasteries and slandering any person with a vocation different from their own. He reiterates his appeal to the eminent patronage Erasmus enjoys in England: John Fisher, "no less famous for culture than for virtue"; Colet, than whom no one among us has been more learned and more holy for centuries; John Longland, dean of Salisbury, who is another Colet both by his preaching and his behavior. Who do Batmanson and his clique think they are, to indict a book which such enlightened churchmen read with gratitude, and which the Vicar of Christ has twice pronounced useful? (p. 192/993f).

Counterattacking with vigor, More evokes the religious who abuse Holy Scripture by weaving dirty stories in Vulgate phraseology; a monastic gang who knelt to Our Lady before perpetrating a horrendous misdeed; a friar at Conventry who from the pulpit guaranteed heaven to all faithful reciters of the rosary. He thus clears the field for a proper bout of jousting under the livery of Erasmus: ''Not that I purpose to write the encomium of Erasmus. This is above my powers, and all over the world the best and most learned vie with each other in his praise; and if they were to keep silent, the fruits of his good deeds to all mortals commend him now to good people and will commend him to all the people when he is gone''[37]. A heart which has inflamed so many others can hardly be cold itself (p. 201/1345). You say he travels too much, but should absolute holiness entail the stability of an oyster or a sponge? Erasmus is no more a vagabond than the Friars Minor, whose order is as holy as any, or than Jerome, who measured the whole way between Rome and Jerusalem. Erasmus voyages as a pilgrim of learning; the frailty of his body, further weakened by age, increases the merit of his thus serving the common good at his own great cost. You have chosen Mary's part, which Christ prefers to Martha's, but beware of ranking that contemplative leisure above the busy life of the apostles (p. 203/1450). After another spirited defense of Erasmus' biblical translations, More takes a severe leave of his correspondent.

Philosophia Christi et Militia Christiana

We have reached a new decade, startlingly different as regards the scene of Europe as well as the lives of our two friends. More is now a senior minister of state and an *eques auratus*. Erasmus is no longer the wandering and needy scholar, but the comfortable guest of Johann Froben in the imperial city of Basel. Nor is he Christendom's leading author any longer: Martin Luther's output is larger, and goes through more editions and translations. More's service to Henry VIII includes ''defending the faith'' against the heresies which come from Saxony. Humanism has won the field, and needs no further defense. Its noblest fruit, Erasmus' bilingual and annotated *Novum Testamentum*, is available to all the scholars engaged in religious controversy: in 1523 More appeals to the undisputed authority of Erasmus in the *Responsio ad Lutherum*[38]. In 1526, he uses similar superlatives when referring Bugenhagen to Erasmus' biblical defense of free-will[39]. More's debt to Erasmus as an apologist of the faith extends to his polemical works in English. I have tried to assess it in the 1529 *Dialogue Concerning Heresies* (*CW6*, p. 459f) and I would like to conclude with the resounding homage published as late as 1532, in the *Confutation of Tyndale's Answer*:

> Tyndale ... asketh me why I have not contended with Erasmus, whom he calleth my darling ..., for translating of this word *ecclesia* into this word *congregatio* ... I have not contended with Erasmus my darling because I found

no such malicious intent and purpose with Erasmus my darling as I find with Tyndale ... But I find in Erasmus my darling that he detesteth and abhorreth the errors and heresies that Tyndale plainly teacheth and abideth by, and therefore Erasmus my darling shall be my dear darling still (*CW8*, p. 177/10 – 23).

The next two pages of the *Confutation* are devoted to defending Erasmus as translator, and to endorsing the spirit of his *Moria*: in her assault "upon the abuses" of society in matters both "spiritual and temporal," Dame Folly, says More, does not go "so far ... as the messenger doth in my *Dialogue*." If readers are scandalized, it is because Tyndale has "envenomed their hearts ... with the infection of his contagious heresies ..., turning all honey into poison." In such an atmosphere, when men "take harm of the very scripture of God, ... if any man would now translate *Moria* into English, or some works either that I have myself written ere this, albeit there is none harm therein ..., I would not only my darling's books but mine own also help to burn them both with mine own hands" (*CW8*, p. 178/3 to 179/15). The tenfold repetition of *darling* conveys, in my opinion, the same affection as the *Erasme mi erasmiotate* of 1517 (Allen III, ep. 683). The shrillness and stridency of the taunt reflect the same tone as More's vindication of Origen and of Aquinas when Tyndale provoked his indignation by slighting these giants (*CW8*, pp. 153 – 54 and pp. 707f): thus More's longest and harshest work places Erasmus in the best imaginable company.

NOTES

1 Thus in the 25 August 1517 letter to Froben: "I see that all learned men unanimously subscribe to my opinion and admire the man's superhuman genius even more warmly than I". Preface to *Utopia*, in the *Complete Works of St. Thomas More*, Vol. 4, p. 3 (Our siglum for this ongoing edition will be *CW* and the volume number). In his 23 July 1519 letter to Hutten, Erasmus quotes Colet's judgment that "More is Britain's only genius".

2 Sixth Birthday Lecture, presented at the Folger Library, 29 October 1985, and published in *Erasmus of Rotterdam Society Yearbook Seven* (1987), 1 – 30.

3 See *Allen* 114, of 28 October 1499; Cf. vol. I, p. 227/9 – 11, of the *Collected Works of Erasmus*, in the ongoing translation (Toronto) for which our siglum is *CWE*.

4 "Subirascebar Moro," he writes to Botzheim in the 1523 *catalogus* (*Allen* I, p. 6).

5 See Thomas More, *Translations of Lucian*, ed. by Craig R. Thompson (1974) as *CW3*, Part I.

6 Nor, for that matter, Giovanni Pico della Mirandola, though he had translated his *Life* and anthologized his works.

7 See Clarence H. Miller's critical edition of *Moriae Encomium*, *ASD*, IV – 3, and his translation of it as *The Praise of Folly* (Yale University Press, 1979).

8 The translator was Robert Whittington in a textbook for Latin entitled *Vulgaria* (London, 1519), and the phrase became a universal pattern when Robert Bolt's play *A Man for All Seasons* (1960) was made into a movie by Fred Zinnemann (1966).

9 They are Nos. 255, 256 and 257 in the Yale edition of More's *Latin Poems* (*CW3*, Part II).

10 Our references to More's letters will be to E.F. Rogers, ed., *The Correspondence of Sir Thomas More*, Princeton, 1947. We shall indicate page and line numbers.

11 It is *CW15* (1986), entitled *In Defense of Humanism*, and containing three other letters to which I shall turn. My translation here deliberately involves occasional compression or paraphrasing, and does not claim to match that of Daniel Kinney in *CW15*. I have in places preferred his text to that of Rogers.

12 Moriam insimulas et . . . institutum eius de emendando Nouo Testamento ex Graecis codicibus tam parum probas, tam angustis limitibus vt coartet suades, vt pene in vniuersum dissuadeas (*Rogers*, 29/48–51).

13 Neque enim quaedam tam acerbe ad amicum tantum, neque tam neglectim ad hominem tam doctum (p. 31/98–100).

14 litteratum, cuius officium per omnes litterarum species, hoc est, per omnes sese disciplinas effundit (32/154–55) . . . qui nec illas quaestiunculas ignoret, et . . . longe vtiliorem bonarum litterarum, id est sacrarum maxime, tum caeterarum quoque, peritiam adiunxerit (33/174–77).

15 Tantum abest ut Erasmus, cuius et ingenium et doctrinam mirantur omnes, futurus sit in disputando omnibus prorsus Dialecticis, hoc est, etiam pueris inferior (34/217–19).

16 qui preter sophisticas nugas nihil didicerunt (42/488), Dorp's own phrase, which More repeats twice on p. 44/565–67.

17 The allusion to Apocalypse (5/1–10): in hoc libro quem signacula septem clauserunt . . ., occurs on p. 49/743ff.

18 Mutauit vero Hieronymus . . . si quid in sensu fuit, quo Latinus codex discreparet a Graeco (57/1040–41).

19 Tam ergo nunc opus correctione est, quam olim fuit (59/1099–1100).

20 In his inaugural lecture on St. Paul's epistles, Dorp confessed the necessity of Greek for a New Testament scholar. More's letter congratulating Dorp has been preserved by another Louvain theologian, Thomas Stapleton (*Rogers*, ep. 82).

21 See E.L. Surtz, Introduction to *CW4*, and *Erasme et Thomas More: Correspondance*, trad. Germain Marc'hadour et Roland Galibois, Sherbrooke: Centre d'Etudes de la Renaissance (1985), pp. 49–52.

22 To echo More's own phrase translating Pico's *sancta ambitio*, see references in my *Thomas More, ou la sage folie* (Paris, 1971), p. 22.

23 *Allen* 999, a response to the German knight's weariness with aulic employment under Cardinal Albrecht of Mayence.

24 *Allen* 1233. Erasmus stresses that More, just knighted and appointed Under-treasurer of England, gives the *bonae literae* the credit for all his promotions.

25 For *obliquus ductus*, see the Yale edition of *Utopia*, *CW4*, p. 98/30, p. 102/2, 13 and p. 128/25.

26 In *Epistolae aliquot eruditorum* (Antwerp, May 1520) and, more completely, in *Epistolae eruditorum virorum* (Basle, August 1520). More's share in the collection includes three letters to Lee, and a very long one "to a certain monk," so sharp that More concealed the addressee's identity.

27 Daniel Kinney has edited only the first of More's letters to Lee, *CW15*, pp. 151–95.

28 Erasmum, fateor, vehementer diligo, nec id ob aliam ferme causam, quam eam de qua totus eum Christianus orbis amplectitur. Nempe quod inexhaustis eius vnius laboribus omnes vndique bonarum studiosi literarum, quantum non alterius fere cuiusquam aliquot ante seculis eruditione, cum prophana, tum etiam sacra promouerint (141/105–110). Cf. *CW15*, p. 158/31f.

29 "which to me is sacrosanct," says More: per sanctissimum mihi nomen amicitiae (p. 153/576).

30   Rogers, ep. 85, p. 209/29f.: *verebar, si ab Anglo impeteretur opus omnibus tam charum gentibus, ne nostra patria traheretur apud aeruditos omnes vndique in inuidiam.*

31   This "learned epistle" (pp. 197–311 in *CW15*) is only a little shorter than More's letter to Dorp.

32   And *CW15*, p. 198: *respondet indoctis ac virulentis litteris monachi cuiusdam.*

33   *Quid periculi est, si eorum librorum lectione delecter, quos doctissimi quique maximeque pii velut vna uoce collaudant? Quos Pontifex maximus pariter et optimus bis iam pronunciauit vtiles esse studiosis?* (166/35–38). To Lee already, More had coupled the two august epithets in speaking of Leo X: *Pontifice non maximo solum, sed etiam optimo* (144/217).

34   *I nunc et Erasmum clama nouatorem esse verborum, cum audias doctissimum patrem ac sanctissimum athletam Christi, Verbum Dei, pro quo fudit sanguinem, et legisse et appellasse 'Sermonem' plus annis mille priusquam nasceretur Erasmus* (183/668–71).

35   *Nam si boni sunt libelli, cur damnas? Si mali, cur legis?* (189/913, cf. John 18:23).

36   He repeatedly evokes the "common foe" of mankind, Satan, the *callidus hostis,* "the wily old serpent," as he also does in writing to Lee (v.g., 170/184, 190/928, 194/1074, 195/1114, 199/1294).

37   . . . *non est tamen in praesenti consilium vt Erasmi scribam encomion. Nam et nostrae vires tanto sunt operi impares, et vbique gentium optimi atque doctissimi pro sua quisque virili certatim faciunt, quibus alioqui tacentibus, sua illum benefacta cunctis fructuosa mortalibus, vt viuum commendant bonis, ita . . . vita functum commendabunt omnibus* (p. 200/1324–30).

38   *uir citra ullam controuersiam eruditissimus, et de ecclesia Christi optime meritus, Erasmus Roterodamus annotauit . . .* (*CW5*, p. 196/18f).

39   *Scripturas illas, quas eruditissimi viri et de Christi Ecclesia bene meriti Diatribe pro Arbitrii Libertate protulit* (*Rogers,* p. 357/1192–3).

PART THREE

IMAGES

INTRODUCTION

La troisième partie de ce recueil est plus modeste que les autres. Ici, il ne s'agit pas d'Érasme lui-même ou de ses idées sur la foi, la politique ou l'éducation, mais de l'image ou plutôt des images d'Érasme. Sans doute existe-t-il une relation entre l'homme et ce que l'imagination fait de lui: la personne fournit matière à l'interprétation, les images n'existent pas sans un *fundamentum in re*. Ensuite, la fameuse fonction fabulatrice de Bergson fait son jeu et l'image s'aliène de la réalité. Cependant, le désir de découvrir et de montrer le vrai Érasme a toujours existé. La question se pose donc de savoir qui choisira de façon définitive entre la vérité et l'erreur dans les projections lumineuses de l'imagination. Personne, bien sûr, puisque tout le monde voit Érasme à partir d'une perspective particulière qui pose des limites à ce que l'on voit. Et pourtant, on ne peut s'empêcher de croire que certaines images sont plus proches de la réalité que d'autres.

Dans les articles précédents, nous avons déjà trouvé des images d'Érasme, mais elles n'étaient pas présentées en tant que telles. Dans la troisième partie de notre recueil, elles sont l'objet privilégié de la recherche.

Cornelis Augustijn (Vir duplex. German interpretations of Erasmus) décrit trois images d'Érasme en Allemagne. Tout d'abord, le prestige de l'humaniste est énorme. Puis, surtout après l'*Expostulatio* d'Ulrich von Hutten (1523), cette image très favorable va changer. Érasme, qui semblait être le champion de la vérité et de la liberté, s'avère être un lâche, un hypocrite, il s'entend avec l'ennemi et laisse ses amis à l'abandon. Cette image est affirmée par Luther qui, dans *De servo arbitrio* (1525), est même plus négatif que Hutten. Érasme est un fin renard, un *vir duplex*, instable, louche: "at noster rex amphibolus sedet in throno amphibologiae securus". Entre l'image projetée par Hutten et celle de Luther il y a des différences, mais l'une est aussi négative que l'autre.

Bruce Mansfield (Erasmus in the age of revolutions) donne un aperçu très intéressant des images d'Érasme à l'époque des révolutions, c'est-à-dire vers la fin du dix-huitième siècle. En général, l'image est très favorable: Érasme fut le champion courageux de la modération, de la tolérance, de la raison et de l'humanité, il a combattu les préjugés de la religion médiévale, il a anticipé l'âge des Lumières, etc., et pour Edward Gibbon la vraie Réforme fut inaugurée par Érasme. Mais à côté de cette image favorable, l'image créée par Hutten est également reprise, notamment par Herder. Les images se complètent, elles se contredisent en partie, et derrière ces images on devine toujours Érasme, cet inconnu, qui dépasse toutes les images.

Enfin, *Nicolaas van der Blom* (Rotterdam and Erasmus) a recherché les vicissitudes de la fameuse statue d'Érasme à Rotterdam. Il y voit reflétée la relation de Rotterdam avec son *civis omnium praestantissimus*. Ainsi ce livre finit là où il a commencé: dans l'*urbecula concinna*, la petite ville de Rotterdam.

J.S.W.

CORNELIS AUGUSTIJN

VIR DUPLEX
GERMAN INTERPRETATIONS OF ERASMUS

In 1939 Joseph Lortz published the first volume of *Die Reformation in Deutschland*. It created a sensation among historians and theologians: for the first time a catholic Church historian treated Luther favorably and gave evidence of understanding Luther's action and theology. But this was not true in the case of Erasmus. Lortz had a long list of derogatory terms for Erasmus: lack of clarity, a threat to Christianity and the Church, a relativist, a moralist—an endless list.[1] Lortz is not alone in this evaluation, nor is his characterization of Erasmus typical of Catholics only.

One could well say that his characterization of Erasmus was generally accepted in Germany, by Protestants no less than by Catholics. In this paper I shall answer the question of the source of this conception of Erasmus. The best studies of the image of Erasmus over the centuries[2] either treat the period of his lifetime very briefly or omit it altogether, since the writers are interested in the image that developed after his death.

My study is concerned with what happened before, the development of an unfavorable image of Erasmus during his lifetime in Germany. The study is divided into four parts. The first looks at the original favorable image; the second deals with Hutten's view; the third with Luther's idea of Erasmus; the fourth presents a summary and some conclusions.

1. *The original image of Erasmus in Germany*

Erasmus suddenly became famous in Germany in the summer of 1514.[3] In that year he travelled from England to Basel to meet Johannes Froben about a number of projects he had in mind: publications of classical writers and of early Christian writers (an edition of St. Jerome in the first place) and of the New Testament.[4] His trip through the Rhine valley was triumphant. Erasmus was honorably received in Mainz, Strasbourg and Schlettstadt by notable humanists such as Jakob Wimpfeling, Jakob Sturm, Beatus Rhenanus and Ulrich von Hutten. Significant for our study is the fact that he was celebrated as a German. To Hutten, Johannes Reuchlin and Erasmus were "the two pearls of Germany, because through them this nation ceased to be barbarian".[5] When he went back to England half a year later it was the same. The knight Eitelwolf vom Stein, ill with a kidney stone, was unable to attend his reception in Frankfurt. He complained bitterly that he had not seen "the greatest man of Germany".[6] Erasmus did his part to promote this image. He paraded as a German, spoke about "my Germany" and praised Germany to the skies.[7]

What sort of image of Erasmus did these German humanists have? We can get a good idea of it from the *Epistolae obscurorum virorum*, in which several humanists ridicule the scholastic theologians of their time by publishing supposed letters.[8] In the first enlarged edition of 1516 there is a lengthy report, fictitious of course, of a doctor who goes to Strasbourg and meets Erasmus.[9] It is a wonderful story, but I must spare you the details here. The doctor makes himself ridiculous by making pedantic remarks on Latin literature in a large company, where Erasmus is present. He has no idea of how foolish a figure he cuts and presents himself as a marvel of learning. He does not think much of Erasmus: he is small of stature and so he cannot know very much. Moreover he speaks low, so that the doctor does not understand a word of his discourse. His concluding evaluation is significant: "After I had said this and much more ..., Erasmus laughed and did not reply. I had squelched him with such clever reasoning". Sure of himself he continues: "And I contend by God that Erasmus isn't all they say he is. He does not know more than the next person". The letter shows the image that existed among German humanists: a small man with a soft voice who laughs knowingly at the stupid remarks of a phoney and is otherwise silent. Other passages in the same work reveal more clearly what the humanists admire in Erasmus. He is the author of the *Adagia*, but above all, the editor of the *New Testament*, the "bulky book" which the scholastic theologians fear the pope will approve.[10] Erasmus' *New Testament* is especially important. Another letter demonstrates this thus: "And if they (the humanists) say that they know Greek and Hebrew, you should answer that theologians do not concern themselves with such languages, because the Holy Scripture has been satisfactorily translated and we need no further translation. We may not even study such languages, out of contempt for Jews and Greeks".[11]

The authors of the *Epistolae obscurorum virorum* understand very well where the greatness of Erasmus lies, in the combination of *bonae* and *sacrae litterae*, i.e. the combination of the study of classical writers and of the Bible and the early Christian writers. But they do evoke a distinct image of the man Erasmus, the man with the enigmatic half-laugh who disdains to respond to nonsense, but who does not identify himself entirely with the friends of Reuchlin. This is very evident in a letter which names all the supporters and defenders of Reuchlin. In answer to the question whether Erasmus is one of them it is written: "*Erasmus est homo pro se*. But it is certain that he will never be the friend of those theologians and regular cler-

gy, and that he definitively defends and justifies Reuchlin both in speaking and writing".[12] *Homo pro se*: he is his own man, he stands apart. The
conclusion we can draw is: although he defended Reuchlin, he did not
identify himself with him. This was in the years 1516 and 1517, when to
be for or against Reuchlin was the best way to indicate where one stood,
to which side one belonged.

Did the picture change after Luther made his stand? In those years most
humanists supported Luther. Although Luther was never deluded and
never considered Erasmus as a supporter,[13] their friends were often inclined to see them as equals. As a result the image of Erasmus began to
change in humanistic circles. It did not change in essence, but to these humanists Erasmus involuntarily took on characteristics of Luther. Typical
of the phenomenon was the reaction of Albrecht Dürer in 1521 on hearing
a rumor of Luther's death: "O, Erasmus of Rotterdam, where are you
now? . . . Hear, knight of Christ, ride forth with the Lord Christ, defend
the truth, gain the martyrs' crown . . . O, Erasmus, stay on this side, that
God may take pride in you".[14] Huizinga remarks that there is a note of
doubt in Dürer's words as to whether Erasmus would really carry out such
a purpose.[15] But the words of Dürer were not meant for the outside
world; his first thought was that only Erasmus could finish Luther's work.

Erasmus and Luther were not always associated so closely. However,
the research by Holeczek shows that in these years Erasmus enjoyed considerable reknown, especially as a Bible commentator who, in his commentaries, criticized the Church of his time.[16] Moreover he was the
writer of the popular *Enchiridion*. The image of Erasmus remains very
favorable and is almost similar to Luther's, in any case.

2. *Hutten's image of Erasmus*

The radical reversal of Erasmus' image occurs in 1523.[17] Erasmus' letter
to Marcus Laurinus was published and so incited the wrath of Ulrich von
Hutten that he could not remain silent.[18] Hutten was adversely influenced by Erasmus' refusal to receive him when he arrived in Basel late
in 1522, seriously ill and destitute after the complete failure of his attempts
in armed combat against the Roman Curia. Although in Erasmus' view
this refusal was simply an act of caution, it took on symbolic meaning to
Hutten. Earlier Erasmus had been his idol; he had praised him as the
"German Socrates, as important to us in literature as Socrates was to his
Greeks",[19] and had offered him his services. He had been happy when
Erasmus had mentioned his name in one of the notes to the edition of his
New Testament.[20] Since then everything had changed. In the summer of
1520 he had visited Erasmus in the Netherlands, had laid before him his

plans for an armed crusade and had asked for his support. Erasmus would have none of it even then; now he seemed to have been completely written off.

In this state of injured self-conceit and offense because of rejected friendship Hutten wrote, in the spring of 1523, his *Expostulatio*. In this accusation he discusses Erasmus' relation to Reuchlin, to the heretic-hunter Hoogstraten, to the Louvain theologians, to Aleander, the Pope, Luther, in short to all those who had played an important role in the tragedies of recent years. He always reaches the same conclusion: Erasmus has schemed and played the hypocrite, he is not to be trusted and is ready to bargain with the winning side. He has made peace with enemies and addresses them with titles of honor such as "reverend father" and "dear sir". He has turned away from his former friends now that they are in trouble. The following quotation illustrates his engaging style and whipped-up pathos: "Up until the present you inwardly stood at a fork in the road, careful as a second Mettius, waiting for the best opportunity. That is why, now that our opponents have so tremendously increased that you despair of our victory, you join the party you think will win. You have no conscience; you make your plans according to the way the wind blows. Or perhaps you have surrendered on these conditions. Or do you act from fear that our adversaries will treat you as roughly as they will treat us, once they will have defeated us? I do not doubt it: that will happen!".[21] Hutten's image of Erasmus is sufficiently clear from this passage alone: a man of great knowledge without moral strength. Erasmus knows the truth but turns against truth out of cowardlinesss and weakness, against better knowledge. One can well imagine that Erasmus was shocked.

But that is beside the point, for we are here concerned with the Erasmus' image which Hutten projected, fully convinced, and thereby also convincing. To him Erasmus is the weak man with no conscience, fearful and grasping, ready to join the winning side. According to Hutten this is especially true of Erasmus' attitude with regard to Luther. Even though it seemed clear enough that Erasmus agreed with Luther, he never spoke of this in public and now withdrew in fear. Behind this lay a certain conception of the Reformation. To Hutten it is essentially a freedom movement. He had discovered this struggle for freedom from the Curia, the Church, Rome and Italy in general—to him the determining motive—in the work of Erasmus in his criticism of various abuses in the Church and in his rejection of meaningless ceremonies. In such an interpretation of Erasmus, the negative, critical elements of his writings predominate. Erasmus is the man who criticized abuses in the Church, who raised his voice in protest against them before Luther did. Hutten is neither the first nor the only person to give us this interpretation of Erasmus. Already in the spring of 1518 Martin Bucer had produced the same picture. He attended the Disputation at Heidelberg and gave an enthusiastic report of Luther's presentation. In the middle of his praise of Luther these words stand out: "He (Luther) agrees with Erasmus in every aspect. He seems to surpass him in that he openly teaches what he (Erasmus) whispers".[22] These words of Bucer indicate his reservations with regard to Erasmus: Luther takes a firmer stand. This bias became the dominant motif in Hutten's *Expostulatio*: Erasmus the coward.

If we define more exactly the image of Erasmus presented by Hutten we see that it is comprised of two elements. The first is the positive significance of Erasmus. He opposed the abuses in the Church, but more than that, in his opposition he rejected the Church as a hierarchic and sacramental institution. He divested the Church of the things that gave it stability. The second aspect is negative. Erasmus knows the truth; in his heart he admits that Luther is right, for Luther maintains the same ideals that Erasmus himself maintains. But he lacks moral courage and firmness of conviction and so betrays the whole cause, actually his own cause.

Nowhere are both aspects expressed more clearly than in the famous story of Erasmus' answer to Elector Frederick the Wise in the Fall of 1520, at a most critical moment. Luther was condemned by the Church, and the princes had to decide on their position with regard to him. The Elector asked for a meeting with Erasmus. The account of this meeting is given by Georg Spalatin who was an eye-witness. By way of Luther's stories in the *Tischreden* it has filtered down into all the literature on Erasmus and Luther. When the Elector asked why Luther was condemned by the Church, Erasmus replied: "Luther has committed terrible sins. He has attacked the bellies of the monks and the crown of the Pope".[23] In one sentence Erasmus is revealed by his criticism of the Church, but also by the detachment evident in his irony.

3. Luther's image of Eramus

A new image of Erasmus soon took form, as negative as Hutten's but having different features. No less a person than Luther produced it and in *De servo arbitrio* of 1525 it is already clearly revealed.[24] Luther acknowledges that Erasmus has many gifts: education, mental maturity and eloquence. But mentioning these positive characteristics only serves to illumine the negative ones. That is already clear at the beginning of the tract when Luther explains why he waited so long to respond to Erasmus' *De libero arbitrio*: Erasmus was so cold and lifeless that Luther could not muster the enthusiasm to answer.[25] After that the same image recurs continually in *De servo arbitrio*: Erasmus is a Lucian, an Epicurus, in the words of Horace, a pig from the herd of Epicurus.[26] Erasmus is a scoffer who, like Lucian, does not believe in God or order, and who, like Epicurus, is only concerned with the present world and its pleasures. What Luther misses in Erasmus is certainty of conviction. It is not without reason that he concludes his tract by declaring that he is not prepared to undertake research and let others draw the conclusion, as Erasmus had done. He will make firm statements and he will require obedience. In short, for Erasmus there is no firmly established absolute truth concerning God, that man must accept and defend. In Luther's table talks, recorded only from the early thirties onward, this image recurs frequently. In 1533 Luther says: "At my death I will forbid my children to read the *Colloquia* of Erasmus. He expresses his utterly godless opinion, opposing faith and the Church in the roles of others. I should prefer him to laugh at me and other people".[27] Most revealing and representative is certainly his famous remark: "Erasmus is an eel. No one but Christ can catch hold of him. *Est vir duplex*".[28] This last remark is a reference to James 1:8, where Luther translates "vir duplex" as "ein Zweiveler". A note in Luther's translation explains clearly what is meant: "One who is not steadfast in his faith, who begins many things but does not stay by them". This accusation of *amphibologia*, ambiguity, is often repeated in like terms. Luther finds Erasmus puzzling, enigmatic, so learned, yet making poor use of his knowledge. In early 1533 he says: "It is the duty of a doctor to instruct and to fight. Erasmus does neither. He is a double minded man".[29] This utterance of Luther combines his criticisms. In Luther's mind theology has the duty to communicate and defend the faith and in this regard he finds Erasmus totally wanting.

At this time Luther often spoke to his friends of his determination to oppose Erasmus in writing.[30] When he became ill he spent entire days reading Erasmus' edition of the New Testament, and he was much displeased. When Erasmus' Commentary on the Apostolic Creed was published he again made the criticism *Wankelwort*, instability.[31] The following year in a letter to his close friend Nikolaus von Amsdorff,[32] meant for publication, he burst out against Erasmus. Allen describes that letter as "a piece of masterly invective".[33] He accused Erasmus in no uncertain terms of being unstable and unreliable in doctrine. Luther named all sorts of concrete examples. Erasmus had pointed out that in his speech recorded in Acts, Peter called Christ a man and said nothing about his divinity. Erasmus had also pointed out that the Holy Spirit was not called "God" by the theologians of the early Church. Erasmus had used the word "coitus" in reference to God and the virgin Mary. Erasmus had declared that Christ, in comparison to heathen wisdom, had brought nothing new. Erasmus had complained that the apostle John wrote poor Greek. Luther places all these points in a special framework about which he is very clear. Erasmus does not frankly state opinions; he is contemptuous of Christianity, indeed in his heart he is contemptuous of all religion. He is a Lucian, an Epicurus, even the devil in human form. To put it in one sentence: "*At noster rex amphibolus sedet in throno amphibologiae securus*".[34] This letter contains Luther's last and most bitter denunciation of Erasmus.

We wish now to formulate exactly the image of Erasmus as given here by Luther. It can be stated in a few words. Erasmus is a relativist, a subjectivist and a skeptic; his work is negative, a mere denial. He destroys, he censures, he knocks down without establishing a standard or a norm. He lives from negating. On this sort of interpretation Erasmus is judged according to what he has accomplished: what doctrine did he teach? Behind this is the verdict that for Erasmus there is no absolute truth. Therefore he is a greater threat to the Church than a Catholic opponent. It is interesting to see that this image of Erasmus was drummed home by Luther, but that Erasmus' opponents in the Catholic camp had formed the same image before Luther had. It had already become dominant in the twenties in Paris and Spain, the two centers of opposition to Erasmus.[35] Luther had even used Alberto Pio, Count of Capri, one of Erasmus' most formidable opponents, in writing his letter.

4. *Conclusion*

When Erasmus died, all the elements were present for the formation of a negative image. We have seen that Hutten's concept differed widely from that of Luther. Yet in the passing of time, traits of one image were often combined with traits from the other. This was not difficult since untrustworthiness and instability were common to both. Hutten also considers Luther a *vir duplex*. The way in which Hutten and Luther work out these traits leads to a crude caricature, but nevertheless it is part of a genuine portrait of Erasmus. Huizinga expresses it in this way: "Erasmus was a master of reserve ... In all questions of the human mind he recognized the eternal ambiguity".[36] Of course, that is something quite different from what Hutten and Luther made of it in their portrait. It is understandable, however, that this ambiguity came over as skepticism to those who were in the middle of controversy.

Only one possibility remained for a positive image. One can see Erasmus as the man of the *bonae litterae*, whose services to mankind were to be found in the field of literature. In 1523 Luther had already typified him so: Erasmus had his merits in the field of literature, but he should steer clear of the Bible. He would die like Moses in the land of Moab.[37] Melanchthon made the most of this argument. He pictured Erasmus as

226 CORNELIS AUGUSTIJN

the outstanding philologist, of great significance in preparing for the work that Luther would do.[38]

NOTES

1 Joseph Lortz, *Die Reformation in Deutschland*, vol. 1, Freiburg im Breisgau 1939, 133–134.
2 See Andreas Flitner, *Erasmus im Urteil seiner Nachwelt. Das literarische Erasmus-Bild von Beatus Rhenanus bis zu Jean le Clerc*, Tübingen 1952; Bruce Mansfield, *Phoenix of his Age. Interpretations of Erasmus c 1550–1750*. Erasmus studies 4, Toronto – Buffalo – London 1979.
3 Cornelis Augustijn, *Erasmus von Rotterdam. Leben-Werk-Wirkung*, München 1986. An English translation will be published in 1988.
4 See Cornelis Augustijn, "Erasmus-Promotion Anno 1515: die Erasmus-Stücke in Iani Damiani . . . Elegeia", *Boek, bibliotheek en geesteswetenschappen. Opstellen door vrienden en collega's van dr. C. Reedijk geschreven* . . ., Hilversum 1986, 19–28.
5 Ulrichi Hutteni Equitis Germani *Opera*, ed. Eduardus Böcking, vol. 1, Lipsiae 1859, 106, 8–9.
6 Ulrichus Huttenus, *op. cit.*, 44, 2–8.
7 Cf. e.g. *Allen* 305, 214–217.
8 The best edition is *Epistolae obscurorum virorum*, ed. Aloys Bömer, vol. 1 Introduction, vol. 2 Text, Heidelberg 1924. Important is the study by Walter Brecht, *Die Verfasser der Epistolae obscurorum virorum*. (Quellen und Forschungen zur Sprach- und Culturgeschichte der germanischen Völker 93), Straßburg 1904. Probably Hutten was the author of all the passages mentioned here. For a review see Hans Rupprich, *Die deutsche Literatur vom späten Mittelalter bis zum Barock*, part 1 (Helmut de Boor und Richard Newald, *Geschichte der deutschen Literatur von den Anfängen bis zur Gegenwart*, vol. IV, part 1), München 1970, 712–718.
9 Epistola I, 42.
10 Epistola II, 38, cf. also II, 33; Epistola II, 49.
11 Epistola II, 33.
12 Epistola II, 59.
13 Cf. Cornelis Augustijn, *Erasmus en de Reformatie. Een onderzoek naar de houding die Erasmus ten opzichte van de Reformatie heeft aangenomen*, Amsterdam 1962.
14 Albrecht Dürer, *Das Tagebuch der niederländischen Reise* . . . Introduction and annotations by J.-A. Goris and G. Marlier, Brüssel 1970, 97–98.
15 Cf. Johan Huizinga, *Verzamelde Werken*, vol. 6, Haarlem 1950, 143.
16 See Heinz Holeczek, *Erasmus Deutsch*, vol. 1, Stuttgart-Bad Cannstatt 1983, 13.
17 Cf. for the following *ASD*, IX–1, 93–113; für Hutten Hajo Holborn, *Ulrich von Hutten*, Göttingen 1968²; Heinrich Grimm, *Ulrich von Hutten. Wille und Schicksal.* (Persönlichkeit und Geschichte, vol. 60/61), Göttingen – Zürich – Frankfurt 1971.
18 This letter was printed with the first edition of the *Catalogus lucubrationum* and a letter to the Louvain theologians in April 1523. For these writings and for Erasmus' purpose in publishing this volume see Augustijn, *Erasmus en de Reformatie*, 103–106.
19 See *Allen* 365, 4–5.
20 In the note on I. Thess. 2,7: "Sed pene exciderat unicum illud musarum delitium Udalricus Huttenus adolescens et imaginibus clarus . . .".
21 Ulrichi Hutteni Equitis Germani *Opera*, ed. Eduardus Böcking, vol. 2, Lipsiae 1859, 232.

22 See *Correspondance de Martin Bucer*, ed. Jean Rott, Leiden 1979 (Martini Buceri *Opera Omnia* 3,1. Studies in Medieval and Reformation Thought 25), 3, 54–56. In this Disputation Luther presented his ideas in the sharpest possible way.
23 D. Martin Luthers *Werke. Kritische Gesamtausgabe, Tischreden*, vol. 1, Weimar 1912, 55, 34–35.
24 See D. Martin Luthers *Werke. Kritische Gesamtausgabe*, vol. 18, Weimar 1908, 600–787.
25 D. Martin Luthers *Werke*, vol. 18, 600, 19–21.
26 With these remarks he offended Erasmus deeply; cf. *Allen* 1670, 30–37.
27 D. Martin Luthers *Werke*, Tischreden, vol. 1, 397, 15–18.
28 D. Martin Luthers *Werke*, Tischreden, vol. 1, 55, 32–33.
29 D. Martin Luthers *Werke*, Tischreden, vol. 3, 3, Weimar 1914, 260, 21–22.
30 See D. Martin Luthers *Werke*, Tischreden, vol. 3, 149, 32–34; 150, 3–6, 18–21; 260, 25–26, 34–35.
31 D. Martin Luthers *Werke*, Tischreden, vol. 3, 260, 27, 35.
32 D. Martin Luthers *Werke*, Briefwechsel, vol. 7, Weimar 1937, 2093. Cf. also the answer of Erasmus, in *ASD*, IX–1, 427–483.
33 See *Allen* 2918, introd.
34 D. Martin Luthers *Werke*, Briefwechsel, vol. 7, 2093, 305.
35 See Augustijn, *Erasmus*, 131–142.
36 See Huizinga, *op. cit.*, 123.
37 D. Martin Luthers *Werke*, Briefwechsel, vol. 3, Weimar 1933, 626, 14–25.
38 See e.g. "Oratio de Erasmo Roterodamo", in Philippi Melanchthonis *Opera quae supersunt omnia*, vol. 12 (Corpus Reformatorum 12), Halis Saxonum 1844, 264–271, cf. Mansfield, *op. cit.*, 89–93.

BRUCE MANSFIELD

ERASMUS IN THE AGE OF REVOLUTIONS

In a curious chapter of the *Decline and Fall of the Roman Empire*, Edward
Gibbon introduces Erasmus thus:

> Since the days of Luther and Calvin, a secret reformation has been silently
> working in the bosom of the reformed churches; many weeds of prejudice
> were eradicated; and the disciples of Erasmus diffused a spirit of freedom
> and moderation.

This chapter follows—from its beginnings in Asia Minor in the seventh
century—the so-called Paulician heresy of which the sixteenth-century
Reformers were the remote heirs. Of those Reformers Gibbon asks how
far they had freed Christians from articles of faith "*above* or *against* our reason". He concludes that, though they had levelled "the lofty fabric of superstition", they remained themselves authoritarian and give an impression less of freedom than of timidity.[1] Hence arose the need for the
"secret reformation" associated with the name of Erasmus.

Gibbon is in effect proposing the idea of two Reformations, the limited
but well understood Reformation of Luther and Calvin and the more profound and far-reaching one begun by Erasmus. In a note, he defines an
apostolic succession of rational theology—from Erasmus through the Ar-
minians of Holland and the English latitudinarians. The outcome has
been liberty of conscience and religious toleration, at least in Holland and
England, a setting aside of presumptuous theological questions and an
honest acceptance of the limitations of the human mind.[2]

In Gibbon's view then the Protestant Reformers carried through a useful, salutary reform; it fell well short, however, of true Christian enlightenment. The deeper currents began with Erasmus. This is one form of
what might be called the Protestant Enlightenment interpretation of Erasmus. It is the most radical or "advanced" form of that interpretation:
Erasmus broke more decisively than the Reformers with medieval religion
and better anticipated modern (eighteenth-century) ideas.[3]

J.S. Semler made a similar judgment in other connections. Early in the
career that was to make him a leader in the historical and critical method,
Semler encountered Erasmus' *Ratio verae theologiae*. Many years later he
edited it—a work, he said, "deserving of canonical recognition"—with
an introduction.[4] In his church histories he argues that Erasmus was the
true source of the sixteenth-century reforms and that the bearing of those
reforms was not to be judged by the standard of Luther, let alone by that
of later orthodoxy.[5] In the introduction to the *Ratio*, he goes further:

Erasmus pioneered the distinction—critical to Semler's thought—
between inner religion and external forms. This religion of the spirit requiring no particular outward expression went well beyond the Reformation as it actually occurred.[6]

An alternative form of the Protestant Enlightenment interpretation was
more confined. In this version Erasmus was closely tied to the Reformation as it actually happened; the revival of learning which he represented
and the Reformation worked together for the liberation of the human
mind. William Robertson, the Scottish historian and divine, whose position in his own church—affirming ecclesiastical loyalty but also promoting
cultural openness[7]—corresponded to an acceptance of Renaissance and
Reformation as mutually reinforcing, called Erasmus Luther's "forerunner and auxiliary":

> There was hardly any opinion or practice of the Romish church which
> Luther endeavoured to reform, but what had been previously animadverted
> upon by Erasmus, and had afforded him subject either of censure or of
> raillery.[8]

Within this version differences were possible. On one view, Erasmus
served the Reformation but ultimately failed it—through weakness of
character, misplaced loyalties or an excessive love of peace. On another
view—closer to Gibbon's—it was to be regretted that the Reformation
had not been large enough to embrace both Luther and Erasmus, since
both served the one enlightenment.[9]

Nevertheless, when allowance has been made for all possible differences
across the range from Gibbon to Robertson, there existed common
ground among the writers of the Protestant Enlightenment: Erasmus was
a liberator of both the intellect and Christian piety from medieval bond-
age, the one by his satires and critical work on the scriptures, the other
by teaching a piety at once more·personal and more expansive and toler-
ant. He joined the Reformers in posing the issues that were the womb of
the modern world. By the end of the eighteenth century these views were
commonplaces, an orthodoxy in enlightened circles generally.[10]

Well before the end of the century, however, this orthodoxy had been
challenged and the tremors of the revolutionary age anticipated. In 1776
amid the turbulence of the *Sturm und Drang* Herder made a fierce attack
on Erasmus in defence of Ulrich von Hutten. Over against Hutten, who
is presented as an authentic hero sacrificing everything for the good (patri-
otic) cause, Erasmus is covered with demeaning phrases: "the faintheart-
ed Erasmus, who always lived simultaneously on land and water", a mere
critic and classical wit.[11] The contrast between the two portraits is bald:
Erasmus was fearful, devious, self-regarding, a bloodless intellectual;
Hutten was straightforward, a fighter, clear as light.

Herder set a pattern for nineteenth-century biographers by making Erasmus' character a central issue. C.M. Wieland, who had published the essay on Hutten in a series on German sixteenth-century heroes in his literary periodical, the *Teutsche Merkur*, replied (in an essay on Erasmus himself in the same series) that character can be judged only in relation to circumstances. Erasmus' circumstances were such as to give him a strong temperamental preference for measure and moderation. Generally, Wieland restates the Protestant Enlightenment view of Erasmus' historical significance: he prepared the way for the reform of the Church and actually supported Luther's Reformation, until it contradicted his own values of disinterestedness and toleration.[12]

Both Herder and Wieland were to refer to Erasmus again in their reactions to the French Revolution, as we shall see. Wieland's defence of Erasmus' character was available to those making a conservative response to the Revolution and following, as they saw it, the example of his response to the Reformation.

One would not expect the name of Erasmus to be much used by apologists for the Revolution. An English pacifist used it to curb the counter-revolution. In 1794 Vicesimus Knox published in London a translation of "Dulce bellum inexpertis" under the title *Antipolemus; Or, the Plea of Reason, Religion, and Humanity, against War* with a long and declamatory preface.[13] Providence, Knox says there, had given Erasmus not only great intellectual capacities but also "a GOOD and FEELING HEART" and a "warm philanthropy", which led him to write as he did for an age "when man, free-born but degraded man, was bound down in darkness, with double shackles, in the chains of a two-fold despotism, usurping an absolute dominion, both in church and in state, over the body and the soul". Knox made a clear continuity between Erasmus' activities and the Revolution: "Liberty acknowledges him as one of her noblest assertors"; he exposed despots "to the derision of the deluded and oppressed multitude". He also promoted the unity of mankind and was, therefore, against war, planting on the rock of religion "the artillery of solid arguments against it". That his struggle against war remained incomplete is, Knox concludes, demonstrated by the counter-revolutionary war (and its accompanying propaganda) against France.[14] We have in this pamphlet a rare case of the use of Erasmus on behalf of the Revolution and also, for its time, an unusual interest in his political writings.

The eminent Scottish philosopher Dugald Stewart, though a Whig and an early sympathizer with the Revolution, finished up ambivalent towards it and expressed that ambivalence through the person of Erasmus. Leaders in the new (classical) studies like Erasmus, Stewart says, contributed to the progress of the human mind and, in particular, aided

its escape from the "melancholy blank" of the middle ages and "the un-
substantial subtleties of ontology or of dialectics".[15] For Stewart the expansion of the mind's powers through empirical learning was the primary
subject of interest and he linked with it the notion of irresistible progress:

> From the Revival of Letters to the present times, the progress of mankind
> in knowledge, in mental illumination, and in enlarged sentiments of human-
> ity towards each other, has proceeded not only with a steady course, but at
> a rate continually accelerating.[16]

However, Erasmus and his colleagues—and at this point the conjuncture
with the Revolution begins to appear—lacked the daring of the Protestant
Reformers who really confronted the errors of the Catholic Church.

In thought and in his appeal to thinking people Erasmus, says Stewart,
was the most advanced of the reformers but his hope of gradual improvement could not provide the needed revolutionary thrust:

> The writings of Erasmus probably contributed still more than those of
> Luther himself to the progress of the Reformation among men of education
> and taste; but, without the cooperation of bolder and more decided charac-
> ters than his, little would to this day have been effected in Europe among
> the lower orders.[17]

The realization of his hopes depended on a wider freedom of debate than
then existed.

Indeed, the defensive response to the Reformation of Erasmus and his
friend Thomas More served to narrow intellectual freedom. That, says
Stewart, cannot be extenuated but something may be said on their side
against the proponents of violence and in support of "their estrangement
from some of their old friends, who scrupled not to consider as apostates
and traitors all those who, while they acknowledged the expediency of ecclesiastical reform, did not approve of the violent measures employed for
the accomplishment of that object".[18]

The revolutionary experience can then be traced in Stewart's comments on Erasmus. The pattern of analogy between Reformation and
Revolution is: intellectual preparation (Erasmus/the *philosophes*); revolutionary thrust (Luther/1789); reaction against violence (Erasmus/1794).

A progressive view of history is to be found also in the work of Charles
Villers which won the prize offered by the Institut de France in 1802 for
an essay on the influence of Luther's Reformation.[19] Attracted by German idealism while an *émigré*, Villers believed that the upward thrust of
the human spirit must over-ride the catastrophes of history.[20] In all
revolutionary upheavals, there are "men of temperate natures" who wish
for amelioration without commotion. Thus Erasmus failed to recognize
that good could come out of the "Lutheran tragedy" (as he called it), as
it would come also out of the apparent evils of the Revolution:

> But to expect that good should be wrought out of good only, is to make of
> human nature a romance, to turn history into a pastoral, and the universe
> into an Arcadia.[21]

While Stewart recoiled before the violence of the Revolution, Villers took
it, so to speak, in stride.[22]

As already observed, Erasmus was more commonly used to defend
frankly conservative positions. Gibbon wrote:

> I beg leave to subscribe my assent to Mr. Burke's creed on the revolution
> of France. I admire his eloquence; I approve his politics; I adore his chivalry;
> and I can almost excuse his reverence for church establishments. I have
> sometimes thought of writing a dialogue of the dead in which Lucian, Eras-
> mus, and Voltaire should mutually acknowledge the danger of exposing an
> old superstition to the contempt of the blind and fanatic multitude.[23]

How is this use of Erasmus to be related to the earlier presentation of him
as a destroyer of superstition more radical than the Protestant Reformers?
Already in the chapter on the Paulicians Gibbon had expressed alarm at
the prospect of a boundless scepticism, the complete unravelling of faith
by "men who preserve the name without the substance of religion, who
indulge the licence without the temper of philosophy."[24] Does Gibbon
see Erasmus as in some sense the antecedent of these men?

The answer to this question depends on a judgment about Gibbon's
relation to the Christian tradition. On one side, he seems to stand above
or beyond any religious persuasion or conviction. He associated himself
with what he and his contemporaries thought to be the "universal Pyr-
rhonism" of Pierre Bayle.[25] On the other side, he remained obsessed
with the religious questions that had attracted him from his youth. If his
rejection of bigotry was complete, he had not broken with all the Christian
traditions and in much that he said remained in the line of liberal Protestants like Jean Le Clerc, the editor of Erasmus.[26] The phrase "only supposed infidelity", used of him by his friend William Hayley, may have
been his own.[27] If this understanding of him is correct, he did not associate Erasmus with Joseph Priestley and others he accused—however
unjustly—of sedition and of seeking the complete destruction of Christianity.[28] He has not secularized Erasmus. He genuinely admired his religious sincerity, openness and universalism. In face of the Revolution,
Erasmus appeared as the enemy of both stunted orthodoxy and revolutionary enthusiasm.

Herder's ideas about Erasmus began to change almost from the time
of his piece on Hutten.[29] He commended his biblical work in very strong
terms.[30] He came to associate him with his own developing idea of "humanity" and its connotations of universalism and continuity. It is no surprise that, after Herder's early sympathy with the Revolution had given

way to a deep reserve, Erasmus should be included among those who helped "build the garden of the graces and muses in tranquillity".[31] Peace was a positive human value. Herder's view of the Reformation also changed in the 1790s. His preference now was for moderate spirits and the "progressive, natural, reasonable evolution of things".[32] In these circumstances, he revised the piece on Hutten. He still admired Hutten's forthrightness but without denying the merits of Erasmus who, with Grotius, had become his idol. The wounding expressions were moderated or removed.[33]

For both Gibbon and Herder Erasmus had come to represent their own positions on attempting change by revolution. Though himself misinterpreted and tormented, he stood for restraint and civility; he was the man of the measured response. This was Wieland's view of Erasmus and that Gibbon and Herder should adopt it, the latter to the extent of rewriting his declamation on Hutten, demonstrates the reappraisal forced by the Revolution. That view lent itself to use by pragmatic conservatives.

Wieland himself had said in 1793: "If I had been Luther's contemporary (as I have many times frankly said), I would have taken the party of Erasmus".[34] Making comparisons between the Reformation and revolutionary eras was commonplace among nineteenth-century writers on Erasmus.[35] Curiously, the most elaborate of such comparisons was made at the beginning of the century by Samuel Taylor Coleridge.

Coleridge had early on been a supporter of the Revolution. He connected the Reformation and the Revolution as stages in a growing enlightenment. This was a progressive understanding of history like Stewart's and—in Coleridge's case—associated with the unitarianism and political radicalism he had embraced as an undergraduate. By the late 1790s he had turned against the Revolution and complicated his understanding of history. In particular, he saw the relation between Reformation and Revolution, which still preoccupied him, not as a simple continuity but as a pattern of repetitions or imitations, real or presumed. The pleasure of studying history, he says, is like that of listening to a musical composition:

> The events and characters of one age, like the strains in music, recal those of another, and the variety by which each is individualized, not only gives a charm and poignancy to the resemblance, but likewise renders the whole more intelligible. Meantime ample room is afforded for the exercise both of the judgement and the fancy, in distinguishing cases of real resemblance from those of intentional imitation, the analogies of nature, revolving upon herself, from the masquerade figures of cunning and vanity.[36]

The effects produced by historical figures of different character, indeed of different worth, can be strikingly similar, once one has penetrated beneath "the altered drapery and costume" from age to age. The same may be said of the methods they employed. Coleridge respected no historical figures more than Erasmus and Luther, "though for very different qualities"; by contrast, he had now great aversion for Voltaire and Rousseau.[37] He developed at length the contrasts Erasmus/Voltaire and Luther/Rousseau but also drew out the parallels, similarities and analogies between them. Coleridge's judgment on Erasmus and his historical significance arises from the comparison and contrast between the two eras; to that extent at least the Revolution impinges directly on his judgment.

Between Voltaire and Erasmus "the *effects* remain parallel, the *circumstances* analogous, and the *instruments* the same." Thus, the effects of each man's activity extended over Europe and were augmented by the patronage of the powerful, the circumstances were in each case "supplied by an age of hopes and promises" and the intruments "chiefly those of wit and amusive erudition". But in character and historical significance the two were essentially different; the difference parallels that between the Reformation as constructive and the Revolution as destructive change. Erasmus was pioneer of one and Voltaire of the other. The former's knowledge is "solid through its whole extent," his wit, "always bottomed on sound sense, peoples and enriches the mind of the reader with an endless variety of distinct images and living interests" and "his broadest laughter is everywhere translatable into grave and weighty truth". By contrast, the latter's knowledge was superficial, "extensive at a cheap rate", his wit lacking character, imagery and pathos. The object of one was to purify, of the other to destroy. Coleridge concludes with the summary judgment:

> Exchange mutually their dates and spheres of action, yet Voltaire, had he been ten-fold a Voltaire, could not have made up an Erasmus; and Erasmus must have emptied himself of half his greatness and all his goodness, to have become a Voltaire.[38]

Coleridge presents in his Erasmus the image of an authentic reformer. He had both good sense and depth of feeling and addressed society on matters of substance. Coleridge in fact assumes a broad reforming movement which had roots in both scholasticism and the classical revival and to which both Erasmus and Luther belonged. Luther is described as "immediate agent", Erasmus as "pioneer".[39] If Coleridge repeats the standard Protestant view that only Luther's earnestness and not Erasmus' wit could achieve reform,[40] his characteristic position is that the two were connected; to that extent he shares a certain Enlightenment view that Renaissance and Reformation are parts of a whole and integral or at least continuous with one another.

Erasmus and Luther, so understood, were of more than historical interest to Coleridge. They were part and parcel of his reaction from the Enlightenment and the Revolution. It is not by chance that, when in 1818 Coleridge reissued the periodical *The Friend* in which the essay on Erasmus and Luther had first appeared in 1809, he rearranged the material to place the piece immediately before the first full exposition of his fundamental ideas. Germane, above all, is the distinction between the Understanding, which orders our knowledge of the external material world, and the Reason, "an organ of inward sense", by which man has the power of acquainting himself with "invisible realities or spiritual objects". The tragedy of the modern world has been that the Understanding, though unfitted, has produced a religion and a theology—natural theology and so-called "rational religion".[41] Voltaire represents this change in an extreme form. From it came the catastrophe of the Revolution. Luther and also Erasmus remained, by contrast, true to the higher Reason. Because they and the Reformation itself were committed to revealed religion and the scriptural principle, they could produce a genuine rejuvenation of society and culture.

In our present connection, the point of interest is Coleridge's use of Erasmus against the Enlightenment and the Revolution. In the longer history of Erasmus interpretations, he offers—for the period—a portrait of unusual depth and character. He presents Erasmus as a positive reforming force drawing on the vibrant life of his time.

Under the Restoration, the alternative views of the later eighteenth century were presented again with the refinement that, at least in Germany after the wars of liberation against Napoleon, nationality had become an issue and, for many, a dominant value. The Protestant Enlightenment understanding of the Reformation as an intellectual liberation, a work essentially of enlightenment and moral purification, had still its exponents; for them Erasmus was one of the Reformers, comrade-in-arms of Hutten and Luther.[42] On the other hand, the sharp division between Erasmus and Hutten, which Herder had made in 1776 and which G.H.A. Wagner had repeated in an intemperate biography of 1802,[43] was reiterated by biographers of Hutten: Erasmus was weak and hypocritical, Hutten was the noble defender of the Reformation and the fatherland.[44] At the same time, Erasmus became a sympathetic subject for those who saw themselves as survivors of the Revolution, who still felt threatened and clung to the precarious balance of the Restoration settlement. These people, often Catholics, were sceptical of the revolutionary ardour the previous generation and some of their contemporaries found attractive in Hutten. It revealed, said one, "the deep degradation of our age that one dares to depict such a character as an example for young people". By contrast,

Erasmus both worked for betterment in the church and stood by it in crisis.[45]

From Gibbon's siding with Burke to Catholic apologists under the Restoration, Erasmus was associated with conservative responses to the Revolution. This Erasmus is recognizably kin to the Erasmus of the Enlightenment; he is a moderate, preferring toleration and peace to ideological enthusiasm of any kind. There was, however, another side to the Enlightenment picture of Erasmus, the side epitomized by Gibbon's reference to the "secret reformation" which destroyed—more thoroughly than ostensibly more revolutionary Reformers could do—the fabric of authoritarian religion. This side reappears in two works written, though from very different standpoints, in a new era of revolutions (1830–48). It is best expressed in Ranke's description of Erasmus as "the first great writer of the opposition in the modern sense".[46] The remark must be read against the background of oppositional politics in the 1820s and 1830s, the emergence of a political press and demands for wider and freer discussion of public issues.

Ranke's discussion of Erasmus in his history of Germany during the Reformation is brilliant, compelling but one-dimensional. This Erasmus is a journalist and critic, the shrewd judge and skilful master of public opinion. That opinion, says Ranke, was already agitated before Erasmus appeared—by the pressing of reform demands, a spate of books popular and learned and the clash of educational ideologies. To great literary talents he added in time a fine sense for what the public liked and wanted. His attraction for that public lay in the tendency of opposition running through his work and expressing his experience which was in "ceaseless inner contradiction" with established views and interests. His satirical works helped entrench the anticlericalism of the age.[47] This is the portrait of a liberal, not a revolutionary publicist, claiming to work only for reforms and concealing the revolutionary abyss yawning beyond. Ranke did not find the type congenial. What is missing is any study of Erasmus' piety. That is surprising in one of Ranke's interests and sensitivities but the outlines of the portrait were determined by the role Ranke had given Erasmus to play.

The second work was Karl Hagen's study of literary and religious relations in Germany during the age of the Reformation. Like Ranke, Hagen found the source of Erasmus' opposition to established interests in his own experience. He also saw him as the master of public opinion; indeed, he was the unifier of the three reforming movements deriving from the mid-fifteenth century, the popular, the humanist and the theological.[48] But Hagen differed from Ranke in making Erasmus, not Luther, the high-point of the movement. Erasmus was more than an opposition figure; he embodied the hopes of the age for fundamental reform and, further, anticipated modern rationalism and freethought.[49] Hagen has restated in a more revolutionary form Gibbon's doctrine of the second, more sweeping reformation. The "secret reformation" has become a broad reforming movement, frustrated finally by Erasmus' vacillating character and the reversion to dogmatism among the Protestants. The portrait, like the whole work, belongs to the pre-revolutionary ferment of the 1840s.[50]

Summary and conclusion

The purpose of this paper has been to show the effect of the revolutionary age on interpretations of Erasmus. The interpretation across the writers reviewed has been consistent: Erasmus stood for moderation, toleration and rationality. The uses made of this interpretation differed considerably: for some, Erasmus prefigured moderate conservative responses to the Revolution; for others, his views were a measure of weakness and, for others again, a salutary revolutionary solvent of established ways. What is striking is how close the interpretation—whatever the use made of it— remains to the Enlightenment one: Erasmus was the progenitor of modern toleration and even rationalism. Only Coleridge breaks out of this framework by recognizing that on the one hand Erasmus remained within the main Christian tradition and on the other he wanted a thorough reform of the manners and institutions of his time.

NOTES

1 *The History of the Decline and Fall of the Roman Empire*, ed. J.B. Bury, 6 (London, 1912), pp. 131–133. For a critical assessment of Gibbon's view of the Reformers, especially the presumed link with the Paulicians, see A.G. Dickens and John M. Tonkin, *The Reformation in Historical Thought* (Cambridge, Mass., 1985), pp. 134–137.
2 *Ibid.*, p. 133.
3 Gibbon's most extended treatment of Erasmus is to be found in his journal for September, 1762, and arose from his reading of Burigny's *Vie d'Erasme* (Paris, 1757). It deals with Erasmus' character, contribution to learning and relations with the Reformers. "Extracts from the Journal" in John, Lord Sheffield, *The Miscellaneous Works of Edward Gibbon, Esq* (London, 1837), pp. 446–449.
4 *Lebensbeschreibung von ihm selbst abgefasst*, II (Halle, 1782), pp. 233–234; *Ratio seu Methodus verae theologiae. Recensuit et illustravit S. Io. Sal. Semler* (Halle, 1782), p. viii.
5 *Versuch eines fruchtbaren Auszugs der Kirchengeschichte*, II (Halle, 1774), pp. 221–222; *Neue Versuche, die Kirchenhistorie der ersten Jahrhunderte mehr aufzuklären* (Leipzig, 1788), p. 43.
6 *Ratio*, pp. viii–xii.

7   Robertson was a leader of the Moderate party in the Church of Scotland which stood for a Church "disciplined yet comprehensive'. Ian D.L. Clark, "From Protest to Reaction: The Moderate Regime in the Church of Scotland, 1752–1805", in N.T. Phillipson and Rosalind Mitchison, eds, *Scotland in the Age of Improvement* (Edinburgh, 1970), p. 207.

8   *The History of the Reign of the Emperor Charles V* in *The Works of William Robertson, D.D.* (London, 1837), p. 467.

9   The former was the view of Robertson and of J.M. Schröckh in his *Christliche Kirchengeschichte seit der Reformation* (I, Leipzig, 1804), the latter that of G.J. Planck in his *Geschichte der Entstehung, der Veränderungen und der Bildung unsers protestantischen Lehrbegriffs* (I, II, 2nd ed., Leipzig, 1791–92).

10 They are found in the two late eighteenth-century biographies deriving from enlightened circles in Zürich: Johannes Gaudin, *Leben des Erasmus* (Zürich, 1789) and Salomon Hess, *Erasmus von Rotterdam nach seinem Leben und Schriften* (Zürich, 1790).

11 "Hutten" in *Der Teutsche Merkur*, July 1776, pp. 11–12; also in *Sämmtliche Werke* (*SW*), ed. B. Suphan, 9 (Berlin, 1893), p. 481.

12 "Ein Fragment über den Charakter des Erasmus von Rotterdam", *Teutsche Merkur*, December 1776, pp. 262–272.

13 As a boy, Knox had been associated with John Jortin, Erasmus' latitudinarian biographer. A good classical scholar and schoolmaster, he valued Erasmus in that connection, as well as for his love of peace. *Works*, I (London, 1824), "Biographical Preface". On Knox' broad sympathy for Erasmus and use of his writings on peace, see now Emile V. Telle, "In the Wake of Erasmus of Rotterdam: An Outcry for Perpetual and Universal Peace in England in 1793–1795", *Erasmus of Rotterdam Society Yearbook Three* (1983), pp. 104–129. Cf. J.E. Cookson, *The Friends of Peace. Anti-War Liberalism in England 1793–1815* (Cambridge, 1982), pp. 32–33.

14 *Antipolemus*, pp. vi–x, xiv.

15 *Dissertation: Exhibiting the Progress of Metaphysical, Ethical, and Political Philosophy, since the Revival of Letters in Europe*, in William Hamilton, ed., *Collected Works*, I (Edinburgh, 1854), pp. 25, 27. On Stewart, see Mary Fearnley-Sander, "The Emancipation of the Mind: A View of the Reformation in Four Eighteenth Century Historians", unpublished PhD thesis, University of Western Australia (1977), pp. 192–202.

16 *Dissertation*, p. 487.

17 *Ibid.*, p. 27.

18 *Ibid.*, p. 530.

19 *Essai sur l'esprit et l'influence de la Réformation de Luther* (Paris, 1804).

20 See Yvonne Knibielher, "Réforme et Révolution d'après Charles de Villers", in Philippe Joutard ed., *Historiographie de la Réforme* (Paris, 1977), pp. 171–181.

21 Eng. tr. by James Mill, *Essay on the Spirit and Influence of the Reformation of Luther* (London, 1805), pp. 31, 34. Mill criticized Villers for overlooking the analogy between Erasmus as a preparer of the Reformation and Voltaire and Rousseau as preparers of the Revolution. *Ibid.*, p. 15n.

22 J.M.L. Coupé, in a long and somewhat muddled essay written under the Directory, used Erasmus to demonstrate the perils of literature in times of violence and the difficulties of moderate spirits. "Erasme. Notice sur sa personne et sur ses ouvrages", *Les Soirées littéraires*, VII (Paris, 1797), pp. 155–216.

23 *The Autobiography of Edward Gibbon*, ed. Dero A. Saunders (New York, 1961), p. 203.

24 *Decline and Fall*, 6, p. 134.

25 *Autobiography*, p. 89.

26 Owen Chadwick, "Gibbon and the Church Historians", in G.W. Bowersock, John Clive, Stephen R. Graubard, eds, *Edward Gibbon and the Decline and Fall of the Roman Empire* (Cambridge, Mass., 1977), p. 221.

27 Paul Turnbull, "The 'supposed infidelity' of Edward Gibbon", *The Historical Journal*, 5 (1982), pp. 23–41. Cf. David Dillon Smith, "Gibbon in Church", *Journal of Ecclesiastical History*, 35 (1984), pp. 452–463.

28 Gibbon interpreted Priestley's attack on the alliance of throne and altar as an attack on political order (*Decline and Fall*, 6, p. 134n.).

29 Cf. Werner Kaegi, "Erasmus im achtzehnten Jahrhundert", in *Gedenkschrift zum 400. Todestage des Erasmus von Rotterdam* (Basel, 1936), pp. 223–226.

30 *Briefe, das Studium der Theologie betreffend,* in *SW*, 10, pp. 187, 252.

31 *Briefe zur Beförderung der Humanität,* in *SW*, 17, pp. 67–68.

32 Quoted from a late ms. *SW*, 18, p. 332.

33 *SW*, 16, pp. 273–293.

34 *Wielands Werke*, 15, ed. Wilhelm Kurrelmeyer (Berlin, 1930), p. 772.

35 Edmund Burke himself had made this comparison in *Thoughts on French Affairs* (1791): "The present revolution in France ... is a revolution of doctrine and theoretic dogma ... The last revolution of doctrine and theory which has happened in Europe is the Reformation". Everyman's edition (London, 1929), p. 288.

36 *The Friend* (1818 edition), in *Collected Works* (*CW*), 4.I, ed. Barbara E. Rooke (London/Princeton, 1969), p. 130.

37 *Ibid.*, pp. 130–131.

38 *Ibid.*, pp. 131–132.

39 *The Philosophical Lectures*, ed. Kathleen Coburn (London, 1949), pp. 291, 316–317, 305.

40 *Ibid.*, p. 308.

41 *Friend*, in *CW*, 4.I, p. 156. Cf. James D. Boulger, *Coleridge as Religious Thinker* (New Haven, 1961), *passim*; J. Robert Barth, *Coleridge and Christian Doctrine* (Cambridge, Mass., 1969), pp. 15–24; L.O. Frappell, "Coleridge and the "Coleridgeans" on Luther", *Journal of Religious History*, 7 (1973), pp. 308–310.

42 E.g., Gottfried Wilhelm Becker, *Luther und seine Zeitgenossen oder Ursachen, Zweck und Folgen der Reformation* (Leipzig, 1817).

43 *Leben des Desiderius Erasmus* (Leipzig, 1802).

44 C.J. Wagenseil, *Ulrich von Hutten nach seinem Leben, seinem Karakter und seinen Schriften geschildert* (Nuremberg, 1823), quoted by Joachim Wulschner, "Erasmus von Rotterdam im 19. Jahrhundert. Sein Bild in der deutschen Literatur, vornehmlich gesehen im Hinblick auf seinen Gegenspieler Ulrich von Hutten", unpublished dissertation, Free University of Berlin (1955), p. 43.

45 Carl Kieser, *Der Streit zwischen Ulrich von Hutten und Erasmus von Rotterdam; ein Beitrag zur Charakteristik Ulrichs von Hutten und seiner literarischen Zeitgenossen* (Mainz, 1823), pp. xii, 146–147.

46 *Deutsche Geschichte im Zeitalter der Reformation*, in *Sämmtliche Werke*, I (Leipzig, 1873), p. 176.

47 *Ibid.*, pp. 176–180.

48 *Deutschlands literarische und religiöse Verhältnisse im Reformationszeitalter*, 3 vols (Erlangen, 1841–44), I, pp. 254–257.

49 *Ibid.*, p. 309, III, pp. 42–43, 86–87.

50 Cf. my "Erasmus in the Nineteenth Century: The Liberal Tradition", *Studies in the Renaissance*, XV (1968), pp. 211–213.

NICOLAAS VAN DER BLOM

ROTTERDAM AND ERASMUS.
SOME REMARKS*

Roterodamus ego, non inficiabor, Erasmus

The State University at Rotterdam, named after Erasmus[1], is organizing on the occasion of her "Founder's Day", November 8th, a symposium to commemorate the death of Erasmus. I assume that no objections will be raised to my making, this time and here,[2] a contribution under the rubric "tradition" regarding some aspects of the history of the relationship of Rotterdam to her *civis omnium praestantissimus*—her most preeminent citizen.

I. "It is unimportant where a person is born. In my opinion it is empty bragging when a city or country makes boast to the fact that it has procreated a person who through his own efforts and not through the support of the country of his birth, has risen to greatness and fame" (*Allen* 1147, 29ff). A quote from Erasmus, with which I ought to begin.

Rotterdam has indeed ample reason for modesty. On August 7th, 1503 the Town Council granted to "Heer Jerassimus" a weekly discount of 2½ "groats" on his excise duty, and this in such a manner that it was to be deducted from the duties on beer owed by his mother and father.[3] Alas, this could not have been our Erasmus, who complains, does he not, for example in the letter to Prior Servatius (*Allen* 294, 13) that he was manoeuvred into the monastery by his guardians.[3]

On the contrary, it is rather Rotterdam who profits from Erasmus when she is lyrically praised, on his account, in the letter written by Chrysostomus of Naples to Duke Nugarolo relating the events of his journey through Holland[4]: in that *urbecula concinna*, that little town, the climate is delicious, which surprises the author until he hears that Erasmus was born there! Nogaroli are known, but I found no Nugaroli. *Nugae* means i.a. nonsense. Thus I suspect that the Chrysostomus who reports to "Nonsense man", is a proto-Hythlodaeus (in whose name, with a change of function, the ironic tone of Nugarolus has been taken over) and that in Holland at any rate Rotterdam was a proto-(and mini-)Utopia. Was the writer John Sixtinus who travelled here at that time? Or Caraffa from Naples who had been papal nuncio since 1513 in England, where he may have heard about Holland? "Chrysostomus" was away from home for 16 months. And Erasmus, when, later, he inquires of Caraffa how he is faring in the rigorous climate of Zeeland and among its surly inhabitants, seems to give a wink at the man who had so complained about the Dutch coachmen and innkeepers, but had so praised the climate of "Rothoroda-mum" (*Allen* 640). Erasmus was acquainted of course with this letter which may be taken as an amusing example of Erasmus-promotion— which meant at the same time: Rotterdam-promotion!

In April 1514 Erasmus hears that Philip van Spangen, his *conterraneus ac plane vicinus proximus* (*Allen* 291, 68f), has read with interest his *Lucubrationes*. Whether he followed the advice to approach the latter for support, we do not know. Philip's uncle, Antony van Bergen, Abbot of St. Bertin, gave Erasmus some help at least around 1514. However, Rotterdam had no part in this.

Meanwhile, Erasmus' fame began to spread here. The rector of the townschool, Ursus (Beren), teaches Greek in 1526 and asks Cornelius Aurelius to provide him for his pupils with an edition of the *Paraphrasis in Elegantias L. Vallae*, and this indeed appears in 1529. This evidence of his influence, although he came to hear of it in circumstances which gave him no cause for joy, must have pleased Erasmus. And it would have amused him to learn that students from here, on their matriculation at the Natio Germanica of the University of Orléans, called themselves initially *Rotterdamensis* (1511), later *de Rotterodamis* (1520) and finally, with a hint of pride (4 ×, 1529/33/40/46) *Roterodamus*.[5]

In 1532/33 the time has finally come and the States of Holland, of which Rotterdam formed part as one of the "small cities", send Erasmus the not inconsiderable sum of 200 guilders. All this proceeded not without some frictions, for which the States and Rotterdam, however, could not be reproached, and the Grand Old Man finally accepted the gift with thanks.

On Erasmus' death in 1536, Bishop Nausea urged in his high-tuned *Monodia* that, just as our ancestors honoured Christ and his disciples with (i.a.) statues, his generation and posterity should honour Erasmus, but no, "not with a statue as of one of those canonized by the entire church", but with a *memoria* which would evoke in them the thought and spirit of his work, in the manner in which the *imagines maiorum*, the statues of ancestors, did for the ancient Romans—"In contemplation of them they were, to quote Sallustius, inspired to match their honours and virtues". Nausea's rejection of a statue as of a saint, and his recalling of the Roman *imagines maiorum* must have given someone here in Rotterdam a hint!

When in 1549 Prince Philip visits Rotterdam, he is greeted, as was the customary practice on the occasion of "joyous arrivals", by a wooden statue. The statue chosen here, represented Erasmus—what a bold idea!—holding a pen in his right hand. In his left hand he held up a board upon which was inscribed the verse: *Roterodamus ego, non inficiabor, Eras-*

mus/Ne videar cives deseruisse meos . . .: Rotterdamer I am, I do not deny it—let no one think that I have deserted my fellow-citizens! An *imago* of a citizen of Rotterdam representing his fellow-citizens and swearing allegiance to the prince in their name.

In 1557 another step is made, in a different direction, which characterizes Erasmus himself and his work to perfection. The wooden occasional statue of 1549 is replaced by a stone image of Erasmus presenting him with "the book". The book in question is—a truth so simple as it is, but so little known!—the Bible, or rather: the New Testament or possibly the *Paraphrases*. Upon the house in which he was born and which already in 1540 was shown to Charles V's retinue, the words could be read: "In this house was born Erasmus renowned, who the Word of God to us so finely did expound". And from that time Erasmus has stood here, first as the fervent preacher in the pulpit we know from a drawing of the wooden copy of the statue of 1557 which was destroyed by the Spaniards in 1572, and finally as the learned exeget "reciting the breviary" on his pedestal, which since 1622 has crowned the series of in total five statues and which survived the fire of Rotterdam in 1940—an Erasmus in the spirit of Grotius, who took the initiative for the erection of the "copper Erasmus".[6] Did the Spaniards in 1572 repent of their misdeed? A galley fitted out by the city-elders loyal to Spain and intended to be used in the struggle against the Beggars, was provided at the bow with a figure-head of San Jago, patron-saint of Spain, and at the stern with a statue of "Erasmus Roterodamus", especially made for the occasion. This combination did not prove to be a success. The role intended for Erasmus was in any case unfitting. The galley had to be abandoned and shortly afterwards the Spanish troops left, never to return. Is there a connection with the famous "Japanese Erasmus", the taffrail figure of the ship De Liefde—the Charity (earlier baptized Erasmus) which set sail from here in 1598 and whose journey came to an end, as it happened, in Japan on April 19th, 1600? In any case there is a certain harmony between the original and the later name of the ship and the figure on the stern.

Concerning the statues of Erasmus may I further refer to my illustrated article in *Erasmus in English* VI (1973) 5ff. An important study in the history of art in particular concerning the bronze statue by Hendrik de Keyzer was contributed by Dr. Jochen Becker.[7]

All in all, Rotterdam has repaid Erasmus in a unique manner for the fact that he named himself after his place of birth and so "has given her a name" (Vondel).

II. Rotterdam has had her share of the religious-theological conflicts of the 16th/17th century. That Erasmus' influence made itself felt, goes without saying. I cite the case of our pastor Duyfhuis (translated: Dove House) who became Protestant, and later a member of the Family of Love. The Museum Boymans-van Beuningen has in its collection a tile which according to tradition depicts the latter whilst holding the sermon which marked his transition. The figure 84 can be read on the pulpit. Psalm 84 (later a word-play is made on his name, after verse 4: he was "The Heavenly Dove who inhabited the House") contains Duyfhuis' program which follows Erasmus' exegesis of this psalm, *De sarcienda ecclesiae concordia*. If my hypothesis is correct,[8] then this tile was made on the occasion of the commemoration in 1678 of the fact that this sermon was given one hundred years earlier, and one may suspect the tile-maker/poet Joachim Oudaan, Arminian, yes even Socinian,[9] to have been behind it.

Halfway through arose the dissensions between the Remonstrants and Contra-Remonstrants. The latter gained the final victory at the Synod of Dordt in 1619. The erection in 1622 of the bronze statue, brain-child of the opposition, could not but cause uproar! The calvinistic preacher Levius is traditionally derided here whenever the statue is written about, because of his fiery reproaches of Erasmus, "libertine, 'vrijgeest' and mocker of all religions". The social side of his protests, his denunciation of the corrupt government of the regents who commissioned this expensive statue whilst extreme poverty prevailed amongst the townspeople, has always been suppressed, whilst precisely this protest is purely erasmian. Selective indignation at a distance!

In 1674 the pedestal was in poor condition and the bridge upon which the market-place was situated with the statue to one side, needed repairing. The statue was removed to a builder's shed along the river and returned in 1677 to its original place in the city. Erasmian Rotterdam which received the commission and ample freedom to provide the new pedestal with inscriptions, became very active, with Oudaan in the forefront. On the jury was teacher and journalist Pieter Rabus, editor, commentator and translator of the *Colloquia* and the *Conflictus Thaliae et Barbariei*. François van Hoogstraten, translator of i.a. the *Laus* and *Utopia*, probably took part in the deliberations. The teacher of the Erasmian School Johannes Sylvius contributed a Greek verse, for which there was finally no room. Oudaan was joined by Nicolaas Heinsius. These two men placed on record on the pedestal for posterity the vision of their circle concerning Erasmus, both in Latin and in Dutch. They drew their inspiration from Grotius' praise of Erasmus: *tuus ille sol primus illuxit*, and from *Allen* 3139, 89ff, and 3141. Erasmus is *tantus vir*, the great man who bested barbarism—the philologist, the moralist, the theologian: the "light of languages", the "salt of morals", the "radiant miracle, the pride of charity, peace and theology". In his writings shines *ingenii coeleste iubar*, the heav-

enly light of genius from "that Great Sun", which rose here and set in
Basel. There they have his grave, here the city where he was born gives
him, with this statue, second life. To adequately honour Erasmus, the
Great Sun, it can but be the heavens which here roof his head. Beautiful
rhetoric. Erasmus stands here *sub templo*, under the canopy of heaven—
which suggests that here Rotterdam at least equals Basel where he lies *in
templo*!

III. Basel and Rotterdam! In Pierre Bayle's *Dictionaire Historique et Critique*, published here by Reynier Leers in 1697, are to be found i.a. the
article "Erasmus" and the article "Rotterdam". In the 2nd edition,
1702, Bayle added to the latter the following story. In 1672 there was both
elsewhere and in Rotterdam an uprising amongst the people and for a few
days anarchy prevailed in the city. During these disturbances the statue
of Erasmus was removed as bearing testimony of "Papism". It was carried to a "maison publique" and deliberations took place as to whether
it would not be "à propos" to melt it down. The magistrate of Basel who
got wind of this, immediately ordered a correspondent of his in Rotterdam
to make an offer for the statue. The sale almost went through. Basel then
gave instructions to pay our magistrate what he asked. However, in the
meantime, they had changed their minds here and decided that the statue
was neither to be sold nor melted down, but to be restored to its place.
And this is what shortly afterwards took place. So far the story which
Bayle took down on July 26th, 1699 from the lips of the very merchant
from Basel himself.

In my opinion, "Mr. Bayle pourra être critiqué".

1. As appears from his verse on the pedestal, Oudaan was alert to the
contrasts which, notwithstanding the mutual agreement to honour Erasmus, existed between Basel and Rotterdam. In the festive poem with
which he celebrated the return of the statue to the city nothing is mentioned about any attempt from Basel to buy the statue. He only speaks—
and this in quite rhetorical and colourful terms—about the masses of people on, and the masses of water under the bridge which had threatened
Erasmus and forced him to step aside, very much against his motto Cedo
Nulli. How angry would Oudaan not have been if a purchase by Basel had
even for a moment threatened and utterly destroyed the balance between
the two cities, emphasized by him in the verse on the pedestal. As poet
he has taken the liberty to encompass in one scene the few days of anarchy
of 1672 and the event of 1674 when the authorities decided to repair the
bridge and to house the statue somewhere else for the time being. This was
a liberty which to Bayle as historian cannot be permitted.

2. The statue "ressentoit le Papisme" in the eyes of "la populace",

"der Pöbel". One would not so much have expected this reproach in 1672, as in 1621/22, when during the commotion around the erection of the statue, it was said that someone had been seen kneeling before it.

3. In 1818 J. Scheltema reports the incident and suggests that the purchase was only rejected by a majority of two votes. Drs. R.H. Krans of the municipal archives, in his letter of March 5th, 1986 to Dr. Jenny of Basel, has pointed out that this is probably an echo of 1621 when a majority of the Council decided on October 29th to place the statue, notwithstanding protests, and of 1622 when, according to Gerard Brandt, Uitenboogaert informed Grotius in a letter of June 3rd that this majority had amounted to exactly two votes. To this I add that Scheltema also mentions that there were ecclesiastics who urged that the statue be not replaced on the market: which is clearly a replica of 1621/22 when Rev. Levius protested so strongly against the placing and the member of the Town Council Van Berckel, as a compromise, proposed placing the statue somewhere other than on the market-place. That Scheltema perhaps derived some details—which Erasmus' biographer Hess does not possess—from archival sources (Basel catalogue H 35 note 4) would in my opinion not seem to apply for his statement that the fact that the purchase did not succeed at once, was imputable to "a chance diffidence on the part of the mandatary". This is precisely the answer that one would devise when asked why ever it did not succeed: the merchant just had a "fit of modesty", which does him honour, since he did not on his own authority dare to agree to the tacitly implied, not inconsiderable price asked by Rotterdam, and fell back on his mandators. In an archival document his price would have been stated, to the uttermost farthing!

4. According to Scheltema, Gerard Brandt the elder wrote a letter to burgomaster De Brauw in order to avert the shame around the sale of the statue. "Whether this achieved any effect, remains unknown". I wonder myself, as does Drs. Krans, whether in the course of the years this letter has not replaced the letter to Grotius of 1622, since it was mentioned by Gerard Brandt the younger. The uncertainty concerning the effect of this letter—of which no trace can be found—suggests that De Brauw perhaps did not wish to or did not dare to act—to both these attitudes it applies that they need archival substantiation. In any case it pleases us to see that De Brauw is included in the list of magistrates at the back of the pedestal.

5. Bayle did not verify the story of the Basel merchant by further inquiries and in particular with the magistrates (something which he did do with respect to another report, also concerning Basel; see below). He was at odds with the Council who had dismissed him. I suspect that he may have derived pleasure from the story of how Rotterdam almost committed an offence against "son camarade de bronze". This was a story of which he did not wish to be deprived.

Thus, with what it says in the Basel catalogue 1986: "it may be assumed that it is largely (*weitgehend*) thanks to the demarches of Basel that the Rotterdamers decided to desist from their *Vandalenakt* so that the statue was saved", I cannot agree. It is quite possible that some individuals in Rotterdam during the troubles of 1672, when the French attacked and the cry for Orange echoed, carried away by their emotions, may with clenched fists have reviled and cursed Erasmus, whom they took as being on the side of the regents, and possibly have wished him far away, even as far as Basel. However, *the* Rotterdamers, in other words the responsible authorities would in 1672 have protected the statue had that indeed been necessary—I know of no archivalia. And in 1674/77 their successors indeed went to a considerable amount of trouble on account of the statue. The question is: if indeed it is true that the Basel merchant in 1672 began negotiations with the authorities—and I deem this to be unlikely—, how far did the latter take the matter? And how serious was their reaction? Not one single magistrate, whatever his political or religious colour, can ever have seriously considered selling or melting down the pride of the town, this statue which was depicted on every map of the town, yes had even become the symbol of the city, this "must" for every tourist (apart from everything else that it was and is). In short, I cannot believe this—as far as we can see now, it must be a legend. *Multis mutandis mutatis*, this case brings to my mind 1965, when the Governors of the Nederlandse Economische Hogeschool, the Dutch School of Economics, proposed to the Municipal Executive that the statue be transferred to their campus on the outskirts of the town, at Woudestein (we have moved a considerable number of things here in the post-war years!). One "letter to the editor" was sufficient: nothing more was heard of this proposal. It would of course not have stood a chance, had the matter come up for discussion. At any rate it is a good thing that in this case there are documents! They will at least prevent the later birth of a legend which in time could grow into another story, exciting I dare say!

Bayle has yet another story about Rotterdam. In his *Dictionaire* I.2 (1697)1070 he writes in the article *Erasmus* about a gift from Basel to Rotterdam, kept here "en un lieu public": a portrait of Erasmus about which he read in R. Telle's Latin translation (1616) of Guicciardini's *Descrittione di tutti i Paesi Bassi*[3], 1588. In this case he made extensive inquiries, but no one could tell him anything.

In Merula's *Vita Des. Erasmi*, Leyden 1607, the dedication to Council and People of Rotterdam reads: " . . . that his portrait is kept with you at a public place, true of life (*ex ipsius vultu*), four years before his death

engraved (*delineata*) and by Council and People of Basel sent (*transmissa*)''.
Bayle apparently was not acquainted with this dedication which only appeared in the first edition. And Telle did not mention it as his source.

Notwithstanding this *delineata*—such terms are in his opinion somewhat loose—, according to Dr. Jenny (his letter of June 6th, 1986) it must have been a painted copy after the ''Erasmus in eim Rund'' from 1532, whilst I argued that it was a copy of ''Erasmus in eim Ghüs''.

However, the *Icones Leidenses* (Leyden, 1973) mention that in 1597 a portrait of Erasmus was donated to the library there, ''a painted copy (*transpicta*) of the portrait that the Council of Basel had sent in earlier years (*superioribus annis*) to Council and People of Rotterdam''! This dates the Rotterdam portrait before 1597, while the ''sending'' (*transmissa*) took place in ''earlier years''. The dating in Merula's dedication: ''four years before Erasmus' death'' applies in my opinion only to *delineata*, and not also to *transmissa*—the account by Caluete de Estrella of the ceremony of 1549 would certainly have made mention of this. One may think for example of 1550/54, when Sebastian Münster's *Cosmographia* spread the fame of Rotterdam and mentioned this ceremony and the statue. Such a portrait, just as the stone statue of 1557, were essential to the status of the city. Or one may think of the ninetees, when Rotterdam became rich and erected the second stone statue of 1593/94. Did Rotterdam at that time commission a portrait through the Council of Basel? Or was it a spontaneous gift for the purposes of strengthening the bond between two Erasmus-cities and, not to forget, two thriving centres of trade? Also at that time there were Basel merchants here! For the time being I assume that it was a gift. Although one would expect two documents on the occasion of an official gift. Questions enough!

Indeed, there is yet another problem! The Leyden portrait is of the same type as the specimen in Parma: a half-portrait of Erasmus, behind a table, gazing out over an open book which lies before him, the text of which is half covered by his left hand. This does not tally with the portrait we have here! It is indeed hardly likely that this was the model for the Leyden piece. Thus another portrait must have existed here, of the Parma-type, of which tradition has it that it was a gift from Basel,[10] and the portrait in the Historical Museum looses this status!

Rotterdam, just as the Leyden Library, must have received or bought in that time more Erasmus portraits—there was a good market for them and therefore a good supply. In 1639 Maria de Medici saw in the Town-hall a portrait ''de la main de ce grand paintre Hollebeen'', probably the piece which is now missing. What happened to it before 1654? That is when the painter Sorgh restores the portrait from the Historical Museum, which apparently was to replace the Holbein.

IV. Bayle provides me, finally, with the stepping stone to my last theme. He informs us that Guy Patin had written to him saying that the rumour was circulating in Paris that the magistrates of Rotterdam had commissioned the printing of a new edition of Erasmus' *Opera Omnia*. "Voilà", says Patin, "une nouvelle qui me rejouit fort. Il y a encore de la vertu au monde, et d'honnêtes gens que ont du courage" (art. Erasmus (1697) 1068). What happened in fact was that the Rotterdam magistrates paid the printer Pieter van der Aa for his "LB", when this edition in 10 volumes was completed in 1706, the sum of Dfl. 1400,- as contribution from the city. Next to the titlepage of volume I, a double sheet had been inserted upon which appeared i.a. the statue, the armorial bearings of Rotterdam and the dedication of the work *inclytae et florentissimae Reipublicae Roterodamensis Consulibus*.

V. *Laudem aeternam nancisceris princeps ad illam rem accessisse*—eternal praise shall you receive because you were the first to take this matter in hand, wrote Dr. A. Horawitz in Vienna on September 2nd, 1888 to Dr. Johannes Benedictus Kan, Rector of the Gymnasium Erasmianum of Rotterdam. The matter he referred to concerned the repudiation by Kan—contemporary of Cobet!—of the authenticity of the *Vita Des. Erasmi*, the so-called *Compendium Vitae* (CV), published by Merula in 1607.

From Kan dates, after Rabus, the most recent scientific activity around Erasmus in Rotterdam. Between 1878 and 1901 Kan received letters from *viri Erasmiani* from many countries. In our Record Office only one is to be found. It appears that the rest has been preserved by the family. Recently, shortly before his death, a grandson, Dr. W.G. Kan AHzn, physician in Bennekom, sent me everything. Rector Kan did not keep copies of his own letters, but copies of letters from Kan to Dr. L. Sieber were sent to me from Basel at my request. And very recently my attention was drawn to the existence in the Record Office of correspondence from the solicitor G.M. Ballari of Turin, who there in September 1876 organized a commemoration of Erasmus' promotion, with the city of Rotterdam— and also with Kan.

During the summer-holidays of 1877 Kan met (by accident?) Dr. L. Sieber, the librarian of Basel, on the Rigi. Their "Schwur auf dem Rigi" had results! When Kan publishes his *Erasmiana* on December 8th, 1877, casting a stone into still waters—he considers the CV, up to then the basis for every biography of Erasmus, to be false, and Merula to have been deceived, and later even: to be a deceiver—, he distributes offprints. Sieber translates the text and discusses this at the Historische Gesellschaft of Basel, after which he has the text published in a journal. Pierre de Nolhac, whom Kan approaches in Latin ("which provides better protection against indiscretions to-day than in Erasmus' time", he writes back), has the French translation by Kan's collegue P. Delinotte inserted in a periodical. F. de Nève of Louvain apparently receives from Kan, besides the offprint, some reflections on Erasmus—he answers in any case: "Possibly I do not share your view. In my opinion Erasmus remained, notwithstanding his polemics, within the Mother Church". Vischer was delighted to hear that his study had stimulated Kan, but he has some objections. Sieber reports a similar reaction from the Gesellschaft. However, he says, you have attained your objective, one is alert to the problem, and it remains now to prove the authenticity of the CV. Kan also, on the advice of Vischer, approaches Horawitz, Knaus and Geiger. Horawitz reacts: he has seen a copy of the CV dated 1520–1530 in a Library, "Was the CV already at that time a forgery? But then, why indeed not?!" Etc. Later correspondents are K. Hartfelder, A. Richter, M. Reich and J. Lupton. I have not (yet) found any report on a meeting between Kan and Allen, neither do I know the source of Allen's statement "that Dr. Kan abandoned (his) opinions at the end of his life" (I, App. I, p. 576, n. 8). Kan, who died in 1902, was never to see Allen's Volume I. Kan's opinion concerning the CV is here, as we know, extensively and fairly discussed and finally rejected. Thus Kan's objective, as Sieber wrote, was nevertheless achieved; he who believes in the authenticity of the CV, does this, after Kan and Allen, no longer naively, but with full deliberation.

The CV says that Erasmus was born in Rotterdam, and that his father Gerardus, hoping for a marriage, held secret intercourse with his mother. *Et sunt qui dicant intercessisse verba*: there are those who say that promises of marriage were given.[11] Further we hear that the father of Gerard was called Helias . . . We know of the recent find by G. Avarucci and A. Campana. In the colophon of two manuscripts copied in Fabriano in 1457/58 it says that *Gerardus Helye Hollandrinus civitatis Rotterdammis* (variant: *G.H.*, *theothonicus hollandrinensis provintie*) with thanks to the Virgin Mary and to the martyr Erasmus, concluded his work.[12] I think: the father of Erasmus[13]. The CV gives the same names and also mentions that Erasmus' father was a scribe. The information therein that he attended the lectures of Guarino, causes Allen, who did not know of a sojourn in Italy so long before the birth of Erasmus, to remark: "This must refer to the younger Guarino at Ferrara"—but Guarino the elder taught there until his death, December 4th, 1460; this also tallies.[14] It would be naive to argue, as Avarucci does, that Gerard must have become father of Erasmus in the same year as that in which he copies these manuscripts; which forces on Avarucci the tour de force of adding ten years upon Erasmus' life! The CV suggests that Gerard was working in Rome. That may well have been the case around the time of Erasmus' birth (1467, according to tradition in Rotterdam). Someone who worked in Fabriano and then returned to Holland, would, as circumstances dictated, have gone back to Italy, where Rome, more than any other city, offered work. These circumstances remain obscure. Dr. J. IJsewijn thinks it may have been a quarrel[15] and he may well be right. The CV connects this departure with the fact that Gerard's family opposed the marriage. We note here that Gerard was from Rotterdam. *Puer alitus est apud aviam*—the child was nursed by his grandmother—it further says. Which was echoed by Rhenanus with his *Roterodami alumnus*, nurseling of Rotterdam.

VI. Kan continuously published Erasmiana from the University Library of Basel in the Program of the Gymnasium Erasmianum, with a text of the CV from Vienna. He was also responsible for an edition of the Laus, which Cl. Miller praises in the *ASD*. Further he made a translation of the *Laus* which was reprinted up to 1969, but which will now be replaced by the lively translation of Dirkzwager-Nielson, accompanied by the Latin text, [1]Asd. 1949, [2]Rdam 1986. Rector Dr. Y.H. Rogge wrote about Erasmus and M. Lipsius. The librarian Dr. W.L. de Vreese (1919/34) brought bibliographic knowledge and enthusiasm with him from Flanders and induced many a Rotterdam Maecenas to donate Erasmiana. Thereupon Dr. F.K.H. Kossmann (1934/58) organized the Erasmus congress-1936 and recorded the considerable collection of Erasmiana in his *Overzicht*.[16] Dr. C. Reedijk, whose *The Poems of Erasmus* was born in the Library, succeeded him. Drs. E. van Gulik (1961/73) was co-organizer of the commemoration-1969, to which the museum Boymans-van Beuningen, under the direction of Drs. J.C. Ebbinge Wubben, contributed splendidly, while the Gymnasium made its own contribution with the performance of the play written by Rector Drs. R. van der Velde "Erasmus sprekend" (= "Erasmus speaking"): texts of Erasmus placed within the context of Beatus Rhenanus' biography of Erasmus. Van Gulik recorded in a short-title catalogue which editions of Erasmus (– 1703) are known to exist and where in the world copies are to be found. For the series Erasmus Studies he is at present preparing a paper on Erasmus' own library. Dr. V.W.D. Schenk who later taught at the University, diagnosed "narcissism" in Erasmus,[17] which diagnosis was reiterated recently by Minnich-Meissner. Etc.

Most important: in 1960 the Historical Society "Roterodamum" propounded before the municipal authorities the desirability of a new edition of the *Opera Omnia*. The Royal Dutch Academy of Sciences took this task upon herself in 1963 (*ASD* 1969 – . . .). The City Library of Rotterdam is rendering considerable services and assistance to this undertaking with her collection of Erasmiana, to date the largest in the world—a cultural asset of the first order, to be carefully conserved and extended.

Hoc alumno Roterodamum oppidum se semper iactabit et doctis erit commenda-tum—because of this nurseling, Erasmus, the city of Rotterdam shall ever be proud and recommended among scholars. Thus says Beatus Rhenanus in his preface to Charles V in the first *Opera Omnia*, that from Basel, 1538–1540. May the last part of this prediction be fulfilled for the sake of Erasmus. But also for what a grateful Rotterdam did for Erasmus with statue and Library. And for the work which was done here on Erasmus at the Gymnasium Erasmianum and in the City Library—and hopefully, for what will be done in the future both there and at Erasmus University.

NOTES

* My heartfelt thanks to Mrs. Louise H. Baker-van Herk, who kindly translated this paper for her former master of classics.

1 The name Erasmus University was probably launched by burgomaster W. Thomas-sen at the New Year's reception at the Town-hall on January 1st, 1968. At the open-ing of the University by H.M. Queen Juliana on November 8th, 1973 mention was made in passing of the fact that there had been some objections to the name. Cf. M.J. Petry, *Wijsbegeerte in Rotterdam* ..., Leiden 1982. Tradition in the Netherlands speaks indeed of: "De Rijksuniversiteit te Leiden", etc. But since then the name has become established. The University proudly displays as her 'logo' on all correspondence Erasmus' signature, as he wrote this in the *felicissima manus*, the beautiful hand which perhaps he inherited from his father. At the time it pleased me to see that the two "Erasmian" adages for which I had been asked and which were to be inscribed on the honorary doctors' medal, had been accepted: AD FONTES and SUIS OCULIS CERNERE: to the sources, and: to discern with one's own eyes (*Allen* 182, 187ff), which adages together formulate the requirements to be imposed on science (my letter of May 5th, 1976).

2 In the summer of 1986 I published on Erasmus' *Carmen Votivum* in Washington's *Year-book Five* (1985) 52–64 and in *Hermeneus* 58, 3 (1986) 191–198. Due to a lack of time and space, the key-stone of my argument is missing there. That Erasmus deposited with Amerbach a copy of his letter to his friend, the physician Cop, seems to be some-what exceptional considering the safe route Basel-Paris. In my opinion the reason is to be sought in its special contents and I think that in May 1531 Erasmus, in view of Cop's advanced age, meanwhile sent him the *Carmen* in manuscript. Not until 1532 did Emmeus find the opportunity to print this text, based on the one returned by Amerbach to Erasmus. Cop died in December 1532—he probably also received the printed *Carmen*: an extra delight for that other old man.

3 Municipal Record Office Rotterdam, OSA 14, p. 63.

4 Was it the student matriculated in Cologne, of *Allen* 48, introd.? In 1496 he was not yet "Heer", i.e. Priest, Dominus; but in 1503 perhaps he was.

5 In: Martinus Dorpius, *Dialogus*, Louvain (1514).

6 Some art historians prefer to label the statue a "scholar's portrait". They seem to neglect the fact that De Keyzer linked up with the Rotterdam tradition, in which Erasmus was not generally speaking a scholar, but specifically the—learned!—exeget of the New Testament.

7 "De Rotterdamsche heyligh", in: *Vondel bij gelegenheid, 1679–1979*, Middelburg 1979, 11–62.

8 *Bulletin museum Boymans* 15 (1964) 39ff.

9 B. van Dam-Heringa, in *De nieuwe taalgids* 77 (1984) 484ff.

10 P. Ganz, *Gedenkschrift Basel-1936*, 264, and *Icones Leidenses*, no. 4.

11 Wrongly translated by A. Godin: "Des racontars, disent quelques-uns, intervinrent". Causing herewith also a tragic point to be lost from sight: Erasmus, as we know, disapproved of this ground for marriage then in force, *LB* V, 627C "O matrimonia non Christiana!" and IX, 1069 CD, cf. *ASD*, I–3, 381.217n and C.R. Thompson, *Colloquies* 196. Marie Delcourt led the way here: *Corresp. de Bruxelles* I 46. See Godin's "L'Enfant bâtard et la langue du père", in: *Réforme, Humanisme, Renaissance* XV.2 (1982) 87.

12 In: *Italia medievale e umanistica* 27 (1983) 215ff.

13 In the address of the dispensation, *Allen* 518,44, Erasmus is called: *Rogerii filius*. In CWE, *The Correspondence* . . . , 4 (1977), CV, p. 405, 54n, therefore the father of Erasmus is called: Roger Gerard. Cf. *Allen* I 577 f.

14 Did Gerard obtain his master's degree at Ferrara? Cf. *Allen* I p. 581, 30n, on magister Gerardus Goudensis who at Deventer negotiated with Agricola about a commentary on Virgil: "possibly Erasmus' father, but the name occurs too frequently at Gouda to allow of any certain reference". I suggest that this was a ms written by Gerardus himself. And I ask: how many Gerardi who were *magistri*, dwelt at that time at Gouda?

15 In: *Wolffenb. Renaissance Mitt.* 9 (1985) 127ff.

16 Cf. the introduction to the *Short-title Catalogue of the Works of Authors Edited, Translated or Annotated by Erasmus in the City Library of Rotterdam*, compiled by Johanna J.M. Meyers, 1983.

17 *De Baanbreker* 22.6.1946, cf. NdGk 91, dated 22.3.1947; and Minnich-Meissner 598 n. 2.

INDEX OF NAMES